10837069

SERMONS

BY

THE RIGHT REVEREND

STEPHEN ELLIOTT, D.D.,

LATE BISHOP OF GEORGIA.

WITH

A Memoir,

BY

THOMAS M. HANCKEL, Esq.

NEW YORK:
PUBLISHED BY POTT AND AMERY.
1867.

RIVERSIDE, CAMBRIDGE:
STEREOTYPED AND PRINTED BY
H. O. HOUGHTON AND COMPANY.

Memoir.

THE Right Reverend Stephen Elliott, for more than twenty-five years Bishop of the Diocese of Georgia, and whom God has recently called to his rest, was born in the town of Beaufort in the State of South Carolina, on the 31st of August, 1806. He was the oldest son of Stephen Elliott of South Carolina, who was known in that day as a scholar, an eloquent writer, and an enthusiastic student of science, especially of the beautiful science of Botany; and whose name and character are among the grateful traditions of the society in which he lived. His mother was Esther Habersham of Georgia; and his family have always maintained close and affectionate relations with that great State. He himself claimed that he belonged to both States. Especially after he was called to preside over the Diocese of Georgia, with that gracious wisdom which was eminently characteristic of the man, it was his habit freely and heartily to declare that he was a true son of Georgia, and that he was ready to serve her with the love of a grateful child, as well as with the zeal of a faithful Bishop.

When his father removed to Charleston in 1812, young Stephen Elliott came with him, and was prepared for College at the school of Mr. Hurlburt, at that time a distinguished and successful teacher in that city. In the Fall of 1822, he went to Harvard College, and entered the Sophomore Class in that Institution. He remained at Harvard until the Fall of 1823, when, at the desire of his father, who wished him to graduate in his native State, he took an *ad eundem* to the South Carolina College, and in November of that year was there admitted to the Junior Class. Among his classmates was the late Hon. James H. Hammond, afterwards widely known as Governor of South Carolina, a gifted writer, and an eloquent debater upon the floor of the Senate of the United States. Another was the late Hon. Thomas I. Withers, who became a distinguished jurist, and one of the ablest and most learned judges of the Supreme Court of South Carolina. He graduated in 1825, with the third honor of his class. Upon his graduation he studied law in the office of the lamented James L. Petigru, the foremost lawyer of his day, who was the intimate friend of his father, and for whom he retained through life a most affectionate reverence and regard. He was called to the bar in 1827.

It was at this period of his life that the great political questions of State Sovereignty and Free Trade arose, and shook the country by the weight and magnitude of the argument. Subsequent events have given grave importance to the opinions he then formed on this agitating subject. Our readers would be unable to understand or appreciate a most eventful portion of his life and a well-known phase of his character, if we were to pass over these early impressions. The ardent and talented young scholar and lawyer took a keen and active interest in the momentous issues of that high debate. Upon clear conviction, he was a States' Rights man in the highest and best meaning of those words, and was through life the warm and unwavering supporter of that school of political doctrine. He believed in the simple story of the Sovereignty of the States of the Federal Union as he read it in every child's history of the early settlement of the Colonies, and the later independence of the States. He believed that this Sovereignty was the true and almost the only conservative element of the Constitution, and the only effective check upon the usurpations of the central Government, when the latter should be controlled by the selfish interests of classes, the mad passions of party, or the wild delusions of the populace; — that conservative element which alone made a free and magnificent republic possible. He believed that the liberty of the States was the Heaven-given shield of the liberties of the peoples; — that the freedom of the Union was the real strength and perfect health of the Union. He loved his own State very dearly, and he believed that an honest, genuine and practical love of the country, was best felt and expressed in a just and generous love of the State. Some will call this weak, will call it narrow; but let us consider if it is not that weakness and narrowness of Nature itself, which is stronger and broader than the fictions of men, which is deeper than the creed of the philosopher and wiser than the calculations of the statesman. It is the sacred and unchangeable love of the child for his home, and, through his home, for his *father-land.* But let us not wrangle over his bier to pass judgment on these opinions. There is enough else that all can admire, and honor, and love. It were well, however, for Christian people to remember, that these opinions have been held by men who have served the whole country with unquestioned devotion and illustrious success, and of whom history must speak with unqualified honor. It would be wise, it would be happy, for the country to respect at least the honesty and earnestness of their convictions and their self-sacrificing devotion to what they believed to be truth.

It was at this time also, that, as a junior colleague and one of the younger friends and companions of the gifted Hugh S. Legare, he shared in the fortunes of the renowned old "Southern Quarterly Review," and the brilliant literature it illustrated. His father had founded this Review, and he worked enthusiastically for its success. He was probably too young at the time to have contributed many articles: it is known, however, that he wrote, and wrote well, for its pages, and helped to make it what it was. In after years he always spoke with pride and enthusiasm of the power and brilliant though brief career of that famous journal, as a noble monument of the scholarship of his native State at that day.

He practised law in Charleston for several years, when, upon the retirement of a distinguished practitioner from the Bar of Beaufort, he removed to the latter place to succeed to his office and business. His return to his birthplace was a happy hour for him. He dearly loved the old place and its people. He loved the bright waters and the broad bays of the country round; and through life it was the delight of the stately Bishop to come back among those scenes from time to time, and, wandering along the neighboring seashore, breathe again the boisterous breath of the Atlantic, while he gathered with the keen zest of no mean naturalist the beautiful shells and the curious things which the seething surf brought to his feet: nothing loath, either, to join with eager energy in the bold and stirring sports of the sturdy young boatmen around him.

He came back to Beaufort to practice law, but a different destiny awaited him there. At this time, not long after the period when the Church of England had roused itself from its lethargy to a deeper and quicker sense of its high mission and duty, and the teachers of a more active and energetic faith had become a power in the Church, and when the eloquent energies of CHALMERS had begun to wake the Church of Scotland also from the deep slumber of the "Moderates," the truths of religion known as *evangelical* were preached with unusual fervency, power and effect in the ancient and secluded town of Beaufort. Aside from the mysterious breathings of the Divine Spirit, as accepted by many, it was a community peculiarly open to impressions from such a source. Thoroughly educated, cultivated and refined; isolated from the turmoil of life and from the tide of the world; bred to a high, self-reliant and unflinching sense of duty and a generous devotion to truth: the solemnity and pathos, the overwhelming obligation, the supreme necessity and the self-sacrificing spirit of the doctrines then preached, appealed with irresistible power to its people.

Among a somewhat remarkable group of young men, not unknown, who, at that time, made open profession of their faith and high resolve, and have since truly kept the word and honor they then pledged, was the gifted, accomplished and graceful young advocate who had recently come back to his early home. Not many days later he turned away from the allurements of pleasure, and the hopes, honors and emoluments of public and professional life, to enroll himself as a teacher of the truths he believed, and a Minister at the Altars of the Church in which he worshipped.

Early in the year 1833 he became a Candidate for the Ministry of the Protestant Episcopal Church, and entered with characteristic ardor upon the work of preparation for the duties of the sacred office. He threw himself into his new studies with all the devotion of a most earnest Christian, the vigor of a profound thinker, and the high aims and disciplined tastes of a scholar. To save the souls of sinful men he esteemed the greatest and noblest work that could engage the energies of earnest men, — the most necessary work, indeed, demanded of man by the piteous wants of his race. To teach the truth and preach the Gospel of God's grace and Christ's Atonement, he believed to be the ordained and most effectual means of saving men and reforming the world. His work of preparation for his duties, therefore, was honest, thorough, varied, and unsparing, as knowing that the teacher and defender of the Truth must win power over strong men. He was ordained a Deacon by the Right Reverend Nathaniel Bowen, Bishop of the Diocese of South Carolina, at Charleston in that State, in the Fall of 1835. He officiated as minister in charge of the Parish of Wilton, South Carolina, for one month, when he was elected by the Trustees of the South Carolina College to the chair of Sacred Literature and the Evidences of Christianity in that Institution, to which also the Chaplaincy of the College was attached. He was ordained Priest in the year 1836.

Thus early was he called to high offices. And perhaps the reader who never saw him will follow us more fully and easily in what we have further to say, if we here endeavor to describe the very striking form and presence of the late Bishop. Long of limb and tall of stature, with a full and vigorous frame, thoroughly yet easily erect, with full high brow, finely chiselled features and lofty crest; with a soft, beaming blue eye, and a complexion fair and fresh, without being ruddy; exquisitely graceful in his carriage, and quiet and easy in his movement, with his thin dark hair floating lightly around and from his head: his was a figure, as he passed along the crowded thoroughfare, upon which men turned to gaze, and the eyes of women rested with tenderness and veneration.

His presence, though graceful, was eminently dignified and commanding. It quietly expressed a very sensitive deference for the opinions and feelings of others, ready to hear and quick to appreciate: yet a full and steady reliance on himself. It is told of him that once, at a country tavern where he had stopped for the night, a poor inebriate was recklessly bantering the bystanders, when his attention was arrested by the appearance of the stately Bishop, and awed and sobered for the moment by his commanding look and towering form, he turned to him and exclaimed, "And who are you? Are you a Judge? or a Member of Congress? or Governor of the State? Well, if you ain't any of these, you ought to be!" That which was felt by this poor fellow has been felt by the highest and wisest and best in the land in the same presence. Often have we watched that tall and graceful figure come swinging along the College grounds in company with grave professor or cheerful student, in serious talk, or with his rich, soft, hearty laugh ringing out at some merry jest, and been conscious that a living grace was added to the picturesque scene within the bounds of the venerable school.

It must be left to his biographer to speak fully of his career as a Professor, and of the manner in which he performed the duties of his Chair. But we can say that each and every one of those whose names stand upon the roll of the proud old College in those bright days, as well as all others who watched and cherished its progress at that time, learned to love, admire, honor, and revere him there. He was the pillar, the pride and the ornament of the College. It was his *Alma Mater*, and he took the deepest interest in its welfare. Its students formed the congregation to whom he preached the Gospel, and over whose expanding thoughts and hearts he watched and prayed. He yearned to make it a school of high learning, a rich source of truth and refinement, and the centre of a generous intellectual citizenship to the State. "Will you let other States breed your scholars?" exclaimed he, on one occasion to one of the classes, "and will you be content to be hewers of wood and drawers of water to them?" In his own person he showed them how high and gracious and precious a thing was the pure gift of learning and the culture of letters, the charm and the power of the scholar. In the lecture room his clear and vigorous analysis, and his rich, polished, and often passionate words, taught them how to think, and how to utter their thoughts. His hopeful voice cheered everybody. And he here exhibited a marked characteristic of his whole life. He deeply and gladly sympathized with every aspiration after a higher culture, however humble. He encouraged each to do his best, although that best might be but little. To him the aspiration itself was a grace, the effort itself was elevating. To him there was every imaginable difference between the high aims of even the weak, and the dull recklessness of aimless strength. Among the best scholars in the College, there came at that time from the rural districts many uncouth and awkward youths. No man had a keener sense of the humorous than our lamented Bishop, the then Professor, or found it harder to keep from laughing when moved by mirth. It was not in nature, therefore, for him not to laugh heartily sometimes, at these queer fellows. But while he laughed, he loved them. The very grotesqueness of their simple and earnest strength seemed to charm him. It was like the joy of a mother in the babbling blunders of her brightest child. It was beautiful to see how tenderly he protected them, how hopefully he guided them, how quickly he felt the weight and caught the gleam of the pure gold in the rugged ore. We here recall an incident which illustrates the exquisite tact and kindness with which he cheered and guided his scholars. A young student, little more than a boy in years, but among the foremost in his class, was standing his first examination in mathematics before the assembled members of the Faculty. He was nervous and excited, and as he answered the questions which were propounded to him, he kept snapping and wasting the piece of chalk which he held in his hand, until there was but a scrap left, with which to write his figures and draw his diagrams. Professor Elliott was watching his examination with curious and pleased interest, when he saw the predicament in which he was placed. Rising quietly from his seat, he strolled down the room, picked up a handful of chalk, which could neither be broken or wasted, and with a droll and inimitable grace, handed it to the excited youth. A smile, a grateful look, a "Thank you, sir," in reply, and the frightened probationer was at his ease before his examiners, and passed triumphantly through the ordeal, without any more faltering, or again scratching his nails on the blackboard. It was but a little thing to do; but it was kindly and wisely done, and shows us, in miniature, the gracious arts, the gentle wisdom, and the practical sagacity, with which afterwards, as a Bishop, he governed his Diocese, and by which he won the confidence and affection of all portions of his State, all denominations of Christians, and all classes of men. He dearly loved books; to be among them, and to handle them. He was a connoisseur in print and paper and binding. He took an eager and active interest in the new library building, the foundation of which was laid under his auspices. He sedulously watched and pushed forward its construction. And when it was finished and all was ready, carefully were the books carried under his eye from the old room where they had stood so long, to a fitter resting-place. Right gladly he called his pupils around him to help him to receive and arrange them. When the great boxes which contained the recent importations of the best and richest English editions of the best and greatest authors — brought there by the prodigal bounty of the State to her favorite Institution — were opened, his enthusiasm broke forth, and he dwelt with all a scholar's delight upon their beauty and value. And when all the work of arrangement was nearly done, he turned to the group around him and said, in his own rich tender tones: "Now, young gentlemen, I will expect in after years, each one of you who can afford it, to bring some work of art, some statue, bust or picture to adorn these alcoves." It was thus he taught the young novices of his school to love books, and art, and letters, and learning. We turn sadly away to think how many proud hopes and glad anticipations, which then swelled in his generous heart, have been crushed and buried under the red floods of war, in ruin, grief, desolation and blood.

But it was for a comparatively brief period that he was permitted to fill the Professor's chair. The Church at whose Altar he served, and to whose Ministry he had been ordained, summoned him to her work. She called him to a higher and larger sphere of usefulness. He obeyed without a question. In the summer of 1840, he was elected the first Bishop of Georgia. In December of the same year, not without some natural regrets, he took leave of the College which he had loved and served so well, and early in 1841 he was consecrated to his Bishopric at Christ Church, Savannah, by Bishops Meade, Ives, and Gadsden.

The limits of this Memoir will not permit us to speak fully of the manner in which the duties of his holy office were discharged. The task of organizing and building up a new Diocese was a trying one. We know that his Dicoese loved him sincerely, and was heartily proud of him. It has recently declared its sense of bereavement at his death, " as too deep to find expression in the common terms of grief and mourning ; " and that they " desire to place on record their high appreciation of his remarkable qualifications for the Episcopal office, exercised for more than twenty-five years ; his profound acquaintance with human and divine learning; his pre-eminent power as a preacher of the Gospel of the grace of God ; his keen insight into the motives and instincts of men ; his tact and ability in administering his Diocese ; his watchfulness and tender sympathy for all the flock committed to his care ; his interest in the welfare of our colored population ; his careful avoidance of party issues and all extremes in doctrine, discipline and worship ; and his cautious endeavors to pursue the quiet, conservative paths trodden by the wisest and most honored Fathers of the American Church."

As a pulpit orator, without aiming to be subtle or metaphysically profound, he was clear, vigorous, eloquent, and often strikingly original in the defence and illustration of accepted truth. His style was passionate as well as exceedingly pure and graceful. He had rather the rich, massive and commanding manner of Milton, South, and Jeremy Taylor, than that of the polished wits and piquant essayists of Queen Anne's reign ; with some touch, also, of the quaintness of those earlier worthies. To his students he always commended the first as the better models.

It was in the earlier days of his Episcopal administration that he sacrificed his private fortune, and reduced himself to poverty and want, in his uncalculating efforts to establish an eminent school for female education at Montpelier, in the centre of his Diocese. No man had a higher estimate of the blessings of a healthy and thorough education. His zeal in this work rose to enthusiasm. He therefore established this school at Montpelier, for the instruction of the young women of his Diocese in that learning and those accomplishments which, according to his conception of her character and duties, a Christian woman, whose station in life permitted it, ought to know and acquire. Large sums had to be expended in the erection of suitable buildings and the necessary outfit of the Institution. It was his ardent wish that every thing should be thoroughly done. When the funds at his disposal were exhausted, he unhesitatingly pledged his private property and credit for the completion of the undertaking. His obligations were all faithfully met, and the debts he incurred were all paid. But it left him without a dollar; and he had scarcely the means of providing the daily bread of his family. He had been accustomed from early youth to the refinement, independence and dignity of an ample fortune. He had never known what it was to owe what he could not punctually pay. The cares, anxieties and heavy burdens therefore of this period of his life were keenly felt, and his spirit was deeply wounded. But he met them all with the firmness, patience, gentleness, and humility of one who had counted the cost of his holy service. Up to this time he had received but a comparatively small salary as Bishop, and this had been chiefly expended for Church objects and for charitable purposes. The people of his Diocese now came forward affectionately and generously to his aid, and provided an adequate income for his support. It was well done, and was gratefully received. We spoke only the simple truth when we said that his people loved and honored him.

At a later period, in the same spirit of generous and untiring devotion to the cause of education, together with the heroic Bishop of Louisiana and the gentle and eloquent Bishop of Tennessee, — and when these three stately men stood together it was a group for the painter's pencil, — he projected and labored earnestly to lay the foundation of a great Southern University, which he trusted would one day become a beneficent centre of learning and letters to our Southern land. And this he did in no spirit of narrow prejudice against other sections or other seats of learning. As we have said before, he did indeed dearly love the South. He cherished and honored her traditional spirit of social order and conservative republican liberty. He believed that there was much that was peculiar and valuable in the life, society, character, traditions and history of her people that ought to be fostered and sheltered. But, besides this, he was also firmly persuaded, that even as regards the development of a national life embracing all sections and latitudes of the Union, a better, healthier and nobler national life and character would be developed by the establishment of many centres of wealth, power, education and influence, than could be produced under a system by which whole territories — equal each of them in extent to great European kingdoms — should be overshadowed, provincialized, and materially, morally and intellectually enfeebled and impoverished, by an abject dependence on one stupendous, turbulent and despotic centre of commerce, arts, manufactures, publication, science, literature, learning and government. It was in this faith that he labored so earnestly for the establishment of a great Southern school as a balance of power in the country.

The work was begun. But the fair prospects of the splendid enterprise were blighted by the opening of that tremendous struggle for the political independence of the Southern States — their society, institutions, civilization, constitutional law, and traditional policy — which was to agitate and overshadow the closing scenes of his life. In this struggle, holding the views of public law and policy which he did, trained in the political school to which we have referred, it was not difficult to see where Bishop Elliott would stand.

But the story is too sad to dwell upon. He shared in the labors of a thousand other heroes who suffered, or bled, or died, all in vain. He placed his Church by the side of the State. He cheered and comforted his suffering, bleeding, fainting people with words of the deepest pathos and tenderness. He sent his sons to the battle, with his pure kiss on their brows and a father's blessing in their hearts. And when all was over — and all in vain — and the cause was lost, he bowed his head without a murmur to the will of his God, and turned to the new duties which lay before him with the hope and energy of an unflinching faith, and the calm dignity of an unconquered heart.

In looking back at the life of Bishop Elliott, there are one or two points of his character upon which it will be grateful to touch.

In Church and State he was eminently conservative. He dearly loved that which was old as well as excellent — the truth and the practice that is taught by ancient precedent, and established by ancient custom. But so ardent a temper, and a nature so sensitive, æsthetic and enthusiastic, could not but sympathize with all honest and genuine progress. In matters of religious faith he rested in Revelation, believing that a Creed was perfect at the time it was revealed. In questions of public liberty he rested immovably in great principles. But in other matters of Church and State he clung to the ancient landmarks of history, rather as tests by which to measure the truth and the earnestness of the new and progressive, than as impassable barriers to change. And in the fields of science, and commercial and material progress, he was full of enterprise and enthusiasm, and passionately anxious that his fair Southern land should press forward with unflagging stride in the great march of modern civilization.

His, too, was an exceedingly happy temper. "The lines have fallen unto me in pleasant places," were words which not unfrequently dropped from him in confidential intercourse. It was this buoyant, happy nature which so often brought the healing of life to the sad and wounded spirits of his people. Doubtless there was in this a deeper, ghostly joy in his holy office, on which we dwell reverently; but there was also, we can see, a human and exulting gladness in the vigorous exercise of his intellectual gifts, and in the beneficent use of the graceful power which he wielded.

In harmony with this conservative yet aspiring nature, this steadfast yet progressive spirit, this faithful yet happy temper, this love of the true combined with an enthusiastic appreciation of the beautiful, was the grace, dignity, justice, and kindness of his personal and official intercourse with his colleagues on the Bench of Bishops. They will gladly and affectionately bear witness, that he was courteous and generous in debate; that he was too well aware of the imperfection of human language in the expression of spiritual ideas, too profoundly conscious of the mystery of religious thought, and yet too clearly convinced of the essential harmony of a Scriptural faith, to be indignant at formulas which were not altogether like his own, or alarmed at methods of argument which, while they embraced the whole circle of Heavenly truth, might begin and end at a part of its circumference different from his own stand-point; that he was too earnestly devoted to fundamental truth to be vindictive towards error that was less than heresy; that his was too great a heart and too noble a nature to suffer him to be the adherent of a clique, or the follower of a party; that in his judicial acts, he was fair, wise, gentle, clear in his knowledge of law and his perceptions of right, and utterly scornful of a shade of selfishness or malice; and that in counsel he was a peacemaker among his brethren, and a bond of union amidst discordant opinions and conflicting policies. The heart of many a venerable prelate has been made sad by the thought that they shall see his face no more.

Such is a brief outline of the life and the nurture, culture and graces, of the distinguished Bishop for whom Georgia mourns.

In contemplating his character, we feel that he was the representative of much that is highest and best in Southern society; and we rejoice that so much at least of Southern history is safe beyond danger or question. Such a life and character ought to be the full and sufficient answer to those who believe or declare, that the traditional institution which has heretofore existed in the South, and which has been made the occasion of so much grief and agony to the country, was of necessity degrading to all classes and conditions of its people. If we turn to the higher forms of a cultivated social life and a beneficent civilization, and look at the representative men of the South, the country may well remember and rejoice, that nothing can strike from their history the life and the labors, the name and the fame, of Georgia's great Bishop, and men like him. If we consider on the other hand the results to the African race, of the institution under which they lived, as it was practically administered, even here, — whatever may be our abstract opinions as to its policy or our moral judgments as to its justice, — all right-minded and candid men who know the facts, will admit that, under the providence of God, the negro has been greatly benefited, his best qualities have been developed, and the whole race has been greatly elevated. Whether that institution was righteous or not, it has been mercifully administered. The South received from the coast of Africa about one million of degraded savages; and under its generous and wholesome discipline, they grew to be four millions of skillful, thrifty, cheerful and industrious laborers, a larger number of civilized and christianized people than have ever been directly reclaimed from the barbarian heathen, since the early days of Christianity: — not wholly contented with their lot, it may be, but as contented, perhaps, as the poor of any country are contented with their poverty. The South received them, a debased, brutish and repulsive people, to whom chastity was an unknown virtue and a strange idea, and honesty was the fear of punishment or the want of opportunity; whose notion of public justice was the trial by poison; whose native tongue was a barbarous gibberish; who trusted in fetishes, believed in greegrees, and alone of human kind worshipped the Evil Spirit. These are the people whom their Southern rulers, by their mingled kindness and discipline, by their justice and their gentleness, have made such a people as to call forth the extravagant eulogies of those who now have charge of their welfare, and who now claim for them the full rights and the highest privileges of the proudest and most enlightened American citizen. It is not our office nor is this the place, to say whether these eulogies are wholly merited, or these claims well founded. But what these people are, all men can see; and such as they are, no man will deny that the South, under God's providence, has made them. No other portion of the world has contributed a man or a dollar to the work; while eminent scholars of the South like our gifted Bishop, as masters and teachers, have been conspicuous laborers in the merciful though humble task. He was earnestly devoted to the duty of preaching the Gospel to the negroes of his Diocese. He summoned his whole people to the work, as the great mission to which they were called, the special field of Christian labor to which they were dedicated. Some of his most eloquent and impassioned addresses were devoted to this theme. He spoke often and plainly, earnestly and solemnly, on the subject. He held his people to a strict responsibility for the spiritual and eternal, as well as the physical and temporal, welfare of those over whom they ruled. He sent missionaries and established missions among the negroes wherever he could. He led the way by his personal labors. He founded S. Stephen's Church for colored people in the city of Savannah. He placed its secular affairs under the charge of a colored vestry. They looked up to him as their firmest, wisest, and noblest friend. At his burial they gave a touching and beautiful evidence of the love and reverence they bore him. The colored vestry of S. Stephen's asked to have the honor of carrying him to the grave; and it was granted to them. It did honor to them, and to their Bishop. Considering the peculiar and momentous issues of the time, we think it was the grandest and most instructive spectacle, amidst all the solemn, mournful, and agitating ceremonies of that day, on which the city of Savannah was hushed to listen to the footfalls of those who thus bore their Bishop to the tomb.

We have paused to speak of this feature of Bishop Elliott's character, because no readers of the following pages will be able to forget that he was a Southern slaveholder, and a representative of Southern society. The sinfulness or the righteousness of African slavery, its evils or its wisdom, are no longer practical questions. Under the Providence of God, the institution itself has been decisively and forever ended. The questions pertaining to it belong to the issues of the past, to be reviewed only at the judgment-seat of God, and before the tribunal of History. But the real character of Southern society and Southern men is indeed at this time a most practical question. It is of momentous import that the country should see it as it is, and judge of it with wisdom and with justice.

Since the close of the fearful struggle which has shaken the very foundations of American society, the people of the South have exhibited a kindly sympathy with their former dependents, an intelligent submission to necessity, an obedience to law and a regard for social order, combined with a firm self-respect, which have merited, we think, the approbation of all men. What it has cost them to do this, is known only to God. That they have been able to do it, has in some measure been the result of the habit of self-control, the daily sense of responsibility, the patient encounter with necessary evils, the carefulness for the welfare of their laborers, and the frequent interchange of acts of kindness, to all of which they were compelled by their Anglo-Saxon education, by the spirit of liberty and Christianity within them, by the very necessities of their anomalous institution, and by its practical administration in the presence of Christendom. Of these great qualities, in their grace and power, Bishop Elliott himself was a splendid example. And when the representatives of these Southern Dioceses shall again enter that august Council of the Church, which will meet not two years hence, they will think mournfully and regretfully of him who, by right of age and service, would have stood at their head. They will recall the exquisite grace, the sensitive delicacy, the lofty wisdom and charity, the calm dignity, the unblenching crest, and the commanding presence which could neither be overawed by the disapprobation of others, nor yet could ever needlessly and unbecomingly offend their opinions or provoke their prejudices. May the full and complete folds of his shining mantle fall on other shoulders equal to the high office which would have devolved upon him!

In looking at his completed life, there was one remarkable gift of this remarkable man on which we dwell with deep and grateful emotion, and which all who ever knew him will recognize at once. We speak of the thorough humanity of his nature: and by this we mean the wealth and strength, the breadth and fullness, of the deep human sympathies in which the learning, wisdom and graces of his nature were veiled — veiled as light is veiled in color, as thought is veiled in words, as feeling is veiled in music. His life seems to have been the rich, healthy growth of early training and happy influences. He grew as the tree grows from the bursting germ, outwards and upwards, year by year, circle upon circle, into strength and majesty: yet with the life and form of the germ all there, with the fibre and firmness of each circle there, all thoroughly sound, — sound to the core; all lending strength to its growth, proportion to its column, and grandeur to its sheltering arms. His childhood took on his boyhood, and his boyhood his manhood, and his manhood passed into the wisdom of years, all complete in the fullness of that great and bounteous nature, whose deep, broad, human sympathies thus made him the friend and companion of young and old and of all classes and conditions of men: made him, too, as mindful of the gentle courtesies and sweet charities of life with little boys and girls[1] and humble men, as he was easily at home amidst the grander graces of social and official intercourse with the wise, the great, the learned and honored in the land.

Doubtless to the eye of that Omniscience which heeds the life and service, the death and fall, of the humblest sparrow among all the feathered tribes that praise Him, the whole life of a man is the man. As the spirit of the living man penetrates and is bounded by every nerve and atom of his living body: so, to that Eye, the soul of every man is incarnate in his life, from the first wail of the infant to the last sigh before the grave which thus completes the full measure of his being, and the perfect "image and superscription" of his identity. So, to some special natures, it is given to carry in their memory a clear and sensitive consciousness of each period of their lives, and each vital shape of their humanity. And thus did the gifted man whom we mourn seem to have grasped the full outline of his own life, and with the sensitive glance of genius, conceived and realized each part and character in which he had lived, and was thus vividly conscious of himself to himself. His merry childhood, his bounding boyhood, his lusty youth and aspiring manhood, were all the familiar companions and friends of the genial man, the allies and counsellors of the august sage. And so the happy child that climbed to his breast laughed and kissed with the happy child which, as from a mirror, laughed and kissed back again; and the gallant boy shouted to the bright lover of fun within, who shouted back in echo; and the vigorous youth felt his outstretched hand clasped by the hand of companion whose steady grasp closed faithfully over his own. And the pale and impassioned student met the answering glance of youthful student with "eyes of speculation" rapt in study. And the

[1] In a memorial sermon by the Rev. Henry K. Rees, Rector of Christ Church, Macon, Ga., we find the following characteristic anecdote: —

"And well might children love him, for he saw in *them* the purest and truest representatives of his Holy Master on earth. In illustration of his reverent tenderness towards them, a touching and beautiful incident occurred during his last visitation, when in an hour of home relaxation, he watched the play of the little one of the household, who in her glee threw off her shoe. The venerable Bishop knelt before the child and was replacing it, when the father said, "Little Mary, you are greatly honored." "Honored," said the kneeling Bishop, "O no, whose shoe's latchet I am not worthy to unloose, for of such is the kingdom of heaven."

struggling man found, in this wise confessor, one who could understand the story of his life, because he retained a vivid memory of his own. Higher than all, he seemed to have kept the memory of mother and sister; and the shrinking maiden might look into that loving heart without faltering, to see a pure, sweet image of herself reflected there, and to feel that she shared in the knightly tenderness for the ideal woman there enshrined. But yet deeper and holier still was kept the memory of his own errors and frailties; and the penitent Magdalen and the contrite man met, in that true soul, a fellow-sinner who knew how to forgive, as he had known what it is to be forgiven.

It was this humanity of his nature, these pure, strong, earthly sympathies, this veil of the flesh in which his piety was clothed, which added so much to the power of his life and doctrine. His was, indeed, a truly and deeply spiritual life, in the religious sense of that word. But there was, besides this, a human soulfulness, a sensitive sympathy with all that was charming in Nature, beautiful in Art, inspiring in life, or useful to his country, which won for him the regard and affection of men, who were afterwards subdued by the teachings of his faith and the example of his piety. Thus it often happened that the generous host or the genial friend who received him as the gentleman, the scholar, the lover of art, the student of science, or the unselfish patriot, learned to know that there was something deeper and holier still; and it softly stole upon his consciousness that, in entertaining this gifted stranger, he had "entertained an angel unawares." Nor was the grateful influence of his teaching less felt because it was thus associated with the human sympathies of common interests, the winning courtesy of a gentleman, the charms of a graceful nature, and the strength of a vigorous and comprehensive intellect.

We have thus endeavored to present to our readers a true likeness of this faithful son of the Church, this noble child of her nurture, this chosen ruler over an important portion of her heritage, this Father in God to a large number of her people. It has been our wish to describe him just as he was, — as he lived, and acted, and spoke, and worked. Bishop Elliott held opinions which are not held by some who will read this volume; he believed it to be his duty to do things which we know they have not approved. We have not felt at liberty to disguise these opinions, or to pass over these acts, or even to soften the sharpness of their antagonism. We have endeavored to speak of them in words and in a manner that might not offend the convictions or the feelings of others.

We have desired to be as respectful to their opposing opinions, as we earnestly crave them to be respectful to his. But we have deemed it our duty to present him, as he himself would have wished to stand before them, — modestly, respectfully, but frankly and manfully, himself. In these things he must be judged as he stands. In how many other things can the whole country and Church unite to praise and honor him!

After a laborious life freely spent in the service of God, the Church, and the country, Bishop Elliott, being in his sixty-first year, died suddenly in the city of Savannah, Georgia, on the evening of the 21st of December, 1866. He had been absent from home in the discharge of his Episcopal duties, and had just returned to the welcome of those who loved him so dearly and reverently; he had just taken his last meal with those who were the objects of his tender solicitude: when, suddenly, he fell lifeless, and was at rest. To close and dear friends, he had often dwelt upon the blessedness of a sudden death to the faithful Christian. This blessing was granted him. Amidst the cares and labors of his holy office, amidst the yearnings of his heart for his country, amidst the peace and beauty of his domestic happiness, "in a moment, in the twinkling of an eye," his earthly life was ended, and his soul was with God.

It is interesting to recall that thrice, during one year, has the name of Stephen Elliott been borne in mourning through two States, and each time with words of honor, regard, and profoundest respect. On the first occasion, the young hero and soldier and humble Christian "was laid gently and reverently upon the bosom of the State he loved," with the eloquent words of genius for his requiem. But a few days later, and the pious and scholarly father of the noble youth, the Rev. Stephen Elliott, — who had trained him for his high duties, and who could truly and proudly say with Lord Ormond, "I would not give my dead son for any living son in Christendom," — was laid by his side. And then, alas! the shining name of Georgia's great Bishop was added to the fatal list. This last startling message carried gloom and sorrow throughout the limits of Georgia and South Carolina, and to many churches, hearts, and homes, in every portion of the country. Men seeking for sympathy met and repeated the mournful intelligence, and the mute but eloquent gesture of grief gave token of their love and reverence for a great and good man thus snatched away, and of their bitter sense of irreparable loss and bereavement.

It was keenly felt that a brilliant light and representative of

Southern life, society, tradition and history was suddenly gone; and that from Churches, and States, and disciples, and friends, a prop upon which they had used to lean, had silently sunk away: and that they must henceforth learn to stand in their own strength, or look elsewhere for support. And in the first blindness of their grief they knew not where to look. The Church which he governed will mourn the loss of the calm, clear, just and graceful wisdom which guided her, and the great heart which cheered her. The society in which he moved will lament that its pride and ornament is veiled. Many a younger man, struggling in the battle of life, will miss his voice from among the good and wise, whose approbation is reward, whose praise is wealth. And hundreds have lost forever their friend, example, teacher, guide and comforter — a comforter whose rich, sweet, happy voice of itself brought cheer and hope amidst sorrow and despondency.

His death was very sudden. And yet, to those who knew and considered the man, it was what might have been looked for. We have said that his life was the rich growth of the cherished memories of the past. And the tempest of desolation and ruin which had scourged the face of his loved Southern land had torn also through the branches of this stately tree, and strained it to its foundations. The scathing bolts of war had fallen deep amidst its roots. Many ties of kindred had been broken. Many proud and generous associations with the past had been destroyed. The homes of many of his blood and lineage had been made desolate; the accustomed fires of their hearths had gone out in bitter ashes; and their sons and daughters were wandering among strangers. His hopes of constitutional liberty had been defeated. His aspirations for his country had been blighted. Thus, all unseen, the great roots of his mortal life were snapped, and the rich sources of his earthly strength were dried up. And although, like a beautiful tree with its roots all broken and bruised, he still, for a time, stood poised in the perfect balance of his character and the symmetrical proportions of his nature: yet the great props of his life had been taken away. And so it happened that, stirred by some cold, mysterious breath of the night, with the growth and foliage of his life all heavy with the dew of heavenly cares, he tottered and fell — fell with perhaps one last, loving pang, for the cruel blow with which his sudden and resounding fall was to crash upon the trembling hearts of Churches and States and friends and family.

And thus he lay in the majesty of death; and little children and pure women, young men and old, the meek and the gentle, the proud and the lowly, the rich and the poor, the great and the wise, Bishops, priests, patriots, soldiers, scholars and statesmen, came to mourn around the bier of Georgia's great Bishop.

Fortuna non mutat genus, was the rallying cry of the ancient worthies. From father to son, is the law of Nature. From generation to generation, is the promise and commandment of God. Amidst the private ruin, social change, and political disaster which now surround them, let those that bear the unsullied name of the soldier of Christ who thus in full armor has fallen on sleep, and names like his, remember, — let every true Southern heart remember, — *Fortuna non mutat genus*. If their fathers, in their day, have trusted in God, submitted to His will, and conquered difficulties; they, in the same faith and with like patience, can retrieve disaster, bring good out of evil, and triumph over misfortune.

The time is surely coming when it will task all the virtue, wisdom, strength and courage of the whole country, to save the ancient liberties of the people, and to purge the administration of the Governments from legislative corruption and official rapacity. The time is not far distant when the true children of God's Church, and the whole brotherhood of Christian men, will be compelled to stand together for the defence of their faith, against the assaults of an infidel philosophy and a material humanitarianism on the one hand, and the narrow despotism of priestly power on the other. Let the country remember that the people of the South have always been ardently attached to the great principles of constitutional liberty, social order and conservative law, and that they can proudly and thankfully call the country to witness, that their public men have ever been uncorrupted and incorruptible in the discharge of their public duties. Let the Church remember that her children of the South have been simple and reverent in their Creed, honest in their piety, and the staunch defenders of the great doctrines of Christ's Divinity, Resurrection, and Atonement; and that, like this beloved Bishop, "they have endeavored to pursue the quiet conservative paths trodden by the wisest and most honored Fathers of the American Church." Ere the time of trial come, let the country and the Church remember *Fortuna non mutat genus*.

T. M. H.

Editor's Preface.

Of the great mass of manuscript sermons left by the lamented Bishop Elliott, nothing was prepared by him for the press; nor was there the slightest indication as to what selection from them he would himself have preferred. Yet it was rightly judged by all that the reputation of so great a Preacher should not be left to go down to futurity only upon the unsubstantial basis of oral tradition.

Of the few sermons printed during his life some were of too transient an interest to justify their being inserted here: but others are given, and among them are the *Twelfth* and *Thirteenth*, on *The Busy Man's* and *The Busy Woman's Religious Difficulties*, which were printed by request in New Orleans in the year 1859. The *Twenty-fifth*, on *Our National Sin of Proud Boasting*, is the second of two sermons preached, and printed by request, in 1843, on the occasion of the deaths of eminent personages occasioned by the explosion of the *Peacemaker;* and it is a discourse the predictions of which will be read with singular interest in the light of the present day. The extract on the *Apostolic Succession* is from a printed sermon; and the *Pastoral Letter* sent out by the House of Bishops from the Southern General Council in 1862, and the *Address at the Funeral of Bishop Cobbs*, were both printed. All the rest of the volume is now first published from the Bishop's manuscripts.

In regard to the selection here made, it was impossible for the Editor to read through the great mass of material placed at his disposal; and the cherished recollections of two happy years passed under the Bishop's roof, from 1842 to 1844, were a very insufficient guide amid the wealth of more than twenty years' subsequent work in the very prime of his splendid powers. The larger part of these Sermons, therefore, are such as were chosen by the various members of his family, or by other relatives and friends, or by his

Clergy, and members of the Parishes in Savannah, as the discourses which had printed themselves the most deeply in their hearts at the time of their delivery. As to the rest, the choice has been made partly with a view to give greater fullness to the imperfect outline of the Church Year, but especially to include as many as possible of the sermons written during the last and ripest years of the Bishop's life.

In regard to the arrangement, the sermons on general subjects are placed first. Then, beginning with the *Eighteenth*, follow a number of discourses arranged in the order of the Church Year, though its circle is by no means completed; and of these, many were written during the last year of his life, including those for Christmas-Day, for the Epiphany, for the first two Sundays in Lent, for Good-Friday, and Easter-Day, with others. From the *Forty-third* to the *Fiftieth* inclusive have been grouped several which are peculiarly interesting from their connection with the closing scenes of his own Ministry. The *Forty-third* is the first that was preached by him on his return to Savannah after the War. The *Forty-fourth*, though written previously, is an admirable expression of his own spirit, and of the spirit which he labored to promote in others, under the calamities of the War. The *Forty-fifth* and *Forty-sixth* are, unitedly, his "last will and testament" touching the great question of the political troubles of the country, in which he had been so deeply interested. The State of Georgia had appointed a fast-day for the sufferings and deprivations of the people of the State; and the President of the United States had appointed a Thanksgiving on the same day of the week following, in recognition of National blessings. Christ Church was open for Divine Service on both days; and these are the two sermons that were preached by the Bishop on those two occasions. The *Forty-seventh* is the last sermon preached by him in Savannah, on Sunday night, December 9th. The *Forty-eighth* in the morning, and the *Forty-ninth* at night, were preached by him on the last Sunday of his life, December 16th, in Augusta. The *Fiftieth* was the last ever preached by him, being delivered at Montpelier — the scene of his heaviest sacrifices in the cause of Church Education — on Thursday, the 20th of December, only the day before his departure. And what more beautiful choice of subjects could be found to close the career of a faithful Preacher? The first of the four — that in Savannah — gives the triumphant key-note: *Look up, and lift up your heads; for your redemption draweth nigh.* Then, almost as with a conscious apprehension of the coming glory: *In Thy Light shall we see light.* Along with this light comes the great *Cloud of Witnesses* — the

> Bright array,
> Round the altar night and day; —

and the full recognition of Christ as not only *the Author* but also the *Finisher of our faith.* Last of all is the solemn repetition of the Master's warning: *Watch ye therefore: for ye know not when the Master of the house cometh, at even, or at midnight, or at the cock-crowing, or in the morning.* And these were the closing words: "Instead of sleeping because the world is troubled and agitated, rather stand upon your watch-tower, and await in faith and patience the Coming of your Master." Almost while the voice of the Preacher was yet sounding, the Master of the house came, "at even," and found the Watchman not "sleeping."

The extract on the *Apostolic Succession* is valuable for its clear doctrinal teachings, though a large part of the printed sermon from which it is taken is of less general interest. The *Pastoral Letter* of 1862 is inserted, not only because it is of so great beauty; not only because it breathes such a heavenly spirit in sending forth, from the midst of the alarums of war, its "greetings of love to the Churches of God all the world over;" not only because it declares in the most plain and pointed terms, what was taught and held by Churchmen as their religious duty towards the colored people even before emancipation: but rather because it was wholly the work of Bishop Elliott's pen, written by him at one heat in the course of an evening, and adopted the next morning by his Brother Bishops with hardly the alteration of a single word. The *Address delivered at the Funeral of Bishop Cobbs* is placed last, because so large a part of it is applicable, with wonderful exactness, to Bishop Elliott himself, although his character was marked by elements of commanding brilliance and intellectual power to which the pure and gentle and lovely Bishop of Alabama could lay no claim. The closing paragraph of that *Address* especially — the utterance of a longing and yearning for *rest* — expresses the dominant feeling of his own heart, no less than that of the saintly Man of God over whose sleeping body they were spoken.

Bishop Elliott was a remarkably rapid and fluent writer. The manuscript leaves of sermon after sermon of his may be turned over without detecting the slightest sign of erasure or interlineation, and, with an evenness of hand as perfect as if written all at one sitting and with one penful of ink. Certain cardinal words, such as Heart, Life, Love, and Heaven, are invariably spelt by him with a capital letter, as if to give them that prominence to the eye which they hold in the mind. The date of composition or delivery was not always placed by him upon his manuscript; but where given it has been printed at the end of the sermon, and will be an additional element of interest to the reader. It was not often that the Bishop repeated his sermons: yet one of those written in the last year of his life — in this volume numbered the *Sixteenth*, on "*Ephraim's Altars to Sin*" — was preached no less than seven times in different places during the course of a few months: a striking proof of the degree to which the Bishop believed the teachings of that sermon to be needed by the people.

It is with inexpressible sadness that we do our humble part in laying before the Church these mute utterances of a voice that shall be heard among us on earth no more: and with many a misgiving lest the selection may not be altogether such as shall do him the most honor or the Church the most enduring service. But there is one consolation; and that is, that this volume contains such singular proofs of his earnestness and eloquence; such melting tenderness and terrible grandeur of spiritual power; such a mastery of the Word of God, which pierces "even to the dividing asunder of soul and spirit, and of the joints and marrow, and is a discerner of the thoughts and intents of the heart;" such vivid and graphic presentations of the Gospel of Christ, and the claims of His Church: that a loving and a faithful People "will not willingly let it die."

J. H. H., Jr.

New York, *July*, 1867.

Contents.

SEVENTH SERMON.

EIGHTH SERMON.

NINTH SERMON.

TENTH SERMON.

ELEVENTH SERMON.

TWELFTH SERMON.

THE BUSY MAN'S RELIGIOUS DIFFICULTIES.

THIRTEENTH SERMON.

THE BUSY WOMAN'S RELIGIOUS DIFFICULTIES.

TWENTY-SIXTH SERMON.

PALM SUNDAY.

TWENTY-SEVENTH SERMON.

GOOD FRIDAY.

TWENTY-EIGHTH SERMON.

GOOD FRIDAY.

TWENTY-NINTH SERMON.

EASTER-DAY.

THIRTIETH SERMON.

WHITSUN-DAY.

SERMONS.

First Sermon.

And I said, Oh that I had wings like a dove! for then would I fly away, and be at rest. — PSALM lv. 6.

AND whither, O sweet Psalmist of Israel, couldst thou fly, even if thou hadst the wings of the dove, and be at rest? Dost thou not know that there can be no rest for the soul of man, save in reunion with God; and that no flight, however distant, however far away from the haunts of men, can give thee that heavenly boon? Hast thou not told us thyself, in thine own beautiful language, "I shall be satisfied, O God, when I awake with thy likeness?" And canst thou, with thy rich and deep experience, expect the wings of a dove to carry thee away, not only from trouble and trial, but from sin and its curse? Alas, no! royal Minstrel: no wings can carry thee away from thyself, — can separate thee from thine own heart, — can give thee rest in a world like this. For unrest is not only in the things outside of us, which harass and perplex us, but has its throne in our own hearts. It is the fruit of our own natures, begotten of the corruption in which we are born; and never to be quieted until the peace of God shall enter into the soul, and calm its struggling elements. And even then shall there be, so long as life shall last, a law of the members warring against the law of the mind, and ofttimes bringing it into captivity to the law of sin which is in our members. Hunt for rest in this world, with wings! It can never be found! "Traverse in imagination the extent of creation," — if I may use in this connection words applied by another to a very different subject, — "wander over the most beautiful landscape, pluck the most fragrant flower, select the most costly gem, glide upon the surface of the fairest lake, scale the highest mountain, soar to the furthermost star: still the question rushes back upon the mind, — 'How shall I find rest among these glories of creation?' Poor, anxious searcher for peace, all Nature unites in testifying: 'It is not in me! it is not in me!'"

We cannot flee away, my beloved hearers, from trouble, from temptation, from sorrow, from sin. They must be met, and overcome. There is a rest promised to the children of God; but it is not to be found in this world. There is a home, reserved for the faithful in Christ Jesus; but it is in heaven. God has prepared, for those who love Him, mansions in which beauty will never fade, in which sorrow will never dim the eye, in which love will never change: but they await His children who have part in the resurrection of Christ. We can enjoy slight foretastes of their happiness through faith and hope; but it is like the sun gleaming through a troubled sky, and only flecking the landscape with spots of sunshine. All is bright to-day, — but only to-day: to-morrow brings its shadow of trial or of sorrow. All is quiet in the home and in the heart this hour: the next, there rests upon both some dark cloud, which scatters the fond dream of Peace or Faith. For trouble comes alike to all. "There is one event to the righteous, and to the wicked; to the good and to the clean, and to the unclean; to him that sacrificeth, and to him that sacrificeth not."[1] Such distinctions could not be made

[1] Eccles. ix. 2.

here without miraculous intervention, because the righteous and the unrighteous are so mingled in domestic and social life, are so bound together by ties of association and love and relationship, that the punishment of the one reacts upon the other, and the sorrow of the one is the affliction of the other. True justice can only be meted out at the last. Rest — that may deserve the name — can only be obtained when mortality shall be swallowed up in life.

This is the mistake which man is ever making, dreaming that he can find rest by flying away from the present, Whenever harassed and perplexed, whenever sad and sorrowful, his feeling is that of the Psalmist: "Oh that I had wings like a dove, for then would I fly away, and be at rest." He forgets that the trouble, or the trial, or the sorrow, or the temptation, is not in the mere accidental circumstances: but in the nature of things. He supposes that if he could change this condition of things, or get rid of that evil, — that if he could fly away from this place, or hide himself from that calamity, — he should be at rest. But he ever finds that the world is the same wherever he goes, because he himself is the same. *Cœlum, non animum, mutant qui trans mare currunt.* He ever finds that the thing which has been, is that which shall be; and that which is done, is that which shall be done: because Nature is ever the one unchangeable impress of God. And when he has shifted all the scenes of life, and played his part now in poverty, now in riches, now in obscurity, now in power, now surrounded by friends, and then deserted and alone: he learns, at the last, that rest is nowhere, and can be nowhere, but in himself; that peace is not the product of earthly combinations, but is the gift of Christ, — the quiet sleeping on the pillow, while the winds are howling, and the waves rolling, and destruction hovering around. But what a long chase man has, ere he finds this out; how he toils and sweats away the best years of his life in looking for rest in change; how he chafes against the fetters which he supposes are keeping him away from happiness and peace! Oh, that I might be rich! Oh, that I might reach this honor! Oh, that I might win this object! Oh, that this crook in my lot might only be taken away; that this skeleton might be removed from my house! These are the desires of men, even when they have been so often disappointed in change; even after they have found no rest in any thing God has done for them. And it will go on so forever. Nothing can alter it, for it is in man himself, and in the condition which sin has forced upon the world. The like cry arises from rich and poor, from known and unknown, from peasant and prince: "Who will show us any good?"

When we hear this wish of the Psalmist uttered by those who are not Christians, we are not surprised at it; for many of them have not God at all in their thoughts, and look upon the world as their only home. If they cannot find rest here, they do not expect to find it at all. But when it is uttered by the Psalmist, or when it is reëchoed from the lips of Christians, it does surprise us, for they ought to understand the purposes and arrangements of God. It was wrung from David under the pressure of troubles and calamities; and it is wrung in like manner from Christians by the sore trials which often come upon them: but still is it the cry of Nature, and not of Faith! For whither could the wings even of the dove bear any Christian, safer and better than the place where God has put him? Whither could he go, to be further from himself, or nearer to his God? It is only God and himself that can give him any irremediable trouble. Nature is alike everywhere,—cursed and smitten. Man is alike everywhere, — unbelieving and wicked. What use in flying? Who has put you where you are? Who has surrounded you with the circumstances which are your trial and temptation? Who has planted the crook in your lot, — the skeleton in your house? Is it not God? And cannot He transfer them wherever you go, or raise up worse in the place to which your wings have carried you? You cannot escape from God. This very Psalmist, who wished that he had the wings of a dove, has told thee that "if thou take the wings of the morning, and dwell in the uttermost parts of the sea; even there shall his hand lead thee, and his right hand shall hold thee."[1] If you believe that God rules and superintends every thing, — that He has disposed the circumstances which surround and harass you, — why fly at all? They must be best for you, because He has promised to make every thing work together for good to them that love Him. It is quite lawful for the Christian to pray, as S. Paul did, that the thorn in his flesh, whatever it may be, may be removed: but not to fly away, as Jonah did, from the cross which has been laid upon him. In the one case he would most assuredly receive the answer: "My grace is sufficient for thee:"[2] in the other, he might find that it was "as if a man did flee from a lion, and a bear met him; or went into the house, and leaned his hand on the wall, and a serpent bit him."[3] In the anguish of some severe trial, the words of the Psalmist might come as the strong cry or wail of Nature from the lips of the believer; but it would soon be followed by the quiet of submission: "Not my will, but Thine, O God, be done!"

A Christian ought to know that rest cannot be found in attempting to fly from God; and flying from His allotment, is flying from Him. It can be found only in submission to God; in doing faithfully that which He has given us to do; in suffering patiently that which He has called us to bear. The Scripture speaks of the Christian life that now is, as of

[1] Psalm cxxxix. 9, 10. [2] 2 Cor. xii. 9. [3] Amos v. 19.

something set and arranged for us by God, just as Christ's life was set and arranged for Him. And if we would receive the rest which remaineth for the people of God, and would catch now and then the foretastes of it which come as streaks of light upon our hidden path, we must —

> "Trust in Him who trod before
> The desolate paths of life;
> Must bear in meekness, as He meekly bore,
> Sorrow and toil and strife.
> Think how the Son of God
> These thorny paths hath trod;
> Think how He longed to go,
> Yet tarried out, for thee, the appointed woe;
> Think of His loneliness in places dim
> Where no man comforted nor cared for Him;
> Think how He prayed, unaided and alone,
> In that dread agony, *Thy will be done!*
> Friend, do not thou despair!
> Christ, in His Heaven of heavens, will hear thy prayer."

We do not understand the true philosophy of Christianity. Where we ought to see it, in the life and character of Christ, we do not look for it, thinking of Him always as God our Redeemer, and not as Man our example. How much divine wisdom we lose in this misconception! His was the true life of man upon earth. How clearly He saw His work; how bravely He went up to it; how patiently He labored in it; how humbly He submitted to the will of God; how meekly He bore every thing which was laid upon Him! He had no rest, — in the sense in which man cries out for it, — no rest, night nor day: but He had the peace of God, which is, in this world, the foreshadowing of the heavenly rest. And this peace — the peace arising from walking submissively in the work assigned to us — is all that we may look for here. And Christ made us no larger promise. He never said that His disciples should have rest. He could not say it; for He said, "The disciple must be as his

Master;" and the Master had no rest: but He did say, "Peace I leave with you, my peace I give unto you."[1] And this peace is our exceeding great reward in this life; never to be got, however, by taking the wings of the dove and flying away, but only by imitating Christ, and setting our faces like a flint towards our work, leaving it with God to portion out our happiness. And when we do appreciate the glory of submission, when we in our work go straight forward whither the Spirit leads us to go, when we, in our sufferings, see God's love ever as a bow in the cloud, and are led to say, "It is well, for the Lord hath done it:" then do we read aright the lessons of Christianity; we know its meaning; we understand its life; we snatch from it its blessings; we look up and see Heaven opened. We are no longer groping amid the beggarly elements of this world; its philosophy we have cast aside as fruitless; its hopes we have trampled upon as vanity; its practice forever feeds unrest. We have found at last the true happiness of man; and we have found it, where man had never looked for it, in labor, in duty, in suffering, in humility, in looking to God's directions, as a maiden looks to the hand of her mistress. Man had supposed that it lay in ease, in wealth, in honor, in freedom of will, in independence of action: but the Christian, in following Christ, has found that his way to rest lay not among these, but turned aside to the humble in heart, to the lowly in spirit, to the meek in nature, to the suffering and the smitten; and ended ofttimes in shame and the cross. But with all these was peace, — peace that passeth understanding; peace which the world can neither give nor take away.

How hard it is to do our part in life patiently and submissively, in the true spirit of the martyr! Oh, how little man knows wherein true greatness lies! He is looking for

[1] S. John xiv. 27.

it in action: God sees it in obedience. He is measuring it by deeds: God is measuring it by suffering. He is embalming it in song and story, because of its glitter and display: God is embalming it in His book of life, because of its quiet faith and its unmurmuring trust. Man sees not the truest glory of his fellow-man: that is hid away in the secrets of his own heart, and is known only to God. Man's noblest and hardest conflicts are with himself, and his noblest victories are over his own nature. His temptation is to take wings and fly away from whatsoever is painful, or irksome, or self-denying. His victory is in overcoming this allurement, and standing firm at his post of duty or of suffering. We are surrounded by humble, unknown beings, whose lives are truly sublime, whose triumphs over self are more glorious in God's sight than all the victories of earthly conquerors. When His books shall be opened, and His record of goodness and of greatness shall be displayed to the world, how many names of which the world has never heard shall stand high upon that roll of life?—here a young heart, which smothered its affections that it might devote itself to the duties which home exacted of it; there a wife, who bore in secret, scorn, contumely, contempt, persecution, for the sake of Christ and His sacred cause: here a hero, who despised the shame of the world, that he might bear the cross of Christ unsullied through the world; there a sufferer, who lay for years without murmuring, in the hands of God, helpless, desolate, with no comforter but his Saviour: here a daughter of affliction, from whom has been stripped the dearest objects of affection, and yet who, kissing the rod, looks submissive into the face of God; there a victim of calumny, who bears for a whole lifetime unmerited reproach, and leaves vengeance and vindication to the pleasure of God. Oh, cases like these abound in the world;

are found everywhere in secret places of which that world never hears; are the true poetry of religion, sweet music in the ear of God, rich fragrance of prayer and faith rising up before His presence. Could the heart-life of such as these be written, — obscure, nameless people, — it would flash upon the world a moral heroism second only to the life of Christ, — a sublime self-devotion, learned only from that inimitable Master. These are the beings — sufferers and martyrs though they seem to be — who know what rest is. They have ceased their struggle with the world; they have subdued their own restless unbelief: and now they have quieted themselves upon the bosom of God, just as little children sink to sleep upon the bosoms of their mothers, their hearts still sobbing out their griefs, their eyes still wet with the tears of their young sorrow.

This is the path to rest, my beloved hearers, and the only one which God has marked out for man. Even if the wish of the Psalmist could be gratified, and you could have wings like a dove, you could not fly anywhere that would give you rest. That must be wrung out of labor, out of duty, out of suffering, out of an imitation of Christ. That must be won, not by flight, but by endurance; not by a cowardly desertion of the post at which God has placed us, but by standing to it through every privation and every suffering. Submission to God's will, whatever that may be, is the first step toward it. In due time will come the fruits of this submission, — peace, and even joy: and then will man learn, what is the true lesson of life, — that unrest is within himself, and is the child of unbelief and vain desires; that it has but slight connection with the circumstances of life; that it can never be quieted by change of scene or condition, or by gratification of its wishes; that even the wings of the morning cannot bear it away from the heart. David's wish was vain; it was one, nevertheless, in which we all sometimes indulge. Let us drive it away from us as a temptation; and seek for rest — where Christ found it — in running with patience the race that is set before us, looking unto Jesus as the Author and Finisher of our Faith.

Second Sermon.

And I said, This is mine infirmity: but I will remember the years of the right hand of the Most High. — PSALM lxxvii. 10.

THE Psalms are what may be termed, in modern phraseology, the "experience" of David. In them we are permitted to trace the workings of a Christian heart as distinctly as if they were the pulsations of our own; to examine minutely the dealings of God with a man whom He declares to have been, despite his infirmities, a man after His own heart. And an unspeakable privilege it is, to be allowed to read a soul in which God delighted, and to analyze feelings which were acceptable with Him. Left to ourselves, we should often be sadly disturbed at our own spiritual condition; we should be tempted to believe that no other Christian had ever experienced the sad variations which disturb our religious life. But having before us such an example as David; possessing what may be considered the daily journal of his feelings and emotions; studying them as they are laid bare in their weakness, as well as exhibited in their power: we can feel "the pulses of our Psalmist's passions beating their ditties as we lay our hearts unto them."[1] They become a standard for us; a spiritual mirror in which we may see our own affections reflected. His experience of God's dealings with his soul is written for our instruction in righteousness; and the phases of his feelings are indications to us of what we may expect in the progress of our spiritual life. Just as we see him

[1] Jackson.

full of joy and peace in believing, to-day; and then to-morrow cast into despondency and unbelief: so may we anticipate changes in our perceptions of God's relation to us. Our comfort, our sorrow; our fear, our confidence; our hope, our despair: are all exhibited to us in some one or other of those exquisite Psalms which he poured forth as indicative of his own emotions; and their rapid and often fearful variations are just as clearly marked in the vicissitudes of our condition. Many a Christian heart has found reason again and again to thank God for having condescended to unfold to us, through His Spirit, the inner workings of a human heart, as it was growing in grace and becoming assimilated to Himself. The sanctified heart, the heart already made meet for the inheritance of the saints in light, is not what the Christian craves for his contemplation. He wants to study the heart in its struggles after sanctification; — in its throbs and pulsations as it battles in the stern strife with temptation and sin, and the enemies of its inner life. It is not the conqueror with the crown upon his head and the palm-branches of victory in his hand, that is the most useful exemplar to the warring child of God: but it is the man of infirmity, and yet the man after God's own heart, whom it craves to look upon, as he rages in the midst of the battle-field, — now in the dust, and anon flashing the sword of the Spirit in the face of the adversary; now crying for help with the feebleness of a child, and anon shouting forth the praises of Him who hath delivered him from the power of the enemy. The soldier who is girding on his harness for the field cares not to look upon the triumphal car, save as it may prove an incentive to his ambition; but rather loves to fight over with the veteran the battles he has won, and to learn the arts and contrivances by which he overcame the foe and laid him prostrate in the dust. It is in the Revelation only — the last and consummating Book of the Gospel of our Lord — that we find those pictures of victory and of Heaven which are so glorious for the Christian: as if to teach us that the greatest portion of our lives, like the largest portion of the Bible, is to be occupied with the good fight of Faith; while victory, triumph, rest, reward, are to be left for the consummation of all things.

Hence is it so very interesting a feature in our Liturgy, that such large portions of the Psalms of David are appointed to be read upon every Lord's day; — enough to ensure to every Christian soul the "meat in due season" which it requires. So intermingled are the Psalmist's joys with his lamentations; so rapid is the change from the full assurance of hope to the deep despondency of a forsaken soul; so frequently does he run the gamut from the lowest notes of a sinner humbled in the dust to the highest outbursts of thanksgiving and of praise: that almost every selection of Psalms will furnish its tone for every heart, and the mourning Christian and the peaceful Christian and the rejoicing Christian will each find something that shall harmonize with his own condition and satisfy the cravings of his own soul. Sadly ignorant must be that mind, or miserably dull that spirit, which can find no music in the tones of David's harp; which can pass uncheered through such a flood of Christian light. Still more forlorn the condition of those who can quarrel with the Church, because she brings these glorious ditties so daily to her children's minds; — because, like a tender mother, she gives them line upon line, and precept upon precept, from the song-book of the sweet Psalmist of Israel.

How cheering to us that David had his infirmity! — that he was not a being of perfection, and that his infirmity was just the infirmity which is most common to us all, — that of distrusting God; of not believing in His promises, because they seem, for a little while, to lack fulfillment. The burden of the Psalm from which my text is taken, is a declaration of his distrust of God; and he recovers himself by confessing that it was his infirmity, and by casting himself back upon the memory of God's mercy and loving-kindness in the years that were gone. "I said, This is mine infirmity: but I will remember the years of the right hand of the Most High. I will remember the works of the LORD: surely I will remember thy wonders of old." I say, how cheering this is, that it is not only we who have our infirmities, who are filled with murmuring and distrust, who require to look back to past experience for our comfort and our assurance: but that this veteran servant of God, this chosen child of grace, this man of Christian struggle from his boyhood, this spiritually-minded saint, is compelled to make the confession of his weakness, and to pursue the very course which we must pursue for the resumption of his faith and his peace. Such confessions are our life, not because we rejoice in iniquity, not because we are glad over the infirmities of the Saints, but because it gives us hope that as they conquered those infirmities, through grace, and "obtained a good report," so may we overcome ours through the strength which is in Christ Jesus, and rejoice through hope of the grace of God. This feature runs through Christianity, and makes it the precious Gospel which it is. The infirmities of the Saints are never concealed, but are made manifest, so that the struggling saints of God, conscious of their weaknesses, may not despair, but may rather rejoice that they have a God who has unveiled the infirmities of His chosen children; that they have a Saviour who can be touched with a feeling of those infirmities; that a Spirit has been vouchsafed them, who is promised especially to help those infirmities.

It is frequently made an objection to the Bible that such

and such individuals, patriarchs, prophets, kings, apostles, have been exhibited therein as men of very great infirmities, and, in some instances, as men who have committed enormous sins. The impression seems to be left upon certain minds, that such individuals could not be accepted by a holy God; nay, more, that a religion must be worth very little whose chief Saints could have been guilty of such weaknesses, — to use no harsher word. The fact I shall not controvert; but that it ought to be an objection to the scheme of religion contained in the Bible, I cannot admit. To me it is one of the clearest proofs of the inspiration of the Bible; for, if the Saints of the Bible had been represented as faultless men, their conduct would not have harmonized with the plan of salvation, with the scope and purpose of the economy of grace. As I understand Christianity, it has come to save sinners, and to change them into saints meet for the inheritance of Heaven. These sinners are to be saved through grace, not by any merit or deserving of their own. And when this grace has worked upon the heart, it is only the beginning of a growth in grace, which is to go on through a lifetime of discipline until it shall be perfected in glory. "And he said, So is the kingdom of God, as if a man should cast seed into the ground; and should sleep, and rise night and day, and the seed should spring and grow up, he knoweth not how. For the earth bringeth forth fruit of herself; first the blade, then the ear, after that the full corn in the ear."[1] If, according to the plan of salvation, the children of God were to be perfect at once, why a Saviour, continued in Heaven to be their Advocate? Why such a precious promise as this, "If any man sin, we have an advocate with the Father, Jesus Christ the righteous: and he is the propitiation for our sins?"[2] Why a Spirit sent to earth to witness with our spirits, to cheer, to

[1] S. Mark iv. 26-28. [2] 1 S. John ii. 1, 2.

comfort, to sanctify us, to help our infirmities? Why the chastening rod of a Father held perpetually over us, and the solemn declaration sounded in our ears, "Whom the Lord loveth he chasteneth, and scourgeth every son whom he receiveth?"[1] Why the constant injunctions of the Apostles to "work out our salvation with fear and trembling,"[2] — to "run, not as uncertainly," — to "fight, not as one that beateth the air," — but to "keep under the body and bring it into subjection, lest while preaching to others," he himself "should be a castaway?"[3] No! this manifestation of the infirmity of the Saints is just in harmony with the Gospel scheme; — especially what ought to have been expected in the development of a "salvation by faith, through grace." It is only when we turn to a spurious Christianity, that we find perfect saints. The Saints of the Bible are all men of infirmity, and therefore it was that they gloried in a "High Priest that might be touched with a feeling of their infirmities"; therefore it was that they cried out for a "Spirit that might make intercession for them with groanings, which cannot be uttered."[4] As the religion, so the saints. A religion of grace: Saints having infirmity. A religion of merit; and, as a consequence, saints pretending to perfection, — "whited sepulchres, full of dead men's bones, and of all uncleanness."[5]

Such is the harmony, as I feel it, between saints having infirmity and a salvation through grace; and such is the attitude which, as all analogy teaches us, should be occupied by those who are in a state of tutelage. What is the necessity of spiritual discipline, if we are already perfect? What of chastening, if we have no faults? What of the means of grace, if we have no evil habits to be rooted out, no good ones to be built up? All the instruction of the

[1] Heb. xii. 6. [2] Phil. ii. 12. [3] 1 Cor. ix. 26, 27.
[4] Rom. viii. 26. [5] S. Matt. xxiii. 27.

Bible, and all the institutions of the Church, teach us that the Church of Christ is a school, planted in the world, in which Christians have to be prepared for their places in Heaven, — prepared through temptation, through weakness, through suffering, through trial. And if this be so, is not infirmity necessarily a part of the very being of a Christian? What the need of placing a child at school, unless it may be trained in knowledge and in virtue? When praising the management of a school, do we say that it is a school whose scholars have no infirmities: or that it is one where those infirmities are gradually cured? Certainly the latter. And we give our faith to it when we see the vicious reclaimed, and the ignorant enlightened, and the weak character made strong; and not when we learn that the entrance to the school has been debarred to all such! When praising the success of a parent's efforts, do we speak of his family circle as well disciplined when we say that his children had no faults: or when we show that very gross faults have been cured under his arrangements? And so with Christianity. So far as the justification of a sinner is concerned, that is the effect of faith in the Lord Jesus Christ; but after we have received peace through that justification, we must be sanctified and made meet for Heaven. Now what should be the praise of the Church, — and this brings us back to the objection we are considering, — that there are no infirmities within the Church: or that she gradually cures them? that as soon as an individual crosses her threshold, his sins are all laid down: or that she is a school in which the teachings of the Holy Ghost are made responsive to the infirmities of the creature, and thus weak sinful men are gradually built up into the image and likeness of Christ? How futile, then, to make it an objection to the Bible, containing the scheme of salvation which it does, that it portrays for our example, and for God's commendation, Saints who have been men of like passions with ourselves!

To return to our subject of rejoicing, — that we find such a Saint as David confessing his infirmity, because each one of us has our infirmity. Who that kneels at this Communion Table, but has occasion to say of some weakness, of some shortcoming, "This is mine infirmity"? "The infirmities of the believer," says a beautiful writer of the present day, "are as varied as they are numerous. Some are weak in faith, and are always questioning their interest in Christ. Some superficial in knowledge, and shallow in experience, and ever exposed to the crudities of error and to the assaults of temptation. Some are slow travellers in the divine life, and are always in the rear; while yet others are often ready to halt altogether. Then there are others who groan beneath the burden of bodily infirmity, exerting a morbid influence upon their spiritual experience; — a nervous temperament — a state of perpetual depression and despondency — the constant corroding of mental disquietude — physical ailment — imaginary forebodings — a facile yielding to temptation — petulance of spirit — unguardedness of speech — gloomy interpretations of Providence — an eye that views only the dark hues of the cloud, the sombre shadings of the picture."[1] Such is the catalogue of infirmities which a Christian of deep experience has drawn up for our consideration; and among them I fear that most of you can lay your finger upon some one and say, "'This is mine infirmity,' this has been the plague of my Christian life, the enemy of my Christian peace. With this have I battled! Against this have I struggled! Again and again hath it cast me down; again and again have I risen victorious over it. But still 'it is mine infirmity.' Shall it

[1] Winslow.

conquer me, or shall I be conqueror, and more than conqueror, through Him that loved me?"

Think not, child of God, whoever you may be, that you are bearing this infirmity alone! Think not that you are unpitied in your lamentations over it, without sympathy in your struggles against it. You have, thanks be to God, a High-Priest who can be touched with a feeling of your infirmities; who is always ready to pour out, upon every sincere struggler, of the fullness of His grace for that very single infirmity which is distressing you. What is it? "Is it sin, is it sorrow, is it sickness, is it want?" What is it? "Is it some fault of temper, some levity of disposition, some lust of the flesh, some temptation of the heart?" What is it? "Is it unbelief, is it despondency, is it faithlessness, is it coldness of spirit?" No matter what it is, my hearer, if you feel it as an infirmity; if you strive against it as an infirmity; if you mourn over it, and would cast it off, as an infirmity: you have the burden carried for you, for the Scripture tells us, "Himself took our infirmities and carried our sicknesses." "Wondrous view of the incarnate God!" as one has beautifully expressed it: "That very infirmity which now bows you to the earth, by reason of which you can in no wise lift up yourself, your Saviour bore. It bowed Him to the dust, and brought the crimson drops to His brow. And is this no consolation? Does it not make your infirmity even pleasant, to remember that Jesus once bore it, and in sympathy bears it still?" It is a blessed consolation to feel that we have a Friend, closer to us than a brother, who is touched with our infirmity; who instead of covering us with reproaches because we are weak, bears those weaknesses for us. How tender is our Saviour! How beautiful our religion! How wreathed is it with the richest treasures of love and of sympathy! How little do they understand it, who would change it into a thing of harshness, and transform the gushing affections of an EMMANUEL, a GOD WITH US, into the stern severity of a God afar off!

And can you not, my fellow-Christians, imitate David, and find in your own experience some consolation for the infirmity which weighs upon you? It was when he was interrogating his gracious Lord in strains like these, "Will the LORD cast off forever? and will he be favorable no more? Is his mercy clean gone forever? doth his promise fail for evermore? Hath God forgotten to be gracious? Hath he in anger shut up his tender mercies?" that he was fain to add: "This is mine infirmity; but I will remember the years of the right hand of the Most High." And have you, my beloved hearer, no such years to remember? Can you not look back to the days that are gone, and consider that in six troubles He has delivered you, yea in seven that no evil has touched you? And, considering this, can you not trust Him for the time to come? Hath He yet permitted your infirmity utterly to prevail against you? Has it ever so cast you down, as that you have let go the anchor within the veil? Then why lament for the future? Why distrust a God who has surrounded you with mercies and blessings, because perchance there remains one thorn in the flesh? Has He not told you, "My grace is sufficient for thee?"[1] Comfort yourself in the past. Remember the works of the Lord,— works wrought by the grace of God and the power of the Spirit within your own heart,— wrought upon feelings, upon affections, upon intellect, upon the whole creature, soul and body, so that you know that you are a new creature in Christ Jesus. Remember His wonders of old,— wonders that you have seen and rejoiced in, when the way of the Lord was in the sanctuary. And even though now

[1] 2 Cor. xii. 9.

"His way be in the sea, and his path in the great waters, and his footsteps be not known,"[1] still trust in Him, and be satisfied that He will put upon you no greater burden than you can bear.

And let the tenderness of God with our infirmities teach us also to bear the infirmities of our brethren. Ah! my hearers, there is a large field of exhortation open for me in this direction, but I can only touch it now. The bearing the infirmities of the weak is a grace too little understood, and yet it is the grace which assimilates us most nearly to Christ. His distinctive mark in prophecy was, "A bruised reed shall he not break, and the smoking flax shall he not quench;"[2] and by these emanations of tenderness—so uncommon and so unknown in the world—was He to be distinguished among the children of men. And shall His disciples be distinguished by any thing so unlike this as censoriousness, as fault-finding, as evil-speaking, as crushing those who are already down, as shooting poisoned arrows at the wounded and stricken heart? The love of Christ forbid! Are you, my hearer, strong in the Lord? Then remember, "We then that are strong ought to bear the infirmities of the weak, and not to please ourselves."[3] Are you yourself "compassed with infirmity"? Then remember, that as you desire the Lord Jesus to bear your infirmities, so should you also bear the infirmities of others. Has a Christian brother or sister been overtaken in a fault? "Brethren, if a man be overtaken in a fault, ye, which are spiritual, restore such an one in the spirit of meekness; considering thyself, lest thou also be tempted."[4] Let us in all things strive to do unto others as we would do unto ourselves. Our own weaknesses we confess to God, but we do not trumpet them forth to men. "We unveil them," as

[1] Psalm lxxvii. 19. [2] Isaiah xlii. 3. [3] Rom. xv. 1.
[4] Gal. vi. 1.

one has exquisitely worded it, "to His eye, and He kindly and graciously veils them from all human eyes. Be this our spirit and our conduct toward a weak and erring brother. Let us rather part with our right hand, than publish his infirmity to others, and thus wound the Head by an unkind and unholy exposure of the faults and frailties of a member of His body, and by so doing cause the enemies of Christ to blaspheme that worthy Name by the which we are called."

There may be some one here present who keeps aloof from the Church of Christ because of some infirmity which may be weighing upon the conscience. Is this wise? How is the infirmity to be cured? Whence is the power to come which is to conquer the infirmity? Is it not better at once to place yourself, in all humility of spirit, in the school of Christ, under the discipline of Christ, and endeavor there to conquer in His strength? If you are kept away only by some infirmity, will it not lighten that infirmity to roll it upon Christ, to permit the Holy Spirit to share it with you? Oh, keep not away from Jesus because of the very weaknesses which He came to bear for you, which He has already borne for you! "Come unto me," is His especial invitation, "all ye that labor and are heavy laden, and I will give you rest."[1]

[1] S. Matt. xi. 28.

Third Sermon.

Pilate answered, What I have written I have written.— S. JOHN xix. 22.

HOW often a man announces a great truth without being at all conscious of it. His words become words in the mouth of all the world, while he spake them only as the appropriate words of the occasion. In some critical moment of individual fortune, at some turning-point of events whose greatness he does not appreciate, he utters a thought which impresses itself upon the whole future of the race, and is repeated from generation to generation as a solemn reality. These are not inspirations, because they are not suggested by the Spirit of God; they are not the deductions of reason, for they are most often just the words which the circumstances call for. They are not proverbs, for they contain no particular antithesis of words. But they have so shaped themselves, that they forever speak a warning in our ears, and haunt us like a shadow which is eternally connected with us, and which we must one day meet when words shall become terrible realities. They startle us, not because of the present, but because they point us to an unending future; not because they suggest any thing which is immediately fearful, but because they remind us of something which is to be eternally permanent. Their awfulness is not of to-day, but forever. Their sting gives no instant pain, but we feel that it is a worm that shall never die.

When Pilate uttered the saying of our text, he had no

conception what it really imported. He spoke it in the haughtiness of his heart and in the indolence of his temper. He had no thoughts, when he said it, either of God or man. He had no conception that he was fulfilling the foreordinations of God; or that he was putting upon record words which should shake man's soul, whenever he might ponder upon them. He was thinking only of himself; and when he said, "What I have written I have written," he meant no more than that he did not choose to alter what he had already done, or that he did not deem the matter of importance enough to take any more trouble about it.

And yet these words teach us two most solemn truths, truths which I mean to dwell upon to-day, and which we should all keep ever present with us as monitors of duty,— as warnings of what is before us in the days which are yet to come upon us. There are thoughts which are grand enough to make us pause upon them, however little we may be accustomed to think seriously about any thing; and such thoughts are these which arise naturally out of Pilate's answer. If there is any thing which can startle us in life, it is the finding that we are swayed by influences which we have never counted upon; that we are making impressions which can never be eradicated. Both these elements of responsibility are found in Pilate's answer.

The words which Pilate had written were, "JESUS OF NAZARETH THE KING OF THE JEWS." Against this the Chief Priests of the Jews demurred, saying, "Write not, The King of the Jews; but that he said, I am King of the Jews. Pilate answered, What I have written I have written." He had been unconsciously an instrument in God's hands. Caring nothing about God, sneering at all truth, considering the Messiah as a mere Jewish impostor, he was nevertheless made to write the truth, the mighty truth of the times, upon the Cross. The King of the Jews had come, and they were ignorant of it; but a Gentile and a skeptic was made to proclaim it in the most conspicuous manner. It was placed as a title right over the head of the Crucified. It was attached to the Cross, as if to show that it was the royal chariot in which to ride triumphant to his Kingdom. It was written in three languages, that all the world might understand it. And when it was objected to, the objection was met by the stubborn answer, "What I have written I have written." It was the overruling power of God using this infidel as His instrument, and yet using him in such manner as that he felt no consciousness of having been necessitated. He had perfect liberty not to write it at all. He might have altered it after he had written it. But yet he did write it, and would not change it, even while he cared nothing at all about the pretensions of Jesus of Nazareth. Thus is it that God is ever making the wrath of man to praise Him, and is compelling the indifferent and the unbelieving to bring His purposes to pass.

And in like manner are we all the unconscious instruments of God in working out His purposes. We are pursuing, whether believers or infidels, what we consider the regular routine of life. One thing follows another in regular and natural succession, the thought of to-day following as we suppose logically the thought of yesterday, and the action of this hour treading consequentially upon the action of the last. We can perceive no interference with the sequence. Nothing comes violently to break in upon our train of thought, or to change our course of action. If there is any modification of either opinion or conduct, it seems to be produced by circumstances which were altogether ordinary, and in the course of a reasonable probability. No man can say that his will has been violently overruled. No angel has stood — that he was conscious of — in his path opposing him with the sword of the Lord.

No voice has come to him saying, "Go here," or "Go there"; "Do this," or "Do that." Every thing has gone on with him as if he were his own master, the creature of his own will. And yet has every individual of the human race been silently working out the purposes of God in Christ Jesus.

This Christians know and rejoice in. It is their delight and their glory to know that God is so using them. It is their heart's desire to aid Him in the whole mystery of His will. Their exceeding great consolation is, that they are not walking by the light of their own eyes, but are led along paths of safety and of peace. Unbelievers do not know it, and would not perhaps acknowledge it; but it is proved upon them by the persistent progress of God's purposes in spite of all opposition, and by the perpetually visible bringing of good for the Church out of the evil of the world. We cannot trace the history of nations in its connection, for example, with such an event as the advent of our Lord, without being most forcibly struck with the constant recurrence of this very thing. It was not Pilate alone who was made to testify to the identity of Jesus of Nazareth as the Messiah. Individuals and nations, all the way back to the promise in the garden of Eden, had been made to do the same. When Caiaphas, who was the High Priest that same year, said unto the Jews in reference to Jesus, "Ye know nothing at all, nor consider that it is expedient for us, that one man should die for the people, and that the whole nation perish not:" [1] was it of his own will, think ye, that he uttered this prophecy of the necessary sacrifice and death of Christ? Like Pilate he uttered a divine truth; he carried on the purposes of God: but did he intend it? Did not God overrule his wicked purpose of the execution of an innocent Man, to the purposes of His

[1] S. John xi. 49, 50.

will? When a decree issued from the court of the Cæsars that all the world should be taxed, and in pursuance of that decree our Lord's Mother according to the flesh came up to her own City and Tribe, and brought forth her Son in Bethlehem, according to all the prophecies which had been forecast upon Him: was it of his own unguided purpose, think ye, that the Cæsar conceived such a project of taxation? He issued an unusual, but still quite a natural, decree. He ordained what he supposed should redound to his own glory and his own emolument. He had no knowledge of the divine prophecies, nor any idea of fulfilling them. The last thing on earth he should have dreamed of, would have been the giving countenance to a rival King. Nevertheless, this very decree did carry Mary to Bethlehem, and did fulfill the prophecy of Micah: "But thou, Bethlehem Ephratah, though thou be little among the thousands of Judah, yet out of thee shall he come forth unto me that is to be ruler in Israel; whose goings forth have been from of old, from everlasting."[1] When Cyrus and Darius issued the decrees permitting the Tribes of Judah and Benjamin to return from their captivity at Babylon and rebuild the city and Temple of Jerusalem, was it at all in their minds to fulfill the prophecy of Jacob made a thousand years before, that the sceptre should not depart from Judah, nor a lawgiver from between his feet, until Shiloh came? Darius performed what he considered a wise political act, putting a strong people between him and Egypt. That was all his motive. And yet it was the overruling hand of God making all things work most naturally for His own wise purposes. I might cite instance after instance of this sort; but it is unnecessary. These are enough to show the course of God's dealings, and the mode of His operation. The world goes on naturally; each man seems to do as he

[1] Micah v. 2.

pleases; each nation appears to be working out its manifest destiny: but yet in the end, that comes to pass which God has foreordained; and when man does not advance it willingly, he is nevertheless made to advance it unconsciously. He is God's instrument whether he chooses to be or not. The only difference is that, if he coöperates with God heartily and sincerely, he receives the "Well done, thou good and faithful servant."[1] If he does not, he is still made to work for God, even though, at the last, he receive condemnation.

This is one truth which comes logically out of Pilate's answer, and is worth a man's consideration. As I said before, an unbeliever may not acknowledge this truth, so far as any consciousness of his own is concerned. But when he perceives, from the whole history of the world, how every thing has been overruled for the establishment and advancement of Christ's Kingdom, and how naturally it appears to have all come to pass: should he not consider this point, whether he may not be an instrument in God's hand, without being conscious of it? Pilate was not conscious of it. Caiaphas was not conscious of it. Cyrus was not conscious of it. And yet every one of them was the instrument of God, — was a mere tool for the economy of Grace. What a silly position, to be made an agent for doing the very thing you are opposing and fighting against; to be clamoring out your antagonism against the purposes of God, even while you are made unwittingly to work in the traces of the chariot of the Redeemer! If there is one thing more than another that should make an unbeliever gnash his teeth, it is the absolute certainty that God is making his wrath turn to the glory of Christ, and is restraining that which He does not choose shall break forth for the annoyance of the Church.

[1] S. Matt. xxv. 21.

But there is another and quite as solemn a truth contained in these words of Pilate; and it is, that we are all perpetually making impressions which can never be changed. We are all writing, writing upon most impressible materials, upon hearts, upon feelings, upon affections, upon mind, upon character, upon soul, words which we may never be able to alter, and of which we shall be obliged to say in sadness and with trembling, "What I have written I have written." It is there stamped upon friends, upon society, upon dependents, upon children, upon wife, upon all that have been near my heart or have nestled in my bosom: and I cannot change it. I may mourn over it. I may repent it in dust and ashes. Tears, bitter tears, may have been shed to blot it out. Prayers, earnest prayers, may have been poured out to God for forgiveness. I may have felt the balm of comfort and the assurance of pardon: but still, "What I have written I have written," and there it stands forever. It has fallen from my lips; it has been set down by my pen; it has been published by my conduct; my example has given it currency; it has gone forth from me: and I cannot arrest it. It was in my power not to have written it in any of these ways: but having done it, it is out of my power to check the evil. My family has drunk it in. The circle of my acquaintance has seized upon it as truth. I now know it to be poison, rank poison: but I myself have infused it into the circulation, and cannot check its fatal progress. I see it extending and extending, like a circle in the waters: and I stand impotent. The law of Nature about which I have been indifferent or ignorant, is working its terrible consequences: and that law is, that an impulse once given must go on until its force is exhausted. And what is there to exhaust the force of evil words, of evil examples, of evil writings, of evil impressions? They are communicated from mind to mind, and from heart to heart, and from soul to soul, unendingly. They begin from me, or from you, and they cleave their evil track through the generations of men: and they find their home in hell.

It is amazing that any thinking man can be indifferent about the impressions he is making. If he truly considers this expression, "What I have written I have written," he cannot be careless of the consequences of his simplest words. When I speak, or write, or act: my words, my writings, my deeds, are not thrown upon the desert air, are not dispersed and scattered as the mists of a landscape. They are received into pure and tender minds, — minds made more tender by affection and kindred; they are taken hold of by hearts, loving hearts, that are trusting to us and resting upon us; they are caught up by souls, immortal souls, which are looking to us for knowledge and culture: and with these they incorporate themselves. They grow into the nature, and we cannot get them out. Childhood assimilates them. Youth is guided by them. Manhood teaches them. Whatever that childhood becomes, whatever that youth may lead to, wherever the teachings of that manhood may reach to, or whatever they may end in: I am the responsible party. The evil is upon me. The sin is at my door. That mischief which I see expanding, forever expanding, *I* set in motion. Alas for me! "What I have written I have written."

And ofttimes we are writing by authority. We are making utterances (and you must remember that utterances can be made by writing as well as by speaking, by acting as well as by writing, by example as well as by action) which God has commissioned us to set forth as parents, as masters, as teachers, as citizens, as His own commissioned ambassadors: and this adds greatly to the terror of those words, "What I have written I have written." When a man has no special authority, the things he writes upon the world are not so important, do not carry so much force, have not the immense influence which belongs to those who are standing in the position of domestic or social power. They may do great mischief; they may be seeds of evil that shall float upon the air and drop their curse hither and thither: yet they are not likely to make the mark which things written by authority do make. But when it can be said, — This is the writing of a Father upon my mind, upon my heart, upon my affections, upon my imagination, upon all my associations, upon my soul; — This is the writing of a Master whom God has set to guide me; — This is the writing of a Teacher who is given the power to mould me as he can; — This is the writing of a servant of the Lord, who holds a commission above all others: then can we understand the mighty import of the words, "What I have written I have written." Every thing given forth as opinion, as feeling, as truth, as example, sinks deeply into the nature. It becomes a mighty part of the influences which are making up the present and the future of those who surround us. We are graving into the character, we are stamping upon the tender heart, what will remain there for blessing or for curse. We are doing our part towards the making of the generation which is to follow us. We are creating, in a certain sense, the character of the times. We are reproducing ourselves in those who are to come after us; and they will carry us down from generation to generation, onward, onward to the judgment-seat of God. We may choose not to realize this fearful responsibility. We may be unwilling to permit such a load of authority to rest upon our feelings. We may endeavor to laugh it off, or sneer it off, or reason it off; but it will be in vain. Even in this world, when things begin to go wrong with those over whom we have had authority, — when the poison is beginning to show itself in outbreaking corruption in children, in servants, among our companions, in society, — the thought will intrude itself, "Is this my writing? Have I planted the seeds of this perilous evil? Have my opinions, my words, my feelings, my writings, ended in this?" I say, even in this world, such thoughts will intrude; but in eternity, we shall find still more sternly the unalterable words of truth, — "What I have written I have written."

And that indelibility of our writings is the most terrible part of it. We can impress, but we cannot cut out. We can write, but we cannot blot out. We can shape character, opinion, feeling: but once shaped, we have no more power over them. Man's nature is so arranged, that even reason cannot afterwards modify what has been engrained into character; that even knowledge cannot scatter the associations of childhood. It is a miserable mistake to look at man as if he were a being governed by his understanding. That is by far the least influential portion of his nature. He is governed a thousand times more by his feelings, by his affections, by those agencies which work upon him through his heart; and when these have been thoroughly impregnated in early youth, woe unto what is called *reason!* It is a most powerless instrument, weak unto death against such influences as passion, as prejudice, as association!

We shall all have an account to give. All that we shall have written will remain, and come up against us. Let us therefore consider not only our present view of the writings we have stamped upon man and society, but the view which we shall have to take of them upon a dying bed. When we shall be lying there, we shall feel most intensely the power of those words, "What I have written I have written." We are then preparing not only to leave them behind us as seeds of good or of evil, as impressions which cannot be eradicated: but we are preparing to meet them. They remain in the world for all time, and then they follow after us for judgment. What a terrible moment, — that moment, when, lying powerless for all retrieval, we shall be obliged to say, "What I have written I have written."

Fourth Sermon.

And David longed, and said, Oh that one would give me drink of the water of the well of Bethlehem, which is by the gate!— 2 SAM. xxiii. 15.

HOW richly the spiritual evolves itself out of the natural! They dwell together, as the soul with the body, spirit within matter; the one the substance, the other the life; each necessary to the other, each harmonious with the other, each illustrating the other. They coexist everywhere; and while we are not to be led away by fanciful analogies and a crude sentimentalism, a spiritual mind will see in nature, and in its constitution and course, manifold indications of its capacity for spiritual development and spiritual instruction. Our Saviour seized hold of this arrangement, and used it again and again in His divine teachings. He made the fowls of the air, the lilies of the valley, the corn in its progress from the blade to the ear, the summer sky in its play of light, — all preachers of righteousness, by bringing out of their natural developments spiritual lessons of the highest practical value. And His Apostles walked in His footsteps through the same rich field of meditation, and have made plain to us the most abstruse topics of life and immortality, by bringing the obvious processes of nature to the help of divine revelation. Who can see a grain of wheat planted in the earth, and run in thought through its future phases of development, without thinking of the resurrection of the body with which S. Paul has forever linked it in delightful association? Who can study the organization of the body with its union of comely and uncomely parts, with its necessary subordination yet complete harmony, without remembering the like adjustment of functions in the Church and the State, — those two essentials of happiness for man, — with which the same Apostle has indissolubly connected them? Who can guide a ship with a rudder, or manage a horse with the bit, without recalling S. James's spiritual use of them in his denunciation of the tongue? And as they read in nature these rich manifestations, and used them for public instruction, so may we, as we walk amid the works and wonders of God, see Him and His revealed truth in every thing around us. And this is just what we should look for in a world ordered and arranged by Him who gave us His revelation; for if they did not in harmony develop the like truths, how could they proceed from the same Author? But we must remember, in our handling of this beautiful principle, that we are not inspired as were Christ and His Apostles, and that we have no authority to derive from nature a new revelation. We may study them as they lie infolded together in the arrangements of things; we may comfort ourselves with the clearness which they unitedly give to infinite ideas; we may revel in the glories which they flash around the future, as the mind is led step by step through the gorgeous array of nature's most precious gifts up to the Heaven where there shall be no more curse: but we must follow the true laws of logic, and illustrate Nature by Revelation, — the typical wisdom of God by the revealed wisdom. It is a beautiful study, if we are not fanciful; a very dangerous one, if we keep not the Word of God perpetually in our hands. Nature is always true; but difficult to read, because her greatest truths develop slowly, and mature only after long observation: while Revelation gives us conclusions from the Divine Mind, which we can receive at once by

Faith, or have forced upon us by a bitter experience. And it often happens that an imaginative temperament becomes bewildered by attempting to rest in the religion of Nature; to look at God only in His poetical and not in His practical aspect; to worship Him as He manifests Himself as the Architect and Ruler of the Universe: but to reject His teachings when He comes to separate man's obligations and duties from his wishes and fancies.

How beautifully is this connection of the natural and the spiritual illustrated in the longing of David for water from the well of Bethlehem! Bethlehem was his birthplace, the home of his childhood, and the spot around which all his youthful hopes had gathered. Beside that well, he had played as a child. From that well he had quenched his thirst when heated by sport, or wearied with labor. At that well he had watered his sheep at morning and evening, surrounded by laughing maidens and joyous youths, when as yet his mind knew no burden and his conscience no sin. And now, wearied with life and tired of struggle, his thoughts recurred to those days of innocence, and to that well whose waters he remembered as the sweetest he had ever drank: "And David longed, and said, Oh that one would give me drink of the water of the well of Bethlehem, which is by the gate!" That well by the gate, — no other: for none had its associations, none its memories. Other water might be as sparkling, as cool, as pure: but not for him. In that well alone could he see reflected, as in a panorama, all his early life, his days of joy and peace. His heart went out to that spot, and fastened itself upon it with a longing which nothing else could satisfy.

And how that longing for the past of our boyhood cleaves to us all! As age creeps upon us, and we live in recollection more than we do in hope, how the heart goes back to those places and circumstances which became dear to us in childhood! We leap over the intervening gap, and fasten our yearning hearts upon the days which have faded into the distance. And such is life, unless we make it bright with the hopes of eternity. In youth we look forward; in age we look back. In youth, ardent and joyous, our hearts bound onward to action, as if we should surely find happiness there; in age, wearied and jaded, we go back to our wells of Bethlehem, to drink there and be at peace. And thus life is frittered away between anticipation and regret, because we have not learned that its balance-wheel is in Religion, — in re-union with God. If we fail to make that union, we find that neither youth nor age will satisfy us. In the one we shall be deluded by Hope; in the other we shall be cheated by Memory. God has constituted us so, and we cannot get rid of our nature. Without the living presence of God in the soul, we cannot be satisfied in the present. We create an ideal world, when we are young, which we are ever hoping to realize; and when we are old we permit distance to give enchantment to the view, and to gild all the past with a fictitious glow.

Is life worth its struggle under such conditions? Are we willing to live altogether without realities, and, like children, to be clutching at the stars or running after the play of the light and the shadow? We are created for higher things. We were never meant to be at rest amid illusions, nor to spend our time in chasing them. A grand destiny is ours; and upon that it was designed that we should fix our aims. We might find much to interest us by the way, — much to love and much to enjoy. As we journeyed we might pluck the flowers by the way-side, and drink from the wells of Bethlehem; but God was to be ever before us, as the purpose and end of all our movements. Those vast affections with which God had endowed us were not to be lavished upon shadows; but were given us for the reproduction within us of a life which should be eternal because divine, having its centre in God, and its strength through Christ. Those grand faculties of imagination, of hope, of memory, were never designed to waste themselves upon dreams; but were bestowed upon us for the uses of life, and the gaining of eternity. If we dwell in vain conceptions of the future, or rest in false memories of the past, we are equally untrue to ourselves. We are not grasping the divine idea of man's existence. We are drinking water which will never quench our thirst. We are preparing to lie down in disappointment and sorrow.

How that longing of the heart for something we cannot attain, breathes of our divine origin, and our assured immortality! Why is it that our conceptions are always more perfect than our realizations, and that we are never satisfied to live in the stern realities of our true existence? Every one has his dream, his fancy, his hope. Every one sits pensive at times, and builds castles in the air. Every one has an inner life which no one reads but himself, and which goes on within his outer life, a wheel within a wheel. While we toil and labor, we are dreaming. While encompassed by the ordinary routine of every-day life, we are in some fairy land of the heart or the imagination. What we are obliged to do in the way of labor or duty, we do mechanically in the sight of the world, and let it see the prose of our existence: its poetry we keep for ourselves; and thus have always a witness within ourselves that we are more than we seem to be, are born of a higher nature, are intended for a sublimer sphere. And as these dreams are successively scattered by the experience of life,—if we have not found God in Christ, and taken that Reality home to us,—we turn to the past, and long with David: "Oh that one would give me drink of the water of the well of Bethlehem, which is by the gate!"

But there is a much deeper meaning in that wish of David than is contained in the train of thought which I have been pursuing. David was a prophet, and saw in his spirit the fulfillment of that prediction of Micah, then not as yet even uttered, "But thou, Bethlehem Ephratah, though thou be little among the thousands of Judah, yet out of thee shall he come forth unto me that is to be ruler in Israel; whose goings forth have been from of old, from everlasting."[1] And God's Spirit, as he lay there, old, faint and wearied, showed him in vision that Fountain opened for sin and for uncleanness in the house of David, and made him to hear that Voice which declared to the woman of Samaria: "Whosoever drinketh of this water shall thirst again: but whosoever drinketh of the water that I shall give him shall never thirst; but the water that I shall give him shall be in him a well of water springing up into everlasting life."[2] And this water was typified by the well of Bethlehem. And while the Psalmist's body longed for the water in the well by the gate, and his mind clustered all its rich memories and associations around it: his spirit was longing for a draught of that divine Love which should quench all the desires of the unsatisfied heart. Even as Job, in his misery, cried out for a Mediator long before He had come, saying, "Oh that I knew where I might find him! that I might come even to his seat!"[3] so did David, in the solitariness of his spirit, cry out for water from that Well which yet lay hidden from the knowledge of man. His lips, his affections, his soul, all longed for water from that Well of Bethlehem,—true foreshadowing of the unquenched thirst which still haunts the children of men.

How often man longs secretly for spiritual water from this Well of Bethlehem, and lets his want die unknown

[1] Micah v. 2. [2] S. John iv. 13, 14. [3] Job xxiii. 3.

within him! He sighs for something he has never had: and he ofttimes knows not what it is. It is a craving at the heart for something that will fill his desires: and he cannot find it. He supposes it to arise from some crook in his lot, from some disease of temperament, from some ill discipline of his character: when, all the while, it has its origin in the soul, of which he has taken no account. Body and mind are all he has been accustomed to consider; and when he can find no remedy for his longing in any change he can administer to them, he thinks his case to be hopeless. His philosophy is as much at fault as his religion. He has left out of his calculation the highest constituent of his being: and yet hopes to be satisfied. When he has furnished food for his body, and literary or scientific nourishment for his mind, and objects of an earthly kind for his affections, he thinks that he has done every thing which he can for the satisfaction of his nature: and yet he, an immortal creature, has left both God and his soul without any consideration. He has made no provision forever for that part of his nature which is its living part. For that which is corruptible and dying, he has exhausted luxury and pushed science to its utmost verge of development: but that which is incorruptible and undying, which is the breath of the Almighty, which is to expand in greatness through eternal ages, is left, without any spiritual food, to pine and perish from utter inanition. And yet the man who does this, wonders that there is some unsatisfied longing in the heart, some inward burning wish for "water of the well" of some Bethlehem, that might revive his hopes. Why, my beloved hearer, it is your soul longing for God; craving to be united once again to the Eternal Being from whom it sprang; forcing upon you, if peradventure you may understand, its claims to your notice, its influence upon your happiness for time as well as for eternity. May you listen to it; may you recognize the voice of the Divinity speaking within you; may you learn, ere it be too late, at what fountain its thirst may be quenched, and its guilt washed out; and may your feelings find utterance in the burning words of David: "Oh that one would give me drink of the water of the well of Bethlehem, which is by the gate!"

You can satisfy your longing, my immortal fellow-creature, at no other fountain than this of Bethlehem. It is God's Holy Spirit that is causing you to feel that longing for something higher and holier than you have yet attained; and it is God's Son giving you to drink of the Water of Life which alone can satisfy your soul. Unless you can procure water from that Well, you must perish in your unsatisfied condition. Nothing but the Spirit of God can quench the thirst of the spirit of man. And thanks be to the grace and mercy of God, that Water is offered to every thirsty creature; and gushes a free, rich, abundant stream of love and peace. When David uttered this wish, the well of Bethlehem was in the hands of the Philistines, his enemies; and his valiant men of war were forced to risk their lives to fulfill his desire. But this Well-spring of Christ, springing up into everlasting life, can be approached without fear and without hindrance. Christ has conquered all the enemies who made it unapproachable; and every one, — the poorest, and the meanest, and the most degraded, and the most sinful — can come and drink of it, and be at peace. Come all ye that are thirsty, all ye that are weary, all ye that would know God, all ye that would fulfill the purpose of God in your creation: and drink, and go your way rejoicing!

And do not we, my fellow-Christians, who have drank of the water of that Well of Bethlehem, often utter in our moments of spiritual declension: "Oh that one would give me to drink of the water of the well of Bethlehem, which is by the gate!" In the early years of our Christian experience, we were wont to go daily to that Well for refreshment. Whenever joyous, we went there and found our loved companions happy in its satisfying waters. Whenever wearied, we went there and found our fainting fellow-pilgrims reviving under its influence. Morning and evening we carried there all our cares, and all our burdens; and they lost their weight when we had drank its strengthening waters. It was the resort we loved most; and oh, how pleasant were those days of our early love, — how full of innocence and peace! But, like David, we have been separated, perhaps, from the water of that Well, first by our own sins, and then by the powerful enemies who seem to stand between us and its waters. The battle of life has carried us away from it. The cares, the anxieties, the collisions of the world, have changed the Christian into the man of war, or the man of many cares: and now, wearied and battered, our hearts turn in earnest longing to our first Christian love, to our haunts by that blessed Fountain, to the refreshing and comforting draughts we have quaffed from its waters, and the wish comes back to us, "Oh that one would give me drink of the water of the well of Bethlehem, which is by the gate!" And why, my fellow-Christian, should you wish in vain? Like David you may be hedged about for the moment. Lions may seem to lie crouching between you and the object of your wish. Enemies may look fierce upon you, and threaten you if you dare to approach it. But fear not! David's wish procured it for him, through all these hindrances; and your prayers will obtain it for you, if you will cry to God in earnest. "Fear not, O Jacob, my servant," is His language through the Prophet Isaiah, "and thou, Jesurun, whom I have chosen. For I will pour water upon him that is thirsty, and floods upon the dry ground."[1] All that He requires is

[1] Isaiah xliv. 2, 3.

that you bring with you a contrite spirit and a longing heart,—a soul lamenting its departure from God, and craving for the water of the Well of Bethlehem. If you will act in the spirit of the backsliding children of Israel, and say, "Come, and let us return unto the LORD: for he hath torn, and he will heal us; he hath smitten, and he will bind us up. After two days will he revive us: in the third day he will raise us up, and we shall live in his sight. Then shall we know, if we follow on to know the LORD: his going forth is prepared as the morning; and he shall come unto us as the rain, as the latter and the former rain unto the earth."[1]

[1] Hosea vi. 1–3.

Fifth Sermon.

For I am not ashamed of the Gospel of Christ: for it is the power of God unto salvation to every one that believeth; to the Jew first, and also to the Greek. — ROMANS i. 16.

IT required two of the most elaborate chapters of Gibbon's gorgeous work to display the grandeur and magnificence of the Roman Empire under Augustus and his immediate successors. With all that we may have seen of modern luxury, and all that we may have imagined of concentrated power, we find it difficult to grasp the conception which he there labors to embody, — the conception of the whole civilized world united under a great military despotism, with Rome as its heart, from which went forth the irresistible decrees of power, and to which flowed back, through innumerable, well-ordered channels, all that wealth and luxury and art could furnish for its adornment and glory. The world has never since seen so imperial a city; and pilgrims innumerable still wander there to muse amid its unrivalled ruins, and dream of the greatness of the past. It combined every thing which could win for it veneration among its dependent provinces, which would make them look with awe upon even its fashions and opinions. It had the prestige of conquest, — nation after nation, the most powerful and the most distant, having passed under its yoke, and confessed its dominion. It was enveloped in that illusion which pomp and show cast around their presence, especially when they surround the palaces of a successful monarch and a time-honored nobility. It was the focus of literature and of art, the point whither every thing tended which might minister to the senses or the tastes of men. Rome was the Empire: every thing outside of its walls was provincial. To be great at Rome was to be great at the remotest extremities of the world: to meet the contempt of Rome was to ensure the contempt of all that depended upon her. Her smile was power; her approbation was influence; her condemnation withered the hopes of statesmen, of orators, of poets, of philosophers. To go up to Rome from the provinces and face its opinion, — to plunge into that roaring vortex of the wise, the thoughtful, the educated, the luxurious, the powerful, and promulge a new and unheard-of doctrine, — demanded not only a mighty confidence of Truth, but a physical nerve over and above the Truth. It was like casting a die for reputation and for life. If it succeeded, it ensured popularity and power. If it failed, it brought down unmeasured ridicule, and perhaps personal destruction.

No wonder, then, that when S. Paul was contemplating a visit to Rome, — was about to preach the novel doctrines of the Gospel of Jesus Christ in this seat of power and of sensuality, — he should have prepared his heart for the struggle, and that some glimpses of hat preparation should manifest themselves in passages of the Epistle which he wrote to the Christians in that place before he had ever visited them. It is one of these glimpses which furnishes the text for my sermon, — one which draws from him the remarkable disclaimer of being ashamed of the Gospel of Christ. Having been hindered again and again, by providential circumstances, in his intention of visiting Rome, he seems to have feared that the Christians there might suppose that he was kept away from shame; that he was unwilling to proclaim the new and despised doctrines of the Cross in that centre of Roman influence.

"Now I would not have you ignorant, brethren," is the language of his explanation, "that oftentimes I purposed to come unto you (but was let hitherto), that I might have some fruit among you also, even as among other Gentiles. I am debtor both to the Greeks, and to the Barbarians; both to the wise, and to the unwise. So, as much as in me is, I am ready to preach the Gospel to you that are at Rome also. For I am not ashamed of the Gospel of Christ: for it is the power of God unto salvation to every one that believeth; to the Jew first, and also to the Greek."[1] It was not the ridicule which it might cost him that hindered his coming. It was that the Spirit of God had not yet opened the way for him, — that way which afterwards carried him there a prisoner and an appellant to the throne of the Cæsars.

How little the world understands the difficulty which there is in preaching the Gospel! — the struggle which the human heart undergoes in setting forth publicly and faithfully those revealed truths which constitute what the Scripture calls "the foolishness of preaching." It is easy enough to be a philosopher or an essayist. S. Paul would have found no cause for shame or contempt in announcing from Mars' Hill at Athens, or from the tribune at Rome, some novel or eclectic scheme of philosophy, — in uttering any piece of human conception, however wild or fanciful. Man will listen patiently to man's inventions. He will weigh and consider the arguments and reasonings of his fellow-creature, so long as there is any show of reason, and even when there is none. But when you leave the sphere of intellect, and attempt to take him into that of Revelation, he mocks. And it is not only the hearer who rebels against spiritual truth; it is the preacher himself who feels the temptation strong upon him to avoid the

[1] Rom. i. 13–16.

Cross of Christ, and to dwell upon the evidences of Religion, where he may reason; or the morals of Christ, which the common sense of mankind in a manner approves; or the practice of life, which comes home to one's every-day feelings and occupations. In these days of almost universal Christianity, when the Church of Christ is a power in the earth, and the Ministers of the Church are respected and esteemed, the question which suggests itself to most minds upon hearing my text announced, is: "Why should Paul have been ashamed to preach the Gospel anywhere? What is there in such glorious truth that any man should shun to declare it to all the world?" And when the answer is returned, that it was a novelty in the world; that it was contrary to all the received philosophy of the times; that it was exclusive and aggressive: such answers are deemed to be sufficient. As if there was any more temptation to be ashamed then, than there is now; as if the doctrines of the Cross have ceased to be an offence; as if it is not just as unpalatable now-a-days to be dependent upon the grace of God and the mercy of Christ for salvation as it ever was! No, my hearer. The answer to that question lies much deeper, — stretches down into the unbelief of the natural heart, and finds its solution there. What tempted S. Paul to be ashamed of the Gospel of Christ, and what tempts me as his successor, and you as a Christian, to be ashamed of that same Gospel, is the natural antagonism which there is in fallen human nature to any thing which comes from God in Christ. It is not a thing to be reasoned about; controversy can make it no plainer, nor any the more intelligible. The Scripture declaration that "the carnal mind" — that is, the heart which is born with a man before the renewal of the Holy Ghost — "is enmity against God,"[1]

[1] Rom. viii. 7.

covers the whole ground. Sin has made it so: and sin keeps it so, until the power of the Holy Ghost subdues that sin, and gives Christ the dominion! It is a thing that you all feel and know, — not that you hate God, for *that* none of you would admit: but that you despise, so long as you are unconverted, what is called "*doctrinal preaching*" — a dwelling upon the Atonement, and upon Regeneration, and upon Justification, and upon Blood as the great cleanser and purifier of the nature. And if you despise these doctrines, what are they but the Gospel? What are they but the very topics which are the glad tidings of great joy? You complain that you cannot understand them; that they are unintelligible (the very thing which the Apostle tells us you would say); that they are foolishness (the very words of the Apostle again): and if they are pressed, — why, then the preacher is "a fool": or if his standing be too high for that, "a fanatic." And when we who preach the Gospel know all this, is there no temptation to be ashamed of the Gospel of Christ? — no allurement to pass over these great and saving truths, and win your admiration by rhetoric and philosophy? There is enormous temptation: for, besides the crucifixion which it really is to ourselves to force upon unwilling ears ungracious topics, there are plausible arguments enough to be found why we should offer you other themes, and dwell more upon the duties of life than on the doctrines of Christianity.

But while there is this temptation to preach morals rather than doctrine, philosophy rather than Christianity, we must nerve ourselves, as faithful Ministers of the Word, against this shame; because this very Gospel "is the power of God unto salvation, to every one that believeth." It is all in Christianity that has *any power*. The rest of the system has no more power than any other scheme of morals or philosophy. What power, for example, had the philosophy of Socrates over his age and nation? I do not ask you what intellectual force it had, but *what power* had it in restraining individuals or in leavening the mass, in even those things which related to the conduct of this life? And surely it could have none upon the salvation of the soul, when it left his most accomplished disciples doubtful about even that soul's immortality! And what power had the ethical philosophy of Cicero over his times? The moral philosophers of Rome were very remarkable men in their way, — unfolded the topics which they handled with great clearness and completeness; and yet what power had they? Just none at all: and their compatriots went plunging on in sensuality and lust, until Rome presented such a picture at the incoming of Christianity as man has never seen since, as the normal condition of his race. Well, if Christianity had not conjoined with it *this power* of God unto salvation, its morals, and what might be called its philosophy, should have no more influence in leavening the world than that of antiquity. What man needs is not advice, is not instruction in mere worldly duty, is not a constant lecturing upon what he ought to do, or what he ought not to do: but it is *power* to operate upon the will, to make it desire to do right; and then *power* to enable it to do right. It would be very idle for me to employ myself twice every Lord's day in telling such a congregation as you are, about the duties of life. You know them quite as well as I do; and if that was all of Christianity, I should be very glad to sit at the feet of many of you, and listen to your instructions. But when the pulpit is fulfilling its true design, — is calling you to repentance for sins against God of which you are not conscious, and to faith in our Lord Jesus Christ, that you may receive power from on high to subdue sin, — then it assumes a very different aspect. It becomes then a very distinct instrument for spiritual good, and can be wielded only by those who have been taught of God what is His wisdom and His will! If under this view of things you were to assume to become a public teacher, I could no longer listen with patience to your cold disputations upon morals and duties. I should have to say to you, as our Saviour said to Nicodemus when he could not comprehend one of the leading doctrines of Christianity: "Art thou a master of Israel, and knowest not these things?" That is the difference! Any one of you who is a man of good morals and high social character might be a preacher of Christianity, if instruction in morals were all that it required: but when it embraces what S. Paul calls "the Gospel of Christ," and concerns itself about the salvation of the soul, it requires other elements of knowledge than are possessed by a moralist; elements of knowledge attained not through the head, but through the heart; coming not from any thing which man teacheth, but which the Holy Ghost teacheth.

This was the reason why S. Paul was not ashamed of the Gospel of Christ, because it was the power of God unto salvation! God had appointed it so. He that commissioned him had so arranged it. "For Christ sent me not to baptize," writes he to the Corinthians, "but to preach the Gospel: not with wisdom of words, lest the Cross of Christ should be made of none effect. For the preaching of the Cross is to them that perish foolishness; but unto us which are saved it is the power of God."[1] He needed no other reason than this; and when men cavilled at it and despised it, his answer was: "For after that in the wisdom of God the world by wisdom knew not God, it pleased God by the foolishness of preaching to save them that believe."[2] When they attempted to argue against it, to prove that there could be *no power* in such foolish doctrines to affect

[1] 1 Cor. i. 17, 18. [2] *Ibid.* 21.

the world, his reply still was: "But God hath chosen the foolish things of the world to confound the wise; and God hath chosen the weak things of the world to confound the things which are mighty; and base things of the world, and things which are despised, hath God chosen, yea, and things which are not, to bring to naught things that are: that no flesh should glory in his presence." What more could be said? What further argument could be advanced against a man making such assertions? He was not ashamed of the Gospel, and could not be made ashamed of it, because it was the power of God; and the very weaknesses alleged against it were met by the declaration that they were made so of set purpose, to confound the wisdom and the glory of man. Believing this, — and every man who has experienced the converting grace of the Gospel must believe it, — what can make him ashamed? He is God's messenger, and is wielding not his own power but the power of God: is contending with man, not upon an equal platform of intellect against intellect; but with an unknown and unreckoned influence, against the feelings and the affections.

And it is just that unreckoned influence which gives Christianity all its vitality. That unreckoned influence — that influence which man does not recognize — is the Holy Ghost; and He will not honor any teaching with His presence and power, except the teaching which holds up and dignifies the Cross of Christ. And this is the way in which the power of God manifests itself in the salvation of the soul. While "godliness is profitable unto all things, having promise of the life that now is, and of that which is to come,"[1] its great purpose is to save the soul. "This is a faithful saying, and worthy of all acceptation, that Christ Jesus came into the world to save sinners."[2] The soul, the

[1] 1 Tim. iv. 8. [2] *Ibid.* i. 15.

soul it was, that brought Christ down from Heaven, — that "vital spark of heavenly flame" which is undying. He came not to teach morals for the benefit of the few paltry years that we spend upon the earth, but to prepare the soul for reunion with that God from whom sin had violently separated it! For this end, he gave Himself a sacrifice for sin. For this end, He put Himself in the place of man. For this end, He bore upon Himself the full penalty of sin. For this end, He shed His precious Blood, and made peace between God and man. And when He had done all this, and made the Atonement, then was the power which was to give the Gospel its spiritual life sent down from Heaven! And when we look into the history of Christianity, we see at once what is the meaning and force of this word, — "*the power of God.*"

Were the Apostles wiser than our Lord? Were they more eloquent than He who spake as never man spake? Could they do more miracles than He did? And yet their first sermon converted some three thousand souls, while the whole life and conversation and miracles of Jesus attached to Him but a very small band of timid and hesitating disciples! How was this? How do those who would take away from Christianity the doctrines of the Cross, explain this? It has no explanation but that which the Scriptures themselves give, — that these very doctrines are those which the Holy Ghost applies and makes operative upon the heart of the creature. And this is in direct fulfillment of the promise of our Saviour: "Howbeit when he the Spirit of Truth is come, he will guide you into all truth: for he shall not speak of himself. . . . . He shall glorify me: for he shall receive of mine, and shall shew it unto you."[1] And how shall He glorify Christ? By making His Cross, His Blood, His Atonement, the power of the

[1] S. John xvi. 13, 14.

Gospel! By giving His work the glory of salvation. By proving to the world that there is none other Name under heaven given among men, in whom, and through whom, they may receive salvation, but only the Name of our Lord Jesus Christ. By finally bringing every knee to bow before the Name of Jesus, and making every tongue confess that He is Lord, to the glory of God the Father. By gathering together that great crowd of the elect, who are to make Heaven resound forever with the new song of the redeemed: "Blessing, and honor, and glory, and power, be unto him that sitteth upon the throne, and unto the Lamb for ever and ever."

How idle is it, then, where the soul's salvation is concerned, to hope to do any good except through the preaching of the Gospel! We may not expect to have the power of God with us, unless we make that the substance of our instructions. We may have the approbation and admiration of men, but we cannot look for the presence of the Spirit unless we glorify Christ, and make His name honorable. "Whosoever shall be ashamed of me and of my words, of him shall the Son of Man be ashamed, when he shall come in his own glory, and in his Father's, and of the holy angels." And if our Lord will be ashamed of those in the last day who are ashamed of His Cross now, think you that He will honor them with His presence in the Church upon earth? No! A Ministry which hides from the people the doctrines of the Gospel because they are unpalatable or unintelligible, will have the light of God's countenance hid from it, — will be shorn of all power for the salvation of the soul! And in like manner with the private Christian. He will find, in his own experience, that he has *no power* against the enemies of his soul, save in so far as he may be living upon the Gospel. He will learn, perchance through a sad experience, that his profession will not stand temptation and seduction and the days of darkness, unless it rest upon the corner-stone of the Atonement. He may be well learned in all those things which make a Christian scholar and a moral philosopher, and yet be weak as a child when he comes to grapple with the great enemies of the soul, unless he be washed in the Blood of Christ, and sanctified and purified there. The Gospel is the power of God; and nothing else! All the rest is the power of man. And the power of man is nothing against the power of the Devil! It fades away before his wiles, as the morning dew before the heat of the sun. It requires the power of God in Christ to conflict with the enemies of the soul! Therefore is it that the work of the Ministry is, to lead the soul away from itself, to the power of God; to teach it where it shall find true strength for the day of trial, and salvation in the day of Christ's Judgment.

Sixth Sermon.

He calleth to me out of Seir, Watchman, what of the night? Watchman, what of the night? The watchman said, The morning cometh, and also the night: if ye will inquire, inquire ye: return, come. — ISAIAH xxi. 11, 12.

METHINKS it would strike a thoughtful man, when his mind rested upon Christianity, for how long God had been answering, through His commissioned watchmen, the question of our text. If the religion which speaks from the Word of God was a thing of yesterday, a man might reasonably put it aside as unworthy of much consideration. But when, however far back he may pierce into the depths of antiquity, he shall find the watchman standing upon the walls of Zion, and replying to the anxious question of bewildered reason, he may well pause and ponder over the startling fact. If he could get rid of it by running it up through a few years, or even a few centuries, until it was lost in obscurity, he might plausibly say, that God would not have delayed so long a Revelation which was meant for the world.

But the unbeliever has no such refuge as this. If he be honest and true, he will find Revelation cleaving to him through all the changes of the world's history, exhibiting its landmarks wherever his researches may lead him, with a faithful watchman for every age, with an earnest invitation for every period since the Creation. Christianity is not like the false religions of the earth, whose origin and whose authors can be fixed in the mid ages of the world:

but already have eighteen hundred years rolled away since it received its fullest development, and was unfolded in perfectness to man. That period, when we have reached it, is called "the fullness of times," — "the latter days." From that point we ascend four hundred years, beyond the time of the Macedonian conqueror: and the Scriptures which enfolded all the promise and prophecy of the Old Dispensation are closed and sealed, waiting in silence the coming of the Messiah. Even at that remote period enough had been said by the watchman to satisfy the questions of man, and to close up and seal the prophecy. And if we open that volume, what a vista spreads away before us, carrying us up beyond Babylon and Nineveh and Troy, and the fabled Argonauts: while yet Isaiah, and David, and Samuel, and Joshua, were uttering immortal truth, and looking with bright-eyed hope for the coming Redeemer. And when we pass beyond any thing which even human monuments can tell us, though dug from their sepulchre of ages, we still meet Moses, and Job, and Abraham, and Noah, and the men before the Flood, resting upon the promises of that Christ whom we worship to-day. Unbelief, if it travel the path of history, will be sorely harassed. It will meet its enemy at every point. If it take Christianity upon its own hypothesis, — that it is the flower of which Judaism was the bud, — it will find a watchman wherever it turns, who will cry to it: "The morning cometh, and also the night; if ye will inquire, inquire ye: return, come."

And should not this arrest any man of reason? Should he not pause until he has satisfied himself about this unique phenomenon? Before he can rationally pass on with indifference, he must account for the origin, the growth, the permanence of this persistent scheme; he must explain how that which was wrapped up in dark, mysterious prophecies, came all to be developed to the very letter of the record; how that which was the literature of a peculiar nation, chanced to be all spiritual, and true to the necessities of human nature; how, while scorned and rejected by the world until the moment when Prophecy foretold that it would expand, it was taken to the heart of humanity, and cherished as its comfort, its life, its hope; how, as the world continues to change, this religion alone is unchangeable; how, while kingdoms and nations perish and pass away, this Christianity perishes not; how the religious utterances of men as unlike us in every thing external as the Prophets and Kings of Israel, should be the very words in which we have this day, and in this holy temple, poured out before God our religious feelings. Could we use here the spiritual language of the Greeks and Romans — if they had any spiritual language — without jarring upon your feelings, and desecrating the holiness of this sanctuary? And yet they were much younger nations than the Hebrews, and far more assimilated to the world. Christianity may drive you off by the sternness of its requisitions, and the purity of its life; but history, tradition, the monuments of the past, and, above all, your own divine thirst, will force you back, and impel you to ask of the divine watchman, "Watchman, what of the night?" When this question was asked out of Seir, it was asked in reference to the heavy burden of prophecies which lay upon that devoted country, — those prophecies which predicted, when she was yet in the pride of her power and the abundance of her riches, that Edom should be a desolation. It may have been asked in scorn; it may have been asked in faith; no matter which: the answer was alike suitable to both: "The morning cometh," — the morning of light and peace and opportunity; "and also the night," — the night of trouble and calamity. As one has beautifully expressed it: "Is it night? Yet the morning comes, and the dayspring knows his place. Is it day? Yet the night comes, and darkness steals over the world." It is thus in nature, thus in life, thus in spiritual things.

Would to God, my beloved people, that you could be aroused even so far as to ask your watchman, "What of the night?" He is set over you by the Lord. His duty is to see that you are warned of peril to your souls; his pleasure to answer truly, when you ask your condition while encompassed by the deep uncertainty of the present and of the future. His position is one of deep responsibility to you, of serious peril to himself. The Word of the Lord to every Minister is this: "Son of man, I have made thee a watchman unto the house of Israel: therefore hear the word at my mouth, and give them warning from me. When I say unto the wicked, Thou shalt surely die; and thou givest him not warning, nor speakest to warn the wicked from his wicked way, to save his life; the same wicked man shall die in his iniquity; but his blood will I require at thine hand."[1] You hear my peril, if I tell you not the plain truth. Now listen to yours: "Yet if thou warn the wicked, and he turn not from his wickedness, nor from his wicked way, he shall die in his iniquity; but thou hast delivered thy soul."[2] This is our relation, — one created by God, — one irrevocable in its nature, and eternal in its results, — one that will follow us both to the Judgment-seat of Christ. And while such a relation, so solemn and so comprehensive, exists between us, we hold it in the midst of corruption, of infirmity, of temptation, of darkness. We should despair, unless the light of the glorious Gospel of Jesus Christ had ushered in a morning, during which we might return to God, and come back to the Father from whom we had wandered, reckless prodigals!

[1] Ezekiel iii. 17, 18. [2] *Ibid.* 19.

When one out of Seir asked this question, "What of the night?" Christ had not yet risen, full-orbed, upon a sinful world. The sky was brightening over Israel; the rays of prophecy were all converging and becoming a light in a dark place: but the morning, the glorious morning, was only coming. And even then, when the watchman dared only to answer with the voice of promise and of hope, "The morning cometh: if ye will inquire, inquire ye," he felt himself constrained to add, "and also the night." As if he said, "I can cheer you with the promise of a coming Saviour; there are the beams of light thick gathering in the chambers of the East. I can enliven this darkness with glad tidings of great joy for you and for all mankind; tidings of redemption, of time and opportunity for repentance, of the glorious hope of everlasting life. But beyond that, I see approaching another night, darker than this; a night wherein no man can work; in whose blackness of darkness no watchman shall walk his solitary round and cry, 'All's well;' where there shall be no question and no answer, no life, no peace, no hope; but all shall be swallowed up in the wrath of the Lamb. Therefore I cry unto you, 'If ye will inquire, inquire ye: return, come.'"

Should the question be asked to-day, the watchman would answer, "The morning is come." The Sun of Righteousness has arisen upon a world lying in darkness, and there is all around us the bright shining of truth and of salvation. It flashes upon us from every thing in society, just as the rays of the glorious orb of day are reflected to us from every object in nature, the minutest as well as the grandest, the grain of sand and the drop of water equally with the mountain top and the ocean's bosom. Milton's prayer, when through his blindness he would see the visions of the Almighty, "What in me is dark, illumine; what is low, raise and support," has been granted to the world by Christianity, and comes assured to our feelings as well as our reason. Christ has sanctified every relation of life, even while he was modifying the civilization of the world. He has exalted poverty, and sorrow, and humility, and made them the vehicles of his richest blessings, at the same moment that He was scattering the vain philosophy of the schools, and was overturning the temples and shrines of paganism. "Objects remain, and relations are still unbroken," is the rich language of Butler, "but new and lovely lights and shadowings cover them. They move in the same directions as before, but under an atmosphere impregnated with brighter hues, and rich with a light that streams direct from Heaven."

This then, my hearer, is your opportunity. Light is all around you. Truth is sown broadcast. Hope spreads her glittering wings above you. Society, home, your own unquenchable desires, your own thick coming affections, all call you to Christ. You have no need of the watchman to tell you of the morning. The Gospel cannot be hid from you; it seems impossible. Why, it is a part of all you are, and all you love. It is the foundation of your happiness and your peace. Even while you do not see it, you are feeling it in every pulse of your manhood. Even while you are indifferent to it, it is adorning your own nature, and showering blessings upon your ungrateful head! Oh! it cannot be hid from you, — it is too palpable in its glories and its wonders! Oh! let it not be hid; for "if our Gospel be hid, it is hid to them that are lost: in whom the god of this world hath blinded the minds of them which believe not, lest the light of the glorious Gospel of Christ, who is the image of God, should shine unto them."[1] Are you then among the lost? Having eyes, can you not see? Having ears, can you not hear? Is your heart stone, that you can-

[1] 2 Cor. iv. 4.

not feel? Am I ploughing with oxen upon a rock? God forbid! Try and see. Try and feel. Put not yourselves in the fearful category of the lost. Let not the bright rays of the morning shine upon you without imparting to you their warmth and cheerfulness. Let not nature and man rejoice in sympathy with God, while *you* have no part in the divine harmony. Let not the voice of adoration swell from the choirs of the universe, from angels and archangels, and the redeemed of every nation and kindred and tribe and people, and *yours* be one of discord and of shame. Now is your opportunity, — "the accepted time," "the day of salvation." Let the Dayspring which has arisen upon the world arise in your hearts, and bathe them in the sunlight of heaven!

This is your opportunity; but even as the watchman answered, "The morning cometh," he added, "and also the night." Oh! how true, — how true in every thing! How bright the morning is! How every thing is rejoicing around us! How the blue heavens seem liquid with happiness! How the leaves of the forest quiver in the sunlight as if they were dancing for joy! How the birds are caroling their morning hymns, and sending their unconscious music up to the throne of God! How vigorous is man, as he treads the earth in the pride of his manhood, drinking in the healthful sunshine, and reflecting it back upon every thing, as if in the superfluity of his blessings! But the night cometh! Nothing can keep it from following the morning: — not the glory of heaven; not the rejoicing forests; not the music of the birds; not the pride nor happiness of man. It is the ordination of nature! Night must settle over the morning; darkness must follow light; obscurity must take the place of brightness, and blot out all the beauties of the day. And it is not confined to nature. Darkness treads upon the heels of joy in the *moral* world. "If a man live many years," says the wise Preacher, "and rejoice in them all; yet let him remember the days of darkness; for they shall be many."[1] No matter, my hearer, how bright your morning may be, the night cometh also. No matter how long that brightness may continue, be not deceived: the night cometh also. Are you exulting in youth, and beauty, and the freshness of life: "Rejoice, O young man, in thy youth; and let thy heart cheer thee in the days of thy youth, and walk in the ways of thine heart, and in the sight of thine eyes:[2] but know thou" that "the night cometh also;" — the night of sickness, the night of sorrow, the night of death, the night of the grave! Are you nestled in quiet happiness in the bosom of your own home, finding your peace and your rest in the hearts of the loved ones who cluster around your hearthstone, and make it redolent with love? Oh! if there is sunlight upon earth, it is *there*. It has more the impress of heaven than any other image upon earth. But even there "the night cometh also." Art thou rich, and increased with goods, and have need of nothing? Is the morning shining brightly upon thy overflowing barns, and are its rays glancing gayly from thy silver and thy gold? "The night cometh also," when, if it has not been devoted to the glory of God and the uses of mercy, "your riches will be corrupted, and your garments motheaten, and your gold and your silver cankered; and the rust of them shall be a witness against you, and shall eat your flesh as it were fire:"[3] when you shall hear the solemn cry, "Thou fool, this night thy soul shall be required of thee."[4]

Are you a Christian, a professed follower of the Lord Jesus Christ? Is it morning with your soul? Is all light there? Are you saying with David, "In thy light shall I see light?"[5] Christian, the night cometh also: the night

[1] Eccles. xi. 8. [2] *Ibid.* 9. [3] S. James v. 3.
[4] S. Luke xii. 20. [5] Psalm xxxvi. 9.

when no man can work; the night when darkness may rest upon the soul; the night when your dying bed shall be the scene of unutterable struggles between your spirit and the Spirit of God. Oh! think of these things, ye that hear me this day; and, while the light is with you, return and come. "Give glory to the LORD your God, before he cause darkness, and before your feet stumble upon the dark mountains, and, while ye look for light, he turn it into the shadow of death, and make it gross darkness."[1]

"If ye will inquire, inquire ye:" so answered the watchman to him that questioned out of Seir; and so answer I. Inquire!—inquire into every thing I have told you this day, and all the days that shall have to be accounted for between us. Christianity fears no inquiry conducted in a logical and earnest spirit. It dreads only indifference and the spirit of the scorner. It has been subjected all along its course to the most searching and malicious inquiry,—inquiry suggested by the devil, and carried on in the spirit of the devil, with the bitter hatred of the crucified Jesus: and it has survived it all. "They shall perish, but Thou shalt endure."[2] Inquire into it,—its history, its prophecy, its wonderful development, its divine moral and spiritual features, its suitableness to your own nature: and it will rise triumphant from the search. Let not your days slip away in apathy and unmovableness. That is your danger: not positive unbelief, but to-morrow—to-morrow—to-morrow. "Go to now, ye that say, To-day or to-morrow we will go into such a city, and continue there a year, and buy and sell, and get gain: whereas ye know not what shall be on the morrow. For what is your life? It is even a vapor, that appeareth for a little time, and then vanisheth away."[3] And inquire, likewise, into the experience of life. If the days of darkness have never yet come upon you, inquire of

[1] Jer. xiii. 16. [2] Psalm cii. 26. [3] S. James iv. 13, 14.

your neighbors and friends whether the night does not come also. Go from house to house, and search and see if there be one in which there has been perpetual morning. The mournful answer which the stories and the rafters will give you, if the master refuses to unfold his griefs, will tell you that "the night cometh also."

And when you have inquired and are satisfied, then return to the Father from whose love you have wandered. Take up your pilgrim's staff, and, armed with the resolution of going to your Father and confessing your sins, tread the way back. It may be a rugged, thorny way, that way of repentance; but it leadeth to everlasting life. It may be a way of humiliation and sorrow; but it leadeth to our Father's house, where are peace and joy for evermore. Return, come! The voice of love is calling to you from Bethlehem, and Gethsemane, and Calvary! Its accents are "Come unto me, all ye that labor and are heavy laden, and I will give you rest."[1] Come *now*, while the light of morning is leaping upon the mountains: for this same loving Saviour said, "Yet a little while is the light with you. Walk while ye have the light, lest darkness come upon you: for he that walketh in darkness knoweth not whither he goeth."[2]

[1] S. Matt. xi. 28.

[2] S. John xii. 35.

Seventh Sermon.

The woman saith unto him, Sir, thou hast nothing to draw with, and the well is deep: from whence then hast thou that living water? — S. JOHN iv. 11.

ONE day," say the Arabs, "King Nimrod summoned into his presence his three sons. He ordered three urns, under seal, to be set before them. One of the urns was of gold, another of amber, and the third of clay. The king bade the eldest of his sons to choose among these urns that which appeared to him to contain the treasure of greatest price. He chose the vase of gold, on which was written the word *Empire;* he opened it, and found it full of blood. The second took the vase of amber, whereon was written the word *Glory;* he opened it, and found it full of the ashes of men who had made a great figure in the world. The third son took the remaining vase, that of clay. He opened it, and found it quite empty; but on the bottom the potter had inscribed the word *God.* 'Which of these vases is worth the most?' asked the king of his courtiers. The men of ambition replied, it was the vase of gold; the poets and conquerors, that it was the amber one; the wise men, that it was the empty vase, because a single letter of the name of God was of more worth than the whole world."

How beautifully this legend illustrates the judgment of the world in regard to Truth. They search for it, and think they have grasped it, when they have laid their hands upon the vases of gold and the vases of amber, — when they have sat at the feet of the great men of the earth, the Conquerors, the Poets, the Philosophers, the Statesmen. They take it for granted that if there is wisdom, it must be found with those; that if there is truth, it must be hidden somewhere among their treasures. They turn away from the vases of clay, never dreaming that the name of God may be written upon them; they turn away from the humble of heart, from the meek in spirit, from the suffering, from the lowly, from those to whom God is speaking in silence and in sorrow, who are working out Truth in the only way by which it can be won, — through the chastened experience of life. These, with whom God loves to dwell, they pass unnoticed. Nothing attracts them there. The well of Truth is deep, and these seem to have nothing to draw with. They press on, and instead of water to quench their immortal thirst, they find blood; instead of food which shall endure unto eternal life, they find ashes!

And yet, methinks, God should have taught all Christian men, through the life of His Son, where to seek for truth. "I am the Truth,"[1] said Christ: and Christ was "meek and lowly in heart."[2] "I am the Truth," said Christ: and Christ was "a man of sorrows, and acquainted with grief."[3] "I am the Truth," said Christ: and Christ was "brought as a lamb to the slaughter, and opened not his mouth."[4] "I am the Truth," said Christ; and He bowed His head and cried, "Not my will, but Thine, O God, be done!"[5] It seems strange, with such indications as these, that man should not know where to seek for Truth, — that he should be at all at a loss about the conditions of human life in which he should be most likely to find it. To discover Truth, we must walk in the footsteps of Truth; and they lead, in this world, through paths from which human nature shrinks, unless it be sincerely earnest. The disciple

[1] S. John xiv. 6. [2] S. Matt. xi. 29. [3] Isaiah liii. 3.
[4] Isaiah liii. 7. [5] S. Luke xxii. 42.

must be satisfied if he be as his Master; and this Master we have introduced to us in the story from which my text is taken, as a weary traveller, seated upon Jacob's well, alone and thirsty, having nothing to draw with, while the well was deep, and the water unattainable.

The conversation which took place under these circumstances is full of interest and instruction. "There cometh a woman of Samaria to draw water: Jesus saith unto her, Give me to drink. Then saith the woman of Samaria unto him, How is it that thou, being a Jew, askest drink of me, which am a woman of Samaria? for the Jews have no dealings with the Samaritans. Jesus answered and said unto her, If thou knewest the gift of God, and who it is that saith to thee, Give me to drink; thou wouldest have asked of him, and he would have given thee living water. The woman saith unto him, Sir, thou hast nothing to draw with, and the well is deep: from whence then hast thou that living water?"

This is the question of man in all generations to Jesus Christ. "The well is deep, — the well of Truth; thou art, to all appearance, an obscure man, of an obscure nation. To the eye of sense, thou hast nothing to draw with. Thou hast neither philosophy, — for we know not thy school; nor power, — for thy father was a carpenter; nor glory, — for thou diedst a felon's death; nor riches, — for thou hadst not where to lay thy head: from whence then hast thou that living water, — that truth which is to be a fountain within us, opening up into everlasting life? We know not truth, unless it comes to us from the wise, or the mighty, or the noble of this world. We look for it where glory illumines the path, where gold glitters in its dust, where learning stains it with its sweat, where poetry and philosophy strew it with their creations. Thou art only a vase of clay. Should we take the trouble to unseal thee, we should find thee empty." And the world sweeps on, never dreaming that the Almighty potter has written the name of GOD upon that humble, weary, thirsty wayfarer.

Our Saviour, as He sat upon that well, was both man and God. As man, He was, like man, powerless to reach the water in that well of Truth: it was deep, and He had nothing to draw with. He could see it lying far beneath Him, calm and pure. He could perceive heaven in its bosom, reflected as in a mirror. He thirsted for it with an unquenchable thirst: but all in vain. It was there, — but not for Him; not for Him, at least, in that way, and under those circumstances. It had been there from the beginning, and man had always longed for it: but it seemed unattainable. Many a traveller, weary and thirsty, had come to it as to a shrine: but not one had ever drawn water from its depths. Each one had gazed into its beauteous face, had seen heaven there, had stretched out his hands that he might clutch it, and carry it to his burning lips: but they all grasped emptiness, for the name of God had not yet been written upon it. Truth was not yet for man. The fullness of times was not yet come: and philosophy speculated in vain, and poetry created in vain, and wisdom cried in vain at her portal. There was no answer. Man described truth, bedizened truth, counterfeited truth, adored truth: but all that was very different from drinking it in, and assimilating it to himself. Yet this was what man wanted, — truth as a satisfying reality, as a substantive good which should enter into his being, and become a part of his nature, and give him assurance of everlasting life. All this Christ represented, in His human nature, as He sat upon the brink of that deep well. He was the type of fallen man, weary and thirsty, with the water gushing in his sight, and nothing wherewith he might reach it. Sad image of our condition: until He came and gave us another side to the picture.

The vase of clay, which the woman of Samaria saw there, had the name of GOD written upon it! He looked like any other man; He was weary like any other man; He was thirsty like any other man: but He was nevertheless God! He might be poor; He might be obscure; He might be suffering: but nevertheless, He was God. And as God, Truth was His own, grew in His own bosom, was the very essence of His Nature. He needed not to draw for it out of any well, not even the well of Jacob. It was a fountain forever gushing within Himself, wherewith He might supply all that should come. "If thou knewest the gift of God, and who it is that saith to thee, Give me to drink; thou wouldst have asked of him, and he would have given thee living water." What glad tidings for man! No more vain hunting after truth; no more vain yearning after its pure refreshing waters; no more sitting and gazing into that deep well, from which we have nothing that can satisfy us. Here is a man — a man like ourselves — who is Himself the Truth; who will give us, for the asking, enough to create within ourselves a well-spring, springing up into everlasting life. "Whosoever drinketh of the water that I shall give him shall never thirst; but the water that I shall give him shall be in him a well of water springing up into everlasting life." And how lovingly he calls us to that divine Fountain! His prophet had foreseen it when he sang, "Ho, every one that thirsteth, come ye to the waters;"[1] had foreseen this very Man of Sorrows, opening a fountain in the house of David: but He Himself proclaimed it on that day when the Israelites sang their joyful thanksgiving: "Behold, God is my salvation; I will trust, and not be afraid: for the Lord JEHOVAH is my strength and my song; he also is become my salvation. Therefore with joy shall ye draw water out of the wells of

[1] Isaiah lv. 1.

salvation."[1] "In the last day, that great day of the feast, Jesus stood and cried, saying, If any man thirst, let him come unto me, and drink."[2]

What a blessed conjunction of Natures! — as man, sitting upon the well of Truth, as cheerless as any of us, having nothing to draw with: but as God, having Truth at his command, and ready to bestow it upon every one who will ask for it as becomes a thirsty, dying creature. Why, oh! why will not man lay aside his pride and his unbelief, and come to the feet of this loving human Brother, and receive the treasures of His wisdom? Because, like the Samaritan woman, he thinks that truth can come only out of earthly wells; and whenever Christ proffers him truth, his question is, "Sir, thou hast nothing to draw with, and the well is deep; from whence then hast thou that living water?"

And this brings up, as you perceive, the whole question of a Revelation. The Jews had this trouble very early in our Saviour's ministry. When He had been teaching in the synagogues, speaking as never man spake, they "were astonished and said, Whence hath this man this wisdom, and these mighty works? Is not this the carpenter's son? (the vase of clay, you see; — that was the difficulty!) is not his mother called Mary? and his brethren, James, and Joses, and Simon, and Judas? And his sisters, are they not all with us? (still harping upon the clay). Whence then hath this man all these things? And they were offended in him."[3] How soon it began! — and it has never ceased, and never will cease. It is the question of Unbelief; and unbelief never dies, — unbelief in a God that cares for His creatures, that will provide for His creatures: for what provision does man need so much as Truth? And where is he to get it, unless it come from God? Has he not been searching for it long ages, and is he any nearer to it by

[1] Isaiah xii. 2, 3. [2] S. John vii. 37. [3] S. Matt. xiii. 54–6.

those researches? Have there not been as many schools of Truth, as there have been men of ability? Have not the wise men of one age assaulted and overturned all that was deemed truth by the wise men of another? Has it not been overturning, overturning, overturning, from the days when speculation was born in the East until now? And is not the warfare still going on? Oh, how pitiful to see those poor, worn, weary, thirsty men, struggling by the side of that deep well of Truth, having nothing to draw with, and striving to pass off the muddy water which they have taken from their own cisterns, for the pure refreshing water that has heaven always reflected in it! They will not receive it from Christ. *He* seems to be but a man, for He was born, and had infirmities, and suffered, and died: whence then has *He* living water? And why is this, my hearers? Why this reluctance to believe in a Revelation? Surely now, after nearly six thousand years, you may give up any hope for Truth from any source save God! You have tried long enough, O man! to draw it up from the depths of the earth. That has been *your* plan. Now try God's, — to receive Truth from the heavens above, from God the fountain of Truth; and cavil not if He offer it to you in a vase of clay, if so be you can only see His Name written upon it.

And is there not abundant proof that GOD'S Name is written upon Jesus of Nazareth? Was that man, who sat upon Jacob's well, wayworn and thirsty, unheralded? A whole nation, unique in its history and peculiar in its institutions, was set apart and miraculously preserved through long ages to predict His coming. Epochs which man could not arrange nor modify, were fixed centuries before He came, to declare His Birth. Miracles accompanied Him from His cradle to His grave. Wisdom flowed from His lips, such as man never spake, such as man can never imitate. His life enlightened the world: His death converted it! What mark does He want, to certify Him to be from God? He is not a vase of *Gold*, and has not *Empire* written upon Him! But remember, that vase was full of blood, — the blood of the oppressed, of the conquered, of the murdered; and He came to bring peace on earth, good-will towards men. He is not a vase of *Amber*, and has not *Glory* written upon Him. But remember, that vase was full of ashes, — of the ashes of hope, of desire, of love, of greatness; and He came to renew hope, to satisfy desire, to enkindle love and make it immortal; to raise men to the true greatness of being the sons of God. He came to give us beauty for ashes! How can you expect to see Him in any shape so contrary to the purpose of His coming? He could come only as He did come, if He would redeem man and restore him to Truth and God!

Until He came, man was indeed a vase of clay, empty and worthless. God had no part in him, save in his creation, after sin had destroyed the likeness of God. How could the Name of God be once again written upon him? The Bible tells us: Only by the Son of God taking our nature and redeeming us back by His own Blood. He, as man, must satisfy God for the race of man; and because, in doing this, He appears on earth as a man, are we to reject him? Are we to despise that humiliation, when we learn that it was the only mode by which we might attain unto glory? Suppose you that humiliation is any the more pleasant to God, than to man? Was not, then, the form He took, the poverty He endured, the scorn He underwent, the cruel death He died, the most striking evidence of His love to us? And because of His love, are you so short-sighted, so earthly, as to despise Him? Can you not see the moral, the spiritual glory of God, breaking out through that tenement of clay? Could a mere man have lived as He lived, without spot and without blemish? Could a mere man have placed Truth upon such a basis as that neither Philosophy, nor Science, nor Time, can shake it? Could a mere man have assumed all the lowliness of His circumstances, and dignified them, and made them honorable, — nay, sublime? Could a mere man have died as He died, making the Cross a very chariot of glory? A vase of clay He was, because it was necessary He should be: but on it was clearly written — too clearly for any one to say he cannot read it — the Name of GOD, the great unchangeable I AM.

And He has arranged in His Church the means whereby we may attain to Truth. It is no longer necessary that any human creature should thirst; the living water can be his for the asking. Christ is ready to communicate with us through His Spirit, — that Spirit whom He sent into the world when He took His place as our Advocate at the right hand of His Father. "Howbeit, when he the Spirit of truth is come, he will guide you into all truth: for he shall not speak of himself. He shall glorify me: for he shall receive of mine, and shall shew it unto you."[1] Truth now comes down to us. No more digging cisterns that can hold no water! No more peering into deep wells to look for Truth! No more watching of those old wrestlers after the good and the beautiful, to see if perchance they might find out any thing for guidance or for comfort! We have now a better well than Jacob dug; one not of the earth, earthy; but "a pure river of water of Life, clear as crystal, proceeding out of the Throne of God and of the Lamb."[2] Let us drink of that, and be satisfied. Let us bathe in that, and receive new life. It is the true fountain of youth. "They that wait upon the LORD shall renew their strength; they shall mount up with wings as eagles."[3] And we are not without something to draw with. "Say not in thine heart, Who

[1] S. John xvi. 13, 14.

[2] Rev. xxii. 1.

[3] Isaiah xl. 31.

shall ascend into heaven? (that is, to bring Christ down from above;) or, Who shall descend into the deep? (that is, to bring up Christ again from the dead.) But what saith it? The word is nigh thee, even in thy mouth, and in thy heart: that is, the word of faith, which we preach."[1] And not only is it nigh us through the Spirit: but we have prayer, the great instrument for drawing Truth out of the wells of salvation. It was that which gave the weary Man who sat upon the well of Jacob, power for all His work of love. "Oh, my Father!" was His constant cry. Whole nights He spent in prayer. All His miracles were accompanied by prayer. He prayed in the Garden, until great drops of sweat, like unto blood, fell upon the ground. He prayed upon the Cross, until He cried, "It is finished." That is our instrument. It brings the Holy Spirit to us, and He gives life to all the ordinances. We feel His Presence in the House of God. We experience His power at the Sacred Feast. We rejoice in the flood of truth which He strikes from the Word of Truth; and while we revel in the love of God which He sheds abroad in the heart, we are made sensible that although we are but vases of clay, yet nevertheless is the Name of God written upon us.

[1] Rom. x. 6-8.

Eighth Sermon.

And in the days of these kings shall the God of heaven set up a kingdom, which shall never be destroyed: and the kingdom shall not be left to other people, but it shall break in pieces and consume all these kingdoms, and it shall stand for ever. — DANIEL ii. 44.

OVID said of the Roman Empire in his day, which was contemporary with the birth of our Saviour, that when Jupiter looked down from the pinnacles of heaven he could not descry any thing throughout creation that was not Roman. This was, of course, poetically extravagant; but much soberer writers than Ovid speak of the Empire under Augustus as embracing all the world that was considered worth having. It was the widest dominion which had been then known; and if it did not equal the great Empires of the present day, — the Russian, the British, the American, — it surpassed them all in the compactness of its power, in the command of its resources, in the terror of its arms, in the celerity and certainty of its blows of conquest or vengeance. It was not the growth of a day. It had been consolidating for seven centuries. And when Augustus closed the gates of the temple of Janus, it numbered among its subjects all the civilized nations of the earth, while the savages who hovered around its frontiers were ready to acknowledge its dominion, and careful to avoid its anger. It seemed, so far as man then knew, to be limited only by the horizon; and its strength was of a piece with its extent. It was no loose disjointed mass, without unity and harmony. Although embracing within its wide circumference various climates and innumerable tribes, it had carried with it in its progress its civil and military institutions, and had knit together all these diversified nations with bands of iron, so that each was made tributary to the fullest extent of its wealth and power. And all this vast accumulation of riches and legions was subject to a single will, and could be hurled with irresistible force upon any point either of resistance or rebellion. The world seemed to have reached that condition when all nationalities were to be swallowed up, and one iron rule, fierce and stern, was to mould every thing into its own shape, and keep that hopeless of change.

Under this aspect of things there was born, in a remote corner of this powerful Empire, a Child, seemingly of very obscure parentage. His mother, it is true, was of the house and lineage of David; but so reduced in circumstances that her husband was a carpenter. One of the decrees of Augustus, expressive of his universal dominion, — that all the world should be taxed, — brought this humble pair to Bethlehem, where the Child came to the birth, and was cradled in a manger. From this time until John appeared in the wilderness of Judæa, we hear no more of this Child; except that once, when a mere Boy, He strayed from His parents, and was found in the Temple among the Doctors, amazing them by His wisdom and answers. After He had been announced by John, we can follow His history for three years, when we find Him accused before Pontius Pilate, the Governor of Judæa, who permitted Him, — although he could find no guilt in Him, — to be crucified between two thieves, as a common malefactor. During His short career, He had attracted great attention among His countrymen. But their interest in Him was only short-lived; and when He died, He left but few friends, and they of the lowest classes of the people in rank and consequence. To them and to all who would listen to Him He declared Himself to be the Christ, the Anointed of God, the long-promised and prophesied Messiah, who had come to set up in the world the Kingdom predicted by Daniel in the words of my text: "And in the days of these kings shall the God of heaven set up a kingdom, which shall never be destroyed: and the kingdom shall not be left to other people, but it shall break in pieces and consume all these kingdoms, and it shall stand for ever."

What a contrast between these two kingdoms! The one throned in power, mighty in resources, surrounded with the prestige of a thousand victories: the other, finding as its only earthly support a few illiterate countrymen, and they disheartened by the ignominious death of their Leader. The one illustrious in its historians and poets and orators, who scattered its fame broadcast among the people, and embalmed its glories in immortal verse: the other known only to the few whom its preachers might attract, and whose only literature was the volume of their Master's sad and painful story. The one with a gorgeous worship, whose officers were statesmen, and whose rites were national, and who received into their tolerant Pantheon every deity who might increase their popularity: the other with nothing to attract save naked Truth; whose temples were the desert and the cave, and the blue vault of heaven; whose priests were unlearned men, save as God might inspire them; whose faith was a declaration of war — war to the bitter end of martyrdom — against idolatry and false philosophy, and every thing that exalted itself against the Name of Jesus of Nazareth. The one offering to its votaries pleasure, power, rank, office, with the delights of the present life: the other, concealing nothing of the ruggedness of the way of Life, but sternly presenting to its disciples poverty, and humiliation, and suffering, and often death. Could any one, who looked upon these antagonists as they stood face to face upon the day of the crucifixion of Jesus Christ, doubt which would prove victorious, Cæsar or Christ? — which would endure the longest, the Roman Empire or the Kingdom of Righteousness? If each was to depend upon what man could see, the idea that Christ would prevail should have been the merest mockery of human experience!

Let us now overleap the centuries which have intervened between the moment when Christ cried upon the Cross, "It is finished," and our day, and see what has been the result of the conflict. Daniel, who called himself the prophet of the Most High God, prophesied of this antagonism six hundred years before these parties were arrayed against one another; prophesied of it while yet the Roman nation was in its cradle upon the Tiber; while yet the Son of God was in the Bosom of His Father: and he said, after enumerating the great monarchies of the earth which should succeed one another, the Babylonian, the Persian, the Macedonian, the Roman, "And in the days of these kings shall the God of heaven set up a kingdom, which shall never be destroyed: and the kingdom shall not be left to other people, but it shall break in pieces and consume all these kingdoms, and it shall stand for ever." And in the preceding part of the same prophecy he described that kingdom of righteousness, figuratively, as a "Stone cut out without hands, which . . . . . became a great mountain, and filled the whole earth."[1] Standing where we do to-day, let us see what is the state of the world and what has wrought the effects we perceive.

What has become of the two kingdoms of the Cæsars and of Christ? We look around us in vain for the great Empire of Augustus. It is utterly broken to pieces, as Daniel foretold it should be, — broken into fragments, whose greatest glory are its ruins. Its noblest monuments are those which attest its utter destruction! Its language

[1] Dan. ii. 34, 35.

remains to us, dead to all the uses of life; unhonored, save as it is embalmed in the inspiration of genius. A hundred nations divide the heritage of Cæsar's Empire; and the imperial city, whose name was a terror to the world, is now guarded by the nations, not because it contains the ashes of the Cæsars, but because he is seated there who calls himself the representative of Christ upon earth. How wonderful! The successors of that mighty man who strode our world like a colossus, utterly lost, — clean forgotten: and the successor of the Bishop of Rome, the representative of the humble Nazarene, seated in his place of power. The simple fact is in itself an argument, not for the supremacy of the Bishop of Rome, but for the supremacy of Christ's Kingdom over Cæsar's kingdom, the Kingdom of righteousness over that of power! The fact is patent. The one has displaced the other. The strong has been broken in pieces, and the weak has been exalted. The Empire which overshadowed the world has disappeared; and the Kingdom which was cradled in humiliation and sorrow has taken its place. This single circumstance — were there none other — should speak volumes to the thoughtful mind. This issue to the contest, even upon its surface, is so unexpected, so startling to all experience, that it wakes up inquiry, and forces us to ask: "Has Christ really conquered in such an unequal struggle?"

We cannot find the Empire of Augustus; but we do find everywhere the Kingdom of Christ. It meets us at every turn. All Europe, with a very trifling exception, is Christian. All America, save the few wild tribes of the wilderness, is Christian. Half of Asia is Christian; and Christianity is now thundering at the gates of the remaining Empires of the East. Africa is encompassed with Christian missionaries, who are gradually working their way, through disease and ignorance and barbarism, into its dark mysteriousness. And that still newer world than ours, which lay so long hidden in its unique singularity, is rapidly rising into a great Christian nation. This is one view which strikes us; but there is another still more important in this connection. Not merely is Christ acknowledged and worshipped already over a surface ten times as great as the Roman Empire, but all the rising nations of the earth — those which are ordained to sway its destinies — are Christian. The Russian Empire, which is destined to blot out Mahometanism and rule over all Northern Asia, is a part of the Kingdom of Christ. The British Empire, which already holds the sceptre of the East, and which will one day rule over the whole Eastern Archipelago, is another part of the Kingdom of Christ. The American Republic, which even in its infancy is making itself felt throughout this whole continent, is another part of the Kingdom of Christ. And Rome, with her spiritual sceptre influencing more minds than ever did Rome with her imperial eagles, is, however corrupt, another portion of the Kingdom of Christ. Every influence is tending to enlarge this Kingdom, and none to diminish it. What Daniel said of this Kingdom is, to all appearance, true: "And in the days of these kings shall the God of heaven set up a Kingdom, which shall never be destroyed." It has gone on enlarging and widening through all the changes of the world; and to-day its sphere is larger, its glory brighter, and its prospects fairer, than they have ever been during its eventful history.

Daniel's prophecy embraced all the peculiarities of this Kingdom. It occupies only three or four verses; but in that brief space it is pictured in all its most striking characteristics. He calls it a "Stone cut out without hands," rising, spreading, increasing, without any visible means. No man lent his power to it. All power was against it.

No man carried it forward by his worldly wisdom. The greatest scholar who was converted to its cause wrote to the Corinthians: "And I, brethren, when I came to you, came not with excellency of speech, or of wisdom, declaring unto you the testimony of God. For I determined not to know any thing among you, save Jesus Christ, and him crucified. . . . . . That your faith should not stand in the wisdom of man, but in the power of God."[1] No one seized upon it as his chariot in which to ride to Empire. For centuries every one was against it: and yet, long before the days of Constantine, Tertullian tells us that "Christians filled the cities, the islands, the towns, the boroughs, the camp, the senate, and the forum;" and Origen said that "there was not a nation, whether Greek or barbarian, or of any other name, even of those who wander in tribes or live in tents, where the religion of Christ was not triumphant:" so that when Constantine advanced to power under the Christian standard, it was not he who carried Christianity to the ascendant, but Christianity which floated him to dominion. And this has been its peculiarity ever since. It has ever been a Kingdom within kingdoms, — a spirit pervading nations, but independent of their forms or power. Man has pretended to use it, — has usurped its holy name to cast a sanctity around his ambition or his crime: but it was only the *name* he could defile; the *spirit* fled from his contaminating touch, and vindicated itself by springing up in some new soil, leaving him to corruption and decay!

Another of its peculiarities was, "that it should not be left to other people," but should remain forever under the headship of Christ. All other kingdoms descend from father to son, from one monarch to another, until they pass away and are forgotten. But this should ever be the Kingdom of Christ: should know no change in its Ruler; no

[1] 1 Cor. ii. 1, 2, 5.

alteration in its principles; no mutation in its heaven-descended truths. And how strikingly has it been fulfilled! No matter what corruptions may have stolen in upon the forms of Christianity, yet is Christ the Head of His Kingdom everywhere. When the Papist prostrates himself before the host, it is because he believes that Christ his King is there. When the Protestant bows himself at the Name of Jesus, it is because he worships Him as King of kings, and Lord of lords, and places Him above all earthly rulers. And wherever His Kingdom extends, it is still the same. "It is not left to other people." It is His, and His only: His in the frozen regions of the North; His amid the palm groves of the tropics; His where "the spicy breezes blow soft o'er Ceylon's isle." It is His, and His only: whether the earthly ruler be Czar, or Emperor, King, or People. No one disputes His supremacy. No one grasps His sceptre. Although exalted to the right hand of His Father, with none on earth to represent His royalty, He reigns supreme, an invisible King, the Head of His Church, the Strength and Rock of His people.

Another peculiarity is, that "it shall stand for ever:" not for time only, but for eternity. It is not only to outlive the kingdoms of this earth, but it is never to die! And while its past history and present vigor give us assurance that it shall never be destroyed in time: its spiritual life, its spiritual Head, its connection with the unchangeable, all certify us of its future. Christ, its King, is already enthroned. In the spirit world is gathering that multitude which no man can number, of all kindred and people and nations and tribes, which is to form His Kingdom. When the economy of grace is over; when He shall have gathered His elect from the four winds of heaven: then shall the end come; and the Church Militant be changed into the Church Triumphant; and the Temple not made with hands, eternal in the Heavens, be filled with worshippers who shall worship Him in spirit and in truth.

It is this Kingdom which we ask you to-day to extend. It cannot lay upon you taxes for its support, as earthly governments do: it can only appeal to your gratitude and your piety. It is a Kingdom: but its subjects are bound to it only by the ties of love and duty. No coercion is used to make you contribute to its maintenance or extension. You give what you please, subject only to the future judgment of God. Your connection with the Church Militant is one of probation merely. You are undergoing here your trial for futurity in the sight and under the supervision of God. If you fail now in your duty, it may not seem to affect your standing in the Church of God. No punishment immediately ensues; no mark is placed upon you: but it will be brought back to you in the day when Christ shall judge His people. Under the Jewish dispensation it was widely different. That was a spiritual kingdom, carried on upon the same principles as an earthly kingdom. God was their King: and taxes were laid upon them for the support of His Kingdom and His Priesthood. Specific offerings were to be made. Nothing was to be received from Nature, without the return of a certain proportion to God. A tenth of the income was required to be laid upon the Altar of their heavenly King. Under the Christian dispensation, all this specific taxation is done away, — done away, I mean, by the Gospel scheme. Your giving to God is now a work of love, — must spring now from a sense of duty. You are to give, as you receive, — *conscientiously*, in the sight of God; *cheerfully*, as from the *heart; in faith* that it will work out God's purposes upon earth. While the decree has gone forth that this Stone, the Kingdom of the Redeemer, will become a mountain, and fill the whole earth, — will do so whether you help it or not, — still God watches you to see if *you* take any part in the fulfillment of that decree,—if you feel any interest in His work of love. Your active co-operation may not make the issue any the more certain; but it testifies your faith and your love! Never forget, in all your Christian thoughts, that you are only educating here. What you do, is of as little importance as is the literary work of a child in the school-room. But, like him, you are disciplining the heart; you are acquiring habits for your affections; you are being made meet for the inheritance of the saints in light. *Giving* is a part of this learning. It represses selfishness; it cultivates gratitude; it enkindles love; it unites us more closely with God, through His great work of Redemption which we are helping to speed forward. Whether we give or not, the Church will go forward: but we shall have no place in the triumph. "The Lord knoweth them that are His:" and when He comes to judge, and to reward, He will place the crown of glory upon those who have been faithful in life, and unto death.

Ninth Sermon.

But go thou thy way till the end be: for thou shalt rest, and stand in thy lot at the end of the days. — DANIEL xii. 13.

AT the close of that series of magnificent and far-reaching prophecies which make up the book of Daniel, we find him asking "the man clothed in linen, which was upon the waters of the river,"— him who had been the instrument of communicating to him the foreordinations of God: "O my Lord, what shall be the end of these things?" The prophet had heard, but understood not. Touched by the Divine Hand he had communicated to the ear of the world the arrangements of God's will; but, like an instrument played upon, he had not comprehended his own harmony: and restive, as human nature always will be, under this condition of things, he asks that he may be permitted to see as well as to believe, — to penetrate the mysteries of the future, as well as to proclaim them. An answer comes to him, solemn and instructive, of which my text forms the conclusion: "The words are closed up and sealed till the time of the end. . . . . But go thou thy way till the end be: for thou shalt rest, and stand in thy lot at the end of the days."

This seems to be very hard, this duty of the Christian, to be always laboring, and never seeing the fruit of that labor; to be the instrument of God's dealings, and yet be obliged to wait until the end before we can comprehend them: but it has ever been the lot of the faithful. "The just shall live by faith": and it has never been otherwise at any period of the Church's history. The work of the Christian, in his day and generation, has always been as much for those who were to come after, as for himself. S. Peter tells us that when the prophets who prophesied of the grace that should come unto the world, inquired and searched diligently into that salvation, "it was revealed" unto them, "that not unto themselves, but unto us they did minister the things which are now reported unto you by them that have preached the Gospel unto you."[1] And Daniel passed through this trial, in common with all his fellow prophets. Distinguished, as he was, for holiness and for wisdom, so that he is twice selected in the Book of Ezekiel to be placed in the very highest rank of the faithful; given, as he was, the power of looking into dark and hidden things, so that he not only gave the interpretation of dreams, but evoked the dreams themselves, when they had been forgotten, out of the shadowy realms of night; honored, as he was, to declare to the world its whole extended future, until it was lost in the abyss of Eternity: God placed him upon no different footing from that of his other prophets; nay, upon no different footing from any one of ourselves, restricting him to the simple faith and patience of the Saints, and bidding him wait until the end should be. Enough for thee, O man, is it, that thou shouldst be permitted to work for God, and then to take thy rest, satisfied to "stand in thy lot at the end of the days."

How hard it is to learn this lesson of Christian experience; — to understand that we have a work to do, sometimes of active labor, sometimes of patient suffering: and that when it is done, we are to go our way, and take our rest in the grave, and receive our reward in eternity. We are so much accustomed, in the affairs of every-day life, to

[1] 1 S. Peter i. 12.

look for immediate results, that we cannot be satisfied with our labor, if we have to wait for its fruits, — that we are impatient at an obedience which requires us to be led by a guiding hand, and not by the light of our own eyes. We are always for asking, " O my Lord, what shall be the end of these things ? " instead of living in our work, and finding our spiritual peace in that. And so we fritter our years away, seeking for light and comfort in some imaginary end: while God intends us to wring them out of our daily toil, leaving the ultimate reward with Him. Could this be truly understood, how much happiness would spring up around our earthly homes; how much light would be shed upon our Christian path! It would sanctify our most irksome duties, and pour the oil of consolation over our severest sufferings. Instead of writhing under our allotted tasks, because we think them disagreeable, or unsuited, or trifling, — because they weary us with their monotony, or disgust us with their vulgarity; we should feel that they have been appointed of God for our discipline and our duty: and, while we labored faithfully in them, would leave it with God to weave these seeming trifles into harmony with His glorious and comprehensive purposes.

What have we to do with results ? No more than the workman in some great manufactory, who, seated at his bench, labors day after day upon that particular portion of the fabric which has been allotted to him. It may be very wearisome to him, nay very painful to him, thus to sit, through his whole life, doing that one thing; and yet, if he do it well and faithfully, however trifling it may be, he is conducing essentially to the grand result, and receives for it the reward of his toil, and the " well done ! " of the master. And we can well understand how his uninformed mind and his limited view may not perceive the connection between his labor and the perfected manufacture; while yet the master-mind, which has arranged and regulates the whole, shall see that it is essential to the completeness of the work. How much happier for that workman to do cheerfully each day his necessary labor, and to find pleasure and hope in doing it, than to rise up in rebellion against the arrangement of things, and murmur at his allotted task, or refuse to perform it, because he cannot *see* — which it is no business of his to see — how it is conducing to the grand design! And this is just our position. We are all workmen, busily employed in carrying to perfection the glorious purposes of God, — those purposes which shall have their consummation at the time of the end. Each one of us has his appointed work; and, although it may seem to us trifling or wearisome, it is conducing to the perfectness of the Divine Work, and is a thread in the wonderful tissue which our Heavenly Master is weaving for Eternity. Our Christian duty is to do our part well; to labor faithfully in that sphere wherein God has placed us; to bear with cheerfulness the burdens which may be laid upon us: and not to be stubborn, nor wayward, because we cannot work at just what we please, nor understand how what we are doing is the necessary complement of a Divine harmony. Our great error is, that we do not rise up, as we should, to a clear perception either of the wisdom or the love of our Heavenly Father. We say continually, in our public and in our private prayer, "Our Father, which art in Heaven": but never realize what that word "Father" means. We forget His presence and His care. We ascribe to a blind Chance, what has been all arranged by Him. We murmur against man, and fortune; and remember not that man and fortune are but His instruments. Oh, my hearers, if we are indeed His children, — if we can lift our eyes to Heaven, and say with true filial reverence, "Our Father": we may rest assured that our work, and the way in which we are compelled to do it, and the sufferings through which we pass in doing it, are just the very best for us; and even though we may not be able to see what is the meaning of our experience, nor how our poor weak work can help along His mighty purposes: when it is all finished, we shall receive no worse a dismissal than his mightiest prophet: "Go thou thy way till the end be: for thou shalt rest, and stand in thy lot at the end of the days."

The work of life is very wearisome, even when we feel that it is allotted us by our Father. I do not speak now of that holiday life which too many lead, — taking their portion in this world; but of that life of duty and of responsibility which God has placed us here to live. It is very wearisome to be ever schooling and disciplining one's self; very wearisome to be contending against natural infirmities and besetting sins; very wearisome to be swimming against the world's current; very wearisome to be guiding and controlling those who are committed to our charge. But then it is the work which God has assigned us, and we must search for the blessedness which He has wrapped up with the toil. And we can find it even here, in the very dust and turmoil of the battle-field, amid the commonplace cares and anxieties of life, in its severest duties and cruelest sufferings, if we will live in the means instead of looking to the end; — if we will search for life and comfort in the thought that all these things, — the most trifling and the commonest, the most solemn and the sternest, — are our part of God's work, and are conducing to His divinest end. How changed is the whole aspect of life, if looked at from this point of view! What before was trivial and unimportant waxes into greatness, so soon as it becomes connected with the purposes of God. What was bitter and loathsome is deprived of its sting, when we find it a link in the chain of God's glorious love. So long as we are looking to self, — to that connection which our lives may be holding with things around us, — we can find no comfort; for there is a crook in every lot, a skeleton in every house: but when we can look away to God, and realize that our work, our condition, our sufferings, are all from Him and of Him; are not things of caprice, or of fortune, but of His fatherly appointment; are not unnecessary and useless, working sorrow to us while they work good to nobody, but are essential parts of His mighty and incomprehensible will: we change the crook into a source of blessing, we clothe the very skeleton with a divine halo, and we sing songs of gladness even in the night. This is the true charm of life, — to find our happiness in our work; not to be looking for it in the future, but in the present; not to expect it to come only out of great things, or out of prosperous things, but to woo it from our commonest every-day occupations, and to snatch it from the stern grasp of adversity. If we separate happiness from our daily and our present work, we are turning it away from our homes, and reserving it for seasons of excitement, or for a distant future which is always rising — like the horizon — as we approach it. The true peace of the Christian here on earth is in doing every thing, and suffering every thing, as a part of the work he is appointed to finish. In this view all responsibility is rolled from him, because he is a mere instrument in God's almighty hand; all murmuring is hushed, because he could not change his work without an interference with God's omniscient wisdom; all anxiety is put to rest, because his business is only to do or suffer, and leave the consequences to God.

This is the Christian's happiness in life, — his only happiness. But the time will come, when that work shall be done; when the books shall be sealed unto the end; when the command shall come to each one of us, "Go thy way till the end be: for thou shalt rest, and stand in thy lot at the end of the days." The time of work is over; the sun has set upon our day of labor; the hour of rest is come: and the Christian is given that blessedness, — the blessedness of the transition state from the work of earth to the work of Heaven. Oh the sweetness of that word *Rest!* — to cease from all the weariness of life; to be done with its cares, its perplexities, its miseries; to have fought the good fight of faith, and ended the struggle; to have finished the work which God has given us to do, and now to lie down and be at peace! But none can enjoy it who have not labored. The self-indulgent know not what it means. It belongs only to the workman, — to him who has borne the heat and burden of the day! "There remaineth a rest for the people of God."[1] And why for them? Because God's people are expected to be a working people, — working for their own salvation, working for the salvation of others; because they are expected to be a struggling people, — struggling against their own natures, and their indwelling corruption; because they are expected to be a warring people, warring against the world, the flesh and the Devil. For such it is, — the true members of the Church Militant upon earth, — that there remaineth *a rest:* for they need it, they desire it, they deserve it. The Psalmist expressed it when, in the weariness of his struggles, he cried: "Oh, that I had wings like a dove! for then would I fly away, and be at rest."[2] "I would hasten my escape from the windy storm and tempest."[3] S. Paul expressed it when, aged and battered, he exulted in his approaching end: "For I am now ready to be offered, and the time of my departure is at hand. I have fought a good fight, I have finished my course, I have kept the faith: henceforth there is laid up

[1] Heb. iv. 9. [2] Psalm lv. 6. [3] *Ibid.* 8.

for me a crown of righteousness."[1] S. John proclaimed it as an utterance from Heaven, when he said: "I heard a voice from Heaven, saying unto me, Write, Blessed are the dead which die in the Lord from henceforth: Yea, saith the Spirit, that they may rest from their labors; and their works do follow them."[2] And these expressions come home to the heart of every struggling Christian. He feels that *rest* is what he craves; — rest from sin, rest from warfare, rest from responsibility, rest from temptation, rest from the solemn work of life: and God gives him the boon when He dismisses him from his post: "Go thy way till the end be. Thou hast finished thine allotted task: now thou shalt rest. Go sleep in the grave, faithful warrior; when the end of the days shall come, then shalt thou awake, like a strong man from sleep, and stand in thy lot!"

And this is the blessedness of Eternity! The Christian has had happiness in his work, rest after his work, and now shall he have reward for his work. "He shall stand in his lot in the end of the days." He had on earth his allotted labor, and he shall now have in Heaven his allotted reward. The same loving Lord who meted out the toil and the suffering of the world, will mete out the joy and the glory of his Father's mansions. All has been arranged for Eternity; all has been watched and guided through Time: and now shall it be made perfect in God Himself. The Christian lived by faith; was permitted to see nothing but his work; was taught obedience, and submission, and humility, and patience; was made perfect through sufferings; toiled on, fought on, resting in nothing but promises, yet seeing God in every thing: and now faith is swallowed up in sight, and mystery in knowledge, and he can see how every thing worked together for good. Until he stands in his lot, he

[1] 2 Tim. iv. 6–8. [2] Rev. xiv. 13.

could not comprehend the work upon earth which was preparing him for it; until he enters upon the inheritance of Heaven, he could not understand the training which was making him meet for it. The one is the complement of the other. God saw them both from the beginning, and fitted them one for the other. Man could see only the work, and had therefore to do it in Faith: until God introduces him to the other, and manifests the glorious harmony.

And as it is with our individual work upon earth, so is it with the Church's work. The Church is an aggregate of Christian people; and when they move and act in a mass, they move and act upon the same principles as the individual. The Church has its appointed work, — a work given it by Christ, its Head, through those who were its earliest representatives: "Go ye into all the world, and preach the Gospel to every creature."[1] And the Church has no more right than the individual to ask, "O my Lord, what shall be the end of these things?" The Church has nothing to do with the end, save to work for it. *That* belongs to God. If He pleases that the Missionary labor of the Church should seem to be spent for nought; if it is His will — and His will is signified by His command — that the blood of the martyrs shall be the seed of His Church; if it is helping on His purposes that Missionaries shall go out to their places of toil simply to die: He knows better than we do, for His eye scans the whole field of battle, and sees the end from the beginning. The duty of a soldier is simple, unquestioning obedience, — to do whatsoever he is ordered, whether to advance boldly, or retreat wisely, or stand in his post of honor and be shot down. Many a battle has been won upon earth by iron-hearted endurance. Napoleon gained the victory at Wagram, and Wellington at Waterloo, by permitting a portion of their troops to be cut to

[1] S. Mark xvi. 15.

pieces in their positions. To those who suffered, it seemed a cruel fate merely to stand and die: but those master-minds, whose comprehensive glance took in the whole field of vision, saw that the sacrifice of the few was necessary for the victory of the whole. Those well-trained, disciplined soldiers trusted in their commander, faithfully believed that no useless sacrifice was made of them, bravely offered up their lives for the cause's sake: and shall Christian soldiers, the conscripts of the Cross, falter in their obedience when such a voice as God's, and such a wisdom as God's, utters His command: "Go ye into all the world, and preach the Gospel to every creature?" He does not say what shall be the end of your obedience, what its results, or what its success: He merely charges you to do it. He gives the Church her work. He does not ask her to crown that work, but merely to do it. It is no matter whether she sees no fruit of her work. Her life is not a life of sight, but of faith. Still must she continue to do it. No matter whether generation after generation of her children pass away and go to their rest without any recompense to sight: still must she continue to do it. When Abraham was called to go out of his own country, and leave his kindred, that he might possess the Land of Promise, he went; and died without any signs of its fulfilment. And Isaac died, and went his way to his rest. And Jacob died, and went his way to his rest. And Joseph died, and went his way to his rest. And generation after generation died, and went their way to their rest. Then came long years of weary bondage: but, at the end of the days, Abraham's children stood in their lot! This record of faith is given us for our example; and not this alone, but the history, all along, of the Church. It treads an equal path. It never offers any thing to sight. Its unchanging principle is, as generation after generation finishes its work: "Go thou thy way till the end be: for thou shalt rest, and stand in thy lot at the end of the days."

And what, my beloved people, is the duty of every age of the Church, is *our* duty. The command of our Saviour is unrepealed. It stands there in all its imperative force, now, to-day, as when the Apostles first received it. If it were right to encourage you by what should never be your motive of action, I might point you to much in the world that looked favorable to the growth of Christianity; but I refrain, because I desire you to stand upon the one unchangeable principle of obedience to Christ's command. If every thing was as dark and dreary as midnight; if the gates of the nations seemed barred and double-barred against the admission of our Missionaries; if storm and darkness raged around the battlements of Zion: it would be none the less our duty to send forth the glad tidings of great joy. Our preachers might never reach their fields of labor; might only reach them, to knock and be refused admittance; might be let in, only to be slaughtered: still have we done our work, and must continue to do it! Results, success, have nothing to do with our duty. We cannot tell how necessary this darkness, this hindrance, this slaughter, may be. That is not for us to judge. We must do our work as a generation of the Church's children; and, when we have done it, be satisfied with nothing more than this: "Go thou thy way till the end be: for thou shalt rest, and stand in thy lot at the end of the days."

Tenth Sermon.

For who knoweth what is good for man in this life, all the days of his vain life which he spendeth as a shadow. — ECCLESIASTES vi. 12.

THE history of a man is very distinct from the life of a man, — that outside portraiture which a biographer gives, from that inward experience which is known only to himself and God. What appears on the surface in the shape of action, is all that is manifest to the world. The deep under-current of motive and feeling, of weariness and disgust, of repentance and remorse, remains forever secret, unless the barriers of the heart be broken down by the weight which presses upon it, and it is poured forth for the warning or the benefit of others. Every honest diary of the heart-life of a human creature is a precious document for man; sometimes because of the true value of the world which it sets before him, sometimes because of the dangers against which it guards him, sometimes because of the comfort which it affords him. "As in water face answereth to face, so the heart of man to man:"[1] and when an honest heart is truthfully opened with all its rich and sad developments, we read as it were our own hidden life, and are startled at its portraiture of ourselves, just as the Samaritan woman was when Christ told her all that ever she did. We have dreamed perhaps that our experience was our own, that it was a thing of individuality, that no one else had ever travelled just such a road, had walked in the deep

[1] Prov. xxvii. 19.

shadow of weariness and satiety when the skies were bright over us and the flowers seemed to grow in our path, had been weighed down by a sense of the utter vanity of all things earthly when others were enjoying our lot, had mourned in bitterness of spirit over words and acts which others applauded and imitated: and lo! another heart speaks, and tells our inner life as its own, and lays bare before the world all our secrets, and anatomizes for the gaze of mankind all that was most hidden and sacred within ourselves. Well is it for us if we will learn from the experience of another; and, taking the chart which another has sketched of the ocean of life, steer wisely and thoughtfully through all its dangers and treacheries and false appearances, into that haven of rest which is offered to the prudent and the faithful.

How strikingly are these remarks exemplified by the two aspects under which Solomon is presented to us in the Bible. Were we to form our judgment of him from the historical books of the Bible, we should conceive of him as a monarch of surpassing wisdom and power, living proudly, haughtily, luxuriously, magnificently: surrounding himself with every enjoyment which life could give, and interested only in matters of state, or art, or literature. We read of him there as extending the limits of his kingdom from Egypt to the Euphrates, and from the Great Sea to the borders of Arabia; as adorning Jerusalem with palaces, and a Temple of surpassing preciousness; as receiving homage from nations and monarchs of remote and almost unknown regions; as promoting commerce and trade beyond all former precedent; as winning admiration by his wisdom and his knowledge; as floating in an atmosphere of sensual enjoyment of the most Oriental cast. This is the Solomon of history. But how different is the Solomon of the Proverbs and of Ecclesiastes! How the mask falls off when we follow him into his secret chambers, and watch him as he lays aside his robes of state and his aspect of dignity and his assumption of enjoyment, and listen to the deep sighs which burst from his wearied heart, and witness the tears of repentance which course their furrows down his cheeks, and learn his honest judgment of himself and human life! The one is the true and proper complement of the other,—the inner life laid bare as the commentary upon the outer. And herein lay Solomon's wisdom,—that wisdom which God had given him. He was the wisest man the world has known, not because he was a consummate statesman, and an acute philosopher, and knew all Nature's secrets: but because he gauged all this at its true value; and when he had flashed it in the eyes of an unthinking multitude, was honest enough to inscribe upon it, "*Vanity of vanities; all is vanity;*"—was true enough to his own nature and his common humanity, to record his own deep sense of his infirmities, and his disgust! And when, my hearers, you would judge the character of this wise monarch, you must combine the two aspects of his life, and remember that God saw all the secret workings of his heart, its sense of vanity, its heavy weariness, its deep contempt of outward show, its repentance and remorse, as well as the pomp and luxury which were open to the world. God knows that station and office and rank require of men ofttimes what their own conscience disapproves: but God alone sees the sorrow it inflicts, and hears the groans which are uttered heavenward for forgiveness and for peace. Blessed be God that He has given us one honest Book in which we may see our fellow-creatures as they are, and learn what wretched inconsistencies God can endure, what a mass of infirmity and weakness God can forgive. But for this, a faithful reading of our own hearts would drive us to despair, and force us to the question of S. Paul: "O wretched man that I am! who shall deliver me from the body of this Death?"[1]

It is among the wailings of this wise king that we encounter the sad confession of ignorance which we have selected for our text: "For who knoweth what is good for man in this life, all the days of his vain life which he spendeth as a shadow?" What an accumulation of epithets and figures to express his deep sense of man's pitiful condition! Vain life, spent as a shadow! All of it spent so, — promising and not performing, alluring and deceiving, weaving bright webs of hope only as snares and meshes! — and mingled with all this, a profound obscurity as to the blessing or the curse of every movement, as to the good or the evil of every possession. Words could not express a more forlorn prospect, especially when we remember that it was uttered by one for whom life had displayed its most flattering visage, — around whose brows had been wreathed the proudest chaplets of knowledge and of wisdom. If he, with his penetratiag and all-pervading wisdom, knew not what was good for man, who might expect to know it? If he counted all the days of man's life as days of vanity, when every enjoyment of earth was his: who might look for satisfaction in the days of the years of his pilgrimage? Sad sentence inscribed by honesty and wisdom upon the life we are now living! Sad shadow cast by Truth over the path which the young, the gay, the ambitious, the sensual, the wise, are now treading! "Press on!" — is its sad accompaniment as the eager train comes sweeping by — "but alas! ye know not whether the good ye are seeking may not turn to ashes in your hands and bitterness in your hearts; — whether the evil ye are lamenting may not be the jewel in the head of adversity and affliction."

[1] Rom. vii. 24.

God alone knoweth what is good for man, and what is evil for man: and the sooner ye commit yourselves to His omniscient guidance, the sooner shall ye experience the peace of a child under the guidance of its Father, the confidence of a voyager under the direction of his unchanging star.

The wisdom of the Greek, who answered, "that no one could be reckoned happy until his life was closed," was founded upon a dim perception of the truth uttered in my text. I say a dim perception, for the philosopher was only looking to the uncertainty of human affairs, and the instability of fortune: while Solomon was embracing a larger compass, and affirming man's ignorance of what was good for him and what was evil, without any regard to its permanence or its frailty. And it is this feature in my text which makes it so sad,—that darkness is around the path of life; that ignorance hangs like a pall over the results of our actions, our pursuits, and our hopes. It is cruel enough to be so often disappointed, to be so long laboriously rolling the stone up the steep ascent, to be thirsting so many weary years with the fountain always glittering before our eyes: but how much more cruel to be told, as you rush along in eager and rapt pursuit, that even should you reach the summit with your burden, you might find a cold, thin atmosphere of oppressive misery;—that even should you slake your parched lips and craving heart in the waters you have sought, you might find them bitter to the taste and unsatisfying to the soul. And this is just what the wise monarch tells us is our condition,—that no man knoweth what is good for man in this life; that we all play our game in the dark; and that all the fondest objects of man's desire wear a double face of good or evil, according to God's arrangements. It is not therefore merely a lesson of the uncertainty of human possessions, of the instability and vanity of earthly pursuits, that the sacred writer is teaching you: but a more striking lesson of man's ignorance and dependence. The object may be won, the goal may be reached, the prize may be grasped: but is it for good or for evil? — for blessing or for curse?

And whether we look at this truth with the eye of experience, or with the teachings of Scripture, we reach the same conclusion. If man's earthly condition be considered, and that alone, it would be very hard to say whether the objects of his pursuit brought more good or more evil to him and his, even when most successfully achieved. Is constant toil, is incessant care, is weighing every word and action, is reckoning every cent, is sealing the fountains of charity, is hardening the face and the heart, is rearing a family of idlers, is introducing luxury and indolence and vice into your domestic circle, *good:* and yet these are the most usual results which follow an ardent pursuit and successful attainment of wealth. Can man know what is good, when he spends his days and nights for consequences like these? Is a brow wrinkled with thought, is a head whitened with care, is a family neglected, is a home forsaken, is a surrender of individual independence, is an accumulation of envy and slander and calumny, is unceasing abuse and misrepresentation, is the unsteady footing of a fluctuating multitude, *good:* and yet these are the fruits which the ambitious reap, when they devote themselves to the pursuit of power. Can man know what is good, when he sows seed that will grow up into such a harvest as this? Is a body decrepid before its time, a constitution broken and decayed, an old age of pain and of sorrow and of inanition, a fortune wrecked, hopes blasted and expectations crushed, *good:* and yet these are the blessings which follow in the train of a life of pleasure. Can man know what is good, when he sacrifices all the kindly charities of life, all the chaste enjoyments of home and fireside, for such companions as these for his declining years? And even when these things, or any other earthly objects, are bestowed upon man without these visible natural consequences, can he or any other man know whether they will work good or evil for him? Wealth suddenly acquired is almost sure to destroy him who receives it. Power rapidly obtained usually turns the head and corrupts the heart of him upon whom it is bestowed. Idleness and luxury enervate both soul and body, and sink those who are permitted to indulge them into effeminacy and lethargy. Whatever man considers good, has with it toil and care and disappointment if he pursues it; and, if it is thrust upon him, almost certain corruption and ruin. The wisest father who had any true experience, would hesitate long before deciding upon what he would desire for his child; and seldom would he wish to heap upon him any of those things which men count good, without first passing him through those preliminary steps of discipline, which seem necessary to chasten the desire and moderate the passions of men.

And as it is with good, so is it likewise with what men call evil. Looking at this under its various forms of labor, of poverty, of disease, of affliction, of humiliation, of disappointment, it is hard to say, from one's own experience, whether those conditions of things have not been most propitious to us. I know that in the world, — and I know that Christians catch the tone and language, — the man is pitied who is subjected to any of these conditions of being: — pitied without any consideration how much his character may need their discipline, or his habits their restraining influence. Little do we know, while we thus speak, but that these things are in the highest sense the very best which could have come upon him; — not for his present and immediate comfort, but for that long future which he may have to live here upon earth. The solemn experience of the world uniformly teaches us that good and evil are not mere abstract and opposite qualities; but that good is often evil, and evil often good — paradoxical as it may seem — according to the individuals around whom they circle, or the circumstances under which they are cast upon us. And the conclusion is the same as before: "Who knoweth what is good for man in this life, all the days of his vain life which he spendeth as a shadow?"

If we look at this truth with the light of Scripture, it is still more striking. Man may not acknowledge his experience, — may prefer to veil his consciousness from the eye of his fellow-man, and persist in the assertion that he does not call evil good, and good evil: but the Bible speaks always frankly and honestly to man, and places before him his full, true measure. It looks at life not simply in the present, but also in the future; gathers man's immortality around him, and makes him take that into the account of good and of evil: and when that union has been made, and the conditions of his salvation are brought to bear upon the question, no one can hesitate in his decision as to man's ignorance of good and evil. When the Bible tells us that it is harder for a rich man to enter into the Kingdom of Heaven than for a camel to pass through the eye of a needle, and man counts riches one of his greatest goods: well may we say, in the words of our text, "For who knoweth what is good for man in this life?" When the Bible teaches us that not many wise, not many noble, not many learned are called, and men toil for wisdom and honor and learning like galley slaves, sacrificing bodily ease and the comforts and tranquillity of life for their possession: we may again ask: "For who knoweth what is good for man in this life?" When the Bible heaps its blessings upon the meek, the pure, the merciful, the peacemakers, the persecuted, and man reckons gentleness and purity and mercy and peace among the mean things and the base things of the world: we may again ask: "Who knoweth what is good for man in this life?" When, in fine, the grace of God is made in the Bible the highest gift purchased for man by Jesus Christ,—is reckoned above all things else in preciousness and glory,—while man considers its possession as a token of weakness and imbecility: we may put anew the question: "Who knoweth what is good for man in this life?" In the view of Inspiration, as well as in that of our experience, we are satisfied that man's ignorance of what is good for him is profound, and that we may safely challenge human nature to answer: "For who knoweth what is good for man in this life, all the days of his vain life which he spendeth as a shadow?"

If it cannot be known by man, then, what is good for him in this life, we are brought to several practical conclusions of deep importance to us in the conduct of life. And the first of them is this: "that we should place no inordinate value upon those things which are counted among men as good for them, nor should we too carefully desire them, nor should we envy others the possession of them." David himself was sorely beset by this temptation, and details his experience and its cure in the 73d Psalm:—"But as for me, my feet were almost gone; my steps had well-nigh slipped. For I was envious at the foolish, when I saw the prosperity of the wicked. They are not in trouble as other men; neither are they plagued like other men. Verily I have cleansed my heart in vain, and washed my hands in innocency. For all the day long have I been plagued, and chastened every morning. When I thought to know this, it was too painful for me; until I went into the sanctuary of God; then understood I their end. Surely thou didst set them in slippery places: thou castedst them down into destruction. Thus my heart was grieved, and I was pricked in my reins. So foolish was I, and ignorant; I was as a beast before thee." We must not look at things in this world as they seem; but we must look at their end, and that in the light of the sanctuary. What seems to flesh and sense to be good, may be good only for the moment, — may be accompanied by troubles and dangers of the most perilous kind, and may lead to inevitable destruction. If we take only one view of them, — what may be called the fleshly and earthly view, — they wear the aspect of goodness: but only turn their other visage, — place them under the eye of Scripture, — and that aspect changes into one of evil and of curse. Those who possess them are said by the Scriptures to stand in slippery places, to be consumed with daily terrors; and sudden destruction is their threatened doom. From such things a prudent man, foreseeing the evil, would hide himself.

Another most important conclusion is the reverse of this: "That we should not be too much cast down by what the world calls evil, nor murmur against the lot which God has assigned to us." When we hear one of God's servants saying, "It is good for me that I have been afflicted," for "before I was afflicted, I went astray;"[1] — when we see an Apostle deliberately writing to the Hebrews that "whom the Lord loveth he chasteneth, and scourgeth every son whom he receiveth,"[2] and that though "no chastening for the present seemeth to be joyous, but grievous; nevertheless, afterward it yieldeth the peaceable fruit of righteousness;"[3] — when we find God's richest blessings associated with lowliness, and humiliation, and suffering; — when, in fine, our great Exemplar was a child of poverty, and had not where to lay His head, and was deeply acquainted with grief: well may we be satisfied with conditions of being

[1] Psalm cxix. 71, 67. [2] Heb. xii. 6. [3] *Ibid.* 11.

which have such words of comfort and examples of holiness connected with them. We cannot credit the Bible without being satisfied that what man calls evil is ofttimes God's richest blessing; and that the school of humiliation, taking the word in its broadest sense, is the discipline of man's highest good. In our ignorance we cannot know this; but it must be learned, like all our other best lessons, through faith and experience. The flesh revolts against it: but then flesh and blood cannot inherit the kingdom of God, which is the inheritance we desire. Let us then be satisfied with our condition, however lowly, however difficult, however full of toil: for if it be blessed with faith, it must end in everlasting life.

And lastly our ignorance of what is good for us should teach us to place ourselves in the keeping of a Being who is wiser and more far-seeing than ourselves. He has promised to make every thing work together for good to those that love him: and how much better—where no one knoweth what is good for man in this life—to place ourselves under the guidance of a Father who will, by His divine power, overrule every thing to good, whatever it may be in itself, or however it may appear to flesh and sense. Good and evil are indissolubly connected together in this world,—good and evil, I mean, in the sense in which the multitude use these words. They come alike to all, the just and the unjust, the righteous and the sinful. But while we are so blind—such "beasts," as the Psalmist calls it—that we cannot distinguish between these: there is One who can make every thing good for us, however marred its visage or ominous its aspect. Upon Him, then, let us cast our care. In His wisdom let us rest our judgments. Let Him decide for us our course, and all its accompaniments: and whether He dispense to us what the world calls good or evil, let us feel that it is best for us, because the Lord hath ordered it.

Eleventh Sermon.

And the apostles said unto the Lord, Increase our faith.— S. LUKE xvii. 5.

IF we were to select from among men an individual who had signally failed in life, and were to analyze the causes of his failure, we should almost certainly find a neglect of what he considered trifles, a disregard of what he deemed unimportant circumstances, to have been really one of the most prominent of them. While he had been preparing himself for great occasions, and waiting for large opportunities, he had neglected the little things which make up the greater part of ordinary life, and had thus, before trial, proved himself ignorant of the true conditions of his being; and unfitted, because of that ignorance, for success in its conduct. While another man had been carefully watching every occasion of usefulness or advancement, however slight it might appear, — had treated every circumstance, which involved him at all in its effects, as if it might be the most important of his life, — *he* had considered like occasions and like circumstances as too trivial for his notice, as too ordinary to produce any material or permanent consequences. And thus while the one, taking advantage of every little wave which rippled to his feet, had launched his bark, and was far off on his prospering voyage: the other was still waiting for some extraordinary influx of the waters, which was to bear him forth upon its swelling bosom, and sweep him at once to fortune or to fame. And there will he stand until his life shall end: and he learn — when too late — that fortune, fame, nay, character itself, are made up not of accidental or lucky chances, but of a steady and industrious improvement of those opportunities which come alike to all in the usual course of human life.

And thus, my hearers, shall every one of us stand, unimproved in religious character, unadvanced in our soul's salvation, waiting, waiting, upon the shore of the great ocean of God's eternal love: unless we learn, at once, that our advancement in spiritual things is made to depend, like our success in worldly things, not upon any extraordinary manifestation of God's grace towards us, not upon any striking exercise of our faith towards Him, but upon the improvement of that grace which, the Apostle tells us, appeareth to all men; and upon the exercise of that faith which is concerned about the circumstances and contingencies of every-day life.

Christians are very prone to consider the increase of faith as necessary for them upon great and important occasions of human life, — when they are called upon to meet a great crisis, or to wade through a sea of troubles, or to struggle with a storm of temptation. And in this they are right, and God has promised that upon such occasions and under such necessity His grace shall be sufficient for them: but they are wrong in supposing that they do not require a like increase to meet the ordinary trials and temptations of every-day life. For these they consider themselves fully prepared by their consistent Christian life, and do not suppose that such common and usual occurrences demand any special supply of the Spirit's power and influence. And it is just at this point that most of us make the great mistake of our Christian life, and lose alike the comfort and the power of Christianity. And this mistake is in supposing that our duties — those duties in which God has promised us His help and support — consist in great things, in unusual efforts, in extraordinary sacrifices, in uncommon self-devotion. And while waiting for these occasions, we are undisciplined for those trials which we call petty because they come daily, and stumble in our Christian walk because unprepared for the exercise of our graces under circumstances which we deem common only because they are constantly recurring.

The circumstances under which this prayer was offered by the Apostles to their Lord furnish a felicitous elucidation of our meaning. It was evidently an earnest prayer, — one offered impulsively, in reply to what they considered one of the hard sayings of their Master. Had it been one of those hard sayings, — had it been offered in reply to His mysterious declaration that "Except a man be born again, he cannot see the Kingdom of God,"[1] or that other saying which commanded them to eat His Flesh and drink His Blood, — it would not have furnished us with the instruction we are deriving from it: because, under those circumstances, we should not have deemed it either a remarkable or an unnecessary prayer. We should have confessed, at once, that for the reception of such doctrines an increase of faith was alike proper and requisite. But when, upon turning to the context, we find that this prayer was uttered in reply to such a simple, every-day duty as the forgiveness of injuries, we feel at once that there is a meaning in it, which it may be well for us to understand, — a lesson conveyed by it, which we ought to learn at the earliest possible moment of our Christian career.

"Take heed to yourselves," are the words of our Saviour: "If thy brother trespass against thee, rebuke him; and if he repent, forgive him. And if he trespass against thee seven times in a day, and seven times in a day turn again

[1] S. John iii. 3.

to thee, saying, I repent; thou shalt forgive him. And the Apostles said unto the Lord, Increase our faith." And well might they pray so: for it is not so much the greatness of an act which makes it difficult to a Christian, as its frequent recurrence, coupled as it is with an antagonism to flesh and blood. When a great occasion offers itself, when a mighty sacrifice for religion is forced upon us, when some remarkable trial casts its dark shadow over our path, we nerve ourselves for the struggle; we put upon us the armor of righteousness upon the right hand and upon the left. But we are not habitually watchful against little sins, against secret sins, against the trials and annoyances which are the most dangerous, because they are the most frequent, and come upon us unawares.

We run into great error both in life and in religion, when we undertake to determine what are great things and what are little things, — what actions are important, and what unimportant. Our judgment is almost always false upon questions like these; and could those judgments be seen by us as they are seen by God, we should find that we were too often calling good, evil; and evil, good: sweet, bitter; and bitter, sweet. We conclude that things are great and important, when they are public, notorious, of wide fame, of extensive interest; when they are blown upon the wings of the wind; when they occupy the tongues of multitudes; when they adorn, or soil, the page of history. On the other hand, we call things trifling and unimportant, when they are frequent, ordinary, confined to small circles, shut up within the heart and consciousness of individuals. We forget that the daily recurrence of a thing, common and ordinary, may make it of vast moment to our welfare and happiness, while the rare occurrence of an uncommon event may render it — however striking it may seem on the instant — of very little consequence in its results. In

Nature, it is the unfailing recurrence of night and day, of seed-time and harvest, of winter and summer; it is the steady movement of the sun and moon and stars; it is the uniform and unchanging laws of attraction and repulsion, of evaporation and condensation, of motion and inertia; which are most important and therefore greatest: and not the portentous eclipse, nor the fiery comet, nor the extreme convulsions of Nature, even though they leave for ages the impress of their terror and desolation. The one goes on forever, — quiet, silent, sublime, yet giving life, happiness, joy, confidence to a world. The other is only for the moment, — terrible, fearful, overwhelming, exciting the mind, astonishing the understanding, for years perhaps the theme of science and of study: yet never working for man any of the beneficent results which flow from the common, every-day blessings of light and heat, of dew and rain, of summer's breath and winter's blasts.

And as it is in Nature, so is it likewise in life. It is not the poetry of life, nor yet its romance, which make up its blessedness: it is its every-day prose. Wit, eloquence, wisdom, heroism, learning, beauty, — these are the idols of the world. These make men and women great, place them upon pedestals, shrine them in hearts, embalm them in song and story. But when you come truly to weigh these gifts, — to rate their value in the world's advancement or in the world's happiness, — plain common sense outweighs them all. And for the simple reason, that life is made up of common and ordinary things, which demand none of these qualities as essential to their proper conduct. They embellish life; they constitute the fluting to the column or the efflorescence of the capital: but coarser materials than these must bear up the fabric of society. The qualities which make the fireside peaceful and virtuous; which train the young in the paths of duty; which furnish the examples of industry, of obedience, of reverence, of religion; which give stability to society and strength to government: are those which are truly great, and most essentially important. And these are the qualities which God dispenses most freely, and which man despises because they are universally diffused. They give peace at home, but they do not confer distinction abroad. They cast a halo around a happy wife and rejoicing children; but then it is not a rainbow that spans the earth. They protect law, and preserve justice, and keep society from anarchy; but then their names are not blown abroad by fame's noisy trumpet, nor their effects recorded upon monuments of brass. They are not great; because man confounds greatness with notoriety, sublimity with noise and ostentation.

And as it is in Life, so it is likewise in Religion. It is not upon the great fields of ecclesiastical strife that the victories of the Cross have been won; but in the quiet, unobtrusive walks of duty and of suffering. Catching the spirit and language of the world, we call the martyr great; we call the reformer great; we call the ripe and learned theologian great; we call the mitred dignitary great; and we connect with them the advancement of religion and the fruits of the Spirit. For deeds such as they have performed, for works such as they have done, for struggles such as they have waged, for writings such as they have left, we think the prayer of the Apostles, "Lord, increase our faith," must have been appropriate and necessary. But God sees not as man sees: and His eyes look upon many a martyr of whom the world has never heard; and watch the dust of many a reformer who lived before the Church knew any reformation; and behold the brows of many an humble and obedient Christian encircled with the golden crown of immortality, who knew no learning when on earth save the learning of His Word, and wore no crown save the crown of sorrow and of thorns. And He sees, too, that it is their deeds of Faith and of humility which have subdued the earth; that it is the seeds which they have planted of obedience and of reverence which have leavened the world; that it is their works of love and charity which have sanctified the Name of Jesus upon earth. Ask the proud man, who lies in humbled repentance at the foot of the Cross asking for mercy and for peace, what hath brought him there: and he will point you, not to the martyr's ashes, not to the theologian's wisdom, not to the preacher's eloquence: but to the meek and holy life of a sainted mother, obscure to all but him; or to the patient endurance of a long-suffering wife, unknown except by God and himself; or to the unconscious purity of some darling child, whose daily life has breathed more of Christianity than all the forms of religion which have surrounded him. Ask the rebellious youth who is returning after his prodigal career to find comfort upon his father's bosom, what is guiding him back to a long neglected and long forgotten home: and he will tell you no tale of wonder or of miracle, — of supernatural awakening or angelic guidance. His polar star, through all his wanderings, has been his father's fireside, hallowed by affection, endeared by tenderness, consecrated by prayer, made lovely as Paradise by the graces of the Spirit which ever rested over it! These are the influences which keep Christ's name divine in the eyes of the world, — which force even wicked men to confess that His life and death have raised humanity to a higher standard than it has ever before attained.

And who are they that have worked and are still working such wonders for the Name of Christ, such blessings for a cursed and smitten earth? They are the meek and humble saints of whom the world knows but little, — the merciful, the pure in heart, the persecuted for righteousness' sake, the imitators in suffering of Him who was the "man of

8

sorrows and acquainted with grief." They are those who have patiently borne all the afflictions which a heavenly Father has laid upon them, and have learned to comfort others with the consolation wherewith God has comforted them. They are those who have labored to cheer the dreariness of poverty, to speak peace to the accusing conscience, to find rest for the wearied spirit, to revive the crushed and despairing heart. They are those who have filled Heaven with their prayers, and whose prayers have returned laden with the blessing and the dew of Heaven, which they have scattered all around them. They are those who have washed their robes in the blood of the Lamb, and from whose eyes God will forever wipe away all tears.

And what are the deeds which have made these saints of God so precious in His eyes, — such a blessing to the whole earth? What are the conquests which shall enroll their names so illustriously among the elect of God? Just such deeds, my fellow-Christians, as any Christian among you may perform; — just such conquests as every one of you is called upon daily to achieve. The deeds of faith which hallow the name of Jesus upon earth, the conquests of love which make His religion indeed glad tidings of great joy to the world, are not limited to great occasions, or unusual opportunities; have not to be waited for until some great religious crisis shall arise, and give fitting scope to the excited energies: but meet us at every step of our Christian life, cross our path daily and hourly, furnishing the means of discipline and the prospect of heavenly glory. Oh! how fatal an error do we commit, when we wait for illustrious opportunities in order to utter the prayer of our text, "Increase our faith!" How fearful is our mistake, when we consider nothing great but what is of public interest and wide-spread renown. We need that prayer at every moment of our lives; for we spend no day in which we are not called upon for deeds of faith, for conquests over self and over the world. We glorify him who confesses his faith in the midst of fire; who bears, for a few hours, the physical agonies of a body devoured by the flames: and think *he* needs, indeed, the prayer, "Increase our Faith." But what is his suffering compared with the martyrdom of a whole life, — with the agony of carrying about day after day, year after year, a crushed and broken heart, — crushed and blighted for the sake of Christ. And yet many a private Christian of whose sorrows the world knows nothing, does this for Christ. We exalt the Name of him, who leaves father and mother and sister and brother, and bears aloft the banner of the Cross in foreign lands, battling for Christ against the powers of darkness; and acknowledge that he needs indeed the prayer "Increase our Faith." But what is his self-denial compared with the self-denial of him who remains in the midst of the world, surrounded by the hosts of the proud, and the unbelieving, and the scoffing, and the lukewarm, and battles for Christ against their indifference and fierce opposition? We place high upon the list of historic fame him who separates himself from the world and dwells in solitariness, devoting himself to prayer and self-denial; and we confess that he requires the prayer, "Increase our Faith." But what is his dreariness compared with the weary spirit that goes forth to his daily cares, tempted on every hand, perplexed, harassed, having to control his temper, to smother his indignation, to walk meekly and humbly in the midst of a gainsaying world. "Better," saith the wise man, "is he that ruleth his spirit, than he that taketh a city:"[1] and yet, who thinks that he needs the prayer "Increase our Faith," when he has nothing more to do than the simple work of ruling his temper.

No, my beloved friends, we have all reason to use this

[1] Prov. xvi. 32.

prayer every day of our lives, because it is the common and ordinary duties of life which are indeed the greatest; — the greatest, because the most frequent and the most influential. Those who are nearest and dearest to us, whom we should rather influence than all others upon earth, are the witnesses of our daily walk. They see our inconsistencies; they watch our infirmities; they mark our deviations from Christian rectitude; and impressions are made upon them which work effects for a whole lifetime. Little eyes are always fixed upon us; little hearts are beating in unison with ours; little feet are treading in our footsteps; little characters are forming under our control. Christianity stands forth daily for trial in our persons and conduct. And when all this influence breathes from our walk, think ye that we do not need the prayer, "Increase our Faith?" We need it *always*, for the government of our tempers, for the ruling of our tongues, for the humbling of our pride, for the control of our desires, for the subjugation of our appetites. We need it for the increase of our trust in God, of our reliance upon Christ, of our confidence in the power of the Holy Ghost. We need it for that struggle with the world, for that battle of life, which we are destined to wage until mortality shall be swallowed up in Life.

Twelfth Sermon.

And after these things he went forth, and saw a publican, named Levi, sitting at the receipt of custom: and he said unto him, Follow me. And he left all, rose up, and followed him. — S. LUKE v. 27, 28.

THE longer the world rolls on, the more does it seem to be involved in worldliness. Only a few years back, and we can remember the comparative quietness of things: how much more time was given by everybody to matters disconnected from business; to amusement, to exercise, to home, to rest. One part of the day sufficed for the transactions of the world; after that, care was rolled off, and the body and the mind were relaxed from their extreme tension. The result of what was done had to be quietly waited for until the operation could travel its required distance, and return with its slow reply. The news of the world came in by degrees, and one thing could be well considered and well digested, before another was hurled upon it, confusing and entangling the past and the present. The thoughts of men were allowed some leisure from external pressure to dwell upon the concerns of domestic life, and they could find a little time to give to such trifling affairs as wife and children, and their souls and eternity. The young grew up then under the shadow of their father's wing, and were taught around the domestic board and at the fireside those lessons of morals and patriotism, which made our forefathers so high-toned and illustrious, and gave to the Republic a race of men which is fast passing away. But all this is now changed. A man of business has no time for any thing except business. Space and distance are annihilated; and news now travels, not upon the wings of the wind, but upon the lightning's flash. There is no rest for the anxious and excited mind. The whole day is a continued succession of new and often startling announcements; and before the one care is disposed of, another comes and thrusts its unwelcome presence upon the harassed and wearied spirit. There is fast getting to be no such thing as Home. It was once the boast of the Anglo-Saxon race, that it had that word in its vocabulary, — that there was a sanctuary for the feelings and the affections, — a consecrated spot, where the mind could be disburdened of care, and the brow could smooth its wrinkles, and the laboring spirit could find refreshment. But alas, while the word still remains to us, the thing is rapidly fading away before the increasing excitement of the world. No place is now sacred, for business thrusts its haggard visage upon every hour of the day, and into every private chamber of the house; and care and trouble cannot be kept at bay, which come with the force and quickness of the elements. Not only in times of difficulty, but at all times, is the system kept in a condition of nervous expectation, because no man knows what the next moment may thrust upon him from the other end of the earth. The toil of the day is never ended; the sweets of home are but half enjoyed. Instead of carrying to that circle of love a calm and cheerful spirit, he hurries there with a disturbed, and perhaps irritated mind: and hurries back to his anxieties, having left no word of comfort, no recollection of happiness, no example of peace, for its unsatisfied hearts. His presence has given no joy, his spirit has received no strength; and thus God's precious relations of husband and wife, of parent and child, of home and love, are worn out under this unnatural condition of things. And when this has gone on for years under the name of "necessary business," with the sacred appellation of "duty" annexed to it, while so many more precious duties have been neglected for it: what has been gained for it all? Perhaps wealth, perhaps bankruptcy; but in either case sure disappointment, because the truest pleasures of life have been sacrificed for it, and what is won is won too late for any true, rational enjoyment.

I have drawn this picture not with any design, of course, of running a tilt against the world's so-called advancement, for no voice of man, even should he desire it, could ever turn that back; nor even of expressing the opinion that it were better not to have been made: but rather to show the extreme difficulty, under such circumstances, of fixing the attention of men upon any thing not wrapped up with their daily routine of business. A mind excited upon one topic cannot be made to attend to another, and if business keeps the mind, as is very much the case now, unceasingly occupied, what is the chance for religious truth? Where is the time, what the hour, for consideration, for prayer, for repentance, for belief? When is the convenient season to come, in which the soul is to be thought of? Formerly, as I said before, there were hours every day which a man might call his own, when he could retire within himself and attend to his own dearest interests, without neglecting, or even seeming to neglect, the interests of others; when, if a man did not attend to the concerns of his soul, it was because he was careless or indifferent. He could not plead the lack of opportunity. But now the case of the man of business is really harder, and does demand of him much greater resolution than of old. He seems now almost compelled to be in a constant whirl of excitement, — to have nothing left him but the necessary hours for his daily food, and his essential sleep, and God's blessed day of rest. And oh! how precious should that day of rest be to him now, when things are so: and yet, with what a jaded and wearied heart, with what an exhausted and collapsed intellect, is he forced to come to it! During the week, — the busy, restless, excited week, — religion and the soul can find no place; and on the Sunday, even when the worn out body does not cry, with nature's cry, for rest and sleep, he brings to the sanctuary of God a heart either unable to cast off its care, or else tired out with its tumultuous pulsations, and careless of every thing save the reaction of quiet. It makes religion almost an unheeded topic: and the minister of Christ feels that he is pleading for men's souls either to a host engaged in the deadly strife of battle, face to face, and hand to hand; or else to that same host when, wearied and exhausted, it has no power left to fight, and is reposing only that it may recruit its strength for the morrow's strife!

The ministers of God have this great comfort, that the Spirit of God is stronger than man or his arrangements; that Christ has gone into the very midst of the marts of commerce, and plucked a soul thence. "And after these things he went forth, and saw a publican, named Levi, sitting at the receipt of custom: and he said unto him, Follow me. And he left all, rose up, and followed him." And what Christ did then, His Spirit can do now, and it can penetrate through all the excitement and turmoil of which we have been speaking, and bring God's children home to Him. This is our comfort, that we are not working alone; that it is not only the voice of man that is crying aloud in the places of concourse, but that a Spirit, subtler than air, keener than lightning, stronger than interest, more absorbing than avarice, is likewise busy there, speaking for Christ with that small, still voice which pierces deeper than a sword, even to the dividing asunder of the soul and spirit and of the joints and marrow. We should faint and grow weary when we looked out upon the world and saw its seeming inattention and complete absorption, if we did not trust in that power of the Spirit, which has come into the world as the gift of God in return for the sacrifice of His Son; if we did not know that He was moving everywhere, inviting in season and out of season, pleading when man has no power to plead, and plucking from every scene of life disciples for the Church on earth. Yes, my hearers! even when you think that you are escaped from the warnings and the exhortations of the sanctuary, there follows you a Preacher far more urgent than your minister, far more intrusive than he can ever be, — a Preacher who shrinks neither from your coldness nor your anger, who fears not to tell you the naked truth, who presses not only into your counting-rooms, and your offices, and your sanctuaries, but into your hearts and souls. And it is this auxiliary who is our Strength and our Power, — who gives us hope when hope would otherwise die, — who bids us be of good cheer, even when all minds seem absorbed in business and gain. It is this auxiliary who can call you, even as Christ called Matthew, from the very midst of your business, and make you leave all and follow Him.

It is very pleasant to observe how Christ went everywhere and found followers; how no pursuit of life escaped His grasp or eluded His love. Wherever He went, He searched for spirits that would obey His voice, and took His disciples from every condition in the world. Matthew was, as we see here, a publican, Luke was a physician, John and Peter were fishermen, Paul was a man of learning and a zealot. No occupation seemed below His call; none so absorbing as to resist it; none too high for obedience and submission to His will. Christianity, my hearers, is for all: and Christ's example is meant to teach us that we should not despise any, nor despair of any; should not neglect to give the word of invitation to the lowest outcast, nor fear to cast it at the feet of the busiest and most engaged. We know not who will hear it and obey. Those whom we least look for may be the first to come out from the worldly throng, and leave all and follow Christ. Men's hearts are as subject to the will of God to-day, under the dispensation of His Spirit, as they were in the time of Christ; and can be bowed down under His voice as quickly as they then were. It is our want of faith which makes us fearful of results. Nothing is more absorbing than was the occupation of Levi, nothing more invincible than the fanaticism of Saul; and yet the one instantly obeyed the voice of Christ, and the other was subdued into humility before His power. Why, then, should we be hopeless of any? Why should we tremble at the world's progress, and be fearful of its influence upon the conversion of men? The Spirit of God is in the world, and He can pluck the sinner thence, snatching him from its whirl and tumult as easily as Christ drew Matthew from the receipt of custom.

But while this is so, and while the ministers of Christ may feel this consolation, there is yet, my hearers, a very great danger for you in this increasing absorption of the world. The Spirit of God is among you, as He has ever been, and is as strong to draw souls to Christ as He ever was; but are you likely to be as attentive to His voice, to be as willing and obedient in the day of His power? Christianity, it is true, is a thing of the heart; but the heart must be reached through the mind. God's complaint against His people of old was, "My people will not consider." And when S. Paul preached to the Bereans, we are told that many of them believed, "because they received the word with all readiness of mind, and searched the Scriptures daily, whether those things were so." And are the times in which we are living, with their constant agitation and excitement, with their rapid influx of new and absorbing matter, with their daily pressure of anxiety and responsibility, propitious to consideration and Scriptural examination? Not at all so: nay, with all the increase of knowledge and books, very adverse; and they demand much greater effort on your part to gain for Christ and your souls the proper attention, than they have ever done before. We talk incessantly of the greater religious facilities and advantages of our day, of the increase of the means of grace. And there is some truth in it, if we measure it by the number of books and tracts which are circulated, and by the accumulation of societies, and by the diversity of benevolent schemes. But I question very much whether more was not done among men for Christ, when we had only the Bible and the Prayer-Book, and time to read and study them, than is done now, with all our books, and tracts, and societies, and no time for any thing but business and gain. We are fast coming to a sort of compact between the Church and men of business, that if the one will support the other, will give money freely for religious objects, the Church will keep their consciences and take care of their souls. Men seem ready to do every thing and any thing for Christianity, except to give it their thoughts and their time. "What do you want?" is the language of the world to the minister of the Gospel: "to build a church? Certainly, I give with pleasure." "To feed the poor? Better still; here is money, as much as you want." "To send missionaries to the heathen? I do not exactly see the use of that, but still you are my pastor, and if you think it right, here is my contribution." "But," replies the minister, "I want something more than this: I want you to give your attention to personal religion — to consider the salvation of your soul, and its unprepared condition." "My dear pastor," is the reply, "I have no time for that; my purse is at your service and the service of the Church, but not my time; I am too busy now for so solemn and grave a matter." But, my hearers, there *must* be a time, and when is that time to come? The world is not going to lose any of its excitement as it grows older. It will be only more and more agitated, more and more restless, more and more unquiet; and if you are putting off this solemn work for any less bustling period, you will find it only upon a bed of sickness or in your graves! The Church can make no compromise for your souls; for the word of God tells us, "They that trust in their wealth, and boast themselves in the multitude of their riches; none of them can by any means redeem his brother, nor give to God a ransom for him: for the redemption of their soul is precious, and they must let that alone for ever."[1] Christ is not satisfied with that. He did not go to the receipt of custom and ask Levi for his money: He called upon *him* to follow Him. And so now. While He will not leave your good deeds unrequited, that is not what He died for, nor what He instituted His Church for, nor appointed His ministers for, nor sends His Holy Spirit into the world for. He wants you to follow Him; to spare time enough to Christianity to save your souls; to give up whatever He may deem necessary to require of you for His Name's sake. To say that you have no time to follow Him, is to give up the question of salvation: for in that respect you will never be any more happily situated. You must *make* the time, if you desire ever to be a Christian. You must break away, if need be, from the receipt of custom. Any thing is better than losing your soul. "For what shall it profit a

[1] Psalm xlix. 6–8 (the last phrase is from the Prayer-Book version).

man, if he shall gain the whole world, and lose his own soul?"[1]

To return to the point whence we set out. Is there not something radically wrong in the framework of a social state which so arranges its work that in order to have it faithfully performed, the higher duties of domestic life must be neglected? This evil is not confined to one class of society, nor to any one kind of pursuit; it is the pervading evil of the whole country. The politician, the lawyer, the clergyman, as well as the merchant, are all so occupied with the duties of their profession, that they must exercise a stern resistance to the exaction of the times, if they would snatch any hours for the blessing of their homes or the improvement of themselves. And it will prove fatal to all the best interests of society unless it be corrected, for there is no authority which can be substituted for the father's. God will not permit the honor nor the glory which He has designed for the parent to be given to any other: and so the child must bear the burden of the neglect, and feel it deeply in himself, even though he does not disclose it to the world in immorality and disgrace. Why is it passing into a proverb that the youth of this country, — which, above all others, demands reverence and obedience, because we have nothing else to protect us from anarchy but a law-abiding education, — is taking things into its own hands, rejecting control and despising authority? Why is it that our academies are scenes of disorder, and our colleges broken up year after year? Why is it that our population is ever growing more lawless and piratical? It is just because the fathers have not had time to give that supervision to things at home, which God and Nature designed them to give: and so the legitimate sceptre of the patriarch is fallen from their hands, and lies dishonored in

[1] S. Mark. viii. 36.

the dust. And no natural relation can be violated with impunity. The sin will find a man out, and a nation out, as surely as effect follows cause in physical things. And there is really no necessity for it. There is no busier land than our Fatherland, no country under the heavens whose commerce is more extended, whose manufactures are more gigantic, whose trade is more exacting, whose professional men are more learned and assiduous, whose politicians have heavier responsibilities upon their minds and their hearts. And yet they do so manage to arrange their work, that they neglect neither their homes nor themselves. Beautiful as is the scenery of England; beautiful as is its rich and perfect cultivation; beautiful as are its parks, its country-seats, its churches: still more beautiful are its Homes, those nests of love and virtue, where are trained up the men of dogged honesty and unconquerable principle, who have carried her up, through trial and trouble, through storm and tempest, to the topmost pinnacle of glory. And this is just where we are going to fail. In looking at great things, we are neglecting what we consider small things. In our onward rush to greatness and power, we are overlooking the natural laws of all our social relations; and they will some day vindicate themselves before all the world with a fearful retribution. Society must and will advance; man's dominion over nature must and will be enlarged; Science will be forever adding new force to our operations, and placing new powers in our hands. But we must never forget that morals and religion do not advance with them; that *they* are immutable; that the great laws which God has established and revealed to us are the same "yesterday, to-day, and for ever." No matter how things may change and advance, THE MAN is still the father, the husband, the master, with duties which none can absolve him from, which none can perform for him. Any work which absorbs him so entirely that he cannot fulfil these, is work more than he ought to do, — work from which he should break away rather than sacrifice his children to it. It cannot be necessary. God will not permit it to be necessary, for nothing can be necessary which violates His laws. Nothing is necessary in this world but duty: and one's duties to home — his moral duties, the duties arising out of his presence, his authority, his example, his instruction — are far more important than the duty of procuring wealth or even comfort for his family.

And then one's own soul! What is to become of that? Is it to be sacrificed to this cry of necessary work? Is Eternity, as well as Time, to be laid at the foot of this Moloch? God forbid! And yet it must be, if you can find no time to pray that your soul may be saved. No time! and what was time given you for? Merely to pass away? Merely to procure meat, and drink, and raiment? Merely to accumulate wealth? No! it was given you for none of these: it was given to prepare for Eternity. The rest should be all by-play, just as a traveller amuses or employs himself while he has his eye steadily fixed upon his Home. That is the end of his journey: other things are only means or accompaniments. And so with Eternity. That is the end of all, the great goal of life: and every thing, save preparation for that, should be handled lightly, so that when Christ passes by and calls you, you may be ready to leave all and follow Him.

Thirteenth Sermon.

But Martha was cumbered about much serving, and came to him, and said, Lord, dost thou not care that my sister hath left me to serve alone? bid her therefore that she help me. And Jesus answered and said unto her, Martha, Martha, thou art careful and troubled about many things: but one thing is needful: and Mary hath chosen that good part, which shall not be taken away from her. — S. LUKE x. 40–42.

WHENEVER we can find a question fairly put to our Saviour, we may be sure, if it be a practical one, of having the proper answer to it for the use and blessing of the world. Idle questions He always put aside with an admonition or with a rebuke; but those which really looked to duty or to holiness received a solution which removed them ever after from the sphere of doubt or difficulty. And it is a great comfort that so many points have been decided by our Lord Himself, — points which lie very near our domestic and social happiness. Nothing perplexes a Christian more, seeing that he is called upon to act amid complicate duties, than to know how to frame his life, so that he may fulfil them all: so that, while acting for God and for the glory of religion in one direction, he may not bring reproach upon that same cause by neglect in some other direction. These cases are continually presenting themselves, and are the cause of much embarrassment to the conscientious child of God. If he knew his proper course, he would be most happy to pursue it. His difficulty does not lie with his will or his resolution to do what is right, but with his knowledge. His duty is not plain before him; he wants advice and counsel; he desires the judgment of one more experienced than himself in the Christian life. Happy for him, if, under such circumstances, he can find a friend who will guide him in his action; — still more happy, if he can be pointed to his Bible, and can read the solution to his difficulty in the very language of his blessed Master.

It is surprising how little Christians look to the Scriptures for a sure rule of duty. They take up the erroneous notion that the teachings of Christ were meant more especially for the age in which He lived, and for that peculiar state of society. Miserable mistake! for the value of the Bible consists in its enunciation of general principles, meant for all people and for all times, and suitable for all. It was impossible, in a Book intended for the world, to take up every single case of conscience, every conflict of duties, every point of casuistry, and settle it upon its merits. The world itself, as S. John says, could not contain the books that should be written after such a plan. Our Lord has adopted the only possible course, — that of enunciating, from a given case, a general principle, which may be afterwards applied to all cases of a like kind. They are the foundation of all Christian ethics, these sayings of Christ; and are to be applied to our doubts and difficulties, as they may arise, for their settlement and removal. They belong to us as much as to any period of the world; they are the inheritance of all Christian people; and if any one fails to use them, because they were proclaimed ages ago, and in a different quarter of the world, he may just as well, for the same reason, refuse to rest upon any of the promises or hopes of the Bible. The morals of the Bible, its rules of practical duty, were promulgated no earlier than the doctrines of the Bible; and if we found our assurance of everlasting life upon the Atonement of Christ, we may surely rest our solution of practical duty upon the principles which

He laid down. Whenever He has spoken, that is enough for man; His sayings are divine, and therefore catholic; are the inspiration of God, and therefore the rule of duty for man all the world over, and in all the changes of the world.

In the verses from which I preach, a case was laid before our Saviour of the simplest kind, and yet covering a vast question, one which demands solution every time that any conflict seems to arise between our domestic and our religious duties. It arose out of the common every-day arrangements of a household, and may, therefore, be a question in every family, concerning every member of that family. Its very simpleness and universality make up its vastness, for what it lacks in seeming importance, it makes up by its wide embrace. Our Lord, it appears, was received by a woman, named Martha, into her house. She seems to have been the elder sister, and a very particular housekeeper. She had a younger sister, called Mary, who embraced the opportunity — letting housekeeping alone for the time — of sitting at Jesus' feet, and hearing His words of truth and eternity. This vexed Martha, and she applied to our Lord for redress: "Lord, dost not thou care that my sister hath left me to serve alone? bid her therefore that she help me." This gave occasion to our Lord to place this domestic question, — one which concerns not only every woman, but every man in this congregation, — upon its proper footing. "And Jesus answered and said unto her, Martha, Martha, thou art careful and troubled about many things: but one thing is needful: and Mary hath chosen that good part, which shall not be taken away from her."

Nothing is more important for the comfort and happiness of the domestic circle than that a house should be well ordered; and this is generally supposed to be the province of the woman. Public duties, professional occupations, the necessity of providing for a family, all force the man away from his home for a very large portion of his time. This casts upon the woman the management of things at home, of children, of servants, and generally of the social relations of the family. Upon her are supposed to depend the neatness, the comfort, the happiness of home. If these are not secured, she receives the blame; and even when they are secured, unless they be secured just in a certain way, after a particular model, she is very apt to suffer from the tongue of criticism. No wonder, then, that there are many Marthas in the world, — mothers, or elder sisters, — who are cumbered about much serving; who are made anxious every day, and almost every hour, lest every thing should not be as it ought; who are tempted to neglect, as Martha did, their religious duties, for fear they may neglect their domestic ones. To all such, Christ lays down the important principle, that if one or the other has to be laid aside, religion is the "one thing needful," and every thing ought to be sacrificed for *that.*

The case of the woman is very hard in this world; and harder than it ought to be, because it is misunderstood. Man expects very often from woman that which he has no Scriptural right to expect. As a quaint old English writer says: "The rib of which woman was made was not taken from man's head, that she might rule over him; nor from his feet, that she might be his servant; but from his left side, next to his heart, that she might be his companion, his friend, the dearest object of his affection." And S. Paul, in his Epistle to the Corinthians, says: "But I would have you know, that the head of every man is Christ; and the head of the woman is the man; and the head of Christ is God."[1] Now mark, the man is the head of the woman as

[1] 1 Cor. xi. 3.

God is the head of Christ: that is, she is subordinate to him, nothing more; he is expected to deal with her as God dealt with Christ, to exact of her her lawful duty and no more; not to make a servant of her whom God gave him for a wife; not to forget that she has duties, feelings, and above all a soul; not to require that she shall sacrifice her conscience to his pleasure, or even comfort; not to derange every thing by his disorderly habits, and then require of *her* all his own deficiencies; not to leave servants, children, household economy, altogether to her weakness. She is his helpmeet. She is only one half of the domestic administration: and unless he support her by his authority and his presence, he is making her a drudge instead of a wife; he is degrading her from her true position, and returning to her toil for her love, discomfort for her affection. Man, too often, thinks that his duty is done, when he provides the money for the expenditures of his household. As if a woman's heart could be satisfied with *that!* — as if it did not yearn for love, for honor, for attention, for companionship, for a heart into which to pour all its weaknesses, for a strong arm on which to lean in all its trials. When man remembers what woman is to him; how much she is called upon to bear and to suffer because of him; how weak her body is, and how inferior her authority: he ought to limit his expectations, if he does not give her his support; he ought to be satisfied with some imperfectness, if he does not strengthen her by his presence and counsel.

It is when a husband gives his wife this love and confidence, that she feels most keenly the conflict of duties which may sometimes arise between her domestic circle and her God. When these are not given her, — when she perceives that she is merely the head servant in the family, expected to minister to the pleasures and caprices of a master, — she loses the sense of her own dignity, and becomes careless of her duties either to God or man. She may, from habit and training, preserve order around her: but the spirit is gone; the life of love has died out, and with it has hope withered and fled. There is no longer any conflict; misery has either driven her entirely to God, or has hardened her heart against him. But to the beloved and honored wife, to the caressed and cherished daughter, to the sister made happy by a brother's affection, the temptation is great to sacrifice God upon the domestic altar; to put His claims aside when the comfort or pleasure of those they love are interfered with; to be cumbered with much serving, when they should be sitting at the feet of Jesus, and listening to His instruction. With them there is a real conflict of duties; and then it is that the conscientious soul would fain understand what is the line of duty, and where serving should cease and give place to religion.

A woman has a soul as well as a man; and, therefore, is entitled to save it. Its salvation depends upon the use of the same means as those which rescue man from destruction. Unless, therefore, she performs her religious duties, — those which are private as well as those which are public, — she endangers her spiritual life. Any serving, therefore, which requires her to neglect those duties, is too much serving. She is not bound to peril her soul for her house. Her relations to God are prior to her relations to her husband, and are of a higher nature. When they come, therefore, into any necessary conflict, her domestic duties must yield. They can never be put as a substitute in the place of religious duties. God is before all, and above all; and husband, children, parents, brothers, servants, every thing, must give way before Him, so far as He has required it. He must be worshipped and served before all others, up to the measure that He has required worship and service. This is the general principle developed by the text: "Martha, Martha, thou art careful and troubled about many things: but one thing is needful: and Mary hath chosen that good part, which shall not be taken away from her."

But while this is the general principle, it must be guarded carefully and conscientiously on all sides. While the wife, or the sister, or the daughter, has the right to claim time and arrangements for all necessary religious duties, for prayer, for private reading and meditation, for communion with God, for public religious worship upon the Lord's day, for the instruction of her children and servants: she has no right to neglect her domestic duties for any thing like religious dissipation. Her husband and children, and the happiness of her home, are not to be sacrificed to societies and meetings, and all the array of benevolent schemes. These are very good, and very necessary: but good only for those who have no duties to interfere with them, and necessary only so far as organization is required for their accomplishment. While a truly harmonious Christian character demands the full performance of all our religious duties, it requires equally the fulfillment of all the requirements of our station and position; and while the one cannot be neglected without danger, no more can the other be thrust aside for the mere excitements of religion. The time for contemplative holiness may be rightfully claimed, but only that it may surround the family circle with the halo of practical religion.

Nor may the woman complain that she has not time for her religious duties, when the want shall arise from her own irregular habits. If by late rising, or a lack of order, or a love of pleasure, she let the time slip for communion with her God, — the precious time which she can never overtake again through the day, — she shall not be able to harmonize her duties. It will be a perpetual conflict; but a conflict of her own making, a trouble of conscience of her own creation. For this there is no remedy save reformation, — save a judging of herself honestly, as in the sight of God. For any neglect arising from this cause, she will necessarily suffer in her feelings of remorse if she be a true child of God; or, if not, in her domestic happiness. The thing is inevitable. The rule of God's government, "Be sure your sin will find you out," will come home under these circumstances, — will terminate in evil, and in misery.

But there is another state of things which calls for a different application of the same principle; and that is, where the conflict does not arise from others, but from within ourselves, — where our religious character is interfered with by our own over-particularity, and by our too great anxiety and carefulness about domestic matters. Women are sometimes so anxious to have every thing around them orderly and comfortable, as to make everybody uncomfortable who comes within their reach; and, in the pursuit of this end, they violate many of the precepts of the Bible, besides sacrificing their own comfort. For life is a complicate thing, and has its duties in all directions; and if we pursue those duties violently in one direction, we are sure to stumble over others in some other direction. Now the Marthas of this world must not forget that husband, children, servants, friends, all have rights in the family; and that towards them they have correlative duties: that if this over-particularity makes them reproachful to the husband, fretful to the children, threatening to the servants, inhospitable to friends, it is a sin, and not the fulfillment of a duty; it is the sacrifice of the comfort of home to a fancied order, which is really disorder in the sight of God. The woman imagines that she is fulfilling her duty; and she finds that her happiness is disturbed, that her home is made uncomfortable, and that her spirituality is eaten out. What must she do? Conquer *herself* and not others; learn to give up her habits, that others may be comfortable around her; adopt the conclusion that her much serving cannot be right, if it lead her to quarrel with her husband, when the Bible says, "Wives, submit yourselves unto your own husbands, as unto the Lord;"[1] — if it induce her to provoke her children to wrath, when the Bible says, "Provoke not your children to wrath;"[2] — if it disturb her to such a degree as to make her unjust and unequal to her servants, when the Scriptures have issued their commands against all these things. Order, neatness, elegance, are very excellent things, but too dearly purchased when paid for by the violation of any of the commands of God's moral law. A notable Martha may make a home very comfortable within due limits, but she may also make it very uncomfortable.

A woman is likewise serving too much when she is careful and troubled about many things. In this case the principal sufferer is herself. A nervous, anxious condition of mind, while it distresses others, is a perfect self-tormentor, eating out the comfort and peace of the soul. And this will agitate itself about domestic matters, — for home is woman's noblest sphere. This may be a natural temperament; if so, it is unfortunate: but have you ever thought that Christ has a feeling for infirmities of this kind, and will help them? It is not irremediable. It may be overcome. Faith and prayer can accomplish much in a case like this. But, apart from natural temperament, there may be an unnecessary anxiety, a preying care, arising out of much serving, which shall eat out the spiritual peace and comfort of the Christian. This is more than duty requires. The highest encomium which our Saviour ever

[1] Ephes. v. 22. [2] *Ibid.* vi. 4.

passed upon a woman was, that "she had done what she could." Be satisfied with this. Let not over anxiety affect your spiritual life. Do your best, in humility and prayer, and leave the consequences to God. You may not satisfy man, but you will satisfy God. He sees your weaknesses; He knows your infirmities. Cast your care upon Him, who careth for you. Sacrifice not your soul before any requirements of man. "But one thing is needful." Choose that part, and it shall never be taken away from you. Fault-finding husbands, surly fathers, ungrateful brothers, shall in the end acknowledge your meekness and your faithfulness, — shall, in the days of darkness, or in the hour of necessity, or when you are laid in the grave, rise up and call you blessed.

You thus perceive, my beloved hearers, that the rule of Christ applies to all these cases, and to numberless others which might be cited, and they must be regulated by it. Serving is necessary, is woman's part of the household economy; and Christ did not blame that: it was only the character and spirit of that particular woman, who was cumbered with much serving, who was careful and troubled about many things, — so cumbered that she could not attend to her religious duties, so careful and troubled that she had not time to sit at the feet of Jesus. Take this principle with you, children of God, regulate your duties by it, and you will find God's blessing to be with you in all your labors, however insignificant. The position of woman is a grand one, standing, as she does, the angel of the domestic circle, the comforter of the husband, the guide of the children, the mistress of the servants, the controlling spirit of the household, the centre of love for the hearts that cluster around her. How holy should she be! how full of the divine spirit! How little does she understand her greatness, when she expends all her energies upon serving! That is but a small part of her duty, — the very smallest part. Her quiet spirit should be prepared to calm the harassed and wearied mind of her husband, — harassed and wearied by its conflicts with the world; to drive away the cares and the troubles which oppress him; to impart strength to his virtue, and courage to his soul; to win him to the service of his God. Her loving heart should be tuned to that Divine harmony which shall make it accordant with the innocent heart of childhood, that she may guide it in the path of truth and Holiness. Her firm principle should be strung to that lofty justice which shall make itself known throughout her retinue of servants, until they shall feel it to be their highest privilege to "look unto the hand of their mistress." And all this, manifold as it is, high and holy as it is, can be done only when she sits first at the feet of Jesus; — only when she is guided by the Spirit of God. Her presence is felt everywhere; vibrates through every nerve of the holy circle of Home: but, oh! how beautiful is it, when she comes, radiant from the presence of her God, her face shining as it were that of an Angel!

Fourteenth Sermon.

How long shall thy vain thoughts lodge within thee? — JEREMIAH iv. 14.

THOUGHT is usually looked upon as an airy and volatile existence, running to and fro with the rapidity of lightning, coming we scarcely know whence, and flitting we scarcely know whither. We understand, in a general way, that it has been made a matter of science; that individuals, whom we sneeringly speak of as metaphysicians, have endeavored to ascertain the laws of its operation, and to establish rules for its government and guidance. We also know, that in severely disciplined minds it is subjected to regulations which control its wanderings and concentrate its energy. But we do not know, or else we do not consider, that like every thing that exists thought has its *natural laws;* and that if it be not disciplined, it will obey those laws as certainly as any thing else in creation answers to the natural impulses which have been impressed upon it by the hands of the Deity. And overlooking this most important truth, we become unconsciously subject to a dominion which rules over us with a rod of iron, making us very slaves to that over which God intended us to be masters and governors. Let us illustrate and justify the expression of the prophet in our text, by briefly considering the laws of thought which stand connected with this subject.

In the question which Jeremiah asks of Jerusalem in our text, his words are these: "How long shall thy vain thoughts *lodge* within thee?" as if certain thoughts might be spoken of as having taken up their abode in the mind; as being privileged residents there; while all other thoughts are treated as mere visitors. This expression seems, at first hearing, to be contrary to our usual conception of thought, — to make that fixed, which we consider variable; certain, which we deem uncertain. A little consideration, however, will convince us that the expression of the prophet is literally and philosophically true; and a few illustrations will satisfy you that there are thoughts — however unconscious you may be of their power — which do lodge within you, and look upon all other thoughts as intruders, whom it is their duty to expel as quickly and as completely as possible.

We habitually speak, in ordinary conversation, of a person's thoughts running in a certain channel, — of their being steadily fixed upon a given subject, — of a man's having no thoughts for any thing else save that which, for the time, absorbs him: and all this is but a truthful utterance of the natural laws which direct and govern the mind. When we speak, however, after this fashion, we suppose all this to be voluntary. We never admit but that these thoughts are entirely under the control of the person of whom we are speaking, and that he can change their train and current whenever he pleases. And here it is — just at this point — that we are so mistaken; — that we are overlooking a natural law, which, operating at first in agreement with our will, quietly gets dominion over us, and rules that will with a terrible and fatal despotism. It is like every other slavery to which we become subject. The transition from freedom to slavery is never abrupt and sudden. It is gradual and stealthy in its steps, seeming to be the result not so much of another's as of our own will; and it is not until we feel the chains around us, and we are anxious to snap them asunder, that we realize how much we had been subject to controlling influences, even while we supposed that we were altogether voluntary agents. Precisely so with our trains of thought. At first these trains are voluntary; they are fallen into either from education, or from interest, or because they are pleasant to us. We indulge them; we connect them with our every-day feelings and affections; they tinge by degrees every thing we look upon or are connected with: and thus an influence is given to them which they could never have attained, save by our own consent. When first adopted, they could have been controlled. We then admitted and dismissed them at our will. But, not preserving our mastery, they soon mastered us; and, instead of visitors, coming and going when their time was out, they now *lodge within* us, as the prophet expresses it, and soon tell us that all other thoughts are to be the visitors, while *they* retain possession, and fully occupy the mind. The laws of habit and of association have done their work, and we become very slaves; unless we have the nerve, — which few possess, — to grapple with the tyrants, and dethrone them.

It is the effect of this law of association upon the religious character, that I desire to develop; and I will confine my illustration of the imperiousness of these *lodgers*, when once they get possession, to cases in which they interfere with our religious duties. Let any one of you — whether a professor of religion or not — be absorbed in occupation of any kind, and I defy you, without an immense struggle, to perform any religious duty, in which these habitual trains of thought do not hurry off the attention and the feelings, and interrupt, if not altogether break up, your communings with God. Place the Word of God before you, realize in large measure its divine Revelation, determine that you will study and profit by that Book;

but, before a very few minutes shall have elapsed, you will be humbled by finding that your thoughts are upon your cares, or your merchandise, or your pleasure, or your interests. You gather them back from the subjects after which they have run astray. You renew your determination not to be disturbed in your religious duties. But very soon you find that thought is more uncontrollable than you supposed it, and that habit and association have become stronger than the will. Disgusted at this condition of things, you suppose that you have not sufficiently realized the sacredness of the Bible, and you determine to engage in some closer act of devotion, — one that shall bring you nearer to the awful presence of God. You fall upon your knees; you begin, in earnest, to pray and to supplicate. So long as you are watchful over yourself, you are praying, you are supplicating; but suddenly you find that some word uttered in your prayer, some topic laid before God, some want, or necessity, or infirmity, — nay, the very prayer you are uttering against wandering thoughts, — has carried away your thoughts upon their habitual train, and that you are offering a lip-service and not a service of the heart. And how terribly these wandering thoughts interfere with the worship of the Sanctuary! How they intrude themselves at every point, interrupting devotion, and deafening the ear lest it should hear and understand, and the soul be converted and live. In all these cases, the conclusion is forced upon us that we are subject to these *lodgers;* that they have become the possessors of our minds; and that, whether we will or not, we are dragged along by them contrary to our better feelings and holier desires.

These are thoughts, then, which lodge within us, — which are the habitual occupants of our minds: and it is against such that the prophet directs his inquiry. But he asks not his question of all thoughts. He confines it to *vain* thoughts! "How long shall thy vain thoughts lodge within thee?" And you may ask, "Are all trains of thought connected with the business or the interests of Life vain? How can life be carried on without such trains of thought? How can a man succeed, unless he fixes his mind steadily upon a given purpose, and pursues it with the energy of a resolute will?" A very fair question, and one which I will answer by gradual approach, keeping in view, meanwhile, the pungent inquiry of the prophet.

What are vain thoughts? What are such trains of thought as we should not permit to lodge within us? This is the first step to the answer of your question; and it must be settled by the balances of the Sanctuary. Providentially, we possess the writings of a man who has himself sounded all the depths of thought, and has determined, from his own experience as well as under the inspiration of God, what thoughts are vain, and what useful, and where the line must be drawn between these classes. The Book of Ecclesiastes seems to have been written for the very purpose of replying to this inquiry. Let us trace the experience and note the decision of Solomon, and we shall then be prepared to state the relation which trains of thought connected with the business and pleasure of life should hold to the mind and heart of the creature.

There are trains of thought which most of you would agree with me in pronouncing vain, and we would deem a man frivolous who made them his constant companions. Even these, however, Solomon did not overlook. In sounding the depths of human life, he turned first to those trains of thought which seemed superficially to present the nearest approach to happiness. He gave himself, he said, to mirth and to pleasure; those were the thoughts which he first made to lodge within him. But these he quickly pronounced to be vanity, and worse than vanity: "I said of laughter, It is mad: and of mirth, What doeth it?"[1] He next attempted to combine pleasure and wisdom, to discover if a proper proportion of ingredients might not take out the sting of vanity from his pursuits. "I sought in mine heart to give myself unto wine, yet acquainting mine heart with wisdom:"[2] but these trains of thought he likewise dismissed as vain. Failing here, he turned himself to the pride of life. All the wealth which the gold of Ophir, and the spices of Arabia, and the rich tributes of the East could accumulate for him, he lavished upon houses and gardens, and orchards and men-servants and maid-servants, and all the delights of the sons of men. He surrounded himself with pomp and luxury, and floated in an atmosphere of homage and idolatry that might have satisfied the greediest imagination. But these he also pronounces as vain thoughts: "Then I looked"—was his lamentable confession—"on all the works that my hands had wrought, and on the labor that I had labored to do: and, behold, all was vanity and vexation of spirit, and there was no profit under the sun."[3] He then turned himself solely to wisdom. He filled his mind with intellectual trains of thought. He compassed all the knowledge of the sons of men. Queens and nobles gathered to his feet to hear his words of wisdom; and when they heard, confessed that they far surpassed his wide-spread fame. These noble trains of thought—the highest certainly which can engage the mind of man—he acknowledges to be as far above all others, as spiritual trains of thought are above *them:* "Then I saw," writes he, "that wisdom excelleth folly, as far as light excelleth darkness:"[4] but at once his clear spirit saw the weak point even of these, and he exclaims in bitterness of spirit: "As it happeneth to the fool, so it happeneth even to me; and why was I then more

[1] Eccles. ii. 2. [2] *Ibid.* 3. [3] *Ibid.* 11. [4] *Ibid.* 13.

wise? Then I said in my heart, that this also is vanity. Therefore I hated life: for all is vanity and vexation of spirit."[1]

How far you may go along, my beloved hearers, with these conclusions of Solomon, I cannot pretend to say. Each of you will have your own *stand-point,* beyond which you will not admit vanity, — about which you will not consent that trains of thought are vain. The grave student will readily consent that the votaries of pleasure are altogether occupied with vain thoughts, which ought to be dislodged; while the industrious man of business will peradventure come to the same conclusion about the student's days and nights of toil, over studies which make no money, and books which bring no return save knowledge. But Solomon includes them all in one sweeping denunciation; allows no exceptions: and, while he gives each its proper grade, he concludes them all to be vanity. And he concludes correctly, even according to man's own estimate when made under circumstances in which all things can be brought to their true proportions.

The first reason why all these trains of thought are vain, is because nothing finite can satisfy the cravings of a creature made a living soul by the inbreathing of the Spirit of the Infinite. The body of man, it is true, was made of the dust of the earth; but his living soul is the breath of God. Nothing, therefore, can ever satisfy man, but reunion with God. He may, like Solomon, drink every cup of excitement to the very dregs, and he shall surely find *Vanity* inscribed within them all: and this, not only with trains of thought that are conversant about the gratification of our sensual nature, but with those also wherein the mind is fixed upon higher and nobler topics. When we read that Alexander wept because he had no more worlds to conquer,

[1] Eccles. ii. 15, 17.

or listen to the wailings of Byron as he sweeps his lyre with the hand of despair, confessing in the anguish of his heart that the vulture of unsatisfied desires is gnawing at his vitals, we perhaps feel that their pursuits were not such as might lead to peace and to rest. And yet they were only following with the impetuosity of Genius, what common minds pursue every day in their own laggard way, and dignify with the name of "honorable ambition" and "rational pleasure." But when we turn to such a man as Newton, and hear him — after a life spent in the acquirement of the profoundest knowledge, in the discovery of the hidden mysteries of things, in converse with Nature and with Nature's God in their most glorious developments — confessing that so far from being satisfied, he could only compare himself to one who had picked up a few poor pebbles upon the shore, while the great Ocean of Truth lay as yet undiscovered before him: we *must* feel, with Solomon, that all our thoughts are indeed vain thoughts. Or if, leaving him, we ask the acutest skeptic of modern times for his estimate of intellectual absorption, the answer will come to you in his own memorable words, — memorable, because illustrating the vanity of a false philosophy; memorable, because confirming the solemn truth, "Be sure your sin will find you out;"[1] memorable, because exhibiting the reaction of skeptical teachings upon the skeptic's own peace: "I know not," were the words of Mr. Hume, "what to believe. I feel myself to be afloat upon an ocean of doubt, without a compass, and without a rudder." If these be the results of the highest trains of thought, the one humbly engaged in the pursuit of Nature's truths, the other presumptuously attempting to shut God out of His own creation: well may we conclude that vanity and vexation of spirit are written upon all the pursuits of men.

[1] Num. xxxii. 23.

Another reason, my beloved hearers, why all these trains of thought are included by Solomon under the general head of vanity, is because they cannot profit us in our hour of greatest need. If there be a future,—if, beyond this brief existence, there stretches an eternity of life,—oh, of how little moment is the present, with all its business, and cares, and pleasures, and petty interests! How every thing ought to look to that moment of departure, when we shall cross the line between Time and Eternity,—when we shall put off this mortal life, and begin the life of spirit and immortality! How every thought should overleap the narrow interval of our threescore years and ten, and concentrate itself upon that solemn moment! Vain must all thoughts be, miserably vain—however seemingly necessary for the conduct of life—all trains of thought, which cannot profit us then. Think you, my hearers, when that dread moment comes,—when, stretched upon your dying bed, you shall be called to make that narrow field the scene of unutterable struggles with your own spirit and the Spirit of God,—that you shall be satisfied to gather about you the thoughts which have lodged within you and made your minds their homes? They may and will intrude themselves, I know; but will not your effort be to banish them, that thoughts more suited to such a time may rest upon your spirit? Is it man's wont, when dying, to summon before him the trains of thought in which he has indulged himself, and pass with them into the world of spirits? Here and there have instances occurred of such a course. Mirabeau's was a striking example: but does not our natural instinct cry out against it as monstrous? Man meets Death, not like a brute, senseless and apathetic; but like a rational creature, who, whatever may have been his forgetfulness of that dread hour, now that it has come, realizes its deep importance. He summons to his bedside the minister of religion; he asks the prayers of the pious and devout; he grieves that so many precious years have been wasted upon vanity; and acknowledges — when too late, perhaps, for remedy — that the only train of thought which was of any real importance to him, was the only one in which he had not trained himself. Unless man's ordinary thoughts were vain thoughts, could this be so? Should he be loth to summon them about him, and die with them in his heart and upon his lips? Oh, that you would heed the warnings of your fellow-creatures, and begin at once to strip away the vain thoughts which lodge within you!

And now, my hearers, I am prepared to ask you the question of the prophet. I have labored to illustrate the natural law by which associated trains of thought take possession of us and lodge within us. I have shown you that all these trains of thought, unless they be thoughts of God and of eternity, are thoughts of vanity, which cannot satisfy the spirit while it is embodied, nor comfort it when it is about to be disembodied, — which answer neither for life nor for Death. And I now demand of you, as rational creatures, "How long shall your vain thoughts lodge within you?" How long will you consent to pursue a course which promises you nothing either for time or for eternity? You desire happiness; you are seeking it hither and thither. Although baffled, you are still pursuing; although disappointed, you are still hoping. Although the peltings of the pitiless storm have beaten down your web; so soon as it has passed, you see the rainbow in every drop that glitters on its broken threads, and weave again. Although the heavens of your bliss are ever rising as you advance, you still, childlike, expect to touch their azure when you reach your point. Why, oh why, children of the Divinity, will you waste your energies upon such baseless Visions? Why, when the Infinite calls to you in love and mercy through the voice of his incarnate Son, saying, "Come unto me, all ye that labor and are heavy laden, and I will give you rest,"[1] *why* will you heedlessly press on, seeking that rest in the finite and the perishing? Why, when the Fountain of living waters is bubbling forth from the foot of Jesu's Cross — that Fountain of which He said: "Whosoever drinketh of the water that I shall give him shall never thirst,"[2] — *why* will you needlessly hew out for yourselves cisterns, broken cisterns, that can hold no water? Why, when Death is cleaving his ruthless track through the generations of your fellow-creatures that he may lay his inevitable grasp upon you, and usher you into the Eternal world, — that world where nothing *here* shall be of any importance, save the single question of time improved or neglected, — *why* will you concentrate, upon mind and heart and feelings, thoughts, vain thoughts, which His presence will scatter, as dreams are scattered when the awakening comes? A mighty work is before you, in the dislodgment of your vain thoughts. It is idle to say to yourselves, "When the time of peril comes, we will gather our strength, and battle with these thoughts, and drive them from their place in our hearts." That time of peril is your dying bed: for any man who reasons thus, can mean *only that.* Alas, my hearers, you know neither your own weakness, nor your enemy's strength! Let not him that girdeth on his harness boast himself as he that putteth it off! Grapple with that enemy *now,* while in health of body and vigor of mind, whom you expect so easily to triumph over when a tortured body and a weakened intellect must be carried into the conflict. Try your strength with the vain thoughts that lodge within you *now,* at this present moment, and see if they can be so easily driven

[1] S. Matt. xi. 28. [2] S. John iv. 14.

from their stronghold. Are the habits and the associations of a long life to be so easily broken? Are thoughts that have come with an every-day regularity for the years of a lifetime, that have intertwined themselves with our very individuality, to be so easily discarded at our wills? The very laws and proverbs of our language should teach you another tale. What means "The ruling passion, strong in death," save that the vain thoughts which lodge within us assert their imperious dominion in that dread hour, and reign supreme? "How long, how long shall thy vain thoughts lodge within thee?" Let it be, my hearers, not a day longer, lest it be forever!

For you, professing Christians, this question has its deep interest. You name the Name of Christ. You call yourselves His disciples. You rejoice in the riches of His grace. You partake of the bounties of His love. What are your habitual trains of thought? What classes of ideas lodge within you; and what classes merely come and go as visitors of duty or necessity? Is the tone of your mind spiritual? Are your most usual trains of thought of God, your soul, and eternity? or have you permitted vain thoughts to take possession of the heart which belongs to Christ, and to drive Him out? Are you mingling in such scenes as foster vain thoughts? Here lies the whole philosophy upon which turn the objections of the Ministers of God to the indulgence of His people in the pursuits and amusements of the world. Too much absorption in any thing not spiritual, creates and cherishes the trains of thought which interrupt meditation, and prayer, and communion with God. The Christian man who hurries ardently into politics or literature or business, the Christian woman who spends her nights in pleasure and her days in the routine of the world, will find alike that vain thoughts are rapidly lodging within them, to the obscuring of

Christ's image, and the destruction of their own spirituality. We cannot be too watchful over ourselves. Even the most legitimate pursuits may be turned into thoughts that shall deface our spiritual character. Hence the continual warnings of the Bible against lip-service, against the chambers of imagery, against the idolatry of the heart. My beloved hearers if any of you feel convicted of these vain thoughts, let the question of the prophet, "How long?" be answered, in the words of the Psalmist: "Search me, O God, and know my heart: try me, and know my thoughts: and see if there be any wicked way in me."[1]

Herein, likewise, lies the philosophy of Christian education. While these habits of thought are forming, while the uncorrupted heart and the unoccupied mind are weaving their associations, how essential that moral and religious ideas should form the materials of those associations! How ennobling to accustom the expanding thought to look upon Nature as one vast Temple, in which are seen everywhere the footprints of the Creator, in which are felt everywhere the breathings of His Holy presence! How purifying to impress upon the fallen nature, ere yet its germs of evil have sprung into life and gained dominion over the soul, that the eye of God is ever upon His creatures, seeing in the depths and in the darkness even as in the light of day! How consoling to be taught, in the very earliest struggles with sin, that a Saviour has died to give us the final victory; to be early strung with the hope that we shall one day be "conquerors and more than conquerors through Him who loved us and gave Himself for us." How elevating to keep ever before the mind, while the character is forming, a perfect model such as Christianity has offered in our Saviour. If such thoughts can only be made to lodge within us in our early days, they will go far to prevent

[1] Psalm cxxxix. 23, 24.

the domination of those vain thoughts against which the prophet warns us. They will introduce into the mind the due subordination of thoughts of business or interest or pleasure, to the more solemn thoughts of the soul and of Eternity. They will become the basis of the character, the lodgers within the man: while all else will be entertained only as it may be necessary, or useful, or obligatory. And when the time of struggle comes — the time that is to test us all — of temptation, of trial, of adversity, of Death: these holy trains of feeling will rise up from the depths where they may have been overlaid, and assert their supremacy! "Train up a child in the way he should go, and when he is old, he will not depart from it." Give him moral, pure, noble, spiritual trains of thought when the mind is budding and the character moulding; and although vain thoughts may seem, for a time, to lodge within him, they will be found to have no dominion; they will be able to exert no permanent supremacy. Neglect not, I beseech you, Christian parents, the power God has placed in your hands for the ennobling of your children, lest you be called to mourn, in bitterness of spirit, over vain thoughts which you cannot dislodge. Weeds will grow in the soil of human nature without any planting, without any culture. Vain thoughts will spring there fast enough, without your fostering hands. Let your effort be to root out these with an unsparing power; to plant in those thoughts which shall connect your offspring with God and with Eternity.

Fifteenth Sermon.

And God requireth that which is past. — ECCLESIASTES iii. 15.

IT requires a firm heart and an awakened conscience to enable us faithfully to weigh our relations to God. For it is not only in the present that we are concerned with Him, nor yet only in the future; but our text tells us that "God requireth that which is past:" so that, while struggling against the assaults of daily temptation, and while casting into the future the glances of an anxious and troubled soul, we have likewise to be trembling for all that is past, knowing that for every work, and word, and even thought, we shall be finally called into judgment. And this accumulation of grave responsibilities too often drives the disturbed spirit away from their steady contemplation; and, instead of meeting them face to face at once, and finding a remedy for all their terrors in the love and mercy of a reconciled Father, the trembling soul buries its painful thoughts in the excitements of life, attempting to quiet itself with the siren song of a future repentance, and a future amendment! It forgets, alas, that, in this very act, it is adding one more to the already accumulated requirements of the past, and is every day making more difficult that which must be atoned for through the blood of a crucified Saviour, or else met, in irremediable sternness, at the bar of an offended and holy God. The present, my beloved hearers, is all that can retrieve the past and brighten the future; and unless you can muster resolution to act upon the Apostolic warning, "Now is the accepted time; behold, now is the day of salvation,"[1] the present will be ever swelling, — the pursuing past will be ever darkening the impending future.

But many do not advance even to this point of consideration, but press on from day to day amid the busy cares of life, without at all thinking of the past. In their estimation it is gone, forever gone; — sunk into the abyss of time, never more to be called up for use or for account. It has been lived; has had its pleasures, its sorrows, its plans, its purposes; and, having been lived, has no further end, save as its consequences give shape and complexion to the present. Living only for time and for the existing world, the past is made to have reference only to the onward course of things, and is merged, in the thoughts of such men, in the circumstances or conditions which have grown out of it. It is, in their view, like one of the ever changing scenes of Nature, in which the fantastic shapes of the present moment are but the fragments of the images which just now rivetted our gaze. What delighted us or terrified us under the aspect of the sunshine and the storm, of the light and the shadow, has passed away; and we forget it in the emotions of the present, and in the anticipations of the future. We never dream that those images can be recalled, that out of the chaos of those conflicting elements the past can ever return with its impressions of terror or delight. Vain man! your reliance has no more foundation than the baseless fabric from which you have woven your imagery. And you will find, when too late, that every passing scene of life, — nay, every detail of that scene, — has been caught, as it passed, with the exactness of a stern reality, and will be made to repass before your conscience, with a distinctness of outline and an accuracy of particulars surpassing any power of nature, or any work of art.

[1] 2 Cor. vi. 2.

"For God requireth that which is past:" and, when He requires it, who can doubt His ability to summon up from the depths of by-gone ages their whole story of sin and of shame? If He can impart to you, one of the weakest and feeblest of His creatures, the wonderful power of memory by which you can evoke, from the years that are gone, such scenes and words and acts and thoughts as you have treasured there; nay more, if He can make the Sun, one of His inanimate creatures, to stamp upon material combinations the images that are subjected to its power: think you that He has not agencies at work that can bring back, for His purpose and your account, every act, every word, every thought, every imagination, every desire? Surely the powers that are in yourselves, vain mortals, — the agencies that are all around you in Nature, — should teach you that the God of man and of Nature has an infinite control over the past, as well as over the future.

But let us reason this matter by easy gradations up to the height upon which I desire to place you. In your own experience of life, is not God constantly requiring that which is past? I would remove you, for a moment, altogether from religious grounds, and place you where there is no demand for faith, save the belief of your own senses and your own consciousness. And I would ask you, Can you separate the present from the past? Are not all the circumstances, the events, nay the feelings of the present, the offspring of the past, having the features, the impressions, the very mould of their parent? Is not your present position in life the result of circumstances that are past? and if that position be infelicitous, is not God requiring of you, in that position, the natural consequences of something which was deemed long buried among the years that are gone? We cannot walk through the circles of social life without seeing this law of past requirement in almost every family. Here, past extravagance is required of its victims, in irksome toil and struggling penury: there, youthful sensuality is working itself out in flame through flesh, and nerve, and muscle, and bone. Here, improvidence demands its pay in anxious brow and whitening hair; and there, society is calling for the past of the criminal through its jails, its fetters, and its gallows. No man is rid of the past! It pursues him from generations that are gone; and when those who gave us birth are buried in their graves, it rises out of them and demands, in a natural way, its inevitable consequences. Independent of the threat of God that He will "visit the sins of the fathers upon the children unto the third and fourth generation of them that hate Him," He has stamped the same unchanging decree upon natural society; and were there no God to execute this threat, the constitution of things is such that it would execute itself, and write its judgment upon the history of individuals and of society. However man and society may have been called into existence,—whatever his end and whatever his future,—this law of past requirement needs no omnipotent arm to bare itself for its enforcement. Man himself executes it upon himself and upon his fellow-men, and society executes it upon the masses which make up her aggregate existence.

Advancing from this position, the truth of which you cannot deny, the next step brings us to all those evils and miseries which life is heir to, and unto which man seems as certainly born as the sparks fly upward. Many of the conditions of human life may be traced, as we said just now, to the operation of natural law, and the established sequence of things; but there are others for which we must seek a different solution. When we perceive the family of a villain writhing under the consequences of his criminality, we need no further investigation to enable us to connect the effect with the cause; but not so when we see the innocent die, and the good suffer, and the noble calumniated, and a world rich in all the beauties of Nature and the blessings of Providence covered with disease, and pain, and suffering, and death. For these results we are obliged to seek some other solution; and we find it in the same general law, but under a higher and more direct development. In all this evil and in all this sorrow we see God requiring that which is past; but we know what that past is, only by Revelation. We bring you, therefore, to Revelation, and we show you, from the operation of the same natural law, a sameness in the God of revelation and in Him who has stamped the law of past requirement upon the constitution and course of Nature. The Bible tells us that in all this misery God is requiring the sin that is past: and the very analogy of the operation should make it more easy for your credence. If you perceive God requiring, in a natural way, the sins of the fathers from the children, to the third and fourth generation, as far as your perception and knowledge can trace the connection: why should you deem it improbable that the same law should be extended backward and backward in the past, till it reaches up to that fountain of sin which has come into the world through our first parents, and brought with it all its crime and woe? And how terrible a view it gives us of sin in its polluting and destructive character, when we perceive that one fatal act still pursuing a whole race from generation to generation; and what an awful aspect it gives to the character of God, that He is still requiring that sin at the hands of man, even while He has given His only beloved Son to die for the destruction of sin, and to rise again for the justification of the past! And can you doubt what is before you in the future, when you look at this development? What must be the wrath of God, and what His vengeance against a lifetime of sin, aggravated too by its commission in the face of knowledge, of light, of mercy and of love? If one sin thus haunts the world, making it wretched, — a very vale of tears: what must be the effect — upon character, upon feeling, upon happiness, upon the future — of a life of sin? Surely, when God comes to require the past of such a life, it will be, it must be, a fearful reckoning.

Let us now take another view of this same subject, and look upon it in the light reflected from the Cross of our Redeemer. The saddest story in the whole history of life is that which details the requirement by God of the past in the Person of His Son, — His only-begotten and well-beloved Son. All other stories of suffering are qualified by the feeling of error, or imprudence, or crime, on the part of the victims; but in Him there was no sin. Spotless innocence was combined with meekness, with gentleness, with submission, — all the qualities which excite pity and move compassion. Nor was it the suffering of necessity, save as that necessity had been laid upon Himself by Himself, out of love for a sinful race. His was not the resignation of one who could not help himself: it was the firm endurance of unutterable woe by One who could have delivered Himself in the twinkling of an eye, had He been willing to consign His brethren to hopeless destruction. His submission was not the submission of one whom fetters and a prison and an armed soldiery could coerce: for He might at any moment have called from Heaven whole armies of angelic spirits, that could have burst all bars of man or Nature for His deliverance. No! It was the holy resolution of Redemption! it was the setting His face unmoved toward the Cross, and enduring, in that progress, humiliation, shame, ignominy, contempt, the desertion of friends, but above all the desertion of His Father, while He was bearing upon Himself the sins of a whole world! And for what? For that same *past* for which humanity has been groaning since the Fall; for that terrible past, which God was requiring, and which could not be expiated save by the sufferings and blood of the covenanted Victim. And this, my hearers, is a more fearful illustration of that inexorable law of which we have been treating this morning, — of that stern, unyielding law of requirement by God which forms the topic of our discourse, — than any which has yet been offered, whether drawn from the course of Nature or from the direct effects of it through the intervention of God. In all other cases we see an indignant Deity requiring the past from those who created that past, or who derived their polluted descent from its creators: in this, we see Him requiring it from one innocent Being, whose past was sinless as His own; and that One His own beloved Son, the delight of His Being from eternity! Ah, my hearers, as you gaze upon that Victim, — as you see Him faint, haggard, bleeding, dying, with no eye to pity and no arm to save, and in that agony contending with the Devil for the souls of men, — can *you* hope to escape this inevitable law? Can you dare to persuade yourself that *your* past will be forgotten? He placed Himself in the room of sinful man, took upon Him the past of the race, and bound Himself in covenant to bear all that the past demanded: and yet, even He, God-Man, was for a moment staggered at the terribleness of His undertaking, — that moment when He said: "O my Father, if it be possible, let this cup pass from me."[1] How awful must be the burden of the past, when such a sin-offering as our Redeemer faltered on approaching His Father's stern requirement of it! Well may weak, erring, sinful creatures, such as we are, tremble as we approach it!

And now, my hearers, that I have illustrated my text for

[1] S. Matt. xxvi. 39.

you, — that I have shown from your own experience, and from the analogy of things, and from the miseries of the world as it lies under the curse of sin, and from the Cross of our Saviour, that God does indeed sternly require the past, let me ask you, in all earnestness, what has been *your* past? You are aware that you form a link in that chain which connects sin with the anger of God; — that you are an inheritor of that corruption which, commencing in Adam, has been accumulating all through the past, taxing to the uttermost the forbearance and long-suffering of God. But it is not of that general corruption I now ask you; it is of your own peculiar past that I make my inquiry. What has been — I ask it of every one here present — your past? If it were required of you now, this instant, what should that past of yours offer to stay the indignation of God, or to disarm His vengeance? Putting it at the very best, would even you dare to say that it was harmless? But your partial judgment is not that which is to pass upon it. It is God that requireth the past!—God, such as He is portrayed in the Scriptures; God the Holy, in whose sight the heavens are not clean, who chargeth His angels with folly; God the Just, who layeth judgment to the line and righteousness to the plummet! Nor is your fallible and partial memory to call up that past. It is to be dragged to light and burned in upon your consciousness by a God who is omniscient, who searcheth the hearts and trieth the reins of the children of men; who has noted not only your deeds, not only your words, not only your thoughts, but every gleam of desire, every vain imagination, every nascent motive; who has recorded not only what you have committed in the course of an active and busy life, but what that very activity and business have caused you to leave undone! Oh! how it will cumulate and accumulate upon you, as it rises up from the abyss of the forgotten, until you will stare in horror at the heap of transgressions, and sink overwhelmed with the idea of meeting them face to face! Ah! my hearers, your actual deeds will form but a small portion of your past. It is thought, feeling, desire, motive, that will make up the hideous mass. You will never realize until that moment comes what an active, busy, restless, burning element of being was your heart! how out of it were the issues of life, while you were measuring only acts; how it was sinning against God in its own deep and unfathomable recesses, while not a word was uttered, not a work performed! how it raged, like a concealed volcano, bubbling and boiling within its own bosom, while, without, it was covered with calmness and with beauty. When all this shall be unveiled, — when that chamber of imagery shall be turned inside out and all its linings displayed as yours, — how unlike shall it be to the self-complacent picture of the past which you now conjure up; as unlike as the faint outline of scenes and circumstances which we can recall in our conception, when compared with those scenes and circumstances themselves as they occurred with all their detail and all their distinct coloring!

Are you prepared, my hearers, to meet that past? You see how terrible it is like to be, how dissimilar from that with which you satisfy yourselves: have you taken the very first step towards meeting it? Nay, have you ever even considered that you will have to meet it? I fear me that every thing connected with your past has yet to be considered; that if you have been able at all to separate your thoughts and affections from the present, they have only turned from its cares and its enjoyments to revel in the hopes of the future. I fear me that you have yet to be convinced that the past is upon your track, that it is hunting you with slow unfaltering pace to the judgment-seat of Christ. And if my fears be true, what a condition is yours! Your boat is gliding swiftly down the current that is hurrying you onward to the abyss. The deep, hoarse murmur of the eternal cataract is sounding louder and louder as you approach its awful brink. If once you are swept into the rapids, nothing can save you from inevitable destruction. The swift waters that are hurrying madly behind you will go over your soul, — will press and break you down under their overwhelming weight! Your only hope is, at once to be aroused to your true position; — at once to face that smoothly gliding current, and, ere it is too late, to escape from its treachery and its doom! Let not the calm present deceive you. Let not the gentle current of life sweep you along, forgetful of what is behind you, forgetful of what is before you. Pause, I pray you, and seek some haven of rest for your struggling, panting soul!

But you may say, "God requireth the past," and how can I meet it in the stern severity of which you have been speaking? How can I meet so holy, so just, so omniscient a God, when He comes to weigh all my past in the scales of His even-handed justice? Well may you ask, "How?" Would to God that I could bring you to ask Him in earnest, and with trembling; that I could make you acknowledge with Job, "I know it is so of a truth: but how should man be just with God? If he will contend with him, he cannot answer him one of a thousand."[1] "The first step in the ascent to heaven," said the ancient inscription upon the Temple of Isis, "is downward to the hell of self-knowledge." Could you only take that first step, — could you be made to see yourself as God sees you; to feel that "if you wash yourself with snow-water, and make your hands never so clean; yet God shall plunge you in the ditch, and your own clothes shall abhor you,"[2] ah! then should I have hope! Then might I point you to a

[1] Job ix. 2, 3. [2] *Ibid.* 30, 31.

Saviour, who has atoned for the past, who has taken it all upon Himself, and borne it already for you, in the mysterious purposes of the Godhead. But I dare not do it while you are unconcerned about that past; for I should perchance be adding to your terrible past this further sin of crucifying afresh the Son of God. What a terrible strait is this! I know that there is none other Name under Heaven given unto man whereby he may be saved but only the Name of Jesus Christ of Nazareth: and yet, to fear that the preaching of that precious Name may only aggravate the past! May God of His infinite mercy arouse you to a true sense of your condition, so that you may indeed ask "What must I do to be saved?"[1] and receive with obedient hearts the joyful response: "Believe on the Lord Jesus Christ, and thou shalt be saved."[2]

And to you who profess the Name which is above every name, let me say a few words of advice and of love. "The heart," fellow-Christians, "is deceitful above all things, and desperately wicked."[3] What a description! Beware of that heart! It may deceive you as to your present condition! It may lead you to believe that your past has been blotted out, while yet it may be pursuing you with all its bitterness and malignity: or it may beguile you to say, with the Antinomian, Let us "continue in sin, that grace may abound."[4] Either of these would be destruction to you! For while it is true that there is a "fountain opened to the house of David and to the inhabitants of Jerusalem for sin and for uncleanness,"[5] it is of no efficacy for those who continue in sin — willful sin. Examine, therefore, yourselves, before the approaching celebration of the Lord's Supper. See that your hearts are right with God; and "so search your own consciences (and that not lightly, and

[1] Acts xvi. 30. [2] *Ibid.* 31. [3] Jer. xvii. 9.
[4] Rom. vi. 1. [5] Zech. xiii. 1.

after the manner of dissemblers with God; but so) that ye may come holy and clean to such a heavenly Feast, in the marriage-garment required by God in Holy Scripture." Upon your sincerity and earnestness will depend God's dealings with you. He will require the past of every sinner; but for those who love the Lord Jesus Christ in sincerity and truth, there shall be no past at the judgment-seat of Christ. His past shall become their past: and their sanctified spirits will not be required to tremble for that which is behind; but will be filled with joy unspeakable and full of glory for that which fills up all the future, — the love of God in Christ, — in the blessed land where there shall be no more curse.

1866.

Sixteenth Sermon.

Because Ephraim hath made many altars to sin, altars shall be unto him to sin. — HOSEA viii. 11.

UNBELIEF, while always the same in essence, assumes a thousand shapes to suit the times in which it may be circulating. A form of infidelity, gross and sensual as that which disgraced the court of the second Charles, could have no currency in an age like this, when at least a show of decency is necessary to give power to any thing which calls itself Truth. Nor would the ignorance and flippancy of the French infidelity find any more countenance among us; because the Scriptures, universally diffused and known as they are, could no longer suffer from the garbling and misinterpretation of shallow profanity. But while this is true, unbelief may be none the less rife, and may be all the more dangerous, because it assumes the cast of thought which is prevalent among educated men. The serpent which can put on the hue of the forest through which it is gliding, steals the more surely and inevitably upon the unwary traveller. While he sees only what appears to him to be the natural motion of the leaves and the twigs, his enemy is close upon him, and is already filling the atmosphere with the poison which is to fascinate and then destroy him. And in like manner that form of irreligion which assimilates itself most closely to the spirit of the times, is the most perilous, because the most natural and unsuspected. It approaches us in such accustomed language, and at such happy moments; it whispers in our ears in such a familiar tone, and its whisperings are so like the voices which we daily hear; it involves us, before we are startled at our danger, with such an enervating atmosphere of corrupt and poisonous sentiment: that we are in the coils of the old Serpent, that subtle Destroyer, before we even conceive that peril is nigh us. And even when we have been warned, — when the finger of experience and of love has pointed out to us the baleful eyes and beauteous skin of the approaching enemy, — those eyes are so like the glittering dew-drops, and that skin so like the colorings of Nature, that we perish gazing upon the insidious foe. Alas for man! — that he cannot learn that the natural stands forever linked, in this world, because of sin, with that which is sensual and corrupt.

There is, perhaps, no form of ungodliness more rife or more dangerous at this present day than that which tempts us to believe that every kind of worship, if it be only sincere, is acceptable with God. The tendency of the times is to strike at every thing positive and distinctive; — to put all systems, all institutions, — nay, all men — upon an ignoble level. Every thing that was considered undoubted and established, is to be once again placed in the scales of judgment, and weighed anew by the present generation; and nothing is to be considered wisdom which is not decided to be so by the charlatans of the current time. If this spirit were confined to science and literature, or even to politics and government, however we might deprecate it even in these, we should leave it to taste, and experience, and interest, to rectify the evil. But when it is unsettling and confounding morals and religion, when it is encouraging men to make experience and utility the basis of truth, it is time for the wise to look about them, and for the guardians of Revelation to strike for their Altars and their

God. Woe to the world, when men learn, — and learn it too from what are *called* "the churches of God," — that right and wrong are not to be settled by the Bible; that there is nothing positive in religion; that God has dictated no form of belief as essentially necessary to salvation; that He looks with no more favor upon one worshipper than another, provided each is equally sincere in his creed and in his practice! Woe to that same world, when such principles as these become the prevailing sentiments of men; for it will inevitably be hurried back, through folly and crime, to anarchy and barbarism!

When we take our first step in sin, we little conceive where that false movement will conduct us. It is only after a sad experience that we come to understand the effects which sin produces upon our own hearts, and appreciate the difficulty which there is in resisting its corrupting and downward tendencies. We imagine that the whole mischief of a sin is in the sin itself; that when it has done its evil, of whatever kind, upon its object, its bitterness is over: and thus it happens that we leave out of view the most terrible consequences of sin, — those consequences which this text indicates, and which I desire to bring distinctly to your notice. The progressive powers of sin are its most terrible powers; and when the restraining influence of God's hand is lifted from them, and they are permitted to come in like a flood, woe to that people or that individual upon whom they exert their overwhelming force! They are swept on, as by an irresistible fate, to utter corruption and destruction. And it is only necessary for God to issue the decree of my text, "Because Ephraim hath made many altars to sin, altars shall be unto him to sin," and the work is fairly begun. There is nothing thenceforward to check its career, either in the nation or the individual, until God's punishment be exhausted, and the entail be cut off through His mercy in Christ Jesus.

When Jeroboam, the son of Nebat, raised a false worship in Bethel, and the children of Israel consented to call upon God there, instead of at Jersusalem where God had appointed that they should worship Him, he established a precedent which, in consistency, he could never oppose when it should be carried to an extent beyond his own intention. It was not the purpose of Jeroboam to lead the Israelites away from Jehovah; he only desired to lead them away from Jerusalem. His object was, not to declare war against the Jewish religion; but only to modify it, so far as was necessary to carry out the separation which he had made of the Ten Tribes from the remaining Two. But the moment that he committed himself to this line of action, he had set the example of disobedience to God's express command that His Temple and Altar and Priesthood should be at Jerusalem; and had infused into every man's mind the principle that a seeming necessity justified the abandonment of God's command, and the substitution, in its place, of man's will and interest. And when this precedent was followed by Ephraim, so that many altars were reared in Israel, these altars were permitted by God all over the land, — altars upon every hill and mountain, and under every green tree, until idolatry the foullest and the most degrading usurped the place of the worship of Jehovah. Altars to Baal and Ashtaroth, to Tammuz and Peor, defiled the land; and it required the direct interference of God, through His prophets, to bring Ephraim back to the worship from which he had thus gradually but surely wandered.

And we can easily perceive, when the thing is brought to our notice, how it comes to pass naturally and inevitably.

The very principle upon which it proceeds, is that by which its final destruction is ensured. Like the brood of Error in Spenser's allegory, the moment it is born it begins to feed upon its own mother. The principle of disobedience and self-will which justified the first deviation, will justify all that follow; until no authority is left, and every one judges for himself, according to his fancy, or his interest, or his passion. If Jeroboam might modify the national worship, so might Ahab, and Jezebel, and Joram, and under cloak of the principle introduce the worst systems of Idolatry. The progress was only natural. Change is delightful to the human heart; especially a change which enables it to cast off established authority, and substitute for what is stern and self-denying something which is exciting and pleasurable. And, growing by what it feeds upon, the appetite craves incessant gratification, and presses on from one degree of licentiousness to another, until Truth itself is abandoned, and every thing established by God is swept away from the altars of men. "Because Ephraim hath made many altars to sin, altars shall be unto him to sin." His act rebounds upon himself; and he is forced, from the necessity of consistency, not only to justify, but to partake of, sins far more gross than any he ever contemplated.

And are we not, in this country, passing through precisely this experience? Is not our religious history fast verging upon this decree uttered by the prophet? Are we not dividing and subdividing into innumerable sects, each one setting up its own altar, and each altar further and still further removed from the doctrine and discipline of Christ? Where is the Unity of Christ? Where is that one Faith, one Lord, one Baptism, of which we read in the Epistles? Has not the progress been rapidly downward, striking in turn at every thing distinctive in doctrine, and bringing in arrangements of religious worship more and more radical? Is not God manifesting the law of His government by permitting these altars to multiply; and, as they multiply, to be more and more irregular and profane? Are not "churches" which we once hoped still clung to the truth of doctrine, abandoning that truth article by article, and adhering only to what suits their interest or their passions? Are not denominations of Christians which once commanded respect by their compactness and their firmness, now losing even that by their innumerable subdivisions and the reception of principles which must lead to still worse and worse? Look at the rapid deterioration of religion in many parts of the United States, once the most rigid and devout! Look at the doctrines which are now publicly proclaimed throughout the land, — which are gathering disciples, — which are forming sects; — doctrines of devils, fit only for execration and condemnation. See the indifference of the people to this rapid corruption of Truth, to this denial of our Saviour, to this blotting out of the Holy Ghost, to this contempt for doctrinal truth, to this irreverence for the word of God and for every thing established by it, to this abrogation of heaven and of hell! Ephraim is making many altars to sin, crowding them over the length and breadth of the land: and, true to the principle of its action, his law is being fast made the banner under which idols of every hue and shape, — idols of imagination, of sentiment, of will, of pride, of lust, — are to take the place of Christ and His Church. And what is worse, Christians themselves seem blinded to the condition of things, and are comforting themselves with the idea that Religion is advancing through the land, when it is really fast running into the foullest corruption. Could the mighty Edwards rise from his grave, and cast his eyes over his own once fruitful field of labor, where should he find the doctrines which he preached, the discipline which he reverenced? Could the eloquent Mason be given back again to earth, how would he thunder against the degeneracy of the times, and ask in vain for the habits of devotion and the morals of life which he adorned and illustrated! Could Whitfield and Wesley survey the masses which have congregated around the altars they erected, how would they shudder at much which calls itself by their name, and mourn, in bitterness of spirit, that they ever turned aside from the good old paths in which they had been trained! And the worst is not yet. It is only beginning: and if these things are done in the green tree, what shall we look for in the dry? Ah! my hearers, if you would only study the aspect of the times, in its moral and religious point of view, you would tremble at what is fast coming upon you,—tremble for your Altars and your firesides! But, instead of that, you are carried along with the current; and conceive that Ephraim has full right to create as many altars as he pleases; and to rend the seamless garment of Christ into shreds and tatters!

But it is not only by a natural law that this deterioration will go on. After Ephraim shall have raised many altars to sin, God's action will become judicial, and Ephraim's sin will find him out in a still more terrible way. Up to a certain point, this erection of altars will be the product of his own will. He shall be sinning against light and conscience, against warning and the Holy Spirit; but when, in defiance of these, he shall have made many altars to sin, "altars shall be unto him to sin." His appetite shall be glutted to its fullest extent. Means and appliances the most ample shall be furnished him for idolatry. Doctrines more false and monstrous, opinions more profane and licentious, opinions more hideous and disgusting, shall meet his eager mind, and he shall rush to their embrace with a greediness which will prove that the Holy Spirit hath left him, and that he is bound up in the wings of the wind! Alas for us! We are nurturing our worst enemy within our own bowels; we are breeding an innumerable spawn of error that will finally consume us. God is our only refuge, and His Church the only ark of safety amid these agitated waves of self-will, of irreverence, and of ungodliness. Unless we turn to them, the sun which rose upon a people who loved and honored the Altars of the living God, will go down in blood upon altars reeking with every unclean and unwholesome sacrifice.

But this text, while its primary reference is to sins against religious worship, has also its stern application to individuals. The Church of the Israelites is often used in Scripture to represent the pilgrimage of the Christian,— to furnish instruction and reproof to the individual as he fights the battle of his soul. Every man may find in Ephraim a warning,—the dealings which God will exercise upon *himself*, if he turn away and make altars to sin. The like process goes on with the individual, as with the people; with the single Christian, as with the believing nation. It begins in what we consider a necessity meeting us in our path of life; and ends in a desertion of the Holy Spirit, the most hopeless which can befall a human creature.

It is an exceedingly dangerous thing for a Christian to tamper with Truth,—to make it at all subservient to any of the interests or passions of life. Truth is one and fixed; revealed by God through his inspired messengers, and written down for the use of man. It cannot be mistaken; for it is united in Christ, with that Life Eternal which we profess to be seeking for. "I am the way, the truth, and the life,"[1] said Christ; and if we will walk in

[1] S. John xiv. 6.

Christ, we cannot miss either Truth or Life. Many, and they among the poorest and plainest people, have found it through simple obedience: have listened to the voice of the Church, saying, "This is the way, walk ye in it,"[1] and have thus drank in all Truth. God has revealed to us in the New Testament a fixed, positive doctrine: "Neither is there salvation in any other than Jesus Christ of Nazareth."[2] "Without shedding of blood is no remission."[3] "Except a man be born of water and of the Spirit, he cannot enter into the kingdom of God."[4] "There is one body, and one Spirit, even as ye are called in one hope of your calling; one Lord, one faith, one Baptism, one God and Father of all, who is above all, and through all, and in you all."[5] A doctrine which, when combined, teaches as settled a system as that of the Old Testament; a system having a Creed, and Sacraments, and Church institutions. What reason has any man who leaves all this solemn truth, and devises a doctrinal system for himself, to expect any other treatment than Ephraim received? Nothing, my people, excuses disobedience. It will always fetch down the denunciation of the prophet: "Because Ephraim hath made many altars to sin, altars shall be unto him to sin."

And what can sound more fearful, my hearers, than such a declaration as this? You are not Christians; because you are trusting in altars of your own, and upon which you are burning your various sacrifices. One builds an altar, and calls it "Integrity," and offers upon it justice, and honesty, and fair dealing between man and man. Another follows his example, but calls his altar "Benevolence," and trusts that the sacrifices which he makes thereon to the poor and the widow and the orphan may enter into the presence of God, and atone for his sins.

[1] Isaiah xxx. 21. [2] Acts iv. 10, 12. [3] Heb. ix. 22.
[4] S. John iii. 5. [5] Eph. iv. 4–6.

Yet another designates his altar by the name of "Good works," and feels assured that the zeal and devotion and bodily exercise which are spent thereon must be sufficient to win the favor of God. Still another altar is seen to rise before us and upon it is inscribed, "God is a spirit, and they that worship him, must worship him in spirit and in truth;" and its worshippers imagine that a service of the heart, without outward profession, without forms or sacraments, must find favor with a spiritual God. How sad that these altars, with their noble inscriptions, with their fragments of the truth, must all fall under the category of the prophet's denunciation; that these blessed truths, which have been snatched from the consecrated Altar of the sanctuary of God, should, by that violence, have been turned into falsehood; that these sightly altars, which rise so proudly from the surface of society, should be altars unto sin! Where is then your hope? You worship not as God has commanded you to worship, because you are trusting in this miserably delusive principle, — that one altar is as good as another in the sight of God; that "His can't be wrong, whose life is in the right"; that the sacrifice of good deeds, of zeal, of devotion, of sincerity, of benevolence, is as potent as the Sacrifice of the Death of Christ." Alas for your fatal error! You will find, at the last, that Christianity is a positive thing; that salvation is by one narrow road, through one straight gate; and that all altars save that One which has been stained with the Blood of the Lamb, are altars unto sin!

You may ask, What is my remedy when I find myself in this condition? If by any means you have placed yourself in a wrong position in this matter, retrace your steps. It may cost you some humiliation; some sacrifice of feeling, or of interest: but any thing is better than to plunge through life in error, and then perhaps to lose your soul.

And you will lose it, just as certainly as you rest in the delusion of being saved because you are "honest" and "sincere." How can you be sincere when you refuse to obey the plain written commands of your God and Saviour: unless you place yourself in the category of infidelity, and say that you do not believe them to be His commands? How can you be sincere when, ranking yourself as a Christian and hoping for a Christian's future condition, you are yet not fulfilling a Christian's duty? But you may answer: "I am trying to live as a Christian, and to perform all my obligations to my fellow-beings, my obligations of integrity, of benevolence, of good works; and I am worshipping God in spirit and in truth." Running back to those old altars, which I proved to you were altars to sin! But have you obeyed Christ's commands? *Have you been confirmed?* Do you *partake of the Sacrament of the Lord's Supper*, which Christ commanded you to do in remembrance of Him? If you were a Christian, or wanted to be a Christian, you would do as Christ commands you:—you would worship God where and as He instructs you; you would connect yourself with the visible Church; you would live upon His Spirit. You may be sincere when you say you cannot believe; but that sincerity will not avail you, because it is a positive command: "Believe on the Lord Jesus Christ, and thou shalt be saved;"[1] and equally as positive on the other hand: "He that believeth not shall be damned."[2] You may be sincere when you say that you cannot repent; but that sincerity will not avail you, because the declaration is positive: "Except ye repent, ye shall all likewise perish."[3] No man *can* be sincere when, with the Bible in his hands, he counts himself a Christian, and yet obeys not the positive commandments of Christ. You are trifling with words and with your conscience. You are laying up for yourself

[1] Acts xvi. 31. [2] S. Mark xvi. 16. [3] S. Luke xiii. 3.

the heaviest of all punishments, — the finding out, at the last, that although you have made many altars and sacrificed diligently upon them, they are only altars to sin. Your remedy is to do with your altars as Elijah did with the altars to Baal, — sweep them from your heart: and turn in faith and humility and obedience to that only Altar which has streamed from everlasting with the blood of the Lamb "that taketh away the sins of the world."

1866.

Seventeenth Sermon.

And take heed to yourselves, lest at any time your hearts be overcharged with surfeiting, and drunkenness, and cares of this life, and so that day come upon you unawares. For as a snare shall it come on all them that dwell on the face of the whole earth. — S. LUKE xxi. 34, 35.

IN many of the addresses of our Lord to His disciples He pursued the plan which had been arranged for the delivery of prophecy, giving His instructions a double sense, the one applicable to the times which then were, the other stretching into a distant futurity. While the substance of His remarks, like the groundwork of prophecy, had its reality in the circumstances which encompassed them, they were couched in language which forbade their limitation to the events of time. As the prophecy, for example, which made David and his earthly kingdom its basis, was at once transferred, by epithets of surpassing magnificence and eternal duration, to the Messiah and His heavenly Kingdom: so the words of our Lord, which applied immediately to the destruction of Jerusalem and the terrible calamities which should accompany its fall, were insensibly passed over, by an intermixture of sublime imagery, to the destruction of the world, and the awful scenes of the Judgment Day. Thus it happened, that language like that of my text was applicable not only to those who heard it, but to those who should receive it until the end of time; — that the exhortation to take heed lest that day should come upon them unawares, was a warning not only to the inhabitants of Jerusalem, but to the people of the whole earth.

The mode in which this coming of the Day of the Lord is spoken of in the New Testament always embodies the idea of suddenness, of unexpectedness; and in our text it has the additional idea of coming as a snare. "But as the days of Noe were," says our Lord in S. Matthew, "so shall also the coming of the Son of Man be. For as in the days that were before the flood they were eating and drinking, marrying and giving in marriage, until the day that Noe entered into the ark, and knew not until the flood came, and took them all away; so shall also the coming of the Son of Man be."[1] And as it shall be with all who shall be alive at the second coming of the Lord, so is it now, even to-day, with us who are living upon the earth. There is, in the coming of Death, a suddenness, an unexpectedness, and ofttimes an ensnaring, which is awful to the very last degree. Take heed lest "that day come upon you unawares."

In this point of view does not the Son of Man find us every day just in the same condition in which our Lord foretells that the world shall be found at His second coming, "eating and drinking, marrying and giving in marriage"? Although Death hovers perpetually over us, although we witness every day the strokes which he inflicts, and follow, in slow funeral procession, his victims to the tomb: we make but little preparation against his coming to ourselves. We are all living under the same sky, drinking in the same atmosphere, engaged in the same pursuits, subjected to like influences: but when Death takes our neighbor or our friend, and leaves us, — not a whit more worthy to live or less exempt from the power of Death, — we never pause in the career of life to ask, "Why was he taken and I left"? We press forward mechanically, like well-disciplined troops, who have to face a certain danger;

[1] S. Matt. xxiv. 36–39.

the gaps are filled up so soon as they are made; and an unbroken front is ever presented, even while an incessant and unsparing carnage is going on around us. We step directly into the shoes of those who have been taken off, occupying the houses they have vacated, filling the offices they have left behind, carrying on the business they have suddenly dropped, never heeding the warning their absence has given us. And thus we press forward, like wave succeeding wave, until we ourselves are broken upon the great shore of Eternity, and we pass away amazed, if we have time left us for amazement, at the unexpectedness of the summons into another world. And yet why should we be amazed? Every illness, every accident, every death of friend or acquaintance or relation, was warning us that it would be so! But we somehow dreamed that we should have some special notice, that disease or Death would creep upon us gradually and give us full warning; that we should see his dart poised at us, long ere it left his hand, and have time for numbering our days and for laying aside our every-day cares and concerns, for setting our houses in order, for making our peace with God, before it reached our hearts. But as all others have found it, save the few to whom God has granted wisdom to live as pilgrims and strangers on the earth, so shall we find it: Death will come on us "like a snare"!

Let us look at this matter in a practical way, especially now, when we seem to be living under a dispensation of Death! There are living in this city of ours many thousands of our fellow-creatures, some of whom die every day, every day. Which of those who die expects it? Here and there is one whose lingering disease would lead you to expect to see him looking for his end; yet even by such a bedside do I find, ofttimes, as little preparation as by that of him who has been arrested in the vigor of his age.

With a certainty upon the mind of every one else, that a few days, or at most a few weeks, must end his course on earth, the sick man is planning for the future; and shows to all who look upon him that when Death finishes what disease has begun, he will come as unexpectedly as to the child or to the healthful. And walk with me the market-place, or the marts of business; thread the crowded streets: and tell me which of those absorbed and eager beings is expecting Death? Which of them has thought of it ere he left his home, and has asked God's protection through the day? Stop one, and tell him that within a few days he will be tolled to his burial, and that he will die in no extraordinary way, by no casualty, by no sudden stroke, but in the common and usual course of disease: and he will be as utterly incredulous as if God had made him immortal! convince him of it, and he will complain of the suddenness of the stroke, and will supplicate for time for preparation! And yet how few have really any longer time than this for preparation, taking the usual course of disease in our climate. And this is no exaggerated case. Take the deaths which have occurred this very summer among our acquaintances, and have they not all exhibited this phase of suddenness, of unexpectedness, if that can be called sudden and unexpected which is ordinary? To-day we meet an acquaintance as busy as ourselves; and the next notice we have of him is, that we are summoned to pay the last tribute to his memory. Did he expect Death any more than we ourselves? Had he any more cause to look for it than we? When we met him, the dart was actually projected against him: but did we perceive that he was the least conscious of it? Was his brow troubled? Perchance it was;—but with the cares of this world. Was his cheek pallid? Perchance it was;—but with anxiety about his worldly interests. Was he setting his house in order, and stripping himself of his absorbing thoughts? Perchance he was; — but it was by laying up for his future comfort and ease, or drowning himself in luxury and enjoyment. Did he speak of Death to you? "Death! why, he was not thinking of Death. He was telling me of his plans and projects for years to come, of his hopes and his anticipations in a long futurity. Death, why, yes! he did speak of such and such an acquaintance who was nigh unto Death; but he had always some good reason why such an one should die, which could not, he thought, be brought home to himself. He had unwisely exposed himself; or his constitution was naturally weak; or he was a stranger to the climate:" something that took *him* out of the category of Death's victims. Is not this within the experience of every one of you? Then why may not his experience be our own very soon? Nay, is it not certain that it must be our own ere long? We shall go, as he went, unexpectedly, to fill our grave, and give our account.

Let us leave the streets, where you may suppose there would not be found much expectation of Death, and enter into the Church, where the subject is unceasingly brought to the notice of the people. Those whom you find upon Sundays in the churches of Christ include probably all his elect people, — those who, in imitation of the Apostles, should truly feel that to them "to die is gain."[1] Which of *you*, my hearers, — for, by your presence here, you stand to-day in this category, — is expecting Death? — is waiting and watching for him as your deliverer from trial and trouble and sorrow? To which of you, if the angel of the Lord were now to say to you, "The Master is come, and calleth for thee,"[2] would the sound come as an altogether welcome one? Who would answer upon the instant, with a shout of joy, as S. John cried, when Christ

[1] Phil. i. 21. [2] S. John xi. 28.

said "Surely I come quickly:" "Amen. Even so, come, Lord Jesus"?[1] I do not ask, Which of you would be prepared to die? That is quite another question; and I answer for you that, I trust, many: but, Which of you is so living, as that it would not come unawares? There is such a thing as dying in a state of faith, while yet we die not in a state of preparation. We go to Christ, but we leave not behind us a testimony to His power over Death and the Grave. We realize our reward; but we glorify not our Saviour in our latter end.

But Christ tells us that this coming of the Son of Man will be not merely unexpected, but "as a snare" upon those that are upon the earth. And this requires a little elucidation, that you may see how fully it is verified before our eyes even in these days.

The snare which expresses the coming of the Son of Man, and to which it is likened, is something which is laid so like the appearance of Nature and the usual condition of things, that it does not alarm those for whom it is spread. And it has likewise another feature which constitutes its peril, and that is, that it is baited with such allurements and enticements as draw men into it, and entrap them to their destruction.

That feature which will make the coming of the Son of Man so sudden and so unexpected is that, as in the days of Noe, the world will be found in its natural and normal condition, eating and drinking, sowing and reaping, marrying and giving in marriage. Every thing will be as it has been every day for ages and generations. Men will be carrying on the same pursuits; will be engaged in the like occupations; will be excited by the same passions, and absorbed in the like pursuits. There will be no visible changes in Nature. The Sun will rise each day as bright

[1] Rev. xxii. 20.

and unclouded out of the chambers of the east, rejoicing as a bridegroom to run his course; and he will sink each night into his bed of clouds, as unchanged as if the world were to endure forever. The moon, which comes in her appointed season, will shed her mild beams of softened light upon stream and tower, upon forest and lake, upon the crowded city and the desert wilderness, as if no change were ever to take place in Nature or Nature's laws. Man will ask, "Where is the promise of his coming? for since the fathers fell asleep, all things continue as they were from the beginning of the creation?"[1] And this is the snare, that men think that coming will be preceded by some tokens which shall mark it, by some shadow forecasting itself upon the world, which will indicate it to all observers. But not so! When it comes it shall have no sign that the natural man can see, no forecast that shall give expectation to the world. The spiritual mind will be looking for the promise; the student of the Bible will have the foreshadowing of Prophecy; the signs of the times shall be such as they have been foretold: but all natural, however intensified; all in the usual course of events, but still such as they have always been, only aggravated. There will be wars and rumors of wars: but when have they not been? There will be nation rising up against nation, but when has that not been? There will be overthrow of governments, and dethronement of kings, and destruction of established things, and the multitude triumphing over order and over law: but all that will be considered as the triumph of popular wisdom, as the introduction of man to his coming age of perfectibility and happiness. The spiritual mind will understand it; here and there one faithful man upon the watch-tower, as Simeon looked for Christ; one faithful woman serving God day and night in His Temple, and

[1] 2 S. Peter iii. 4.

waiting for the coming of her Lord, as Anna did for the infant Jesus: but that will be all. And while the world is rolling on according to its usual and customary course, the Son of Man will come and take it as in a snare, because, having the light of the glorious Gospel of Christ shining upon it, it had suffered the god of this world to blind its eyes and stop its ears. And then the Judgment: and then Eternity.

And what will make the snare more overpowering and certain in its operation, will be the fact that all its usual pursuits will be intensified and more absorbing as the world approaches its end. Do you not perceive that already? Are not the improvements, as they are called, in physical science, the rapidity of movement, the constant flashing of exciting news from the ends of the earth, the never-ending pressure of business, the greed after money as the one necessity of life, all making the snare more complete, the world more enticing? Is not man forgetting that there is any God, much more that there is any second coming of the Lord; — of that Lord, whose first coming he does not believe in? And as the end approaches, shall not this be more and still more the order of things? — wealth concentrated; luxury abounding; money grasped at as the *summum bonum*, the one thing needful; sensuality overflowing; life loved and cherished for the lusts of the flesh; the soul forgotten; Heaven and Hell put aside as idle dreams. And when this is so, — as it is fast getting to be so, — shall not the world so absorb all thoughts and all minds, as that the snare will be stretched over the whole earth, in such wise that nothing shall escape? Woe to the world, — the blinded world! All captured; all so fast bound in prison that they "cannot get forth"![1]

And as it will be at the consummation of all things, so is

[1] Psalm lxxxviii. 8.

it now with us who make the present generation, and who stand in relation to Death as they stand to the second coming of the Lord. Things go on so naturally around us; one day succeeds another so equably and quietly; men are pursuing so precisely the came courses; we sleep, we eat, we do business, we marry and give in marriage, day by day, and year by year, as if there was no end: that it becomes a snare to us. We do not think about any interruption to the course of things. It seems so natural to live, that we do not think of death. If there was any sign or token to warn us, we might take heed; but the world goes on so steadily, and life flows so evenly, and home to-day is so like to what it was yesterday, that we fall into the snare. We cannot anticipate any harm from what looks so pleasant and so agreeable. And therefore we float on upon the tide and current, until Death comes upon us unawares, and we find, when too late, that we have been caught in the snare of natural sequences, and are swept away "unawares."

And just as in the case of the end of all things, the snare was made all powerful through the concentrated interests and lusts and passions and cares which the progress of the world had accumulated and hurled upon its absorbed inhabitants, — absorbing and blinding them: so is it with us. The snare of natural sequences is made so tempting to us through the lusts of the flesh and the interests of time and sense, that we never pause to examine the real peril of our position, but become enveloped in a cloud of pleasures, of enjoyments, of cares, of duties, which swallow up all our time, and enfold us in their ensnaring and seducing arms. The present blots out the future. The cloud comes between us and God. We hope and trust that it will remove: but it only grows thicker and thicker; until, forgetting our religion, our future, our hopes, our fears, even our God, we are taken in the snare, and swept off "unawares."

There are three temptations against which our Lord warns us most particularly, surfeiting, drunkenness, and the cares of this world.

Of the power of sensual indulgences to drug the soul against any preparation for Death, I need hardly speak to you. Surfeiting and drunkenness, or even smaller measures of the same kind of viciousness, are so entirely contrary to the graces of Christianity, that it does not require much argument to show that they must be guarded against by every one who would not have the Day of the Lord to come upon him unawares, and as a snare. S. Paul speaks of those whom he looked upon as the "enemies of the cross of Christ"[1] because they indulged in such things. And when we see how they unfit a man for any duty, whether domestic or social or civil; how they brutalize the character, and injure the mind, and harden the feelings: we can easily understand how entirely incompatible they are with any thing like a spiritual state of mind. Indulgence in them is fatal to all Christianity; therefore take heed, my hearers, lest they overcome your hearts. Be not entangled again with the rudiments and beggarly elements of sensuality!

But take heed likewise to that which is a much subtler temptation to most men, and especially most Christians, because it comes wearing the garb of duty. I mean the cares of this life, which are particularly singled out in my text. Alas! how many, without any vice that one can lay his hand upon, wreck their spiritual hopes upon this rock. And how striking it is that Christ should place these alongside of surfeiting and drunkenness, as most likely of all things to overcharge the heart. What a striking expression, overcharge the heart! Not the mind, not the body; but the heart, the seat of the feelings and affections. And

[1] Phil. iii. 18.

how universal is the temptation! It comes home to everybody. Who has not something to do with the cares of life? The father to his business, the mother to her household, and both to the interests of their children; — the rich to their wealth, having really more care than anybody; the poor to their need; the old to the accumulation of their lives; the young to their plans and their anticipations. It is duty, some of it; but duty which must be watched! No one can live without encountering, in some measure, the duties of life, and therefore the cares of life; but you can live so as to prevent your hearts from being overcharged: *over*-charged — mark the word! — not "charged," for the heart must, to a certain degree, be charged with them; but *over*-charged! Christ rebuked Martha, not because she was engaged in household duties, for that was her legitimate function; but because she was permitting them to absorb her heart, and take that away from rich opportunities of religious instruction. "But one thing is needful."[1] Every thing must be subordinated to that.

The cares of this life must be strictly under the control of a well-regulated heart, otherwise they will overpower us. The temptation is the other way, — to apportion our religious duties according to our worldly cares, diminishing those as these increase: that is, to take less heed as our peril increases. This is folly: for when cares increase, which they always do with years, then are prayer, consideration, thoughtfulness, and other religious duties most necessary for us; for they alone can turn the cares of life into religion, and make that burden light and easy, which would, under other circumstances, be intolerable. It is dreadful to think of a Christian being taken by the coming of his Lord, as in a snare; and yet this will be his condition, unless he take heed of those things which over-

[1] S. Luke x. 42.

charge the heart. Our Lord, you see, places the man or the woman who is absorbed in the cares of this life upon the same footing, as regards preparedness for Death or the coming of the Son of Man, with the glutton and the drunkard. And for this plain reason, that while they operate in different ways, they alike take the heart from God and from eternity; they alike overcharge the heart, and make men forget their accountability, and wrap them in a dream of security: until death enfolds them as in a snare, and they perish! Take heed lest "that day come upon you unawares"!

And to you, who have not yet attended to the concerns of your souls, let me beseech you to secure their salvation while you are in health. Besides the snare which the vigor of life, and the natural sequence of things, and the cares of this life, enwrap around you: even when you are sick, friends, relations, physicians, all who love you and care for you, will cherish and increase that snare. When you are sick, they will not believe that you are going to be dangerously so; when ill, they will not permit you to be disturbed, as they call it, by religious thoughts and exercises, lest you should be made more ill: and when you have reached that stage in which they acknowledge the necessity of your turning your thoughts to your soul, in what condition will you be for preparation,—a preparation which you have neglected? Is the whole period of an ordinary sickness in our climate sufficient for such a mighty work? How much less, then, its closing passages, when the body is weak, and the mind clouded, and the spirit frightened and fluttering at its approaching separation! My hearer, if you would not have Death come upon you "unawares" and "as a snare," prepare for it while you are yet in health! Christ bade us watch, because, He said, we know not when the Master of the house will come, whether "at even, or at midnight, or at the cock-crowing, or in the morning."[1] The pestilence "walketh in darkness."[2] Take heed, "while it is called To-day,"[3] lest Death come upon you unawares, and as a snare!

August 19*th* 1866.

[1] S. Mark xiii. 35. [2] Psalm xci. 6. [3] Heb. iii. 13.

Eighteenth Sermon.

Sanctify them through thy truth: thy word is truth. — S. JOHN xvii. 17.

SO far as individuals are concerned, the main object of revealed religion is the formation of character. Christianity was never intended to be inoperative; but in its very birth was filled with the energy of the Holy Spirit, producing changes which filled the streets of Jerusalem with awe and astonishment. And that divine energy did not expire with the day of Pentecost, but manifested itself wherever the Cross was lifted up by the Apostles of Revelation. Christians were made Christians, in the truest sense of the word, out of every sort of material, — out of fanatics, out of fornicators, out of idolators, out of adulterers, out of thieves, out of covetous, out of drunkards, out of revilers, out of extortioners; for "such," says S. Paul, in his first Epistle to the Corinthians, "were some of you: but ye are washed, but ye are sanctified, but ye are justified in the name of the Lord Jesus, and by the Spirit of our God." [1] And this is still the purpose of our holy religion, — the sanctification of the individual character; the making such fallen creatures as we are, fit for earth and then fit for Heaven. This was a part of that solemn prayer which our blessed Lord made to His Father just before He took His farewell of earth, and was commending to Him His beloved disciples: "Sanctify them, O Father, through thy truth: thy word is truth. . . . . Neither pray

[1] 1 Cor. vi. 11.

I for these alone, but for them also which shall believe on me through their word." He forgot us not in that hour of His deepest sorrow; but recorded for us in Heaven His earnest supplication, that His work might produce in us that richest of all its personal effects, holiness of character and of life.

We should, as Christians, my beloved people, keep this perpetually in our minds, — that unless Christianity sanctifies us, it falls short of its intended purpose. To make our religion a matter of mere sentiment, a thing of feeling and not of practice, is to emasculate it, to strip it of its power and its glory. In the discipline of its children, the world aims at the formation of characters which shall be suitable for its purposes; and so likewise in the Church of Christ, characters are to be created which shall illustrate the mission of our Saviour on earth, and then glorify it in Heaven. It is not he that merely crieth, "Lord, Lord," that is the Christian; but it is he that doeth the will of God. Profession and practice are very widely different things. The one may satisfy man, and may blind the Church while militant upon earth; but it is only the other which can satisfy God. He cannot be deceived by words and sentiment. He must have the imitation of Christ in the life, — the advancing holiness which tells that the Christian is growing in grace, and in the knowledge of the Lord. To be a Christian, and to stand still in character, are incompatible terms. To be a Christian, and not to be struggling to overcome evil feelings, bad habits, wrong temper, idle words, are inharmonious positions. "Onward," should ever be the Christian's motto, for holiness should ever be the Christian's goal. Without holiness, says S. Paul, "no man shall see the Lord."[1] Even in the progress of life, one is expected to grow wiser and more sober and more experienced as age

[1] Heb. xii. 14.

creeps on; and shall the Church expect less of her worshippers? S. Paul says, "When I was a child, I spake as a child, I understood as a child, I thought as a child: but when I became a man, I put away childish things."[1] Christians are not to be always children, to be fed on milk: they must seek after strength; they must search for wisdom; they must rejoice in experience; they must cultivate the graces of Christianity; they must learn to be able to grapple with hard sayings, to digest strong meat. S. Paul's rebuke to the Hebrews was: "For when for the time ye ought to be teachers, ye have need that one teach you again which be the first principles of the oracles of God; and are become such as have need of milk, and not of strong meat. For every one that useth milk is unskillful in the word of righteousness; for he is a babe. But strong meat belongeth to them that are of full age, even those who by reason of use have their senses exercised to discern both good and evil."[2]

Sanctification of character is therefore an indispensable requisite of every Christian, and he must search for the means which have been arranged by God for his advancement. Our discipline, during this first Advent of our Saviour, is to fit us for His second Advent; and the Word of God is that means to which the Church especially calls us to-day. The Collect which has been read to you this morning concentrates in itself the full essence of my text: "Blessed Lord, who has caused all holy Scriptures to be written for our learning;" and the Epistle reiterates the same truth: "Whatsoever things were written aforetime, were written for our learning." And what that learning is, we ascertain by turning to the Epistle to Timothy, where the Apostle says: "All scripture is given by inspiration of God, and is profitable for doctrine, for reproof, for correc-

[1] 1 Cor. xiii. 11. [2] Heb. v. 12–14.

tion, for instruction in righteousness: that the man of God may be perfect, thoroughly furnished unto all good works." [1] When our blessed Lord, therefore, was supplicating His Father for our sanctification, He was also designating the instrument through which it was to be pursued: "Sanctify them through thy truth: thy word is truth." It was truth which was to advance his people in character, and in knowledge, and in spiritual understanding; and that truth was to be found in the word: primarily in Christ, THE WORD; and then secondarily in that which remains to us as the transcript of Christ, the written Word, the Holy Scriptures, the records left us by holy men speaking "as they were moved by the Holy Ghost."

How important then, my beloved people, is it to us, that we should make ourselves intimately familiar with the Holy Scriptures, when we find them presented to us by Christ in this most solemn manner as the great means of our sanctification; and that, because they embody divine truth. Man affirms perpetually that he is in search of truth; that all his efforts are to discover it; that his struggles are hardest when they lie between truth and error: and yet, when absolute unmixed Truth is presented to him, how hard it is to make him either admire it, or receive it. Christ says, "I am the Truth:" and man turns away from Christ. He says again, "Thy word is truth:" and man neglects and despises that Word. What more can be done for man? "Buy the truth and sell it not," [2] is the injunction of the wise man; but we will not receive it when it is offered to us without money and without price. Can any thing show us more strikingly the evil heart of unbelief? What we pretend to crave, what we affirm that we desire more than we can express, we reject, when it is thrown at our feet, a gift from God, purchased at the price of the Blood of His

[1] 2 Tim. iii. 16, 17.

[2] Prov. xxiii. 23.

only-begotten and well-beloved Son! Pilate sneeringly asked, "What is truth?" showing us how profoundly skeptical the world was in his day about truth: and when Christ has answered that question for us, saying, "Thy word is truth," we will not deign to receive it. We press on, looking for that which lies in our pathway, and which has become so precious a comfort to the world. Amazing inconsistency! incredible except upon the hypothesis of the Bible: "But if our Gospel be hid, it is hid to them that are lost: in whom the god of this world hath blinded the minds of them which believe not."[1]

It is the study of the Holy Scriptures which is to sanctify us. They are truth, and truth is God's agent. But in order for truth to produce this transforming effect upon the character, it must be received as truth, really and cordially received, so that the heart can repose upon it with confidence as Truth indeed. This therefore demands of you, my hearers, that you should satisfy yourselves as to the truth of the Holy Scriptures. You think that you believe them; you would be shocked to be counted as unbelievers: and yet, if you examine yourselves, many of you would find that there is no such belief in the Scriptures as makes you receive them as the infallible Word of God; as wiser than all ancients or teachers; as uttering words which no man should be bold enough to gainsay or contradict. Your conduct proves this: for in practical conduct a man's real faith comes out; and when you come to practice, you are found clinging to the laws and proverbs of worldly policy more closely than to the Word of God. The doctrines of the Bible are many of them considered unreasonable and fanatical, not to say foolish; its precepts are deemed not to be suited for life, however much they may be suited to another and more spiritual world; its graces are

[1] 2 Cor. iv. 3, 4.

not reckoned to be such as could be safely depended upon in the whirl and tumult of life. This is what many men consider as belief, — a general acquiescence in the Bible, as the Word of God in some form or manner: but no such trust in it as should make them rest upon it as the guide of their conduct, and the rule of their daily life. In such a belief as this there can be no power of sanctification, for that comes through the very struggles which truth forces upon us when we come into conflict with the world. It is a real, earnest heart-belief; a thing to rest upon in opposition to, and contradiction of, every thing which opposes it; a reception of all which it affirms, — its hard sayings, its supernatural requirements, its spiritual life; an active, living faith in its promises and its threatenings: in fine, an adoption of it as Truth not to be controverted or overturned. Such a belief in the Bible as this, gives it power over the whole character; creates in us a life of faith in harmony with our sentiments; and leads us onward in the divine likeness, and changes us from grace to grace into the image of our Saviour. A vague acquiescence produces nothing. It fades before every difficulty, and is turned aside by every lion in the path. It has no foundation stronger than the current opinion of the society in which one moves; or the force of habit, or education. It may produce a moral life, but never sanctification. That must be the product of Truth; divine, infallible, unchanging, forever operating. To say, "I believe," and then never act up to that belief; to profess faith in Christ and His work, and then never to show any fruit of that faith in one's conduct; to speak of the Word of God as truth, and then to live as if you had come to the conclusion that it was all a lie; is not Christianity: for it can never lead on to the end of Christianity, which is sanctification.

Ere the prayer of our Lord can be fulfilled in us, therefore, my beloved hearers, we must be true believers in the Word of God: otherwise we cannot be sanctified by it. Therefore is it that in the Collect for the Day our prayer is not merely that we may read, but that we may "mark, learn and inwardly digest" the Scriptures; may assimilate them to ourselves; may make them a part of our daily growth. In no other way can they produce in us the result which they are intended to produce. A mere cursory reading of the Scriptures may ease our consciences, as the performance of a daily duty; may awaken interest, or admiration of character, or style, or pathos: but will produce no effect in changing the character to a higher state holiness. No one can understand the inner, life-giving meaning of the Holy Scriptures, unless it be interpreted to him; and no one can interpret it so well as the Holy Spirit who inspired it; and that Holy Spirit can be brought down to us only by prayer. To receive sanctification through the Word of Truth, therefore, we must accompany it by prayer, — earnest, faithful prayer for an enlightened understanding and an obedient heart; for willingness to know the truth, and for still greater willingness to practice it; for faith in it when we have learned to know it, and for reliance upon it when we may be put to the test through some deeper waters or more fiery trials. Some holy men have never studied the Scriptures save on their knees; and such students have ever found the truth to be sanctifying them, and making them more meet for communion with their God. If we would be sanctified through the truth, we must study it in this way. By no other process can we reach the higher steps of the divine life. If we would gain rich views of our heavenly home, we must climb the heights which rise perpetually as we advance in the Christian pilgrimage. There is no reward for indolence, for lukewarmness, for indifference, for carelessness.

These traits of character will always make us slow travellers in the divine life; and will mar our Christian happiness here, as well as diminish our reward in the Kingdom of Heaven.

God's Word, absolute Truth! What a precious consolation for us in a world like this, to know that there is such a thing as Truth! As we advance in life, we grow more faithless in every thing, especially in our conclusions about things intellectual and moral. In early life we form opinions, which we think that nothing can ever shake; but time, and experience, and a maturer consideration, make all our fabrics to totter, and involve in one general distrust every thing upon which we had determined to rest. What can compensate us for such a condition of things? What can once again revive faith and confidence within us? What can renew our youth, and roll us back to the precious hours of believing innocence? Nothing on earth. There is naught that can give us back to ourselves, but the reception of God's Word as divine Truth. How the heart yearns for something to trust in, to act upon, to cling to as a sure anchor within the veil! How the seared and callous spirit longs to soar once more upon the wings of Faith and Hope, and find peace in believing! Well, the yearning of the soul and the longing of the spirit can both be gratified in the Word of God; for, says our blessed Saviour, "Thy word is truth." Oh precious declaration! Oh divine announcement! Well may the angels call it the Gospel, the "glad tidings," and desire to look into it, and understand it! In this Word, O worn and jaded and deceived man, may you find a resting-place; nay more, a place in which you may cast aside the garments soiled by a deceitful world, and array yourself in the robe of truth and of holiness. Your course is not finished because the world has deceived you, because your own understanding has played you false.

Your life is not ended because one phase of it has been a delusive play of error and falsehood. There is something yet untried; a new course to be entered upon, in which you will find no deception and no falsehood; a fresh life to be begun, wherein truth will cause your path to shine brighter and brighter unto the perfect day. Come to the Word of God; study it under the guidance of the Church and the Spirit; embrace it as divine Truth; let it sink into your heart as life-giving and life-restoring: and you will find that every thing within you will be changed under its divine influence; and that every thing outside of you will catch the light which now illuminates you; and will be irradiated, no matter how dark and sombre your prospects may have seemed, with the brightness which Truth reflects upon them. You will then, for the first time, no matter how long you may have lived the life of the world, realize the transforming power of Truth, not only within, but without the soul.

Is this sanctifying process going on within you, and upon you, my beloved hearers? Are you growing in grace as you grow in years? Is Christianity working upon you such changes as it is intended to work? Or are you rather at ease in Zion, satisfied with your attainments and settled upon your lees? Beware of this condition! If you are not advancing in holiness, the probability — nay, almost the certainty — is that you are moving backwards. Religion in the heart needs constant cherishing. It is a plant in an unkindly soil. Every thing is against it. It is like rowing against the wind and the tide: constant exertion may urge you forward; but the cessation of exertion certainly places you at the mercy of the contending elements, and you drift backwards. Christ would never have called upon His Father in that most solemn hour of prayer to sanctify us with His Truth, if He had not known, as a man tempted in all things as we ourselves are, what a struggle it requires in us to advance in holiness! Let us remember this, fellow-Christians, that our aim should be sanctification, improvement in Christian character, an onward movement towards a higher perfection of holiness. Such injunctions as these, "Be ye holy; for I am holy,"[1] "Be ye therefore perfect, even as your Father which is in heaven is perfect,"[2] occur in the Scriptures; and suggest to us the point of attainment after which we are expected to strive. How earnestly the Apostles looked towards perfection! "I count not myself to have apprehended," said the ambitious S. Paul, — ambitious after the image of Christ his Lord: "but this one thing I do, forgetting those things which are behind, and reaching forth unto those things which are before, I press torward the mark."[3] "Toward the mark," was ever his motto! Although humble enough to say, "By the grace of God I am what I am,"[4] he was yet enthusiastic enough to look forward at the "prize of the high calling."[5] Let us endeavor to imbibe this spirit, to drink in of his ardent zeal. Lukewarmness is peculiarly hateful to Christ, the Head of the Church. He spues it out of His mouth! The Word of God is one of the great means whereby we may get rightminded views upon this topic, for it "is quick, and powerful, and sharper than any two-edged sword, piercing even to the dividing asunder of soul and spirit, and of the joints and marrow, and is a discerner of the thoughts and intents of the heart."[6] What an instrument! Sent, too, not for destruction, but for our blessing and comfort; sent to sanctify us; sent to bless us; sent to comfort us; sent to give us the blessed hope of everlasting life; sent to prepare us in heart and soul for the fruition of those joys

[1] 1 S. Pet. i. 16. [2] S. Matt. v. 48. [3] Phil. iii. 13, 14.
[4] 1 Cor. xv. 10. [5] Phil. iii. 14. [6] Heb. iv. 12.

of which it is written: "Eye hath not seen, nor ear heard, neither have entered into the heart of man, the things which God hath prepared for them that love him."

1865.

[1] 1 Cor. ii. 9.

Nineteenth Sermon.

In those days came John the Baptist, preaching in the wilderness of Judæa, and saying, Repent ye: for the kingdom of heaven is at hand. For this is he that was spoken of by the prophet Esaias, saying, The voice of one crying in the wilderness, Prepare ye the way of the Lord, make his paths straight. — S. Matthew iii. 1–3.

IT has struck me very forcibly, in studying the Bible and comparing its prophecy with its narrative, that unless the essential Divinity of our Lord and Saviour Jesus Christ was received as its orthodox teaching, a very grave charge might be brought against the whole Revelation, — a no less charge than that of directly plunging the sincere and the devout into the damning sin of creature-worship. I say of directly plunging; for a Revelation should be liable to this accusation, which, not intending that those who embraced it should receive its proffered Saviour as God, should yet invest him with all the glory with which it surrounds and describes the Godhead. What could the Revelation, which we accept as from God, do more to mislead us upon this point (if it be not the truth), than it has done? What more than give Jesus Christ all the titles of God? What more than clothe Him with all the attributes of God? What more than separate Him, as it has done, from all human creatures and all angelic spirits, and place Him alongside of Jehovah as His fellow and His everlasting counsellor? What more than denounce all worship, save that of God, as idolatry, and not only permit but charge all things in Heaven and earth to worship Jesus?

All this is plainer even than so many direct affirmations of the fact; for it is interweaving the Name of Jesus so closely with that of Jehovah, that one cannot separate them, and must be guilty either of degrading Christ far below any thing which a fair interpretation of the Scriptures will permit, or else of confounding God and Christ continually, in thought, word and worship, to the destruction of his soul. It is impossible to do what the Bible commands us, impossible to worship as the Bible enjoins us to worship, impossible to administer and receive sacraments as the Bible arranges that they shall be administered and received, without being guilty of creature-worship, — if Jesus Christ be not God; without bringing upon us the curse of serving other gods, — if our Redeemer, the Messiah of the Jews, the Christ of the Gospel, be not a Person of that Triune Godhead, which is the great mystery of earth and Heaven.

My text has led me naturally into this train of thought; for, in considering the prophetic and evangelic offices of John the Baptist (to which the Church especially directs our attention to-day), and using them as incitements to urge upon you repentance and faith as the proper preparations for the coming of Christ, it is necessary to observe how the Bible first exalts John the Baptist, and then how it exhibits him as humbling himself before Jesus Christ as his Lord and his God.

As between the Old Testament and the New, with the exception of the Persons of the Godhead, John the Baptist is the only individual noted in prophecy. All the chosen servants of Christ under the Gospel were called after they had reached mature life; but nothing had been spoken of them before in Holy Writ. Not so with John the Baptist. Upon his birth and office and habits had holy men of old spoken as they were moved by the Holy Ghost.

Isaiah had predicted him in those rich verses, "The voice of him that crieth in the wilderness, Prepare ye the way of the LORD, make straight in the desert a highway for our God. Every valley shall be exalted, and every mountain and hill shall be made low: and the crooked shall be made straight, and the rough places plain: and the glory of the LORD shall be revealed, and all flesh shall see it together: for the mouth of the LORD hath spoken it."[1] Malachi closes the volume of Old Testament inspiration with a prediction and description of him: "Behold, I will send my messenger, and he shall prepare the way before me: and the Lord, whom ye seek, shall suddenly come to his temple, even the messenger of the covenant, whom ye delight in: behold, he shall come, saith the LORD of Hosts."[2] And again: "Behold, I will send you Elijah the prophet before the coming of the great and dreadful day of the LORD: and he shall turn the heart of the fathers to the children, and the heart of the children to their fathers, lest I come and smite the earth with a curse."[3] And this at once places him above all the most exalted characters of the Scriptures, even supposing that there was nothing more to distinguish him from his brethren.

But his birth and the inspired blessing of his father Zacharias betoken that a most wonderful personage was born into the world. His conception was supernatural, seeing that his parents were both past age; and that conception was announced, as a special answer of God to prayer, by the mouth of an angel: "Fear not, Zacharias: for thy prayer is heard; and thy wife Elizabeth shall bear thee a son, and thou shalt call his name John. And thou shalt have joy and gladness; and many shall rejoice at his birth. For he shall be great in the sight of the Lord, and

[1] Isaiah xl. 3–5. [2] Mal. iii. 1. [3] *Ibid.* iv. 5, 6.

shall drink neither wine nor strong drink; and he shall be filled with the Holy Ghost, even from his mother's womb. And many of the children of Israel shall he turn to the Lord their God. And he shall go before him in the spirit and power of Elias, to turn the hearts of the fathers to the children, and the disobedient to the wisdom of the just; to make ready a people prepared for the Lord."[1] And when the miraculous birth has taken place, and the Spirit has filled Zacharias, he thus predicts the glorious career of his son: "And thou, child, shalt be called the prophet of the Highest: for thou shalt go before the face of the Lord to prepare his ways; to give knowledge of salvation unto his people by the remission of their sins, through the tender mercy of our God."[2] Of no human being were ever more glorious things than these spoken; upon no creature could be heaped more exalted offices. And when Jesus had occasion afterwards to speak of him, He says emphatically: "Verily I say unto you, Among them that are born of women there hath not risen a greater than John the Baptist."[3] Abraham, though styled "the friend of God," was not greater. Moses, though permitted to speak face to face with God, was not greater. David, though the man after God's own heart, was not greater. And yet see in what relation the Bible places this mighty prophet, to Jesus Christ.

Even when honoring him most, the Bible but gives him the place of a messenger or herald before some mightier Being that was to follow; and that Being is called "The Lord our God;" and the day of His coming, that "great and dreadful day of the Lord." And when the children were yet unborn, this babe leaped in his mother's womb at the salutation of the Mother of Jesus,—leaped for joy; and his mother was filled with the Holy Ghost, and she

[1] S. Luke i. 13–17. [2] *Ibid.* 76–78. [3] S. Matt. xi. 11.

spake out and said: "Blessed art thou among women, and blessed is the fruit of thy womb. And whence is this to me, that the mother of my Lord should come to me?"[1] And in the full tide of his popularity, when multitudes had flocked to his baptism; when the Pharisees and Sadducees, the bigots and skeptics of that day, had combined to do homage to him; when men were musing in their minds whether he were the Christ or no: he cumulates epithets to humble himself before Jesus. He is One mightier than him; One that is preferred before him. His baptism is of water: the baptism of Jesus Christ shall be with the Holy Ghost and with fire. He goes before merely to prepare the way: in the hand of Jesus is the fan, and He will throughly purge His floor. Mighty as he is, — foretold, announced by an angel in the Temple, filled with the Holy Ghost from his mother's womb, — he is not worthy to unloose the latchet of the shoes of Jesus; nay, not worthy to bear them behind Him as He walks. How wonderful that all this humiliation should have no effect upon men to make them perceive the vast distance which the Bible has placed between the greatest of its prophets and Jesus Christ the Lord!

If we examine the passages of the prophets which predict the coming of John, we shall find that in them which bears strongly upon the same point, — the Majesty of the Person whom John was to precede and herald. In that of Isaiah, the office of the Baptist is designated as that of one raised up to prepare the way of the Lord; for what purpose? That "the glory of the LORD" may "be revealed, and all flesh" may "see it together." What is this glory of the LORD?

To us this term "Glory of the LORD" may mean any thing; but to the Jews, to whom Isaiah was writing, it was

[1] S. Luke i. 42, 43.

not so. In connection with His place of worship, it could have but one meaning,—the meaning that had been affixed to it under the Tabernacle and the first Temple. When Moses had finished all the work of the Tabernacle, and had set it up before the Lord, "Then," says the inspired writer, "a cloud covered the tent of the congregation, and the glory of the LORD filled the tabernacle."[1] When all things were perfected in Solomon's Temple, and all things had been arranged according to the pattern of the Lord, and the priests were come out of the Holy place, then the cloud filled the House of the Lord, so that the priests could not stand to minister because of the cloud: "for the glory of the LORD had filled the house of the LORD."[2]

There can be no doubt, in either of these places, who it was that filled those houses with His glory. In Exodus, the context plainly indicates that it was the same Being who had appeared to Moses upon the top of Sinai; who had overthrown Pharaoh and his hosts in the Red Sea; who had covenanted with Abraham, Isaac and Jacob; who had set His bow in the cloud for the comfort of Noah; who had attempered the curse upon the earth in the garden of Eden with the promise of the Seed of the woman. In Kings, the Lord whose glory filled the House of the Lord was thus addressed by Solomon, just after the cloud had filled the Temple, in language which could never have been used, under the Theocracy, save to Jehovah: "And Solomon stood before the altar of the LORD in the presence of all the congregation of Israel, and spread forth his hands towards heaven: and he said, LORD God of Israel, there is no God like thee, in heaven above, or on earth beneath, who keepest covenant and mercy with thy servants that walk before thee with all their heart. . . . . But will God indeed dwell

[1] Exod. xl. 34.

[2] 1 Kings viii. 10, 11.

on the earth? behold, the heaven and heaven of heavens cannot contain thee; how much less this house that I have builded?"[1] The term must be interpreted under the prophetic, as it was under the legal dispensation; and can refer, therefore, to none other in this passage, "that the glory of the LORD" shall be revealed, than to that revealed God who is everywhere in the Bible represented as distinct in Person from the concealed God, and yet identified with Him in titles, in power, in attributes.

Such is the personage before whom John the Baptist was to go as a herald; before whom he was to prepare the way, and make straight the paths. No wonder that before such a Being he should humble himself even to the dust.

In what manner, is our next inquiry, was John to prepare the way of the Lord? He himself explains it, and thus casts the clearest light upon the passages of the Prophets: "Repent ye: for the kingdom of heaven is at hand," was the burden of his preaching. "Bring forth therefore fruits meet for repentance;" for "now also the ax is laid unto the root of the trees."[2] Repentance, for their sins personal and national, was what was necessary on the part of the Jews, to precede faith in their coming Messiah, — in the establishment of that Church of the Gospel which is called, in the New Testament, "The Kingdom of Heaven."

The same call, my beloved hearers, is that which the ministers and stewards of the Gospel make upon you now, in reference to the approaching Advent of our Lord Jesus Christ in human flesh. Every year, as it rolls its course, does the Church bring before us, in her seasons, the great events which together worked out our redemption; and just now does she call upon us to contemplate the Nativity of our Lord as the first manifestation of that "grace which

[1] 1 Kings viii. 22, 23, 27. [2] S. Matt. iii. 8, 10.

bringeth salvation." In view of its near approach do I say unto you, as John said unto the Jews, "Repent ye, for the kingdom of heaven is at hand."

Repentance prepares us for the coming of our Lord, because it makes us dissatisfied with our own righteousness, and drives us to look out of ourselves for some justification before God. And this is evidently the meaning of John the Baptist, when he tells those who came out to his Baptism: "Think not to say within yourselves, We have Abraham to our father." Think no longer to place your justification in your national election, "for now also the ax is laid unto the root of the trees," and every individual "which bringeth not forth good fruit is hewn down, and cast into the fire." And this is the great object and end of preaching, — to dissatisfy you with your own righteousness; to make you see it as God sees it; to tear you from every other refuge as a mere refuge of lies, that you may take hold of Christ as The Lord your Righteousness. So long as man can find any thing to rest upon out of Christ, so long will he remain out of Christ: for such is his nature since the Fall, that he will believe any absurdity which demands not faith, rather than the power of God and the wisdom of God when it has to be received through faith. Repentance is the great theme of the Apostolic preaching. "Repent" begins almost all their sermons. "Repent" precedes every direction which they give to the inquiring crowds. "Repent" opens the door to Baptism, to Church membership, to a participation in the Supper of the Lord. "Repent ye, therefore," my hearers; and for this reason especially, because "the kingdom of heaven is at hand." Once again is Jesus Christ brought before you by the Church, and the mighty claims which He has upon your love and your devotion are presented to you. He is about to be manifested to you in that low estate which He put on for your sakes, when, "being in the form of God," and thinking "it not robbery to be equal with God:" He yet "made himself of no reputation, and took upon him the form of a servant, and was made in the likeness of men."[1] He is about to act out before you that career of love and mercy which had its consummation in His becoming "obedient unto death, even the death of the Cross."[2] He comes "to finish the transgression, and to make an end of sins, and to make reconciliation for iniquity, and to bring in everlasting righteousness."[3] All this, my beloved hearers, would not have been undertaken for you, could you have worked out for yourselves any righteousness that would suffice you in the day of God's wrath; — could you have found any refuge to shield you, when "judgment" should be laid "to the line, and righteousness to the plummet."[4] "Repent ye:" pray the Holy Spirit, whose office it is, to convince you of sin, and to give you that view of your own righteousness, which shall make you cry in anguish of spirit, "What shall I do to be saved?" It is an awful sight to see a human creature resting in a righteousness which the Bible calls "filthy rags;" which the holiest men of old abjured as utterly insufficient for their necessities: when there is a perfect Righteousness, wrought out for him by Christ, which can be his when he may be made to see his own sinfulness and the glorious sufficiency of Christ. O fellow-Christians, in view of this coming of the Kingdom of Heaven, let us unitedly beseech the God of love to pour down upon His Church the spirit of grace and of supplication, that the unbelieving may look upon Him whom they have pierced, and may mourn for Him as one mourneth for his only son, and may be in bitterness for Him as one that is in bitterness for his first born. "Repent ye," all that profess not the Name of the Lord, for the prophet calls it

[1] Phil. ii. 6, 7. [2] *Ibid.* 8. [3] Dan. ix. 24. [4] Isaiah xxxviii. 17.

"that great and dreadful day of the LORD;"—great and dreadful indeed, for it aggravates sin with the rejection of mercy, and brings down upon the impenitent the additional condemnation of having trampled under foot the Blood of the son of God, and done despite to the Spirit of His grace.

"Repent ye: for the kingdom of heaven is at hand." What a call to you, members of the Church of Christ? Hear the words of Malachi: "Behold, I will send my messenger, and he shall prepare the way before me: and the Lord, whom ye seek, shall suddenly come to his temple, even the messenger of the covenant, whom ye delight in: behold, he shall come, saith the LORD of Hosts. But who may abide the day of his coming? and who shall stand when he appeareth? for he is like a refiner's fire, and like fuller's sope: and he shall sit as a refiner and purifier of silver: and he shall purify the sons of Levi, and purge them as gold and silver, that they may offer unto the LORD an offering in righteousness." Are you ready, my hearers, for this Lord? Are you prepared for the refiner's fire? This Lord will come near to you to judgment, and will be a swift witness against all iniquity. How can you stand when He appeareth? Search and examine yourselves, ere it be too late, and see that you are in the faith. Prove your own selves! If you will not, God must prove you: and even though you stand in the day of His appearing, believe me that the trial of your faith, if you put Him upon it in this world, will be like passing through the fire; and the dross which shall be burnt away will be like the tearing asunder of soul and body. When Christ sits as a refiner and purifier, He will not leave His work until He shall see His own image reflected in you. Refine yourselves at once, therefore, lest He come upon you, and judgment be laid to the line. Humble yourselves at once before His awful appearing, and bring forth fruits meet for repentance.

My beloved hearers, the Kingdom of Heaven is at hand. Oh, in how many senses! It is at hand, in that the Gospel circle is once again begun to be run in the Church. It is at hand, in that the means of grace are all around you, freely offered, freely dispensed. It is at hand, in that the Second Coming of our Lord is nearer than when ye believed. It is at hand, in that Death, which terminates our probation, is overhanging us at every moment. Under each and every one of these aspects, the cry is the same: "Repent ye." Despise not the voice of warning, lest the Lord come upon you suddenly, like a thief in the night, and ye find no place for repentance, though ye seek it carefully, and with tears.

1865.

Twentieth Sermon.

As sorrowful, yet alway rejoicing. — 2 COR. vi. 10.

AT first glance, this sentence appears to involve a contradiction; but the longer we think of it, the more will it strike us as describing very faithfully man's condition while on his march to the Holy Land of Promise and of Peace. Sorrow for the present, but joy coming in the morning; weariness as we tread the thorny road, but rest awaiting us at its close; tears sprinkling our path, but our God ready, when our work is done, to wipe away tears from off all faces; darkness embarrassing us, hindering us, putting us out of the way, but light, light from heaven, shining more and more brightly as we fix our eyes upon the Cross. It is the true picture of life as sin has made it, — sin limited and restrained by the power of Man's divine Champion. And we are assembled to-day to commemorate the birth of Him, who has hindered life from being all sorrow, all weariness, all tears, all darkness! It is the true festival of the heart and of the affections, for it awakens every thing to love and joy, and then makes that love and joy undying. It rises above all affliction; and for the time, so long as we can keep sense and memory subject to faith, it places earth with its temporary trials and sorrows at their true value. Every thing rejoices at its coming: from the angels in Heaven who sing the song of "Glory to God in the highest," to the trees of the field which come in hither to clap their hands before the Lord. Every thing rejoices, and ought to rejoice, for it celebrates the reunion of man and God, of earth and Heaven, of the soul with that divine Fountain whence it sprang when Jehovah breathed into it the breath of life.

And what a rich blessing it is, my beloved people, that there should be in a world like this something to break the sad monotony of life; something to relieve the mind from the continued contemplation of trouble, of sorrow, of sickness, of death; to separate us from the necessary work of life; to remove us from the pressure of carking care, from the degrading influence of worldly strife, from the deteriorating effects of selfishness and avarice. What a rich blessing to find a centre of love, around which should be gathered, if only for a little while, the kindliest sympathies of human nature, — a fountain of real joy sending its refreshing waters to cheer the weary path of the mourner, and trickling through all the by-ways of the world, seeking out the children of want and poverty, and creating green spots even in a desert. It is hard to estimate the value of such a season in its humanizing and softening tendencies. How many elements have to be combined, ere we can appreciate the festival we are keeping, even under this aspect. We should be obliged to unlock all the secret doors of sorrow and of shame, all the private recesses of affection and delight, and combine them, ere we could understand how the joys of this season pervade the whole frame-work of society. The chamber of the sick is lightened by its coming. The humble abode of poverty is cheered as this sun rises upon it. The thousand firesides of the land are full of words of affection and the merry laugh of childhood. The whole Christian world rises up and calls Him blessed, who has come upon this mission of love, and has humbled Himself to lowliness, and to sorrow, and to suffering, that the children of sin and death may have rejoicing mingled with their sorrowing.

The coming of this Son of God in human form has been the burden of hope from the beginning of the world. From that moment when the promise fell upon the ear of guilt in the garden of Eden, "The seed of the woman shall bruise the serpent's head," until the morning when the herald angels sang the song of His Birth, has every thing been overruled for His Advent. Upon every thing else in the world were change and decay permitted to place their hand of destruction, save upon this promise. This ever waxed stronger and brighter, even amid wreck and ruin; and was the rainbow that encircled the darkness. Whatever else was overturned, this stood immovable, the corner-stone laid in Sion. When a single family enshrined the promise, that family was watched and guarded by Heaven: for in its bosom was the Word of God and the Hope of the World. When that Family swelled into a nation, God Himself became its King, and guarded it as the apple of an eye, leading it like a flock and protecting it under the shadow of His wing! When that nation sorrowed in captivity by the waters of Babylon, God heard the cry of the people of whom, according to the flesh, His Son should come: and led them back, with songs and rejoicing, to their own land of promise. All the mightiest monarchies of the world — Egypt, Assyria, Babylon, Macedonia, Rome — raged in their madness around the future birthplace of this promised Seed: but each, in its turn, was made to feel that a mightier power than itself had placed a curb upon its fury, and had uttered the decree, "Hitherto shalt thou come, but no further."[1] It was not until this promise was fulfilled at Bethlehem, — until the Seed of the woman was incarnate, — that the reins were thrown upon the neck of these executioners of the Lord, and they were permitted to make the Holy Land a desolation, to raze the Temple to

[1] Job xxxviii. 11.

its foundation, and scatter God's people over the face of the earth. How firmly does this adherence to His promise prove for us the truth of God! How immovably does it establish the future upon the basis of the past! When we follow this promise, struggling to its fulfillment through four thousand years of clouds and darkness, can we doubt but that all the promises of God are "Yea and Amen" in Christ Jesus?

The life of Jesus was an example of the life which is shadowed forth in my text. He was a Man of sorrows and acquainted with grief, yet had He within Himself a well-spring of joy, which carried Him unmurmuring through all He had to bear with for us. He was sorrowing, yet always rejoicing: sorrowing for man, sorrowing under the burden of sin which He was bearing, sorrowing in view of the sufferings He was called to pass through; yet rejoicing for the joy that was set before Him, and for the glory which was evermore to encircle His Name. He was poor, and had not where to lay His head: yet He rejoiced! He was tempted in the lonely wilderness, and had to bear the polluting approach of Satan: yet He rejoiced! He was scorned and despised: yet He rejoiced! He was persecuted and forsaken: yet He rejoiced! He was made obedient unto death, even the death of the Cross: yet He rejoiced! He exhibited to us the double life which it is intended for us to lead on earth; — the outer life by which we touch the world and the things of the world, in which we are called upon to bear and suffer and mourn, through which we are to work out in the strength of Christ our salvation: and the inner life, by which we touch God and heavenly things, in which we are to reap the fruits of the Spirit, joy, peace, love; and through which we are to receive the adoption of sons of God and the glorious inheritance of His eternal kingdom. This double life, if we are Christians, we must all lead. There is no escaping it. Our joy, whatever it is, must go along with sorrow: our sorrow, whatever it is, must be borne in a spirit of rejoicing. We cannot separate them; and therefore does the Apostle enjoin upon us, to act heartily up to what is allotted to us. Any other life will prove to be a forced life, and will turn out to be an abortion — a life of misery to ourselves, of hypocrisy to the world. To be truly Christian; to move in the spirit of Christ, and with the mind of Christ, we must follow His footsteps whether in sorrow or in joy. We must live in the world as not of the world; bearing whatever is laid upon us, as though it was only by the way, and had but little to do — save in the way of discipline — with the real purpose and end of our existence.

When we take the true view of life, — and this festival really exhibits it to us, — I do not see why we should not be always rejoicing even though for the present we go on sorrowing. In an elaborate and complicated piece of machinery, there is a principle which pervades the whole structure, and regulates its action and its use. In a musical composition, there is a key-note upon which depends all the harmony, and without attention to which all is discord and confusion. Well, Life has likewise its principle, which regulates it; its key-note which gives it its harmony: and unless we attend to these, it will be like jangling bells, ringing noisily upon the ear, yet breathing no music either for use or delight. The divine object of life — our eternal future — must be kept in view; or else we shall not be able to understand fully the meaning of the Apostle when he says, "As sorrowful, yet alway rejoicing:" and what is worse, we should not comprehend the life of Christ, into which we are to grow, which was the foreshadowing of this injunction. It was not this life of sin and sorrow that our Lord rejoiced in: it was the joy that was set before Him.

And so with us. The true key-note of our life is that glory which is laid up for us in Christ, and through Christ; — that crown which is to encircle our brow, when we shall have triumphed over our spiritual enemies. This should rule over every thing: over our sorrows, over our troubles, over our temptations, over sickness and death, over corruption and the grave! — should be a bow of promise ever spanning the clouds and the storm, a thing of beauty and of joy, even though it be made up of light and tears. Does not any prospect of earthly bliss — future but sure — fill the heart with joy, and sustain it through toil and weariness and suffering? Are we not all borne up in life by some hope that is before us, — some secret, hoarded bliss, which goes along with us, and clothes with sunshine the rugged path which we are appointed to tread? Every individual has this sustaining though secret joy; and none can have it so surely and so brightly as the Christian. He has a right to rejoice at all times, to keep a perpetual festival in his heart, to make a Christmas of his whole life: for Christ, to him, has not only been born in Bethlehem, but born within him; has not only lived and died for him, but is making his body a living temple, and dwelling there by His Holy Spirit — the Spirit of peace and joy! If he is faithful to himself he can never be without joy: for deep down in his heart is there a fountain always gushing, of which nothing can deprive him but sinfulness and faithlessness. "Holding faith and a good conscience," he can move forward in a spirit of rejoicing, however troubled he may be in the flesh. No stranger can intermeddle with his joy: for it is hidden from all but God, who gives it the full warrant of His inspired Word.

And yet the sorrow of the world does press upon even the most faithful of us, and does often turn us aside from the rejoicing which really belongs to us. Nature leans one way: Inspiration directs us another way. Flesh and Blood would dwell in the low valleys of despondency and depression: Faith summons us to the mountain-tops which look out upon the unclouded skies, and bids us rejoice in spirit and in hope. How shall heavy hearts and anxious spirits be made to lighten themselves of their burdens, and to obey the injunction of the inspired Apostle? In whom shall sorrow and joy be harmonized?

My answer is, "In Christ Jesus our Lord." And the error which pervades the reasoning of the world, and which creeps in upon the Church, arises from a want of proper discrimination between the joy of the world and the holy joy of Christian belief. There is a rude vulgar mirth which the world dignifies with the name of "rejoicing;" and there is a Christian grace which the Apostle entitles "rejoicing in the Lord." These two species of joy differ from each other in every particular, — in their origin, in their occasions, in their nature, in their ends. The one is born of the flesh, and is antagonistic of the other which comes directly from the Spirit of God. The one arises out of those gratifications of sense or of interest which absorb so much our feelings and our affections; the other springs out of considerations connected with Christ's future dominion. The one is dependent upon prosperity for its existence; the other brightens and flashes just when clouds and darkness lower upon us, and is like the lightning, the more vivid because of the darkness out of which it seems to dart. The one has its consummation in the very moment of its production; the other awaits in patience the time when it shall flourish in eternal peace. To be "sorrowful, yet alway rejoicing" the Apostle did not believe to be possible for the world, and in the spirit of the world: but to be "sorrowful, yet alway rejoicing" in the Spirit of Christ, was his daily practice, and his exceeding great reward. And what he had learned from his own wide experience, he exhorts us to learn who may be called to wade, like himself, through a sea of trouble and of woe. "For whom the Lord loveth he chasteneth, and scourgeth every son whom he receiveth."[1]

And how much we have to rejoice in, my beloved hearers, even though we be sorrowful! We can rejoice, because we know that the world has not been left to itself to stagger on in its sinfulness and misrule, but has been given to Christ for His possession. "The Lord God omnipotent reigneth,"[2] — reigneth over all the kingdoms of the universe; and He has promised to set His Son upon His holy hill of Zion. The earth is the Lord's and the fullness thereof; and He ordereth all things according to the purposes of His will. For this we can rejoice, no matter how troubled the world may be. "I will overturn, overturn, overturn it: and it shall be no more, until He come whose right it is, and I will give it him,"[3] is the decree of God: and the Christian, however sorrowing, may rejoice, that every thing is working together to bring in the kingdom of righteousness, and to place Christ, as King of kings and Lord of lords, over every thing in Heaven and in earth. The wrath of man is altogether under the control of Him whose incarnation we are celebrating, and it cannot hurt one hair of our heads without His permission. And in His hands do we rejoice to leave all things, and to trust in Him for the future, as we have for the past. In the midst of the sorrow of the world, we can be ever rejoicing: because we know that the Lord maketh every thing work together for good to them that love Him. Sorrow, sickness, suffering, death, striking us in the current and rush of life, are made to work, together with its events, for good. The expression is a very striking one, and conveys the idea of

[1] Heb. xii. 6. [2] Rev. xix. 6. [3] Ezek. xxi. 27.

many threads interlacing and forming the web of a texture; of many rays converging and constituting a star of promise and of hope. The single thread we often cannot see the purpose of; the single ray gives no positive light amid the darkness: and in the same way any particular act of God's providence may lack its meaning even to the eye of Faith. But when these single threads are woven together by a skillful hand, they form a pattern of order and of beauty: and when these single rays are converged by the unerring law of Nature, they become a centre of light and of glory. So these movements of God's providence, which, as single acts, seem mysterious and severe, change into mercy and blessing when His all-wise hand shall have arranged them in their proper places, and united them with others which are their complement and harmony. "Work together for good;"—not work singly for good, but together: teaching us never to judge hastily or rashly, never to murmur inconsiderately, but to wait patiently; and, while waiting, to rejoice that, in the darkness and misery by which we are encompassed in this world, our Lord is controlling all things, and is holding in His hands the innumerable threads of our complicate Being, and is working them up together for good to those who are the called according to His purpose. And surely, no matter how full of care and grief the present may be, how inexplicable the dealings of God with us: we may rejoice through it all, and lift our hearts to Heaven, feeling that nothing can separate us from a love which could give its only-begotten Son for our redemption.

I trust that you can now feel, my beloved people, that "although sorrowing, you may be always rejoicing," because, while the sorrow will pass away, the joy remains, not only undying, but ever increasing in brightness and certainty! No sorrow, however acute, however deep, can extend beyond this life. Death cuts it off; it has no longer any influence over us. But our rejoicing passes with us, through the grave, because Christ, who is our cause of rejoicing, receives us there to the brightness of His Glory. Our rejoicing here is by faith, that the day of this humiliation will be soon ended, and that He will come again in His glorious Majesty to raise us to the life immortal, and glorify us with that glory which He had with the Father ere the world was! Who can think of sorrow when such a vision rises in the future? Who can count the griefs of this world to be of any moment, when he remembers that Christ has come, and has sanctified all this sorrow, and made it holy? When the angel-song reaches our ears, "Glory to the new-born King!" what other strain can overpower it? It swells from earth to Heaven, and our hearts rise with it, and mingle in the shout which rings through the arches of the skies at the wonderful declaration. Him whom these angels had known in the Bosom of His Father, whose brightness they could not look upon, before whose presence they were compelled to hide their faces with their wings: they now see an infant in His Mother's bosom! Sublime mystery! Incomprehensible work! Angels desiring to look into it; — yet all done for man. The universe receiving it with songs of triumph; — yet all done for man! done for him, — a fallen, sinful, corrupt creature; — for him, a child of shame and of the curse; — for him, born to trouble as the sparks fly upward; — done for him, that he may be rescued from all the evils of sin, and all the penalties of the curse; — done for him, that he may be pardoned, and justified, and sanctified; — done for him, that he may be adopted into the family of God; — done for him, that he may be exalted to Heaven, and made a king and a priest unto God. All this done for him: and yet he going along to this glory, and permitting himself to be sorrowful and despondent, with his knees feeble, and his hands hanging down,—with his eyes fixed upon the earth, as if that were his home and his treasure!

For shame, Christian! You should be "alway rejoicing," especially to-day! For shame, Christian! Your eyes should be turned with joy to Bethlehem, even though they be filled with tears. For shame, Christian! Lay aside all private griefs, all public sorrow, and sing this morning with the holy angels, "Glory to God in the highest, and on earth peace, good will towards men." And you should sing all through your life, and engrave upon your heart as your motto: "Sorrowful, yet alway rejoicing."

1865.

Twenty-first Sermon.

And this Gospel of the Kingdom shall be preached in all the world, for a witness unto all nations; and then shall the end come. — S. MATTHEW xxiv. 14.

THE Scripture has a depth of meaning which is discovered only by those who will compare one portion of its revelations with another portion, and weave out of them a perfect pattern of the mind of God. If we read those divine books hastily, or with preconceived opinions, we may deduce from them conclusions diametrically opposed to their real meaning, and a practice of life which will be contrary to our highest because eternal interests. The mind of man, when spread over various works, it is difficult always, at once, to understand. We are obliged to compare utterance with utterance, and opinion with opinion, and to elucidate them by the life and actions of the writer, ere we can make out the exact meaning of the writings through which he has made himself known to the world. And if this be so with men of our own times, when speaking upon topics familiar to us, and which are made clear to us from our own experience: how much more difficult must it be for us to take in correctly the mind of God, delivered to us as it has been through so many various authors, and treating of spiritual matters not known to the natural understanding, and connected with a scheme of grace which is progressive and perpetually expansive. It requires great attention, not great intellect; much meditation, not critical study; a great deal of prayer, rather than a great deal of learning; much personal experience, more than the discipline of the schools. All the great errors of the Christian world have come from the wise, and not from the faithful; from philosophy, and not from experience; from conclusions drawn from *a priori* reasoning, rather than from the plain letter of the Scriptures: and thus — like the more common opinions which are met floating upon the current of the Church — they are almost always found to have arisen from a lack of Scriptural knowledge, — from a too narrow induction of the disclosures of the Sacred Writers. An idea which is made prominent at a particular moment and under particular circumstances is seized upon by an ardent mind, and is advanced boldly as the central idea of the Scriptures, and every thing else is made to circle around it and is tinged with its coloring. This has been the fountain of all sectarianism, and will ever be the prolific source of error until the time of the end.

Out of this springs the great value of the Church of Christ, with its Creeds, its Formularies, its Liturgy, its Ordinances. These have been gathered out of the Word of God carefully, and through a long sequence of Ecclesiastical experience. They have been harmonized by comparing all portions of the Sacred Writings, and not by grasping one utterance and making that the key to unlock every thing else. They have been weighed, and proved, and illustrated; they have been wet with the tears of repentance, and dyed with the blood of martyrdom: and now they represent, hoary as they are with the marks of antiquity, the united consent of all the purest ages and the holiest men of the Christian Faith. Upon them, steadfast and immovable, may the mind rest itself, and the heart plant its belief: not because they are the teachings of the Church, but because we are satisfied that they are the teachings of God's inspired Word, collected, by the Apostles and the holy men who have succeeded them, out of every book of that Revelation; and representing, not some one idea of the Divine economy of grace, but all the ideas in succession which make up the glorious body of the Gospel of Jesus Christ. Those are grievously mistaken who imagine that we love the Church because we receive from her new developments of faith and practice (*that* is *Roman* doctrine). We reverence the Church, and gladly follow in her sacred circle of truth and order, for the exactly opposite reason: because she maintains unchanged and unchangeable the doctrines of salvation which the Bible promulges, and teaches them in beautiful succession as the year rolls round, never violating the proportion of Faith, but presenting in turn all the features which make Christ the Prophet, the Priest and the King of His elect people in earth and Heaven.

One of the errors which has gained currency in the Church, although it has never advanced to the dignity of a sect, is one which naturally comes up at this season of the Church's services,[1] and which it may be well to put at rest just at this moment in our Ecclesiastical condition. The manifestation of Christ to the Gentiles which the Church now celebrates, and the command which Christ gave to His Apostles to go into all the world and preach the Gospel to every creature, have given rise, somehow, — I I know not how, — to the idea that the world is to be converted to Christianity, ere our Lord shall come a second time to judgment. And this impression has worked evil both to the believers in Christ, and to those who have been looking about for grounds of cavil against Christianity. The former have suffered sorrow and despondency, because they have not seen our holy religion spreading rapidly and

[1] Epiphany.

embracing the whole earth in its arms of mercy and of hope. The latter have triumphed over every discomfiture of Gospel truth, and have rejoiced whenever the events of the world have seemed to countervail this promise of the world's entire regeneration. Both have proceeded upon the erroneous idea that the Revelation of God had declared any such truth; and the one has suffered and the other rejoiced for no reason at all, but because of a popular fallacy derived from Millennial views finding no real support in Scripture.

The influx of Gentiles to the Church of Christ was one of the phenomena which were to mark the Advent of the Messiah. It was the prophetic result of the fulfillment of the work of Christ upon earth; and while it was a stumbling-block to the Jews, was nevertheless their true glory and triumph. That, just in the moment of their seeming degradation, when the sceptre was departing from Judah and a lawgiver from between his feet, — when a nation of fierce countenance was sweeping over them, and destroying nationality, Temple, Altar, Priesthood, and scattering them over the whole earth, — all nations should flow unto them, and find, amid those broken shrines and desolated homes a spiritual worship before which their idolatries should all vanish, a philosophy so much purer and more refined than any which preceded it that wisdom bowed before it even while it corrupted it: was a marvel which furnished evidence for Jesus so strong that the Jews have ever found it an unanswerable testimony. It was an epoch which Prophecy had foretold; to which their sacred writers had all pointed with exultation; which their own Rabbis had interpreted and settled ere the Messiah came. It explained numberless obscure passages in the Old Testament Scriptures, and developed a consistency and beauty in the whole Gospel scheme which one cannot perceive without being ravished at it. But while it promised that the death of Christ should be "as floods upon the dry ground,"[1] and that the offspring of his work should "spring up as willows by the watercourses,"[2] it did not promise that all the Gentiles should be converted unto Christ, and that a spiritual dominion should be acknowledged then or at any subsequent time over the universal earth. Its extent was precisely that which has been accomplished, — that multitudes of all nations, and kindreds, and people should flow up to Mount Zion, and should receive instruction from its fountains of life. And our Lord's command that the Gospel should be preached to every nation went no further than this, and must be interpreted by the text from which I preach: "And this Gospel of the Kingdom shall be preached in all the world, for a witness unto all nations; and then shall the end come."

So far from there being any warrant for any such opinion in the writings of the Prophets and Apostles, the very reverse is clearly taught in many passages of the New Testament; — so clearly that one wonders how they could possibly be overlooked. Our Saviour's own description of His second coming is decisive upon the point: "But of that day and hour knoweth no man, no, not the angels of Heaven, but my Father only. But as the days of Noe were, so shall also the coming of the Son of man be. For as in the days that were before the flood, they were eating and drinking, marrying and giving in marriage, until the day that Noe entered into the ark, and knew not until the flood came, and took them all away: so shall also the coming of the Son of man be. Then shall two be in the field; the one shall be taken, and the other left. Two women shall be grinding at the mill; the one shall be taken, and the other left. Watch therefore; for ye know not what

[1] Isaiah xliv. 3. [2] *Ibid.* 4.

hour your Lord doth come."[1] All this is entirely incompatible with the notion of a converted world living in faith and watchfulness; and brings strikingly before us exactly such a state of things as exists about us in every Christian land, — the godly in contact with the ungodly, the righteous man eating, drinking, working, in connection with the unrighteous. Nay, parts of the Scripture lead us to anticipate a very infidel condition of the world as immediately preceding the second coming of our Lord. Our Lord Himself asked: "Nevertheless, when the Son of man cometh, shall He find faith on the earth?"[2] And the Apostles all foreshadow a state of great iniquity as preceding the day of Judgment. One of them writes: "This know also, that in the last days perilous times shall come. For men shall be lovers of their own selves, covetous, boasters, proud, blasphemers, disobedient to parents, unthankful, unholy, without natural affection, truce-breakers, false accusers, incontinent, fierce, despisers of those that are good, traitors, heady, high-minded, lovers of pleasures more than lovers of God; having a form of godliness, but denying the power thereof;"[3] — a goodly catalogue for a world regenerated by the Gospel! Another, in introducing the scenes of the last day, opens his description in language like this: "Knowing this first, that there shall come in the last days scoffers, walking after their own lusts, and saying, Where is the promise of His coming? for since the fathers fell asleep, all things continue as they were from the beginning of the creation. . . . . But the day of the Lord will come as a thief in the night; in the which the Heavens shall pass away with a great noise, and the elements shall melt with fervent heat, the earth also and the works that are therein shall be burned up."[4] These proph-

[1] S. Matt. xxiv. 36–42.
[2] S. Luke xviii. 8.
[3] 2 Tim. iii. 1–5.
[4] 2 S. Pet. iii. 3, 4, 10.

ecies might easily be multiplied, but these are enough to show the teaching of the Scripture, and to remove the error of which we have been speaking, — that obedience to the command of Christ to go into all the world and preach the Gospel to every creature, is to result in any thing like an universal conversion of a world lying in wickedness.

The question then naturally comes up: "What is to be the result of the Missionary work? Why is the Church so earnest in spreading the Gospel, and why does she press it upon her children as their duty, especially at this season of the year?" Very proper questions, which I am glad to answer; and the reply to which will put the Missionary work upon its true basis, and will remove some of the difficulties of Christians arising out of the slow progress of the Church of Christ, and the continual interruptions which occur from civil discords, and the tumults which unsettle and overturn every thing from time to time in the history of the world.

If there was no other reason why the Church should be earnest and active in the cause of Missions than the command of her Lord, that alone would render it imperative. It was His last and most solemn command to His Apostles. Nay, it was the *only work* which He gave them to do. They were to go and preach the Gospel to every creature, teaching them, and baptizing them in the name of the Father, and of the Son, and of the Holy Ghost. The Church work which has grown up out of this, and which too much absorbs the energy of Christ's disciples, was merely secondary to this command, — the fruits of its faithful performance. The Missionary work was that which Christ Himself arranged, and made obligatory upon the ambassadors whom He left behind Him in the world. And surely, obedience to the arrangements and commands of her Lord is the first and highest duty of the Church, — the token of loyalty which He loves best. Long ago, God said: "To obey is better than sacrifice, and to hearken than the fat of rams,"[1] and it continues true to the end. And for this sufficient reason, that the Head of the Church knows what is her duty better than the members; knows His own plan, knows His means; knows what will be most conducive to the progress and welfare of His purposes. The Church looks to her own ease or dignity: Christ keeps His eye fixed only upon the mighty work which the Church is subserving through all her arrangements. The Church is tempted continually to turn away from spiritual things, and to mix up herself with the world and its concerns: Christ knows the world only as an enemy, and treats it accordingly. The Church is forever in danger of keeping her resources within herself, and using them for her own aggrandizement: Christ desires the Church to be as her Lord, humble, active, working, looking to the real point of the Gospel, and not to those things which have grown up out of its success and power. The command of Christ is therefore enough to guide and control the Church; and where that is positive, obedience is the virtue which most becomes her, and Faith and Grace, which mark her spiritual condition.

But our Lord has condescended to give us a reason as well as a command. This Gospel is "to be preached in all the world for a witness unto all nations." It is salvation, but it is also to be condemnation. It is to be not only a savor of life unto life, but of death unto death. The command of Christ must be carried out, not only that the Gospel of this Kingdom should be freely offered unto all men, but that its offer might rise up against them in the great day of Judgment, and speak for God against them. This Gospel is glad tidings for all the world, and therefore must be delivered in the hearing of all the world. Christ is the

[1] 1 Sam. xv. 22.

Lamb of God, who taketh away the sins of the world; and so He must be pointed out to every nation and people under the heavens. It is a part of the dispensation of Grace that in the fullness of times all things should be gathered together in Christ, both which are in Heaven and which are on earth; and to the Church is assigned the high duty of performing it. What the result of the Missionary work is to be, is not for the Church to inquire. She has received her Lord's command; and whether the preaching of this Gospel in all the world is to be only for a witness unto the nations, or, besides that, is to be for salvation to them, is no question for her. The economy of the Gospel is to be worked out through the Church; and this is a part of the economy of the Gospel. Faith must preside over this part of her work, as well as over every other part. She cannot say, "I will not send this Gospel into the world, and among the nations, because I cannot see such fruits of its preaching as I think should follow it:" because the answer would at once be given her by her Lord: "The preaching of this Gospel is not always that it may produce such fruits as you look for. It is sometimes sent that it may be only a witness unto all nations." The Church must enter into the whole mind of Christ, and must consider His purpose in sending a Gospel. "Many be called," said our Lord, "but few chosen."[1] Many are called in Christian countries; but alas, how few are chosen! Many are called in our cities, and towns, and villages; yet how few are chosen! Many are called in our congregations; but ye yourselves can witness, how few are chosen! And why should it be any different among nations? Why should the Church expect that multitudes should at once flock to her fold from among creatures who have had no Christian teaching and training, whose habits of thought, of feel-

[1] S. Matt. xx. 16.

ing, of action, are all alien from Christianity? Among nations the same rule holds: "Many be called, but few chosen." Nevertheless, this Gospel must be preached as a witness, — must be sent among all nations, that they may know the offer of mercy which God has made them according to the purpose of His will, and may accept or reject it. Christian hearts need not be distressed when they see the Missionary work in which they have been earnestly engaged, and in which they have delighted, interrupted or even broken up. As human creatures, where hopes have been disappointed they may feel the pangs of natural sorrow; but as Christians, looking to the great end and purpose of the Gospel, they have no reason to be despondent. The Gospel of the Kingdom has been preached, at least as a witness: and if God means it for no more, He knows best. The conversion of the world has nothing to do with the end of the world. They stand apart and distinct. The end will come, not in the midst of faith, but in the midst of infidelity; not when men are sober and watchful, but when they are eating and drinking, marrying and giving in marriage. The success of Missions is never that at which the Church should look. It should rejoice when Christ appears to have many people in such and such a land; but it should never measure its work by its results. The Gospel which has been sent and preached, — preached through the Bible, preached through the living voice, preached through martyrdom, — may appear to have accomplished nothing. Grieve not! it has done its work — it has been a witness, and therefore has not returned *void*. It has done that whereto Christ sent it. The Church is guilty, only when she does not send it, — only when, wrapped up in indifference and lukewarmness, she will not obey the command of her Lord, because He will not permit her to live by sight. This is her guilt, — *disobedience*. Want of success, interruption through the civil convulsions of the world, disturbance through the breaking up of Ecclesiastical unions: are all with the Lord. She must bow in submission to them, and be ready, at any moment that opportunity may offer, to resume her labors. She must witness, even though she do it in sackcloth and ashes. She must send the Gospel, even though it be for condemnation. It is not for her to undertake to fathom the ways of God, for they are past her finding out. She must fulfill her work in silence and in awe, trusting to the wisdom of her Lord, and remembering that of Him, and through Him, and to Him, are all things: to whom be glory forever. Amen.

1866.

Twenty-second Sermon.

And these are they which are sown among thorns; such as hear the word, and the cares of this world, and the deceitfulness of riches, and the lusts of other things entering in, choke the word, and it becometh unfruitful. — S. MARK iv. 18, 19.

OF the three classes of unfruitful hearers exhibited in this parable by our Saviour, the position of this third class has always seemed to me the most perilous and the most to be deplored. The first class is careless and indifferent, and therefore has the seed snatched away that was sown in the heart: but carelessness or indifference may be cured. The second class is offended because of the word, and with something like indignation casts it away: but then they understand precisely the position of defiance which they occupy. This third class, however, does not acknowledge indifference, nor consent to occupy the standpoint of defiance; but they suppose that the seed which has been sown in their heart is doing quite well, and will in good time bring forth its proper fruit. It is a case of dreadful self-deception, which is unconsciously sweeping its victims to inevitable yet unnoticed destruction. The seed sown in a heart of this class, has not been snatched away; neither has the plant which that seed produced withered away: but a constant, silent process of emasculation is going on upon a rooted plant and a growing blade, which does not destroy it, but only renders it unfruitful. The evil in the first two cases is seen at once, and may possibly be remedied: the evil in this last case is not discovered until we come to the harvest, and we find that the thorns have choked the good seed, and have prevented the grain from filling, and from producing fruit. Nothing worse is said of this seed than that it is "unfruitful."

The hearers included under this class are not those only by whom no profession of religion has been made, but comprise likewise that large body of Church communicants whose piety is endangered by the affairs of life and of the world. Many of those who worship regularly in the Church of God, who fulfill all the external duties of religion, who commune whenever the Lord's Supper is administered in their presence, come, at times, under its perilous enchantment, and need constant self-examination lest they permit themselves to be deluded by its snares. You must not suppose therefore, while I treat this subject, that my remarks are at all restricted to a class of hearers, who, immersed in business or care or pleasure, take no account except on Sundays of their soul's salvation; but you must understand them as referring to all, of whatever class or whatever condition, who permit the word of religious truth that is sown in their hearts to become unfruitful. And indeed those who have made some progress in religious things would seem to be more particularly intended in this portion of the parable; for the seed is represented as not only sown in the soil, but as actually growing, and in appearance doing well. The effect produced upon it by the thorns is not visible until the time of harvest comes, when the master has a right to look for the fruit; and then it is, and not until then, that it is found to be "unfruitful."

Christianity, my beloved hearers, is intended to prepare and fit us for the duties of life, at the same time that it reunites us to God, and makes us at peace with Him through Jesus Christ our Lord. Its sublime boast is that it is entirely practical; and that its great Teacher taught us, not merely by moral precepts but by His own living example, how we might at once serve God faithfully, and yet fulfill all our domestic and social obligations: thus developing the highest style of life for the human race. With this example and these instructions, Christians err when they would flee contact with their fellow-men, and hide their light under a bushel; — when they would bury themselves away from the uses and employments of their kind. Our Saviour Himself never retired from the society of men, except only for a little time that He might meditate and pray; and His command to His Apostles was to go into all the world, and preach the Gospel to every creature. In His prayer to His Father, in the seventeenth chapter of S. John's Gospel, when He was committing His beloved disciples, with all the earnestness of divine love, to His Father's care, we find Him using language which indicated plainly that He expected them to be in a state of intercourse with the world: for His words are: "And now I am no more in the world, but these are in the world, and I come to thee. Holy Father, keep through thine own name those whom thou hast given me, that they may be one, as we are. . . . . . . I pray not that thou shouldest take them out of the world, but that thou shouldest keep them from the evil."[1] He supposed therefore, that His people would be in danger from the evil of the world; and His supplication for them is, not that they should be taken away from contact with it, but that they should be preserved from the pollution of it, while moving in the midst of it. And this is the true position of all Christians, — a position which they cannot avoid without neglecting their duty; for the most sacred obligations of life force them into connection with it. How is a man to provide for his family, unless he mingle among men, and carry on, in con-

[1] S. John xvii. 11, 15.

tact with them, the business for which he has been trained? And yet the Apostle says: "But if any provide not for his own, and specially for those of his own house, he hath denied the faith, and is worse than an infidel."[1] How is a man to fulfill his relations to wife, to children, to servants, unless he guides them along the path of life, and leads them the way amid its intricacies? Nay, how is he to propagate the very Gospel itself, to spread among men the saving doctrines and blessed precepts of his Master, unless he meet his fellow-man face to face in the streets, in the haunts of business, around the fireside, as well as in the sanctuary of God? "This man receiveth sinners, and eateth with them,"[2] was the taunt which the Pharisees threw out against our Lord, because He mingled with men, and endeavored to win them from what was wrong by teaching them what was right. All this proves that each and every one of us must be placed in the midst of the evil of the world; must hear and receive the Word into soil that is more or less infested with thorns; must be placed in peril of having it choked and made unfruitful, when it has been planted for the express purpose of bringing forth fruit to the praise and glory of God. We cannot perform our Christian duties, and escape this trial. We must pass through this ordeal, if we would be faithful to man, as well as to God.

And the world, of which these thorns are the representative, is a terrible snare to all of us. At some weak point or other, it touches every one of us. If what are called the pleasures of the world and the lusts of the flesh have no temptation for us, then perchance it is the acquisition of riches, and their increase, which threaten to choke in us the good Word. If none of these prove our infirmity, then we are assailed in a subtler way; and the cares of life, aris-

[1] 1 Tim. v. 8.

[2] S. Luke xv. 2.

ing ofttimes out of its most sacred duties, are made to prey upon us. Any thing, — no matter how honest in its purpose, no matter how pure in its inception, no matter how necessary to the conduct of life, — may assume the shape of thorns, and help to choke the seed of grace. It cannot bring forth fruit where the heart is filled with the world, and forgetful of God. It grows, because it is in a soil that has been at one time prepared for it, and because it receives the nourishment of the sanctuary, and such culture as an absorbed heart can give it: but that is all. The food and the strength which it ought to receive from its roots are lacking, because the thorns have been permitted to absorb them all, and waste them in the service of the world.

Our Lord puts forward two things as most likely to interfere with the fruitfulness of Christians, — the "cares of this world," and the "deceitfulness of riches." To these He adds, "the lusts of other things," which will include all those affections and passions of the mind towards earthly things, which are not included under either of the other heads. Let me warn you against each of these in turn.

That which our Lord places before all other things, and which is of all thorns the most dangerous because the most common, is what He calls "the cares of this world;" and that, because every one is obliged to bear some portion of them. They are a heavy burden upon the spirits of men, and an equally heavy one upon their souls. Deceitful as riches are, — and they are fearfully deceitful, — these cares are still more deceitful and treacherous. They assume every form of duty and of obligation, at the same time that, unless strictly guarded, they are alike injurious to the growth of spirituality under whatever shape they may assail us, whether of business or of politics, whether of anxiety about public or private concerns, of restlessness over the affairs of the world, or the household. The father is careful and troubled, lest his family should come to want or to reproach; and the mother is equally troubled about her children, her house, and her servants. The poor man is burdened with the thought of how he shall provide what is necessary for those who are dependent upon him; and the rich man is equally burdened with the thought of how he shall preserve what he has already gained, and increase it. The obscure man is worried by the effort of bringing himself into notice and position; and the honored man by the effort of keeping himself at the point which he has attained. The parents are troubled about the education of their children, and their preparation for life, and their settlement in the world; and the children are looking forward with eagerness to the day when they shall begin the world for themselves. The master is anxious and careful about the conduct and industry of his servants; and the servant is equally anxious how he may please his master, and move forward in the world. The husband is careful how he may provide for his wife; and the wife is equally careful how she may please and satisfy her husband. And so the world rolls on, each one carrying his burden of real or imaginary care; and each one permitting it to weigh upon him to the injury not only of health, of cheerfulness, and of usefulness, but also of spirituality, more, far more, than is at all necessary. And each one excuses himself upon the plea of its necessity; and often contends that it is only the performance of duty: thus endeavoring to convince himself that those cares which are rapidly choking all his religion, are a part of religion itself. How many are kept unhappy all their days through this grievous weight of cares; and how many are wrecked by it, bodily, mentally, spiritually, because they will not proportion it to their necessity or their ability! If they would only learn to see God's hand in every thing which befalls them, God's mercy in every position in which He may place them; if they would only struggle after that which is necessary for comfort and for sustenance, instead of grasping at earthly honors, or greedily clutching at wealth; if they would roll their cares upon Him who has said, "I will never leave thee, nor forsake thee:" [1] how full of peace would that heart be which is now overwhelmed with anxiety, and in which the thorns are rapidly choking the seed of grace which may have been planted there!

The next point upon which our blessed Lord dwells as likely to choke the good seed of the Word, is "the deceitfulness of riches." The expression is a peculiar one. It is not riches, but *the deceitfulness* of riches; — as if there was a quality in the thing which was peculiarly dangerous. And so there is; and it is just this quality of deceitfulness. Riches are deceitful, in that they tempt us to depend upon ourselves, and not to look to God for our daily blessings. They are deceitful, in that they lead us on to indulge in the pride of life, and in the lusts of the flesh. They are deceitful, in that they imperiously require us to devote the most of our time to their preservation and increase. They are deceitful, in that they promise us much good, and give us no adequate return. They are deceitful, in that they hold out the appearance of great blessing to our children, when they bring forth for them, very often, nothing but misery and ruin. They are deceitful, in that they take to themselves wings and flee away, just when all our habits and tastes and pleasures had been made to turn upon them. And their deceitfulness is their danger. In themselves, they are no more a bar to the Kingdom of Heaven than any thing else. A rich man may so use what God has given him, as to lay up for himself treasures in heaven. But the peril lies in

[1] Heb. xiii. 5.

the quality which is singled out in our text. It is *because* we find it so hard to place riches in their true relation to God, and our own souls; to gauge them at their proper value; to use them so as not to entangle ourselves in ruinous pleasures or in overwhelming anxieties; to cause them to procure, for those we love, the blessings which they can command, and yet not involve them in the idleness and the ruin which the early possession of them too often induces: it is because of all this that the Scriptures dwell very frequently upon them as a great impediment in the way of reaching heaven. But while they are an impediment; while they constitute one of the most insidious snares of the human soul: their deceitfulness may be so clearly perceived and appreciated as to render them innocuous. But this is all that can be said in their favor. If riches are at all overvalued; if they are eagerly sought after; if we make haste to get them; if they are anxiously increased; if they are hoarded, so that their rust eats into them, and their meanness into the heart and the soul: they immediately put forth all their power of deceitfulness, and choke all grace and all goodness in the heart. They are thorns, which inevitably make a profession unfruitful. And yet, how eagerly are they pursued, even by those who understand all this! The temptation which pleasure is to the young, riches and the pursuit of riches are apt to be to the more advanced in life.

Whatever ardent desires or affections of the heart may not be included under the cares of the world and the deceitfulness of riches, our text sums up under the words "the lusts of other things," — of other things than the grace of God and the culture of the soul. Any thing which fills the mind, and keeps it from thinking of God and Eternity; any thing which interests the heart, so that it is made an idol of; any thing which inflames the affections and the passions, so that they cannot be restrained within the bounds of sobriety and of prudence: are all thorns which choke the Word of the Kingdom, and make it unfruitful. Clothed in a nature weak and corrupt, surrounded by objects of interest and desire, in a world whose very duties are full of care and of anxiety, we meet these things at every turn: and our only safety is, to grapple with them, and conquer them in the Name of Jesus Christ our Saviour. Run away from them we cannot; evade them we cannot, without sinning in some other direction; overcome them we cannot, in any strength of our own. If we are to be conquerors, it can be only through His power, who has taught us how to live, regardless of the world; how to die, triumphing over it.

These are the thorns which choke our religion, and which make the people of God unfruitful, when they should be glorifying God in their souls and in their bodies which are His. And when we see, not only the careless of our congregations, but even the professing part of them, so anxious about the things of the world; so troubled about gain and profit; so greedy to add house to house, and field to field; so deluded by the deceitfulness of riches; so tossed hither and thither by affection and desire: can we be surprised that so little fruit is brought forth for the Church, and in the Church? Ought we to be surprised that there is so little faith in the promises of God; so little joy in the prospect of the future; so little peace in believing; so little charity in the heart and life? Can it amaze us that so little is done for the propagation of the Gospel,—for the advancement of the Church? Nay, should it not rather fill us with wonder that religion and the Church exist at all? "The fruit of the Spirit," that which is to come out of this seed of grace which the thorns are choking, "is love, joy, peace, long-suffering, gentleness, goodness, faith, meekness, temperance,"[1] but how can they be expected to come to perfection, when all the influences which should be exerted for their production are expended upon things which are adverse to their production, and which are killing them out as fast as they push their blades into the light of day? Christianity, and the Church as the embodiment of Christianity, have the means of culture and the influences which can mature the fruit, — such as the dew of the Spirit, and the gracious rain from heaven; the early and the latter rain; and the sunshine of Christ's presence: but the plant will not flourish where the soil is overgrown with thorns. A fountain cannot give forth, at the same time, sweet and bitter waters; neither can the same heart be overgrown with thorns, and bring fruit unto perfection; be absorbed in pleasure and business and the acquirement of riches or even the essential cares of life, and bring to any perfection the graces of the Gospel. "No man can serve two masters."[2]

You perceive, then, how fruitless hearing is, unless the heart is not only prepared for it, but kept in a condition of order and of culture. Relaxation is necessary for the body and the mind; business is necessary for the support of our families, and for the comfort of our homes; care always rides behind us, wherever we may go; anxiety is as certain to cleave to us, as the sparks fly upwards: but there is no necessity that any of these things should take entire possession of us. All these occupations and pursuits will be helped and relieved by the presence and the exercise of religion in the heart. A merciful God knows our weaknesses, and our inevitable tendency to absorption in whatever we have to do; and He has so arranged the means of grace as to help us to overcome this tendency, and to mingle our Christianity with the necessary duties of life in

[1] Gal. v. 22, 23. [2] S. Matthew vi. 24.

such measure as will enable us to keep down the thorns. He does not expect us to root them out entirely; that is beyond our power: but He does require of us that we should keep them from choking off our religion, and making us altogether fruitless. One simple rule has our Saviour given us: "He that abideth in me, and I in him, the same bringeth forth much fruit."[1] And there is no other rule. Out of Christ the struggle is vain: the thorns will be too much for you; pleasure will entangle you; business will enwrap you; riches will deceive you; the cares of the world will overwhelm and destroy you!

1866.

[1] S. John xv. 5.

Twenty-third Sermon.

O house of Jacob, come ye, and let us walk in the light of the LORD. — ISAIAH ii. 5.

IN the graphic account which the Bible gives us of Creation, — that account which, although brief, is comprehensive and distinct, — the production of Light is the first outward act of the Divine power. In the beginning, ages ago,—as long ago as man and Nature choose to place it, for no distance of time can carry it beyond the existence of God, — the heavens and the earth were created. The material earth was there; but it was without form and void. The great deep was there ; but darkness was upon its face. And there they lay, from the beginning, fermenting, seething, rolling in space, undergoing such changes as their Creator chose to work upon them, until such time as He was ready to prepare them for the habitations of men. Then began the movements of those Divine Persons, whose acts have illustrated our world, and whose glory is to fill forever the universe of God. The Spirit moved upon the face of the waters, — the Spirit of life, — and impregnated it with the germs of being which were afterwards to burst forth for the use and comfort and blessing of His creatures. And when that divine Spirit had brooded long enough to impregnate the seeds of things, then went forth the sublime command, "Let there be Light : and there was Light."[1] Its existence was the prime necessity. Every thing depended upon it; and therefore it must precede every thing. Life sprang up

[1] Gen. i. 3.

beneath its genial touch, — the life of plant and leaf and flower. Life, in every existing being, depended upon it; for when they leave it, they enter the realms of death, and the darkness of the grave. Beauty came forth of it: for without light there is no color; and without color, one dull, gray, leaden hue would enwrap every thing, and swallow up all that rich variety of heavenly dies and earthly shadows which makes our world so charming, even under the withering touch of the curse. Happiness and joy flashed on creation together with its brightness; for what would life be without light? What would be the pleasure of existence, if we were doomed to grope about forever in darkness? No vision to guide us in safety, or preserve us from destruction; no change to gratify the sight, or give variety to life; nothing to satisfy the cravings of the affections; no place for friendship, or for love; no human face divine to look upon, and drink in the thoughts and feelings of the soul! — one despairing sense of hopeless, remediless darkness would swallow every thing, — even hope! The wail would go up alike from Nature and from man; from field and forest, from cave and den; from the heavens above, and the earth beneath, and the waters under the earth: "Roll darkness from us, O Thou who gavest us our being, and restore to us Thy Light!"

And is there no such thing, my beloved hearers, as spiritual darkness? Is a creation, which would send up to its God such an universal cry of anguish at being doomed to unceasing natural darkness, content to abide forever in a condition of corruption and moral disorder which the inspired Word of its Creator designates as "gross darkness"? Have you ever noticed the wonderful analogy which there is, even in language, between that first chapter in Genesis which describes to us the creation of natural light, and the first chapter of S. John's Gospel which gives us what may be called the philosophical presentation of our Saviour to the world as its spiritual Light? Like the chapter in Genesis, it carries us back to those ages of the past which the geologist is always demanding, and which the infidel declares to be necessary for the harmony of things; and is opened with a like solemnity: "In the beginning was the Word, and the Word was with God, and the Word was God. . . . . In him was life; and the life was the light of men. And the light shineth in darkness; and the darkness comprehended it not."[1] It is literally the second Creation. Every thing, save the rough material, was wanting in the moral world, as it had been wanting in the natural. The rude elements were in man, as in the old world of nature; and like them, seething, fermenting, undergoing all manner of hideous change: but there was no spiritual life, no moral beauty, no heavenly joy; for darkness covered the earth, "and gross darkness the people."[2] They groped in the noon day as in the night; they groped for the wall like the blind, and they groped as if they had no eyes; they stumbled at noon day as in the night; they were "in desolate places as dead men."[3] Such is the gloomy description which the sacred writers give of the condition of the world when Christ our Lord arose upon it and said: "I am the light of the world."[4] And the assertion of it was not confined to their prophetic denunciations. The philosophy of the Old World confessed that there was no life in the darkness which enshrouded them; that death ended every thing; that the grave was a pit wherein was no water. And there was no moral beauty in such a world; no beauty arising out of the highest sources of spiritual harmony, — out of purity, out of faith, out of charity, out of holiness: — the dyes of heaven intermingling with the shadows

[1] S. John i. 1, 4, 5.
[2] Isaiah lx. 2.
[3] Isaiah lix. 10.
[4] S. John ix. 5.

of earth! And there could be no true joy; for joy cannot exist without hope, and a future, and an expanding glory spreading away in the visions of promise and of covenant. And that old Pagan world was sensible of it. The earth groaned under the curse of God: "For we know," says S. Paul, "that the whole creation groaneth and travaileth in pain together until now."[1] Nature acknowledges it to-day, — even although Light has beamed upon the world, and is waging fierce battle with darkness, — in the wild fury of her elemental strife, and in the mad rage with which she tears to pieces, and swallows up, and tramples in her fury, the creatures who undertake to harness and control her. She buries navies in the depths of the Ocean; she engulphs cities in her womb of fire; she sweeps away multitudes, as she passes along with her pestilential breath; she disgorges from her bowels the materials out of which man forges the instruments of cruelty. She manifests her misery by her rage; and echoes back to man the truths which he tries not to believe because they come from the inspiration of God: "Cursed is the earth for *thy* sake; — thy sake, because of thy sin! *Thou* hast blotted out the light! *Thou* hast brought darkness once more over the earth." And man, too, in his wild restlessness, acknowledges that Nature has just cause for her madness. His own misery satisfies him of her's, and he too gnashes his teeth against the darkness in which he is enveloped; and, — while he springs upon his brother with the fury of a wild beast, calling evil good, and good evil, deluging the earth with his blood from the days of Cain until now, — he hurls defiance into the face of his Creator, loving "darkness rather than light." But thanks be to God, in spite of all this, Light has come into the world, — moral light, spiritual light, the light of the Lord, — and is growing fast

[1] Rom. viii. 22.

in brightness, and bringing into its focus, for exposure and final destruction, all the hidden things of darkness. The Creator has said a second time, "Let there be light:" and the primal source of life, of beauty, and of joy in the spiritual world, has relumed the old Creation!

And as with light in the natural world, so is it with light in the moral and spiritual world. We cannot do without it. It is a necessity. It is the ornament of man. It is the joy of the world, and its glory! It is a necessity, because we have a rugged, tangled path to tread in life, and we must have light upon it, or we perish; because we are laborers in God's vineyard, and we must have light to do our work aright; because we are preparing for another state of being, and we must have light to exhibit for us the conditions of that being, and the mode by which we are to fit ourselves for it. It is the ornament of man, because it shines in upon our unsatisfied natures, and changes and purifies them, and then fructifies the germs which have been implanted in the heart and conscience by the Holy Spirit, when He brooded over them even while they lay in darkness; because it changes us from grace to grace, causing all the faculties and capacities of our being, which were dead in trespasses and sins, to reflect (as points in nature — the leaf, the dew-drop, the grain of sand — do the sun's rays) the radiance of righteousness, and illumine all around us with the new life of the Spirit. It is the joy and glory of the world; for it opens to man's vision a glorious futurity, when he shall enter upon a higher state of undying existence, in which he is to be a partaker of the Divine Nature, and to grow eternally into the likeness of Him who is the express image of His Father. Spiritual light unfolds to us a new world: a new world outside of us, causing us to look upon Nature and the world with unsealed eyes, finding in them a beauty which was never seen before; a new world within us, wherein the sated or crushed affections may revive and flourish in a higher life, soaring upward and upward until they fold their new-found wings at the Throne of the Eternal. And yet man prefers darkness to all this heavenly light; would rather grovel on the earth, and creep, in darkness, amid the beggarly elements of an effete and worn-out world, the companion of impurity, and sin, and crime! Well might that beloved disciple, who felt in the depths of his own loving heart the joy and the glory of the Light of the Lord, utter, as if lost in amazement, "And the light shineth in darkness; and the darkness comprehended it not."

It is to this spiritual light, this light brought into the world by Christ and now shining in His Word and in His Church, that you, my hearers, are invited to come. "O house of Jacob, come ye, and let us walk in the light of the LORD." How loving and sweet this offer of fellowship! "Let us walk," is the language which the prophet places in the mouth of the Gentiles, who have flocked in to the mountain of the Lord, and to the house of the God of Jacob, to learn His ways, and to walk in His paths. Jacob had been invoking them for long ages; and now they are invoking him. So full of comfort and joy and glory have they found this light of the Lord which has arisen upon them, the Gentiles, that in the exuberance of their new-found happiness they are reflecting it back upon Jacob. How amazing, that even before the Sun of Righteousness had arisen upon the world, while as yet His coming rays were only tinging the east with the early dawn, God should have permitted His chosen heralds of salvation to catch the glory of its hidden fires, and to flash them in prophetic brightness into the besotted eyes of a wicked world! And yet we, now that yon Sun has fully risen and is manifesting His glory all around us, are hiding from it and fleeing the light, like owls and bats, — fearing lest it may make our sins too manifest; preferring darkness rather than light. Beware, my hearers, of that solemn warning of the Apostle: "But if our gospel be hid, it is hid to them that are lost: in whom the god of this world hath blinded the eyes of them which believe not, lest the light of the glorious gospel of Christ, who is the image of God, should shine unto them."[1]

We belong to that Gentile Church, which Isaiah thus saw in vision praying fellowship with the house of Jacob, and inviting them to walk hand in hand in the light of the Lord. How beautiful the picture — the old enmity between Jew and Gentile done away in Christ, melted before the fervent rays of the Sun of Righteousness, their swords beaten into ploughshares and their spears into pruning hooks, and they going up together to the house of the Lord! May that blessed vision soon be fulfilled, when all nations shall flow up to Mount Zion, and the Mountain of the Lord's house shall be established in the top of the mountains, and shall be exalted above the hills: —

> "Hail, glorious day, expected long,
>   When Jew and Greek one prayer shall pour;
> With eager feet one temple throng,
>   With grateful praise one God adore!"

Until then, may we, who call ourselves Christians, have fellowship one with another, and call upon each other to walk hand in hand in the light of the Lord!

Can any thing be more exquisite than this conception of a band of pilgrims walking together in the light of the Lord? Darkness all around, — gross darkness enveloping the world: but one stream of light, flowing from the Cross of Jesus; and they, clinging together in that Light, lest they should be tempted out of it by the powers of darkness!

[1] 2 Cor. iv. 3, 4.

And yet it is true to the very letter. That is our condition; and this close gathering together in the stream of light which flows from Christ, should be our attitude. Because we are in the light, let us not suppose that we can never any more be merged in darkness. Our Saviour was *the Light* Himself: and yet was He tempted in the wilderness, in the garden, on the Cross. He was tempted in all things like as we are, save without sin. And if Satan dared to undertake the task of putting out the Light itself, think ye that he will permit any of us, who are only walking in that light, to escape his wiles and sophistries? In the Gospel for the Day[1] ye have heard read from the Holy Scriptures the whole story of that daring act of the great Tempter, how he struck at every human weakness: at the infirmities of the body; at the pride of the heart; at the aspiring ambition of the earthly spirit. And in the same way will he probe the weaknesses of every one of us, taking them in turn, if so be that he may plunge us once again into dárkness. Darkness! that is the state he glories in. He is the prince of darkness, even as Christ is the Light. They are enemies for time and for Eternity. The one, struggling to envelop the world once more in that gross darkness which enshrouded it when he reigned triumphant over the kingdoms of this world, when every faculty and instrument of man was under his undisputed control: the other, forcing the pure, bright beams of His own divine Light into the dark places of man's habitation, through His Word, through His messengers, through His Church, through the example of those who call themselves the children of Light. Every one of us is engaged in this conflict; is on the side either of light or of darkness; is helping Satan, or working with the Lord of Light; is enlarging the confines of knowledge, of truth and of glory, or is

[1] The First Sunday in Lent.

drawing the curtains of night closer around the world. It is fearful to dwell upon our responsibility: for it extends, beyond ourselves, to children and children's children, along the stretch of time, until it mingles with Eternity.

The exhortation of my text is, "Come ye, and let us walk in the light of the LORD:" and the Church echoes this message at all times; but especially now when she is approaching, nay, is already in the midst of, that exhibition of the power of Satan, of which Christ said: "This is your hour, and the power of darkness;"[1] and which culminated in the Sacrifice upon the Cross. You are now called to especial prayer and watchfulness; to a closer study of the Word of God; to a deeper examination of your hearts and lives; to a renewed exercise of repentance, and faith, and charity. You are invited to walk in the light of the Lord, — in fellowship with his people; in the communion of Saints; in the joy of God; and in the blessed hope of everlasting life. And unless we obey that invitation, we are despising the teachings of our Holy Mother; and we are exposing ourselves on every hand to the encroachments of that enemy who often presents himself as an angel of light, and whispers sin into our ears so plausibly, so seducingly, that we are led away captive, with our eyes blinded that we cannot see, and our hearts hardened that we cannot understand. "Then Jesus said unto them, Yet a little while is the light with you. Walk while ye have the light, lest darkness come upon you: for he that walketh in darkness knoweth not whither he goeth. While ye have light, believe in the light, that ye may be the children of light."[2]

And especially, my beloved hearers, is there great danger, in these days, of mistaking the path of Light. Many are kindling fires of their own, and calling them the Light of the Lord. New doctrines are being hatched all the world

[1] S. Luke xxii. 53. [2] S. John xii. 35, 36.

over, — doctrines of devils; and they thrust themselves across the pathway of the children of Light. Be watchful, and strengthen the things that remain. Hold together, children of Light, and walk hand in hand in the light of the Lord. Edify and strengthen one another. Be valiant for the Truth. "Warn them that are unruly, comfort the feeble-minded, support the weak, be patient toward all men. See that none render evil for evil unto any man; but ever follow that which is good, both among yourselves, and to all men. . . . Pray without ceasing. . . . Quench not the Spirit. . . . Prove all things; hold fast that which is good. Abstain from all appearance of evil."[1] The Word of God and the Church of God, — the two great instruments which reflect the Light of Christ, — are being assaulted on every hand. Cling to them only the more closely, for they are your impregnable strongholds in the day of temptation. Even our Lord himself, when tempted, answered Satan with the word of truth: "It is written;" "It is written;" "It is written." Although the Wisdom of God and the Light of the world, He drew not upon His own Divine Mind to answer Satan, but used only that weapon which is ready at the hand of his poorest and weakest disciple. Bring every thing "to the law and to the testimony: if they speak not according to this word, it is because there is no light in them."[2] And the Church, with her Creed and her formularies and her teaching, is but a concentration of that Light which flows from Christ, kept as a treasury for her children. Keep ever before you the denunciation of the prophet: "Behold, all ye that kindle a fire, that compass yourselves about with sparks: walk in the light of your fire, and in the sparks that ye have kindled. This shall ye have of mine hand; ye shall lie down in sorrow."[3]

The end and purpose of all our Christian knowledge and

[1] 1 Thess. v. 14, 15, 17, 19, 21, 22. [2] Isaiah viii. 20. [3] *Ibid.* l. 11.

exercise is, that we should reflect the Light of the Lord. I close with the words of an Archbishop of Canterbury, one of the holiest prelates that ever sat in that chair: "As the darkest body, when brought near a shining flame, derives a brightness from it; so must it be with those who profess to have been brought nigh to God through the Gospel of His Son. 'If we say that we have fellowship with him, and walk in darkness, we lie, and do not the truth.'[1] As He is Light, so all who are united to Him must be Light. He calls them to be partakers of His own holy Nature; 'and every man that hath this hope in him purifieth himself, even as He is pure.'[2] This is the proof that our hearts are drawn to Him, and united with Him, that we 'cast off the works of darkness,'[3] and walk in the light as 'children of the day,'[4] whose deeds will bear to be exposed; nay, which shine before men, and attract others to the Light to which they owe their brightness. Then are we indeed part of that family which God has created for Himself, through Jesus Christ: 'We have fellowship one with another;'[5] we are joined together as brethren who have 'one Lord, one faith, one baptism;'[6] and 'the blood of Jesus Christ His Son cleanseth us from all sin.'"[7]

1866.

[1] 1 S. John i. 6. [2] *Ibid.* iii. 3. [3] Rom. xiii. 12.
[4] 1 Thess. v. 5. [5] 1 S. John i. 7. [6] Eph. iv. 5.
[7] 1 S. John i. 7.

Twenty-fourth Sermon.

To what purpose is the multitude of your sacrifices unto me? saith the LORD. — ISAIAH i. 11.

THIS question seems a strange one to be asked of the people of Israel by their Lord and King, when we remember the very stringent command and the very minute instructions which that people had received for the offering of almost numberless sacrifices, and when we look forward to the divine Saviour, whom those sacrifices foreshadowed and typified. It appears at first sight casting contempt, as it were, upon their obedience; to be very inconsistent with all that had gone before; nay almost contradictory of the institutions which Jehovah had Himself established. To arrange a worship upon this very basis of sacrifices, and then to ask "To what purpose is the multitude of your sacrifices unto me?" was, to say the least, a very startling proposition, and one calling upon the Israelites to pause and inquire into the purpose and meaning of its enunciation. And this was just the effect which God designed to produce by means of His prophets. The prophetical office was altogether distinct from the priestly. The latter, the priests, were set apart from a particular family to carry on the regular and ordinary routine of the divine arrangements: to offer sacrifices; to mediate between God and His chosen people; to offer atonement for public and private sins. The prophets, on the other hand, were not necessarily priests; but were raised up by God, in an irregular manner, to speak for Him to the people, and startle them from that formalism into which all regular worship is very apt to fall. The former were the unceasing line in which the service of God descended from father to son: the latter were special messengers sent by God to stir up priests as well as people to a clear comprehension of the spirit of the work which they were, too often, smothering under the letter of their performances. The one was necessary for the preservation and due performance of the rites and ceremonies which were to be fulfilled in Christ: the other just as indispensable to bring back the minds of all parties to the gracious purpose which gave to those institutions their true and only meaning.

It is from this point of view that we must look at the words of my text in order to understand them. They were uttered by the Lord through the mouth of one of these special messengers, the prophet Isaiah, and were therefore intended to bring the careless Israelites back to a proper sense of their duty. While fulfilling to the letter the commandments of God; while offering all the sacrifices and bringing all the oblations; while filling the Temple with incense, and keeping the new moons and appointed feasts: the tenor of the chapter proves that the Israelites were utterly forgetful of the spirit which was intended to sanctify these devotions, and were carrying to the Temple unholy hearts, and were lifting up unclean hands to Jehovah. And it was because of these misconceptions of His purposes and will that their gracious Lord asked them the question from which I preach: "To what purpose is the multitude of your sacrifices unto me, saith the Lord?" Of what avail is all this literal fulfillment of my commandments to either of us, to you, or to Me, if you overlook, so entirely as you do, the final cause of their institution? Can you not perceive that the sacrifice of bulls and of goats can be of no benefit to Me, whose are all the beasts of the field and the cattle upon a thousand hills, if you separate that sacrifice from the holiness which it was intended to produce and maintain? What care I for oblations; for incense; for new moons; for appointed seasons: unless they are accompanied by the spiritual results, with which I intended that they should always stand connected? And of what possible benefit can they be to you, unless they lead you to those exercises of repentance, of faith, of holiness, which they were established to produce? Away with them, if they are to be mere forms! Unless the heart is disciplined by them, they are the merest husks, furnishing you no spiritual food, yielding Me no acceptable worship.

In all this, you will perceive, there is no contradiction; the contempt of God is not directed against His appointments, but against their misuse of them. Sacrifices, oblations, incense, the appointed feasts, were full of their original value, when offered aright, and understood aright: still propitiated God; still atoned for sin; still kept wrath from bursting out upon them from between the cherubim; still pointed to a coming Saviour. But all this was made valueless by themselves. They used them punctually as forms, but did not permit them to exert the slightest influence upon their conduct. They went to the performance of them superstitiously, as a task which God had set, expecting no spiritual benefit from them, and therefore receiving none. They were consequently of but little use; and no wonder, therefore, that Jehovah said, though He had instituted them Himself: "Bring no more vain oblations; incense is an abomination unto me; the new moons and Sabbaths, the calling of assemblies, I cannot away with; it is iniquity, even the solemn meeting."[1]

And just as it was between Jehovah and His elect people, shall it be between the Lord and ourselves, unless we are

[1] Isaiah i. 13.

careful in all our worship to preserve the spiritual meaning which it is intended to convey. All regular devotion has a tendency to run into formalism: and by formalism I mean a system which quiets the conscience by the performance of certain religious acts, without any reference to the spiritual meaning of them; just as a child, to still its nightly fears, might hurry over by rote its little prayer. And it would surprise all of us, could we be made aware how much of our worship, both private and public, does run into this very formalism, — this "vain repetition,"[1] as our Saviour called it, of prayers without any spiritual exercise accompanying them. We need no better proof of this than the little result which flows from prayer. We are told in the Holy Scriptures, that God is a hearer of prayer; that He will grant any thing which is asked, in His Son's Name, according to His will. And yet, where is the answer to prayer? We are all of us asking: who is receiving? Surely God cannot deceive us. The fault is with us; and lies in just this substitution of formal, customary prayer, for that earnest, spiritual wrestling with God, which is prayer in His view. Examine yourselves, my hearers, upon this point; consider your mode of prayer; your preparation for prayer; your faith in prayer; your expectations of a return of prayer. Judge yourselves honestly, as in the sight of God, and determine how much of it is the mere hurrying over of a form, so as to quiet conscience and feel that you have knelt in prayer; and how much is real communion with God, to which you go with pleasure, and from which you return laden with a blessing of the dew of Heaven.

And as it is with private prayer, so is it likewise with all religious exercises of whatever kind. Their tendency is to formalism; and the duty of your ministers is, like the office

[1] S. Matt. vi. 7.

of the prophets of old, to rouse you up perpetually to a consideration of the spiritual meaning which is enshrined in all our ritual usages. They are valueless, unless they are looked through, and God is seen as their life and purpose. This very season which we are now celebrating, and which calls upon us for unusual solemnity, can be of no service to any one who keeps it as a mere form: who is satisfied by an attendance upon frequent services. God might well ask of such an one: "To what purpose is the multitude of your services unto me? Do I need your prayers or your praise, when there are myriads of unfallen and glorious spirits who offer it up to Me perpetually from hearts overflowing with gratitude and from lips sanctified by My Holy Spirit?" Its object is to deepen our repentance, to enliven our faith, to stir up all our graces, to call us to the exercise of self-denial, of humility, of holiness. Unless these are the results of it, it is nothing but form: it is only the utterance of an increased number of prayers for which, when we come to reckon up the result, we shall find no return at all.

Twelve days have already elapsed of the period set apart for the observance of our holy solemnity; and can you perceive that you have received any special benefit from it? You have kept it, and perhaps kept it faithfully; but are you conscious of any spiritual improvement? Has your heart been in the work? Has Christ been made the end of it, and your life in Christ its fruit? Lent is not commanded that a certain amount of prayer may be offered to God, nor that a fixed amount of bodily exercise may be passed through; but that your religious life may be solemnized. It is a wonderful provision of the means of grace, that while God delights in the prayers and the praises of His people, He has so arranged those exercises that they are never acceptable unto Him unless they work spiritual benefit to those who offer them. And thus He unites our duty and His blessing together, and fills us with grace at the same time that He receives our humble offerings.

There are three blessings connected with Lent which we ought to experience, and which at this period of the season we should ascertain whether we have begun to experience. The first is, its influence upon the general spirit of our character; upon the tone of our feelings as Christians; upon the atmosphere which surrounds our presence and deportment. This is independent of its effect upon any personal trait of character. The one is like the general sunshine which spreads itself over a whole landscape, giving warmth and geniality to the entire scene: the other like the rays shining upon a particular point of it, and maturing the fruit which is ripening for the Master's use. Each has its separate purpose and its separate glory. The first is intended to diffuse itself over society, and to impart to it a softness and a charity which are the true manifestations of Christianity: the last, to concentrate itself upon ourselves, and to make us more meet for that presence of the Lord, when He shall come as our Master, and call us home to His heart and His service.

A long and continued season of devotional exercises ought to manifest itself in our whole temper and presence. When Moses came down from Mount Sinai, after his long conference with God, his face shone so that he was obliged to cast a veil over it while he conversed with Aaron and the people. When our Lord was transfigured upon the Mount, His face did shine as the sun, and His raiment was white as the light. And the Apostle tells us that "we all, with open face beholding as in a glass the glory of the Lord, are changed into the same image from glory to glory, even as by the Spirit of the Lord."[1] These are the effects of com-

[1] 2 Cor. iii. 18.

munion with God, of dwelling in His presence in spirit and in truth. We cannot be long in the presence of a fellow-creature distinguished for virtue and nobleness, without catching something of the tone which belongs to him: how can it then be possible for us to commune daily and habitually with God in Christ, without drinking in some of the holy influences which flow down from His gracious presence? If we have sincerely communed with Him in prayer; if our spirits have indeed risen up to Him upon the wings of praise and adoration; if we have truly sought unto Him in our silent hours of meditation and thought: we must have brought away from these conferences and this intercourse something of the divine influence; there must breathe around us some of the spiritual atmosphere which envelops His divine Presence. Neither we ourselves, nor others, could exactly say what it consisted in, or wherein it was particularly exhibited: and yet both might perceive and acknowledge it; — a more cheerful spirit; a more loving temper; a diviner charity; a more manifest holiness. Nothing in the individual has changed: the manner is the same; the face is the same; the voice is the same; just as all the features of the landscape are the same. But the sunshine is upon the one, tinging every point with beauty and holiness: is upon the other, giving a softness and a gentleness to every part of the human frame.

This is the first blessing of frequent religious exercise; and I would ask you, my fellow-Christians, whether the season of Lent, so far as it has gone, has produced any of this effect upon you? Are you conscious of having received any general spiritual benefit from your frequent religious exercises? Is there with you a deeper glow of spiritual life? Has your heart been sensibly softened towards man, and elevated towards God? Has there come over you any of that genial glow, which makes your face to shine with the light from Heaven? Has there been awakened within you any higher aspiration towards holiness? Have those about you perceived that you have been dwelling with Jesus, and basking in the sunshine of His Spirit? These are the results of a general kind which ought to flow from a continued dwelling in the Sanctuary, from the reaction of daily prayer and meditation. As one has beautifully said that memory was the echo of perception, so ought holiness to be the echo of prayer and thanksgiving. To give ourselves to devotion, and to exhibit no results as the fruit of it, is the very condition in which might be asked of you the question of my text: "To what purpose is the multitude of your sacrifices unto me, saith the Lord?"

The effect of Lent upon our individual sins and infirmities is the second blessing which we should expect to derive from its faithful observance. Every one of us has some besetting sin: some weakness, some frailty, some dark cloud that hangs over our spiritual life; something that can come forth, perhaps, by nothing but by fasting and prayer. Are we endeavoring to bring this under the influence of the season? Besides the general blessing of which we spoke just now, are we striving to get this particular trouble under our control? It is the fly in the ointment, which is disfiguring its beauty and marring its sweetness; it is the discord in the harmony, which puts every thing out of tune. Our spiritual being is made imperfect by it; and our influence as Christians among men is marred by it. It is some infirmity of temper; some insubordination of tongue; some out-cropping of lust or covetousness; some love of the world and its applause; some affliction to which we cannot be reconciled; some enmity, or jealousy, or injury; some burden of unbelief. It can take a thousand shapes, and molest us under numberless disguises. It is at special sins like these, — sins of which we are convinced, and over which we mourn, — that we should particularly strike, at this season. We should make their subjugation, if not their extinction, an especial object. We should strike such blows at them as they could not well recover from, even though we did not quite extinguish them. What a glorious result it would be of our efforts, if at the close of this Lent we could feel that we had subdued some tyrant sin, some overpowering infirmity, which had been disturbing us all through our Christian life! And thus should we be reaping the true blessing of the occasion, so far as we are personally concerned, — the deliverance of our souls from that thralldom which sin ever inflicts, and the introduction of them into that true liberty wherewith Christ alone can make us free.

Have we, my Christian friends, been combating sin after this fashion, for so much of Lent as we have already passed through? Have we truly discerned our besetting sin, and are we warring against it with heart and soul? Or have we been beating the air uncertainly? Have we been going through our increased services without a purpose? If, so far, you have been looking only to general ends, let me advise you, for the remainder of this solemn season, to keep some special end in view; to have some particular private matter as that upon which your supplications and intercessions should be bent. Besides the general blessing which will flow upon you from the faithful observance of this season, strive to secure some individual favor from God; and then will you understand the value of such an arrangement as the Church has made for you at this season.

There is yet another blessing which you should endeavor to secure through the fasting and prayer of Lent, and that is, the favor of God upon His Church in general, and especially upon the particular congregation to which you belong. The Church has just passed safely through a great trial and has come out of it, as we trust, purified and sanctified. The Law of Charity has been triumphant, and we give thanks and praise that the Spirit of God hath made it so. Let us pray that this greatest of all graces may pervade her courts more thoroughly, and may enter into our hearts, leading us to fulfill that new commandment which Christ left to His Disciples, that they should "love one another." Let us pray that all Christians may be so joined together in unity of spirit and in the bond of peace, that they may be an holy temple, acceptable unto God. And especially let us supplicate Him to give to this congregation here present the abundance of His grace, that with one heart they may desire the prosperity of His Holy Apostolic Church, and with one mouth may profess the faith once delivered to the Saints. The day is fast coming when we shall celebrate the resurrection of our Lord; and upon that day there will be offered, to many in this congregation, the opportunity, through the laying on of hands, of rising from the death of sin unto the life of righteousness. Let us pray that many may embrace it; and that they may come as doves to their windows, bringing to God that sacrifice which He loves above all things, — a broken and a contrite heart. Of such sacrifices He will never ask the question of my text; but will rejoice over them with that joy which fills Heaven when one sinner comes, with true repentance, and casts himself for mercy at the foot of the Cross! Such fruit as this will be the surest proof that we have kept Lent well, and will be the sweetest incense that can enter into the presence of the Lord of Hosts.

1866.

Twenty-fifth Sermon.

Talk no more so exceeding proudly; let not arrogancy come out of your mouth: for the Lord is a God of knowledge, and by him actions are weighed. — 1 SAMUEL ii. 3.

IT is neither an easy, nor yet a safe thing, to read the judgments of God upon individuals, let alone upon nations. The more complicated the subject upon whom the judgment is inflicted, — the more the relations and contingencies of which it admits: the more difficult is it to determine, in many cases, the connection between it and the dealings of God. But, nevertheless, there are such judgments; and there are many, many instances, in which the connection between the sin of the people and the avenging hand of the Lord is so plain, that it strikes at once upon the moral sense of the land, and forces from every tongue the acknowledgment of that connection. So far as the moral feeling of the country has yet been borne to us, in view of the successive strokes with which we have been visited, it is wonderfully unanimous in its confession of the hand of the Lord, and wonderfully harmonious in the cause to which it ascribes these visitations. All, with one accord, lay it at the door of our exceeding pride and arrogancy; and therefore we utter to you, to-day, the words of the Scripture, words spoken in view of the majesty and supremacy of God: "Talk no more so exceeding proudly; let not arrogancy come out of your mouth: for the Lord is a God of knowledge, and by him actions are weighed."

This is the great lesson which we need to learn, — to learn, not as a mere thing of the head, but to learn so as to believe it, and feel it sensibly affecting our lives, — "that the Lord is a God of knowledge, and by him actions are weighed." As individuals we do not realize it enough, but, as a Nation, we do not recognize it at all. Because we could not adopt a State Religion, it almost seems as if we considered ourselves as a Nation without any religion at all! And as the necessary result of our not acknowledging God in Christ as a people, we have come to think that God will not — nay, has no right to — interfere in our concerns, either in the way of mercies or judgments. This view, strange as it may sound, is much more nearly the truth than one would imagine who has not weighed it well; more nearly the truth, because it is merely adopting and diffusing throughout the mass — making that general which before was individual — the common opinion of irreligious men, that because they have not bound themselves to God, in His Church, by direct personal vows, they are, to a great degree, exempt from those spiritual responsibilities and spiritual dealings which are operative between God and His professing people.

But this is a sad mistake, both as it regards individuals, and as it regards a Nation: — sad, because it leads, in both cases, to misery and ruin. Whether man, in his personal or in his social capacity, recognizes or forgets his God, still is He — and no ungodliness of His creatures can ever make it otherwise — "a God of knowledge, and by him actions are weighed." And it is no fault of His that His creatures will not know this and consider it; for besides those manifest strokes of His wrath, — of which we spake just now, and which the Pagans acknowledged and trembled at, — He has given us a plain account, in the Old Testament Scriptures, of His dealings with peoples as well as with individuals; with nations which recognized Him not, as well as with those whom He chose and guided according to the purpose of His own will. That record is history written by the finger of God; and as such should be studied by all who desire to understand the ways of God, — by all who are not satisfied to look upon history merely as the relation of nation to nation, but as a narrative of all the causes which operate to elevate or depress a people in the scale of things. And in this record we see the hand and the sword of the Lord forever at work, dealing righteous judgment upon the right hand and upon the left, rooting out, and pulling down, and destroying, and building, and planting.[1] Before us does the inspired penman make all the great monarchies of the earth to pass in review, and upon their fate sheds a divine light, which the spiritual mind appreciates, but which those who rule nations, for the most part, scorn and ridicule. And as if to leave man no excuse for disregarding Him in the affairs of nations, He has beforehand written, in prophetic characters, the history and fate of many of them, that, when it came to pass, men might confess His hand; and, in their judgment of the causes of their decline and fall, mingle His will and purposes with the secondary causes that have operated to produce the effects which are seen upon the face of the earth. But this will, and these purposes of God, men will not take into the account, even when the event has fully and exactly verified the prophecy: but will rest altogether in the proximate causes which God has used merely as His means and instruments, showing the aversion which they have to acknowledge His immediate interference in the events of the world; and removing, at the same time, by their pertinacious assertion of man's free agency, the most plausible argument wherewith the Devil could furnish them against

[1] Jer. i. 10.

turning unto the Lord as the Supreme Ruler of the Universe in humiliation and prayer,—the argument of an unchangeableness in the Divine decrees!

If we believe the Bible, then, my hearers, we must believe that God weigheth the actions of nations; for it is there all done before our very eyes, and His judgment upon those actions exhibited and executed. If we believe the Bible,—and the great mass of the people throughout this land professes to believe it,—we can resort to it and see, as in a mirror, the sins which most provoked the wrath of Jehovah; and, in His punishment of those sins, read the fate which awaits us, if we indulge ourselves in them. God's ways are without repentance; and the sins which He hated then, He hates now; and the sins which He punished then, will He punish now. The like pride and arrogancy which brought down the stroke of His sword in those days, will cause it to descend upon us; and we shall writhe under it until we confess the sin, and turn aside the wrath. May we be prudent in time, as a Nation, and study those records which can make us wiser than all ancients or teachers![1]

Among the sins which most surely brought down the vengeance of God upon individuals and peoples, was *proud boasting* conspicuous. It was one of those national iniquities which God seems never to have passed over. When Pharaoh said, "Who is the Lord, that I should obey his voice to let Israel go? I know not the Lord, neither will I let Israel go:"[2] he was soon made to know who He was, in his own discomfiture and the overthrow of his hosts. When Moses had brought the children of Israel to the borders of the land of promise, and was pressing upon them his dying admonitions, how frequently he dwelt upon this theme: "Beware," was his language, "lest when thou hast

[1] Psalm cxix. 98–100. [2] Exod. v. 2.

eaten and art full, and hast built goodly houses, and dwelt therein; and when thy herds and thy flocks multiply, and thy silver and thy gold is multiplied, and all that thou hast is multiplied; then thine heart be lifted up, and thou forget the Lord thy God, which brought thee forth out of the land of Egypt, from the house of bondage; . . . . . and thou say in thy heart, My power and the might of mine hand hath gotten me this wealth." And if they did, what was the doom predicted against them? "As the nations which the Lord destroyeth before your face, so shall ye perish!"[1] And when David numbered the people, provoked to it, as the Scripture tells us, by Satan, this seemingly slight reliance upon the arm of flesh brought down the displeasure of the Lord upon Israel, and He sent pestilence upon Israel, "and there fell of Israel seventy thousand men. And God sent an angel unto Jerusalem to destroy it: and as he was destroying, the Lord beheld, and he repented him of the evil, and said to the angel that destroyed, It is enough, stay now thine hand. . . . . And David lifted up his eyes, and saw the angel of the Lord stand between the earth and the heaven, having a drawn sword in his hand, stretched out over Jerusalem."[2] Although God had led up Sennacherib against Jerusalem, yet when he uttered blasphemous words against Him, despising God, and setting himself above Him, saying to Hezekiah, "Let not thy God, in whom thou trustest, deceive thee, saying, Jerusalem shall not be given into the hand of the King of Assyria. . . . . Have the gods of the nations delivered them which my fathers have destroyed?"[3] his answer was: "Whom hast thou reproached and blasphemed? . . . . By thy servants hast thou reproached the Lord, and hast said, By the multitude of my chariots am I come up to the height of the mountains, to the sides of Lebanon; and I will cut

[1] Deut. viii. 11–20. [2] 1 Chron. xxi. 14–16. [3] Isaiah xxxvii. 10, 12.

down the tall cedars thereof, and the choice fir-trees thereof: and I will enter into the height of his border, and the forest of his Carmel. . . . . Because thy rage against me, and thy tumult, is come up into mine ears, therefore will I put my hook in thy nose, and my bridle in thy lips, and I will turn thee back by the way by which thou camest."[1] And in like manner, everywhere throughout the Old Testament, is this sin of putting confidence in flesh, in our own arm, in horses and chariots, instead of trusting in the arm of the Lord, visited with the uniform, unvarying displeasure of Jehovah. "THE LORD THY GOD IS A JEALOUS GOD," is written upon every event of that most awful record of God's dealings with His creatures!

If there is one sin more than another for which we stand conspicuous, as a Nation, it is this sin of speaking exceeding proudly. There is no limit to our *vain boasting!* If it were the boasting of a Christian people, rejoicing because the God of Israel is their God, because the Redeemer promised to ages and generations is their Saviour, because the laws and the statutes of a Holy God are the provisions of their moral code, because all the blessings which Christianity fetches in her train are richly showered upon their heads: it would enter as sweet incense into the presence of the Lord, and crown us and our children with a lasting and a beneficial prosperity. But such is not our boasting! It is not in this God of Israel that we put our trust. It is not in this Redeemer that we rest as our strong tower and house of defense. It is not in the lofty morality of Jesus that we look for our success. It is not in the ameliorations of Christianity that we triumph and exult. No. Our idols are our political institutions; our oracles are our frail, short-sighted fellow-creatures; our tower of strength is our numbers; our shield is the immensity of our domain,

[1] Isaiah xxxvii. 23, 24, 29.

and the vastness of our resources; our rule of life is a tyrannous public opinion. Every day is the ear of God vexed with the arrogancy of our mouths, with our exceeding proud talk. Let what may be the subject, it ends in self-glorification! Our public speakers, from him that addresses himself to his fellow-citizens of the same parish, to him that speaks for the ears of a Nation, all indulge the same exulting strain; — nay, are obliged to indulge it, for a national vanity craves it, and is not satisfied without it. And worse, the pulpit too, that which should humble man perpetually to the dust, prostitutes itself to the same vile flattery, and fears to speak to man the truths which he should hear and feel, if peradventure God may bless them to his soul. For these things God will surely visit. Our sins will surely find us out. And have they not already found us out? In what has our proud boasting of the perfectibility of human nature under free institutions ended? In our being the by-word of the world as repudiators and faithless. In what has our arrogant talk of the superior acuteness of our people resulted? In covering the land, from the one end to the other, with cunning and roguery. In what has our haughty maintenance of the freedom of opinion terminated? In every man's being afraid of having any opinion of his own; so that virtue and vice, justice and injustice, morality and immorality, stand upon the same platform, and are covered over with the same mantle: and that, not a mantle of charity, but of fear. And so will it go on, until we turn from these vanities to serve the living God: until we trust, not in refuges like political institutions, and mortal men, and public opinion; but take the arm of the Lord for our defense, and the Word of the Lord for our rule of life, and the Spirit of the Lord for our counsellor and guide. Subject after subject of boasting will be snatched from us by the withering hand of the

Almighty, until laws, institutions, country, shall all be mingled in one common ruin. And as the nations which the Lord destroyed before our face, so shall we perish.

The natural effect of this exceeding proud talk is beginning to be perceived in a growing contempt for the Word of God, and the precepts of the Bible. No allowance is made for the wisdom of a Being like God, who sees the end from the beginning, and knows the effects of His positive, as well as His moral arrangements, upon the characters and conduct of His creatures: and the wisdom of a people so exceeding wise, as we are every day told that we are, is preferred to that which dictated the Bible, and promulged its morals. Nothing is bowed to, — even though it come from the Bible, even though it be writ there with a pencil of light, — unless it can be shown to be accordant with a limited reason, or a short-sighted utilitarianism. All the positive institutions of religion are beginning to be sneered at. The *Sabbaths are polluted,* because man thinks one day as good as another: although God has directly commanded its being hallowed, and reckoned it among the chief sins of Israel, as ye have heard read in the Scriptures this day,[1] that they were not kept sacred. The *Ministry is degraded,* because man thinks one religious person is as good as another: although God has distinctly set apart an order of men for that vocation, with whom He promised always to be, to the end of the world; and grievously punished those who assumed its functions, under that dispensation where immediate rewards and punishments testified His approbation or disapprobation. The *Sacraments are despised,* thousands going to their graves without Baptism, or the Sacrament of the Supper; because man thinks faith in the heart is all that is necessary: although Christ has said: " Except a man be born of water and of the Spirit, he cannot enter

[1] Ezek. xx. to v. 27, is the Morning Lesson for the 3d Sunday in Lent.

into the kingdom of God;"[1] and, "Except ye eat the flesh of the Son of Man, and drink his blood, ye have no life in you."[2] And, from the positive institutions of the Bible, be assured we shall very soon pass over to the moral precepts; — nay, have we not already assaulted them? — and shall pronounce murder, and adultery, and theft, not such crying sins as God would make us believe. Alas for my country, that it should so soon have run to such crying corruption! Not yet a century old, yet vitiated to the core with unbelief and immorality; and the people loving to have it so!

Whereunto will all this come? It will have first, my hearers, — unless the Spirit of the Lord raise a standard against the overwhelming flood, — a natural punishment; and then be visited judicially by the Lord. These are two distinct results; as distinct as the capital punishment which awaits the murderer at the hands of the law, and the remorse of conscience which he suffers as the natural consequence of his crime. The spirit of pride, leading to unbelief, to self-confidence, to a reliance upon human wisdom and natural virtue, will very soon cover the country with the fruits of infidelity, and the works of the flesh, — with lawlessness, with adultery, with fornication, with uncleanness, with lasciviousness, with hatred, variance, strife, envyings, murders, drunkenness, and such like: until all virtuous persons shall feel that the natural punishment is so sore, they will long and pray for a judicial visitation of the Lord, to purify and cleanse the foulness which is all about them. And it will come, in some shape or other, "for the Lord is a God of knowledge, and by him actions are weighed," — in just such shape as shall be most humiliating to us, as shall cast our pride and our arrogancy to the dust. God is not satisfied that evils shall run only to

[1] S. John iii. 5. [2] *Ibid.* vi. 53.

their natural results. Upon those results He superinduces, in all the arrangements of His punishments, a positive wrath, which will fall in judgment upon those whose actions He has weighed, unless they deprecate His wrath and turn away His fury. Although, for the moment, we see not that wrath gathering around us, still all actions are open before His eyes, all actions are weighed in His balances — the balances of the sanctuary; and when the sins of the people are filled up, the sword descends, and they find the word "TEKEL" written against them: "Thou art weighed in the balances, and art found wanting."[1]

That such may not be our fate, let us strive and pray, my beloved fellow-Christians! What should we do in an emergency like this, — an emergency pressing every day more and more upon us, — but cry unto the Lord for help? Although the prophecy had gone forth against Nineveh, yet when the people turned unto the Lord with all their heart, in repentance, and in sackcloth, God forgave them the wickedness of their sin, and removed His avenging angel from over them. Although He had led up the Assyrians against Jerusalem, yet when His servant turned unto Him in earnest prayer, He sent His sword into the midst of his enemies, and delivered him. Let us turn in like manner now. We know not what may be overhanging us. We know not what the Lord, whose eyes run to and fro in the earth, has seen in us for punishment and wrath. Our consciences fain tell us that He has seen enough! His successive strokes upon our rulers tell us that He has seen enough! Let us take warning from these glimpses which we have had of His glittering sword! If the gleam of that sword be so awful, what must be its full vengeance, when it is poured out in fury upon a people? God avert it from us!

[1] Dan. v. 27.

But "in vain shall we pray, if we do nothing," says old Bishop Hall. "Our prayers serve only to testify the truth of our desires; and to what purpose shall we pretend a desire of that, which we endeavor not to effect?" Let us begin the remedy. Let us "talk no more so exceeding proudly. Let not arrogancy come out of our mouths." Let us clear our skirts, at least, of this vain boasting, of which the country is so guilty. Ten righteous men in Sodom would have saved it; and a few determined Christians may avert the wrath of the Almighty from this land. Will you be these Christians? Will you humble yourselves before God, and give Him the praise and the glory of all the good which we enjoy, and take to yourselves the shame and the confusion of face which belong to the guilty? If ye will, that humiliation will give power to your prayers, and earnestness to your endeavors. If ye will, ye may set an example that shall bless your homes for ages to come.

One question more: Will ye add to this prayer and this humiliation, a Scriptural view of vice? Ah, my hearers, we are all guilty in this particular, calling good, evil, and evil, good,— sweet, bitter, and bitter, sweet. We do not make the distinctions which we should do, in our conversation, in our actions, in our social intercourse, between virtue and vice. Besides the punishment upon vice wherewith God has promised to visit it, there is a punishment which Society is bound to inflict,—*sternly to inflict,*—else will that Society itself reap the bitter fruits of its neglect! Every crime which Society lightly passes over, is, in so far, encouraged by Society; for ofttimes the severest punishment of vice is the social punishment. Man can often better bear death, than the stern severity of the social circle: but that severity is needful, until repentance and a sufficient probation shall have again opened the door for the re-admission of the contrite penitent. But the impenitent sinner should be frowned from its ranks. Its doors should be closed in his face, as the virtue of our own firesides is regarded! His name should never cross the lips of the virtuous, save for reprobation, or for prayer. Hear, Christian, what the Epistle for the day prescribes as your duty: "And have no fellowship with the unfruitful works of darkness, but rather reprove them. For it is a shame even to speak of those things which are done of them in secret."[1] Is this so? See to it that it be so: for if it be not, God will draw His sword against the righteous and the wicked together, and then shall it not return into its scabbard!

1844.

[1] Ephes. v. 11, 12.

Twenty-sixth Sermon.

And the multitudes that went before, and that followed, cried, saying, Hosanna to the Son of David: Blessed is He that cometh in the name of the Lord; Hosanna in the highest. — S. MATTHEW xxi. 9.

THE entry of our Saviour into Jerusalem, described in our text and in the parallel passage of S. Luke, seems, to imaginations filled with false ideas of glory, to have been a very mean and paltry affair. A meek and humble Man, clothed in the every-day garb of the country, seated upon a colt, the foal of an ass, appears but a poor representative of royalty, preceded and followed though He was by multitudes heralding His approach. Accustomed as the world is to imperial processions very different from this, it cannot associate greatness except with pomp and ostentation. There must be tinsel, there must be show, there must be something to strike upon the senses, ere even the most educated and refined among us can be satisfied that we are in contact with something above ourselves. Although the mighty works of God, the most truly sublime with which our experience has made us acquainted, have been performed with a severe and studied simplicity, — although all the mighty processes of Nature, processes confined not to this world but pervading the whole universe of God, are carried on with a quiet harmony which keeps us almost unconscious of their action, — so unstrung are all our conceptions of things that we pass by this natural and therefore true law which has been impressed upon the works of creation and

Providence, and frame one for ourselves, which shall be more vulgar, and therefore better adapted to an uncrowned and disordered manhood. When God would dispel darkness, — would usher into being that agent which was to clothe the world with beauty, — He merely spake the word, "Let there be Light:" and "there was Light." When He would bring order out of chaos, and wake into existence the vast succession of beings that people His universe, "He commanded," says the Psalmist, "and they were created." And now, how simply and yet how gloriously does the universe roll on, obeying the sweet influences of Pleiades, — night and day, winter and summer, seed-time and harvest following in their appointed times! But because we only feel their blessings, and their unostentatious grandeur is not made to strike upon our senses, the lesson which they should teach is unobserved, and fails to bring us back to the divine idea of glory. And therefore when He makes the advent of His Son to be of a piece with all His works, — grand in its simplicity, and its grandeur only seen when its vast influence and its eternal blessings are displayed, — man cannot reconcile it with his distorted conceptions, but turns into an argument for unbelief that which most strikingly proves that the coming of Christ was not an imposture of man, but an ordinance of God, rising quietly, grandly, sublimely upon a world of darkness and of sin.

This entrance of our Saviour into Jerusalem, was no more humble than all the other visible accompaniments of our Saviour's coming. He was humble in His birth, — a carpenter's reputed son, and born and cradled in a manger. He was humble in His training, — growing up among obscure people in the land of Galilee. He was humble in His life, — poor, separate from sinners, having not where to lay His head. He was humble in His followers, — a few fishermen of His reputed country forming His retinue, and

His worshippers coming from the ranks of the despised and the unclean. He was humble in His language, — speaking the words of gentleness, of meekness, of mercy, of charity. To have cast off all this at once, — to have put on His divine glory, and to have entered Jerusalem with royal pomp, — should have been altogether inharmonious, should have been to have confounded the glory of His Second Coming with the humility of His first. He was to appear before the world as the antitype and complement of all God's works, — as His sublimest mystery, and most perfect glory; and was therefore to exhibit in Himself all the marks of the Divine method of proceeding: and this, above all, of manifesting greatness not through that which dazzles, but through that which blesses, — not by an encouragement of human pride, but by sanctifying virtue, and making that the greatness of the earth beneath as it is of the Heavens above!

As the true greatness of our Saviour's mission was to consist in transferring, through His atonement and the power of the Holy Ghost, man's idea of human excellence from outward appearances to inward holiness, it was not only of a piece with God's sublimest works that He should come simply and unostentatiously before the world: but it was likewise necessary that He should embody the lowliness which He had come to teach. Had He been a *mere man*, the simpleness of life and the meekness of carriage which distinguished Him should not have been half so striking as when, proving perpetually, although only by glimpses, that He was "the Son of God with power," He yet maintained it as the rule of His life and the legacy of His disciples. There was no necessity laid upon Him that He should thus live and thus die. It was a voluntary self-denial, from the cradle to the Cross! "Thinkest thou that I cannot now pray to my Father," was His rebuke to Peter when that disciple would have defended Him with the sword, "and he shall presently give me more than twelve legions of angels?" But how then should His great mission have been fulfilled, of being the Exemplar of life for those who could not command the heavens to pour out its embattled legions? He was to teach the world how to be *truly great,* and that was not by encircling Himself with the glory of His Father's kingdom — which was to be the manifestation when the economy of grace was ended, — but by exhibiting those qualities of heart which were afterwards to be called "the fruits of the Spirit," — love, peace, long suffering, gentleness, goodness, —under circumstances in which they should be His only claims to glory. What the world would call a lowly life, — lowly in all its phases and accompaniments, — was the chosen life of Jesus. He humbled Himself, — put away His glory that it might not impede His purpose, — and in every act of His brief life on earth, was teaching us that all that God called great lay in the soul, and that when He should come a second time in His power, He should not take to His glory the mighty of the world, but those who had not been ashamed to tread in His footsteps of lowly virtue and sanctified holiness.

Those, therefore, seem to me to be entirely at fault, who would use this humble appearance of the Son of God while on earth, as an argument against His divinity. It is, to my mind, one of the very strongest in its favor. The simple yet sublime grandeur of His whole demeanor is so in harmony with all that we know of the character and actions of God, that it points Him out, to the spiritual eye, as the image of His Father's glory. And then that total disregard of all human views, — that trampling under foot of all human pride, —that new aspect which He put upon life when He lavished the blessings of God upon the poor in spirit, upon the meek, upon the pure in heart, upon the merciful, — that sanctity with which His example has invested poverty and sorrow and humility, — that new ideal of glory which He has impressed upon the world: all separated Him, by an immeasurable distance, from every other who has assumed the character of a divine teacher. But if any should fail to see, in these things, the marks of His divinity, let me show them that while the advent of Christ was ushered in quietly and unostentatiously to the vulgar eye, and while His presence was unmarked save by its blessings: it was preceded by a chain of the grandest evidence which has ever been piled together, and followed by an influence which has revolutionized the world in its feelings, its habits, its hopes, its religion.

If one were asked to arrange evidence for such a fact as the appearance of the Son of God upon earth, he would say, that the most striking proof of this mission would be His descent from Heaven in august pomp, so that there might be no mistake about His divine character and mission. This would seem to be such testimony as would satisfy anybody. Now, passing by altogether the entire overthrow that this would be of the principle of Faith upon which Christianity is founded, and the complete change it would produce in the Christian probation, it must be, after the extinction of the generation which witnessed this descent, only the testimony of tradition, which soon becomes the vaguest and weakest of all evidence. Our Lord must descend from Heaven for every generation of men, or else the testimony, which, at first sight, seemed so desirable and so complete, would soon vanish, and leave no impress behind. For a mission like that of our Saviour, which was to embrace in its benefits all people and all time, the evidence must be peculiar and permanent. It must have a local habitation, so that it should not be lost amid the rise and decay of nations, amid the migrations of people, in the confusion and desolations of war: while it should be of a diffusive character, capable of exhibition and appliance to the furthest extremities of the world. While it should have its central shrine, it should also have its temples, wherein man might reason and be satisfied, wherever man should exist upon the face of the earth. It should likewise be germinant evidence, such as should produce its blade at one period, its blossom at another, its rich clusters of fruit in the fullness of times. It should be massive evidence, such as man could neither create nor destroy, increasing in its momentum as the world rolled on in years. It should be permanent evidence, written upon the face of Nature, as well as upon the history of nations and in the literature of a chosen people. Such evidence as this should be as much above the direct testimony of a visible and glorious descent once made in the face of the world, as the daily rising of the sun and shining in our very eyes would be a better evidence of the existence of light, than any traditional testimony which might come to us of its creation. Well, such grand evidence has Christianity. Judea is its central shrine, the hallowed spot around which has circled the history of the world; from which, when Christ had come, floated upon the wings of the everlasting Gospel to every nation and kindred and people, the evidence of his Messiahship. And that evidence has found belief everywhere, has built temples everywhere, has made its home in the human heart everywhere, and that because of its nature. It had in it qualities which fitted it for minds of every cast, which adapted it to temperaments of every degree. If one was not satisfied with the traditional testimony of miracles, he could find rest for his spirit in that wonderful train of prophecies which has been fulfilling through the whole history of the world, and is still fulfilling under his very eyes. If the appearance of our Lord in His condition of humility upon earth was distasteful to the conceptions of a man of peculiar mind, he might find contentment for his aspiring thoughts, that around the cradle of that Child earth's greatest nations had been made to play their parts and fulfill their destiny. If one should doubt the records of the people of whom, according to the flesh, Christ came, God has stamped the corroboration of their testimony upon the face of the very earth which they once trod, and upon the character of the nations which encompassed them. And if all of these should fail to convince, there is evidence likewise for the conscience, and the divine truth of the Scriptures is made to pierce into its very recesses, and wring thence the confession of the Samaritan woman, — He "told me all things that ever I did." Every shape which evidence could take, has the evidence for Christianity assumed; and if human nature cannot detect the greatness of our Lord under the garb of His lowliness, cannot see the divinity breaking forth from beneath the shroud of His humanity, he may, at least, find food for his admiration in the wonderful tissue of proof which the Living God has woven together in richest harmony for the identification of His Son. He could not put upon Him the vulgar greatness of pomp and show, for that should have been alien from His nature and works, and subversive of the lessons He was to teach the world: but He could make Him, in His lowliness, the focus of all the action of the world; in His Crucifixion, the radiating point for all its blessings!

We are told by the Evangelist that the multitudes which went before and that followed, cried "Hosanna to the son of David: Blessed is He that cometh in the name of the Lord; Hosanna in the highest." And these voices were but the commencement of that unceasing chorus which has ever since been swelling up from the earth re-echoing these hosannas, and which will go on increasing until it is merged in that triumphant song of "Blessing and honor and glory" which shall eternally roll through the Heavens. And this, my hearers, is another direction in which God has manifested the greatness of His Son, in that the influence of His divine mission has been felt and shall be forever felt wherever there is a wounded spirit or a sorrowing heart or a guilty conscience among the children of men. The noble and the mighty and the prosperous may not have acknowledged it, because they have been offended at the ideal of greatness upon which it required that they should dress themselves: but the multitudes of the earth, like the multitudes of Jerusalem, have ever recognized in Jesus their Friend, their Deliverer, their Saviour. For them — the humble, the lowly, the oppressed, the weak — has His coming been the harbinger of good. Their humility has He exalted; their lowliness has He sanctified; their weakness has He changed into power; the chains of their oppression, whether chains of ignorance, or passion, or lust, or power, has He broken asunder. His example has nerved the hearts of myriads to labor and to suffer for their blessing. His teaching has purified the conscience of the world so that oppression and crime are rebuked, abashed, even though they be not destroyed. His death has opened the portals of Heaven, and brought down the Spirit of God to dwell with them as their Guide, their Sanctifier, their abiding Comforter! To Him are temples raised in every land and by every people. At His name ten thousand times ten thousand knees are bent, and voices which no man can number confess the power of His presence. Under His eternal wings are clustered the contrite, and the penitent, and the returning prodigal. To Him the mourning flee for comfort, and the sinful for pardon, and the dying for immortality! Unbelief may suggest its doubts. Wickedness may hurl its taunts. The scoffer's laugh and the skeptic's sneer may grate upon the harmony of a ransomed world. But they can avail nothing against the multitudes who strew the path of His glory with their offerings, and cry with the earnestness of ransomed joy: "Blessed is He that cometh in the name of the Lord; Hosanna in the highest."

By those who have opposed the religion of Jesus this has been styled the voice of ignorance, — a clamor raised and cherished by priests and hirelings, whose interest it has been to keep alive this shout of divine praise. It is the voice of suffering humanity, rejoicing in the coming of its great Deliverer; recognizing in His life and sufferings the very Saviour whom they needed, one who might be touched with a feeling of their infirmities. The multitudes of the earth — for such are the poor and the lowly — do not ask for cold philosophy or abstract teachings. They ask for sympathy, for the voice of compassion, and the hand of relief! A Saviour who should have come to them in the garb of wealth, or with the pomp of power, should have been separated from them by all the conventionalities of life and the associations of the world. But when the meek and lowly Jesus enters their homes of poverty and suffering, simple in His dress, a man of sorrows and acquainted with grief, His heart yearning with love, and His hand mighty to save and mighty to relieve; they spring to meet him, and shout, "Hosanna to the Son of David: Blessed is He that cometh in the name of the Lord; Hosanna in the Highest." What care they for evidence? They have the evidence of a yearning heart, that this is the Saviour of their necessity! What care they for cavillers? They are immovable as the blind man in the Gospel, and their cry is: "One thing I know, that whereas I was blind, now I see." What care they that He did not put on, while incarnate, His divine glory? They feel that His greatness in Love, in Mercy, in

Charity, in Forgiveness, in Redemption, is far more to them than the pomp which has ground them to the dust, and the power which has forged the fetters of their darkness!

The greatness of our Lord and Saviour must, you perceive, my hearers, be looked for somewhere else than in any vulgar parade as king or conqueror while on earth. If you search for it, you will find it in many directions, but never taking this shape. The salvation which is through Christ is a great salvation, but never in the sense of worldly greatness. It is great, as having been the great mystery of heaven from the beginning, — that which angels desired to penetrate. It is great, as having brought from the bosom of the Father, and shrouded in human form, His only begotten Son, the glory of His Father and the express image of His person. It is great, as having been the charmed centre, around which every thing in creation has been made to turn. It is great, in that nature, and nations, and men, and angels, and devils, have all been constrained to form its chain of evidence. It is great, because an influence has gone out from the Cross of the Crucified which has changed the world, and turned it from idols to serve the living God. It is great, because it is silently rolling on to its consummation, and is moulding every thing to the purposes of God's will. But none of these are effects which the world cares about. There is nothing dazzling about them. They are slow in their operation, silent in their progress, natural in their course, gradual in their effects. Generation succeeds generation, without much apparent result; and yet when those generations have waxed into centuries, the world is seen to have grown in the extent of its Christianity, and in the power of its influence. Three centuries ago, and this whole continent was in the darkness of Paganism: and to-day its citizens stand among the foremost as the worshippers of Christ and the heralds of His salvation. Five centuries since, and Christianity was limited to a single continent, and that corrupted to its core: to-day there is no isle nor continent where the name Jesus is not preached, and His example followed by faithful disciples who for His name and glory's sake are content to be lowly, and abased, and poor, and humble, and suffering! Eighteen centuries ago, and all there was of Christianity clustered around the Cross of the dying Nazarene: to-day, and voices of every kindred and nation and tongue and people are joining in the loud Hosanna, "Blessed is He that cometh in the name of the Lord."

And will not you, my people, speed on this glorious cause? Will you not join in this shout of the rejoicing multitude, "Hosanna to the Son of David," and strew your offerings under His advancing footsteps? His greatness it is, which has made your homes to be circles of refinement and of virtue, of lofty culture and pure devotion. His greatness it is, which has bound your firesides together with the bond of immortality, and made your love undying. His greatness it is, which has given to woman her holy influence, and transformed her from a plaything and a slave into the wise mother, the virtuous wife, the loving child. Great our Lord may not have seemed to be to the eye of sense, when born in Bethlehem, or fleeing into Egypt, or wandering through Samaria and Galilee, or riding into Jerusalem upon an ass, or agonizing in Gethsemane, or bound before the judgment seat, or dying on Calvary deserted and forsaken; but great He was in all the mystery that enveloped heaven ere He became incarnate; great in the promises and the prophecy and the types and the sacrifices which heralded His birth; great in the sublime influence which He has diffused through every department of life, from the private chamber to the royal throne: but greater than all, when, at the consummation of all things, He shall gather together His people from earth and sea and the chambers of the dead, and glorify them with that glory which He had with His Father ere the world was! Arouse yourselves in time, my people, and understand that greatness! Be not so blinded with the false glare of this world's glory, as not to see this outspeaking Divinity of your Saviour. Link not greatness forever in your minds with pomp and power and earthly glitter; but with the refined qualities of the soul,—Virtue, Devotion, Holiness!

Twenty-seventh Sermon.

Then answered all the people, and said, His blood be on us, and on our children. — S. MATTHEW xxvii. 25.

HOW dreadful would be our feelings at times, if, just as we had finished an action, all its consequences were made to flash upon us! What a change would there often be, in a moment, from indifference to terror, from confidence to dismay! Things that under the present arrangement of God seem but of trifling interest, would, under such an operation, acquire an importance beyond conception. Events that appear but of passing moment, would be seen to stretch away into an endless eternity.

How reckless is it, under a dispensation in which a finite mind is moving in the midst of an infinite and incomprehensible scheme, for man to dash on without Scriptural knowledge or a heavenly guide. How daring for him, surrounded as he is by controlling spirits, invested as he is with an immortal soul, capable as he is of infinite happiness or infinite misery, to think or say or do any thing without looking to its consequences. Consequences are eternal, as well as temporal; affect others, as well as ourselves; change their nature and become causes, and are prolific in effects — glorious or dreadful — like themselves; perpetuating to generations yet unborn their blessing or their curse. We do not *see* them. We cannot *follow* them. They circle away beyond our view and beyond our conception. But still they are ours; and one day shall they be traced out for us, by the hand of our Judge, along their pathway of evil or of good, amazing us with their extent, overwhelming us with their awfulness.

How little did the people of Jerusalem, who invoked, at the judgment seat of Pilate, the blood of Jesus upon them and their children, understand what they were doing! How little did they appreciate the *consequences* that were wrapped up in that one rash sentence! Could *these* have passed before them, on the instant, in their terrible array: their tongues would have cleaved to the roof of their mouths, — their spirits would have melted within them for very terror. The personal suffering, the national disgrace, the terrible siege wherein for very straitness they did eat the fruit of their own body, the abomination of desolation standing in the Holy Place, Jerusalem ploughed over, themselves scattered upon the whole earth, ages of widowhood and persecution and reproach and contempt and misery, — no home, no ease, no rest: these in themselves would have made up an appalling picture of evil, for parents to call down upon their children. But when to these are added their spiritual miseries, — that want of a Temple, of an Altar, of a Sacrifice; that absence of Jehovah from the midst of them; that darkness of soul that has settled upon them; that inscrutable purpose of God in regard to their salvation; that trembling of spirit and fearfulness of heart which Mosaic prophecy has fixed upon them: they would at once have realized the woe denounced by the Lord Jesus upon those by whom He should be betrayed; they would at once have cried out, in anguish of spirit: "Would to God we had never been born!"

But hidden as these consequences were from their eyes, — hidden by their unbelief, their malice, their contempt, — their clamorous cry was, "Crucify Him, crucify Him!" And when Pilate washed his hands before them, saying, "I am innocent of the blood of this just person: see ye to it;"

the reckless answer was : " His blood be on us, and on our children."

It is a bold step for man to take any one's blood on himself and on his children; for blood crieth unto the Lord from the earth in a mysterious way, and fetcheth down a curse: but to invoke such Blood as was found upon the Cross, was unutterable madness. If they had the most distant conception that the Being standing with them before Pilate was their Messiah; if the vaguest doubt floated in their minds that He might indeed be the Prince of Peace; if the slightest testimony witnessed to His identity with Him of whom the Prophets had spoken from the beginning; their folly was inconceivable: for the Blood they were presuming to take as a burden upon them and theirs, was Blood which concentred in itself every thing that could make it precious, and sacred, and vengeance-bringing. It was *the blood of the everlasting Covenant,* — that which had entered into the counsel of Peace as the price of man's redemption; which had been accepted, when every thing else in Heaven, and Earth, and the Universe of God, had been reckoned valueless; which had sealed the New Testament of Mercy. It was *the Blood* that was the *substance of all their sacrificial* blood; which had given to their sacrifices their whole value and efficacy; which had made them, for a season, mighty for the remission of sin and the sanctification of the soul. It was *the blood of God,* according as S. Luke tells us in his Acts of the Apostles, when he speaks of the Church of God which He redeemed with *His own Blood:* awful and mysterious theme, — incomprehensible and soul-subduing thought, before which we must bow in humble adoration, — *the blood of God made Man,* prepared, infused, circulated for this very end. It was *the blood* that is *forever offered* at the mercy-seat of God, pleading for mercy, crying for vengeance, the Blood of the Lamb as it had been slain, which the Apostle of the Apocalypse saw in the midst of the Throne and of the Elders, — such was the Blood which this maddened multitude invoked upon themselves, and upon their children; which has cleaved to them as a curse forever since; which still follows them, saying, "True and righteous are Thy judgments, Lord God Almighty."[1]

What a burden for a human creature to bear! The blood of a fellow-mortal upon us subdues our spirit, quenches our energy, furrows our brow, whitens our head, mixes bitterness in every cup of life: but *the blood of God,* oh what a burden! If Cain said, when the blood of his brother was upon him, "My punishment is greater than I can bear. . . . Every one that findeth me shall slay me:"[2] what shall *he* say, upon whom is resting the blood of his God? Surely every thing in the Universe must rise up against him, —Nature, which *that Blood* has freed from its curse; Saints, whom *that Blood* has ransomed from destruction; Angels, whom their King, clothed in a vesture dipped in *that Blood,* leads forth as His avenging host; God Himself, before whom *it* is offered day and night unceasingly: — Lord God of mercy! May none of us ever have the Blood of Thy Son upon us!

But we can have it upon us! we can bring it down upon us, and upon our children. We can crucify Christ afresh, and take upon us, and ours, the whole curse, present and eternal. We cannot escape the *contact of that Blood.* It has been shed *for us;* and upon us, and ours, must it have its operation. We cannot escape it. If we climb up to Heaven, it meets us there. If we descend to hell, it has been there before us. If we cover ourselves with darkness, it tracks us as in the light, having itself shrouded the world in darkness, even when it was laying its terrible

[1] Rev. xvi. 7. [2] Gen. iv. 13, 14.

grasp upon those who shed it. Christ died for the sins of the whole world, past, present, and to come; and our sins formed a part of the load that pressed upon the Soul of this God, and wrung the Blood from his lacerated Body. It has been shed *for us.* The Covenant was, that He should bear the sins of all; and we must answer for our portion of it. Our sins nailed Him to the Cross. Our sins pierced His hands, His feet, His heart. Our sins brought down upon Him the wrath of God, and the darkness of desertion. And we must account for our share in the work. It will not do to lay it upon those who stood around the judgment-seat and cried for His Blood; nor even upon those who gloated on Him as He hung upon the Cross. We are in like condemnation with them. The Blood is upon us: and it must either wash us, and place us among the ransomed of God; or else fetch down upon us the wrath and fierceness of the Almighty. It is not voluntary with us whether we shall stand connected with that Blood. From eternity has *that* been settled. It is the blood of the everlasting Covenant, and we must meet it everywhere and forever, in the shape of mercy, or the form of vengeance. It remains for us only to determine whether it shall glorify us and elevate us to the rank of the redeemed, or whether it shall press us down to utter darkness, the blackness of darkness.

And we *can entail* it upon our children. We can act so that they, as well as we, shall bear *the curse* of this Blood. We can hand down its burden from generation to generation, and it shall lie heavy upon our posterity, and they shall writhe under it, until the grace of God cut off the entail. O my beloved friends, deep and awful are the dealings of God in Christ: but they should be looked at here, in all their depth and in all their awfulness, before it be too late to help ourselves or those we love. God has set before us, in the Jewish people, a living example of His dealings in this regard. "His blood be on us, and on our children:" and we see how it hath dealt with them unto this day, — how it will deal with them, until God "pour upon the house of David, and upon the inhabitants of Jerusalem, the spirit of grace and of supplications: and they shall look upon him whom they have pierced, and they shall mourn for him as one mourneth for his only son, and shall be in bitterness for him, as one that is in bitterness for his first-born."[1] And so are His dealings *now*. Unbelief, contempt for religion, vice, perpetuate themselves, pass down, from father to son, and to son's son, until the horrible succession is lost to the view of the mortal eye that has traced it; but not lost to the Eternal Eye, which never sleepeth. It was a noble lineage of faith which the Apostle ascribed to Timothy, when he spoke of the "unfeigned faith" that was in him, "which dwelt first in his grandmother Lois, and his mother Eunice:"[2] and how often, even with our short-sightedness, can we trace the descent of infidelity from generation to generation, — can we trace the fruits of vice as they break out, age after age, in the blood that hath planted them in the race. The *Blood of Christ* cannot be trifled with. It is destruction to ourselves, destruction to all about us, — it is a plague upon our house: unless we can turn it, through faith and prayer, into a blessing.

And how naturally is the dreadful result worked out. Those who say unto God, "Depart from us; for we desire not the knowledge of thy ways;"[3] who say of Christ, "His blood be on us, and on our children:" themselves produce the horrible result. Their principles, their precepts, their example, are all against religion: and the watchful eye of childhood fixes itself upon its parent's movements, drinks in his unguarded language of irreligion, notes his open marks of scorn, imitates his neglect of all

[1] Zech. xii. 10. [2] 2 Tim. i. 5. [3] Job xxi. 14.

sacred observances, and glories that he is like his father, — a despiser of God, and a scorner of the Blood of Jesus. And the father, too, glories in the manliness of his boy, and chuckles, perchance, at his independence of thought and of feeling, and rejoices — at what? That he has made his child an unbeliever; that he has helped to put the Blood of Christ upon him; that he has doomed him, so far as he can do it, to eternal misery! A man should be thoroughly convinced that Christianity is a fraud, before he takes this responsibility upon himself; should be assured that it is nothing to trample the Blood of Jesus under his feet; before he leads his children to do it. His children God has given him for nurture, for admonition, for eternal as well as spiritual guidance: and he uses his power to make that child, with his own will, — for the child has as yet no will in the matter, — indifferent about religion, if not a scoffer. And even though he be not in himself an unbeliever or a scorner, — even though he show outward respect to religion, and treat its observances with attention, — yet ought he to ask himself seriously whether the keen observation of childhood does not mark the inconsistency between his actions and his feelings; does not graduate his belief and his action according to the example that is most venerated and esteemed in his eyes. Without family worship, without the religious instruction of the fireside, without the father's hand of blessing upon his children's head, without the invocation of the Holy Spirit upon his household, the child will seldom carry into the world the truth as it is in Jesus; will seldom have the Blood of Christ sprinkled upon him by the Holy Ghost, so that the avenging angel shall pass by him in the day of destruction.

But there is yet another class that bring down upon themselves and upon their children the Blood of Christ. And they are *the hypocrites,* — those who use religion as a cloak, and wear it as a garment for convenience. This was the class against whom Christ uttered the only woes, — the only language of harshness that is ascribed to Him in the Scriptures. The opposers of His doctrine He answered mildly. The multitudes that cried out, "Crucify him, crucify him!" He wept for, with compassion. They that stood around His Cross, nailing Him to it, He prayed His Father to forgive. But of the *hypocrites*, who for a pretence made long prayers, He asked, "How can ye escape the damnation of hell?"[1] And for this very reason, — because they have taken upon them the *Blood of Christ*, and use it for vile purposes, desecrating that, which is the most precious gift of God, to lust and to iniquity. And after the same natural way of which we spoke just now, does this Blood rest upon their children, who grow up learning to be hypocrites, taught to look upon the religion of Jesus as a matter of convenience or of interest, odious in the sight of all spiritual souls, a stumbling-block in the way of the irreligious. Lord Jesus, teach these deluded souls the way to escape damnation! — the way to cut off the entail of this Blood from their offspring!

When the people answered, and imprecated this Blood upon themselves, and upon their children, He that was to pour it out stood captive, and bound, at the judgment-seat of Pilate. That was their hour, and the power of darkness. But the Bible tells us that there shall come out of Heaven one clothed with a *vesture dipped in Blood*, whose name is called *The Word of God;* and there follow Him the armies which are in Heaven. "And out of his mouth goeth a sharp sword, that with it he should smite the nations: and he shall rule them with a rod of iron: and he treadeth the wine-press of the fierceness and wrath of Almighty God." And on this same vesture dipped in Blood, "a name writ-

[1] S. Matt. xxiii. 33.

ten, "KING OF KINGS, AND LORD OF LORDS."[1] And when "the wine-press was trodden," "*blood came out of the wine-press,* even unto the horse-bridles."[2] What an awful harmony of sin and of punishment! The garment of the avenger, a *vesture dipped in blood,* — that very Blood which they had despised and invoked upon themselves, and their children: the punishment to be inflicted in the wine-press of the fierceness of the wrath of the Almighty, — that *same wine-press* which He had trodden alone, when the prophet saw Him, in vision, coming "from Edom, with dyed garments from Bozrah," "glorious in His apparel, travelling in the greatness of His strength:"[3] that punishment, to be *trodden under foot,* until their blood should come out of the wine-press, — even as they had trampled under foot in this world the Blood of His Atonement. How shall they appear at that day, upon whom is lying the Blood of Christ? If the Saints that have been slain for the Word of God and for the testimony of Jesus, cry in the Heavens with a loud voice, saying, "How long, O Lord, holy and true, dost thou not judge and avenge our blood on them that dwell on the earth?"[4] shall the Blood of Christ, wrung from Him in His sweat of agony, drawn from Him by the nails in His hands and in His feet, forced from Him by the thorns in His forehead and the spear in His side, cry for vengeance in vain, vengeance upon those who have invoked it upon them and upon their children? It shall, and it will, be heard! Prophecy has uttered the words; and prophecy never faileth. When "the day of vengeance is in mine heart, and the year of my redeemed is come," "I will tread them in mine anger, and trample them in my fury, and their blood shall be sprinkled upon my garments, and I will stain all my raiment."[5]

[1] Rev. xix. 13–16. [2] Rev. xiv. 20. [3] Isaiah lxiii. 1.
[4] Rev. vi. 10. [5] Isaiah lxiii. 3, 4.

My beloved friends, is not this an awful doom for one to bring upon himself, and upon his children? I have not exaggerated a single word. I have not left the language of Scripture for an instant. All that I have said, and more besides, is contained therein; and over all there hangs the feeling that it is language that fails to convey its whole awfulness, and not that the theme is exhausted. What I have given you is the description, such as it can be received into a finite mind. The reality, when we shall become spiritualized and capable of taking in the whole sublimity, will far exceed our worst conception. Until that Day of Vengeance come, and we see the Almighty in His fierceness, and the Lamb in His wrath, and we feel the meaning of those words, "*The Blood of God:*" we shall not understand the horror of imprecating it *upon us*, and *upon our children.* Until then, we can only use the language of the Bible, and — comparing Scripture with Scripture, and gathering the materials of woe — warn you against the *burden of this Blood.* And oh! turn not away from the description! It is the part of true courage, and of true nobleness, to look the matter in the face. Say not, "These terrible things shall not drive me to religion." If they are *true,* they ought to drive you there: and it is your duty, for your own sakes and for your children's sakes, to determine whether they are true. Why should not the terrible things of God drive us to consideration? Is it the part of wisdom to despise what it may one day have to meet? — to rush on blindly, involving with you in one common fate all that you love most dearly, to what may be eternal death and intolerable anguish? If there be a probability in favor of the truth of Christianity, — and even to the most skeptical mind there is a very great probability, — you should at once adopt it and act upon it as if it were demonstration, so awful are the interests which are included under it. And believe me, that every day that probability will increase in your mind until it becomes moral certainty, and you feel as sure of its truth, as you do of your personal identity.

Men and brethren, strive to cut off this entail of the Blood of Jesus! Let it no longer cleave as a curse to you and yours; but, by the grace of God, change it into a blessing! Permit it not to rest upon you as a burden, sinking you down to condemnation; but use it as a fountain for sin and for uncleanness! It has been opened in the House of David for that purpose. To invoke it upon you and yours, is to abuse it, — to desecrate it: but to wash your robes in it, and make them "white in the Blood of the Lamb," *that* is to carry out the purpose of the Godhead. As we said before, this Blood must have its effect upon you, for evil or for good. You and yours cannot get rid of it. The world cannot get rid of it. It hath been shed, and every thing human and divine must submit before it. It is the mark that shall designate for mercy or for slaughter. Let it be upon *you* for mercy! Let it be the blood of *sprinkling*, of which the Apostle saith to the Hebrews, that it "speaketh better things than that of Abel."[1] Invoke that upon you and upon your children. Applied by the Spirit of God, who hath the treasure in His keeping, it cleanseth from all unrighteousness; it purgeth the conscience from dead works, to serve the living God; it purifies the corrupted nature; it turns aside the destroying angel, when he comes upon his work of vengeance. Sprinkled upon your House, you need fear nothing. Evil tidings shall not disturb you. The afflictions of life shall only refine you, as gold tried in the fire. Death, at his entrance, shall not dismay you: for the Blood is upon your lintel and your door-posts, and at the sight his sting grows pointless. The grave shall have no

[1] Heb. xii. 24.

darkness: for He sprinkled the sepulchre with His Blood, and light and immortality are there. The Judgment day shall have no terrors: for you and yours shall all be marked in the forehead, the water of Baptism having changed, under this sprinkling, and shining there a blood-red Cross. Pray, men and brethren, for this Blood to be sprinkled upon you at once, lest some of you be cut off ere it be done, and you go to Judgment with it witnessing against you.

And is not the preciousness of this Blood an inducement to you to cry unto God for the sprinkling of it upon you? If it were doubtful in its efficacy, you might hesitate about taking any especial pains to procure it: but its sufficiency is pledged by the everlasting covenant of God. God hath sworn, and will not repent: that it shall be glorified in His Kingdom; that it shall be the badge of honor in those realms of peace; the token of past forgiveness; the sign of eternal bliss. Its efficacy reacheth from eternity to eternity. It hath power to blot out every thing that is past; to assure every thing that is to come. Once sprinkled upon you and your children, it is forever there; and nothing shall take it from you, — neither man, nor angels, nor devils.

And is not the *freeness* of this Blood an inducement to you to cry unto God for the sprinkling of it upon you? "This is a faithful saying, and worthy of all acceptation, that Christ Jesus came into the world to save sinners."[1] If this was a boon which God were unwilling to grant, there were some better reason why you sought not after it, as you might lose your pains. But nothing can be more freely offered than is this Blood. "And the Spirit and the Bride say, Come. And let him that heareth say, Come. And let him that is athirst come."[2] Christ has been lifted up upon the Cross; and if, instead of scorning Him, you cast

[1] 1 Tim. i. 15.

[2] Rev. xxii. 17.

upon Him a look of *faith*, you shall not perish, but have everlasting life!

And are not the mighty agents that are at work ready to procure for you this Blood, an inducement to you to strive after it? The Throne of Grace is set up in the Heavens. A way to it has been opened by the Blood of Jesus. God sits more ready to hear, than we to pray. Go there; and ask, by the Agony and bloody Sweat, by the Cross and Passion, by the precious Death and Burial, by the glorious Resurrection and Ascension, of your Saviour, for the sprinkling of this Blood: and the Holy Ghost will come forth and subdue your hearts of unbelief, and show you the sufficiency of Jesus, and unite you to Him by a true and living faith. And in making those prayers, we have an Advocate with the Father, Jesus Christ the righteous; and the Holy Ghost intercedeth for us with groanings that cannot be uttered. The cry for mercy through the Blood of Jesus will always be heard there.

Men and brethren, come unto Jesus! He is waiting to receive you; and not only waiting, but He is abroad seeking them that are lost! He stretches out His arms over you, invoking blessings from His Father upon you. He has given you full manifestation of His willingness to save, in the Christians that are now around you. Why should He save us, and not you? We are no better, no worthier! Each one of us has cause to say, with S. Paul, "Christ Jesus came into the world to save sinners; of *whom I am chief*."[2] None of you can be worse than we were; for God does not reckon sin as man reckons it! Be not afraid. Cast yourself upon the Blood of Christ, and it will make you all that you desire, all that you need! Wait not until you are worthier. "They that are whole need not a physician, but they that are sick."[3] Come as you are, burdened

[1] 1 Tim. i. 15. [2] *Ibid.* [3] S. Luke v. 31.

with sin. It is safer that, than to remain burdened with the Blood of Christ. Coming with the burden of sin, you can but perish, having done your duty: remaining with the burden of Christ's Blood, nothing shall ever avail to purge you clean!

Twenty-eighth Sermon.

To this end was I born, and for this cause came I into the world, that I should bear witness unto the truth. Every one that is of the truth heareth my voice. — S. JOHN xviii. 37.

WHEN we recall the events which have made this day the most solemn in the Church's calendar, the most important in the records of our race, we turn with deep anxiety to search in every direction if by any means we may grasp something of the divine purpose for which such a catastrophe was consummated. Why such an Incarnation as this of Christ? Why such a life of wondrous woe, and such a death of terrible suffering? Why such a long array of promises, of types, of prophecies? In answer to this craving anxiety Christ Himself satisfies us, when He saith to Pilate: "To this end was I born, and for this cause came I into the world, that I should bear witness unto the truth. Every one that is of the truth heareth my voice."

To creatures situated as we are, there is nothing so important as truth; and at the same time nothing, I grieve to say, so unpalatable. Without the Truth, placed before us upon divine authority, we are in a most uncertain position, alike ignorant of the present and of the future. Both in the past, and in these days of accumulated knowledge, we have enough of human speculation and man's conjecture; but what we need is a Divine voice, uttering words from the fountain of wisdom and of truth. But while we need it, and in a certain measure crave it, it is nevertheless, when uttered, received with aversion and unbelief, because it does not harmonize with our preconceived views and wishes. But the value of Christ's incarnation is, that, being the Son of God, He cared more for our good than for our gratification; and when He did speak, did not dally with us, nor flatter us, but placed the truth fully before us, whether we would hear or whether we would forbear. His purpose was, to awaken us to our true condition, and then to offer us the only remedy in Heaven or earth for that condition.

Man disputes always the sinfulness of sin. There is no point upon which he continues in such great error, — no point upon which it is less easy to undeceive him. Every thing within him and around him operates to keep him wrong upon this point: his own corruption by the fall; the custom of the world which calls good evil, and evil good; the habits and fashions which surround him from his birth, and which all help to deceive him and to support his own views. Wherever he can see sin breaking out and disturbing society, — wherever he can feel it inflicting pain and suffering upon himself or those he cares for, — he is ready to confess its heinousness; but beyond this, when it affects only God and His spiritual universe, he does not understand why so much is made of it by the Church, and by those who call themselves the ambassadors of God upon earth. "What have I done?" is the question which he puts in connection with his own life. "What is there in my conduct to my neighbor that deserves the threatened punishment against sin? It is to enquiries like these that the coming and life of Christ give the divine answer: the first step towards truth.

How should God — who willed not the death of a sinner, but rather that he should come into the light and life of Truth — satisfy man of the odiousness of sin; — of sin in itself, abstracted from its injury to man and to society?

The effects of sin cannot always be traced. They are beyond our power to follow. They are separated again, at too long distances, from the sin which produced them. They ofttimes do not strike the senses, and so are lost upon us. How was sin to be so connected with its terrible results, as to make its sinfulness in God's view manifest to man? Some striking exhibition of His abhorrence of it must be made in the face of the world; some illustrious example of its horrible criminality, and then of its merciless punishment, must be given to our race. And so God arranged it, in His own Divine counsels, that when the attention of His suffering creatures had been attracted by a long course of events, unique and conspicuous, — events connecting themselves with the most conspicuous nations of antiquity, — He lifted up His own Son upon the Cross, that, dying the death of a malefactor, He might testify to this solemn truth, that sin could not be pardoned even in His sacred Person; — that God would not spare its odious features, even though they must be struck at through His only beloved Son.

Standing then, this morning, at the foot of the Cross, learn, my hearers, your first lesson in Divine Truth: that sin, however lightly you may think of it, will not be pardoned by God, except upon the conditions of the Gospel. If you have ever doubted the fearful nature of sin, because you have not witnessed its dreadful effects, contemplate them here. See in all that passed before the eyes of men upon this day, long centuries ago at Jerusalem, and which the Church brings back to you upon this its anniversary through all her services, what God thinks of that, which you commit so readily, and speak of so flippantly, and expect to obtain pardon for — if pardon be at all necessary — so easily. See how God deals with it when He encounters it in the Person of His only and well-beloved Son; and tremble lest he find you, at the last, subject to a like mercilessness at His hands. Christ upon the Cross is the witness to you, and to the solemn truth, that sin is an evil and a bitter thing!

In what spirit, my hearer, will you receive the truth? It is brought to your notice conspicuously to-day. Never again can any one of you say that you knew not the odiousness of sin in the sight of a pure and holy God. When you look at the Son of God, made Man, and born into the world of a woman; at Him whose glory was equal with the Father's for eternity; at Him whose birth made the Heavens to shine with glory, and the Angels announced; at Him whose pathway was one of wonders and miracles; at Him, whose Death convulsed all Nature: and see Him smitten by God for sin, and for nothing but sin; and that sin borne for us: every mouth must be stopped, and every conscience must be satisfied that God will not look upon iniquity. Whenever you feel inclined or tempted, my hearer, to consider sin as a little thing; to make a mock at it, like a fool; to despise its threatened punishment: only cast your eyes up to the Cross, and you will see that all which the Bible says to you; that all which society, in its universal subjection to the curse, attests to you; that all which your Ministers preach to you about the sinfulness of sin, is far less than the truth: that Christ alone, as He expires upon the Cross, can truly testify of its terribleness.

And should it not startle you, my hearer, when you thus are made to understand with what a dangerous thing you are trifling; with what boldness you handle sin; with what presumption you approach it; with what indifference you regard the committal of it? "The wages of sin is Death,"[1] the Apostle tells you: and you see Christ upon the Cross, suffering that Death for sin. Are you believers? Can you

[1] Rom. vi. 23.

deem this spectacle, which the Church brings before you this day, of your dying Saviour, to be any thing more than a fiction, and yet continue to sin recklessly? Ask yourselves these questions? Christ says: "To this end was I born, and for this cause came I into the world, that I should bear witness unto the truth." Do you believe His witness upon this point? You cannot evade the answer. Either you must deny the faith of your fathers, abjure Christianity, and cast yourself back upon natural religion, which never yet satisfied anybody: or confess that in your dying Saviour you see the certain foreshadowing of your own fate, unless you repent of sin and turn to Christ for succor and salvation!

But perchance you may say: "I see in my crucified Lord the punishment of accumulated sin, while I feel in myself no such monstrous burden." Sin was accumulated upon our Sin-offering, my hearer, because He was the Sacrifice for the sin of the world: but you must remember that it was a single sin which polluted creation, and made that accumulation a necessary consequence. Could that one sin of our first parents, which brought death into the world with all our woes, have been arrested at its beginning by a free pardon from God,—a pardon without an atonement and without a mediator,—think you that He could not, upon the instant, have blotted it out, and thus have rid his guiltless creation of the curse? Your argument only brings out more forcibly the intensity of the poison of sin, showing that when once committed it could not be arrested in its terrible career of guilt and curse and punishment, save through the long process which led up to the Incarnation, and suffering, and death of Christ. It rushed on, like a pestilence, cleaving its hideous pathway through the habitations of men, infecting every thing, polluting every thing, cursing every thing, dooming all men to the fires of hell.

Until our High Priest could cast himself between man and its fury, it threatened universal destruction. Comfort not yourself, therefore, my hearer, with the soothing balm of not being a great sinner! A single sin was enough to pollute the whole creation: and you surely will not say that you have never committed a single sin. A single sin was enough to accumulate all that guilt for which Christ died; was enough to bring about this bloody Sacrifice which the Church exhibits before you this day. A single sin is sufficient to bring down upon you the whole penalty of the Law. Jesus Christ is my witness, for He has said in His Holy Word: "Whosever shall keep the whole law and yet offend in one point, he is guilty of all."[1]

Another point, my hearers, about which you are all skeptical, and which you are most loth to admit, is the corruption of human nature. While you are all ready to admit that there is a vast deal of vice and crime in the world, you cannot consent to any such proposition, as that it is the necessary product of that nature of which you yourself are so fond and so proud. You ascribe it, in the individuals in whom it is exhibited, to some unhappy taint of blood; to some unfortunate conjuncture of circumstances; to some special ill-training; to some overpowering temptation; or, at least, to some natural badness of disposition peculiar to the individual. But this is all false. Come with me again to the Cross, and let your suffering Saviour be my witness. Study that sight! He that is dying upon the Cross is a Being of two Natures, — a conjunction in one Person of the human and the Divine. That which is human in Him is suffering for the sin laid upon Him, — for the corruption of man which has produced that sin. That which is Divine is supporting and sustaining the humanity. The manifestations of sublime thoughts and words which burst

[1] S. James ii. 10.

from His dying lips, are all divine; they belong to Him as a part of the God-Man. You witness submission to God's will; humility under trial; long-suffering under torture; love in opposition to malice; forgiveness in the midst of taunts, insults, and revilings. These manifest his Divinity! Now cast your eyes upon those who stand around that dying Son of God! See those looks of hatred and scorn! Hear those taunts of ridicule! Mark the joy which beams from their infuriated eyes as He evinces suffering and decay! Behold that wretch giving Him vinegar and gall for His thirst! See that soldier thrusting his spear into the side of Him that was already dead! That, my hearer, is your nature! The sufferer is Divine, without sin, worthy to win the crown of everlasting glory as a Conqueror. The executioners and scoffers are human: and Christ is thus made again the witness to you of a solemn truth, that man cannot appreciate Divine goodness; and that the only perfect Man who ever lived, perfect as his Father in Heaven is perfect, was the Man of deepest sorrows, and of the cruellest sufferings; — sufferings even unto death, at the hands of those whom He was sent to save!

"Yes," may you say, "but these were the Jews!" So they were, but that only plunges you deeper into difficulty. They were the elect people of God; and from whom, therefore, should we have expected greater freedom from corruption than from the Jews? Had Jehovah not committed to them His oracles? Did not the covenant, and the adoption, and the law, and the promises, pertain to them? Was not our Lord Himself a Jew after the flesh? Were not His disciples and Apostles Jews? Were not the great company of believers, who first illustrated the Church, Jews? Is there any reply to this? Because the Jews are now blinded and under a curse for this very Crucifixion, they were not always so. They were the only people then upon earth in whom any thing approaching to spiritual life and spiritual holiness could have been found. Think you that any of the Gentile nations of whom S. Paul makes mention in the first chapter of his Epistle to the Romans would have done better! No, my hearers; this is not a door through which you may escape. These miserable men around that Cross were Jews; but as Jews they represented, at that time, the most enlightened and most divinely instructed people upon the face of the earth! It was an exhibition of human nature; of your nature, my hearers, when excited by passion and sin; of that broken and defiled image of the Divine Spirit which was left you when driven, a fallen and corrupted being, from the presence of the Lord!

A third point, which some of you, and many in the world, count foolishness, and upon which you are therefore skeptical, and for which Christ came to be a witness, is the necessity of an atonement for sin through the shedding of blood. You cannot see, you say, how it is, or why it is, that blood should expiate sin, and cleanse from all unrighteousness. No more can I, my hearer, — although I may see more clearly than you, — pronounce otherwise than that so the Lord has ordered it: but this I say, that the Cross of Christ testifies to us of *the fact*. Standing at the foot of the Cross, I am forced to believe it: for I can find no other solution of His sufferings and Death; no other explanation of the effects which flowed from that Death. I cannot understand—if Jesus of Nazareth is a mere example, or teacher, or philosopher — why He should have shed His Blood upon the Cross; and especially why it should have been connected, through long ages, with the blood of bulls and goats, and with the morning and evening sacrifice. Surely the Old Testament, the larger portion of the Bible, has a meaning. God designed not to trifle with His people. He did not descend upon Mount Sinai in the glory of His sublime Majesty, and there detail the minute arrangements of sacrificial offerings, for nothing. Until they pointed to something in the future, they were unmeaning and profitless, not to say foolish. Would Jehovah have instituted these things in His Law, and then have permitted His prophets, those whom He inspired through His own Spirit, to expose their impotence in the letter, unless there was an Antitype to interpret and ratify every thing? All this the Epistle to the Hebrews — especially that chapter which has been read as the Epistle for the Day — argues fully and elaborately and conclusively: "For it is not possible that the blood of bulls and of goats should take away sins. Wherefore, when He cometh into the world, he saith, Sacrifice and offering thou wouldst not, but a body hast thou prepared me." No, my hearers; you must cut out the larger part of the Revelation of God, you must overlay His whole dealings with His elect people, you must charge Him with unmeaning action, ere, standing under the shadow of the Cross, you can deny that the shedding of Blood is connected with His remission of sins!

Nor is there any solution for the effects of Christ's death, save in the sanctifying and converting power of His Blood. Change the scene for a moment, but I will not carry you out of Jerusalem. I will only ask you to advance the time for a few weeks, and then to note the strange scene which is enacting by that same multitude which hurried our Lord so madly to Calvary, and there gloated upon His sufferings. At His Cross, while suffering and dying, we could find but one of His Apostles: the rest were scattered from fear and disappointment. Peter followed, afar off. In this scene to which I now invite your attention, we hear those same Apostles, addressing an amazed and smitten multitude; so filled with a holy enthusiasm as to carry them entirely away; charging home upon them the Crucifixion of Jesus; calling them, to their faces, murderers; fixing His Blood upon them! What means this? What has produced this divine boldness? Do you believe, with the skeptical gainsayers, that they were filled with new wine? Could new wine teach them to speak in other tongues? Could new wine give them the power to make that implacable multitude, stained with the guilt of the death of Jesus, whom every word was piercing like a sword, smite upon their breasts and say: "Men and brethren, what shall we do?" As great a change has passed on them as on the Apostles. From murderers they have been changed into penitents! From being vile sinners who had dared to say, "His blood be on us and on our children," they were trembling supplicants, crying for mercy. From being a rabble polluted with almost every sin, they were now the baptized disciples of Jesus, the redeemed with that very Blood which they had shed, laying broad and deep the foundation of the Church. What is the solution for this? I cannot conceive why the Apostles should influence the same men, whom Christ — the Example, the Model — only drove to malice and persecution; why ignorant and unlearned fishermen and tax-gatherers should so suddenly effect what all the miracles and teachings of Christ had failed to do: unless I receive what I think that the Bible clearly teaches, — that His Blood had cleansed and sanctified both Apostles and multitude, and had worked within them the new life of spiritual power.

Such was the way in which our Lord was a witness to the truth. He was born for that end and purpose. He was a witness to it through His whole life, using its force to break up old opinions, to clear away traditional rubbish, to develop the proper idea of God and His kingdom. He bore witness to it in His death, exhibiting and enforcing the sublime ideas which I have developed in the early part of my sermon. And now He rules by the power of truth, and witnesses to it daily and forever in the hearts of men. It was foretold, in Isaiah, that He should be a witness to the people,—a leader and commander to the people; and so He is. The whole foundation of Christ's kingdom is Truth, Divine Truth: and therefore it is the Rock against which all error is being perpetually dashed to pieces. Its spirit and genius are truth. "Christ conquers," as one has well said, "by the convincing evidence of Truth; rules by the commanding power of Truth; and in His Majesty rides prosperously, because of Truth. It is 'with His truth,' as the Psalmist says, that He shall 'judge the people.' It is the sceptre of His Kingdom. He draws men to him by its cords, and brings their thoughts into obedience to it; and thus He rules over His subjects through conviction and Love." Every one that is of the truth heareth His voice.

Solemn words are these of Christ, with which He closed His answer to Pilate: "Every one that is of the truth heareth my voice." What then of those who hear not Christ's voice?—of the many, many who cling to the old errors of the world's philosophy, or are carried away by the current fancies of the day? Remember that, in the Bible, Satan is called the father of lies; and is in direct antagonism to our Lord who is "the truth." If you hear not Christ's voice, as it speaks to you through His Word and the action of His Church (but especially from His Cross), whose voice are you listening to? The one tells you, by all His sufferings for you, that this world is but a passing show, full of illusions, a vale of misery through which you must pass in darkness and much sorrow: the other, that it is full of pleasures; that it is the only reality of life; that you are certain of nothing better; and that if you give this life up to God, you will be giving up every thing which is really yours. Which voice will you hear? To which kingdom will you belong? Truth and error are offered to you, — the one by Christ, the other by the Devil. There is no middle ground. Truth is one and immutable. Error is manifold, spewing out its horrid spawn in shoals; and, like the chameleon, changing its hue, that it may deceive and elude. There was a time when Error had all the advantage; but the times of that ignorance are passed, and Truth is, for you, manifest in the Person of Christ. The life of Christ has taught the world that virtue, active virtue, finds no favor in it; has but little chance of life or influence; wins no prizes of riches or honor; and often goes down in sorrow to the grave. His Death has taught it, just as plainly, that sin is the curse which is most odious to God, and should be most hateful to man; that we are all sinners, — corrupt, and dark, and allied to error; that His Blood alone can change us, and bring us from darkness into light. If you will hear the Voice which cometh from this Life and from this Death, then shall you be blessed, my hearer, for time and for eternity. Be not satisfied until Truth is a part and parcel of your being; until you are made one with Him who is the Truth, even as He is one with His Father, the Fountain and Source of all things for the universe.

1866.

Twenty-ninth Sermon.

But Mary stood without at the sepulchre weeping: and as she wept she stooped down and looked into the sepulchre, and seeth two angels in white, sitting, the one at the head, and the other at the feet, where the body of Jesus had lain. And they say unto her, Woman, why weepest thou? She saith unto them, Because they have taken away my Lord, and I know not where they have laid him. And when she had thus said, she turned herself back, and saw Jesus standing, and knew not that it was Jesus. — S. JOHN XX. 11–14.

THE grave and a woman weeping over it, is the standing witness of the curse which sin has brought upon the world. Wherever there is a home, there is a grave; and wherever there is a grave there is a woman weeping over it. It would seem as if the keenest punishment visited upon woman, because of her having been first in the transgression, has been inflicted upon her through her affections. Because of the depth of them, she clings to those she loves through every sorrow of life; and because of their permanence, she hovers, weeping, around their graves. Mary, by the sepulchre of Jesus, was the type of womanhood; and her attitude of sorrow, as she stands gazing upon that burial-place of her hopes and her affections, was that of woman wherever we meet her upon earth. Like Mary, she often goes there without faith or hope, looking at the earth which covers all she loves, yet comforting herself by weeping over it. She looked upon the grave as a devouring enemy which had swallowed up all her present joy, and separated her forever from the desire of her eyes. And oh! how long has she stood there without any ground of hope, or any room for faith. Long weary years rolled away, before Jesus came, and in His resurrection opened for her the glorious vision of hope through the dew of His blood! We pity those who, in the ages of that ignorance, stood "like Niobe, all tears:" but our pity gives place to amazement when we see her still clinging to the inanimate dust. For surely the coming of Christ has changed the aspect of every thing connected with death, as well as with life. The grave is no longer what the grave has been. It still hides from us the bodies of those we love: but hides them only as the earth hides the seed while it is preparing to renew its life; only as the chrysalis hides the worm while it is changing into a thing of beauty, no longer to creep upon the earth, but to soar in the atmosphere of Heaven. Woman may still haunt the graves of those she loves and may still weep there, but not as she wept of yore: for "I would not have you to be ignorant, brethren," says S. Paul, "concerning them which are asleep, that ye sorrow not, even as others which have no hope. For if we believe that Jesus died and rose again, even so them also which sleep in Jesus will God bring with him."[1] Once the grave seemed indeed the end of all to man; and as the loving heart stood by it, it had cause to weep, — to weep as those which had no hope. It looked icy and impenetrable. It appeared to bear the motto which the fancy of Dante inscribed over the portals of his *Inferno:* "Let all that enter here leave hope behind." No wonder that even Mary stood by the sepulchre weeping: for she had not yet learned the glorious truth that the weakest Christian can now lay his hand upon the dust of which he was formed and to which he is doomed to return, and can exultingly ask, "O grave, where is thy victory?" and, in the very face of Death, can utter over his dead the consoling strain of prophecy;

[1] 1 Thess. iv. 13, 14.

"Awake and sing, ye that dwell in dust: for thy dew is as the dew of herbs, and the earth shall cast out the dead."[1]

But Mary was not satisfied with mere weeping. She needed more comfort than tears could give her. She must look into the sepulchre, and see the loved Body of Jesus for herself. She must understand the secrets of that dread grave which was closing up forever her heart, and cutting off all the rich hopes which the life of Jesus of Nazareth had waked within her bosom and the bosom of the Disciples. She was not satisfied with the report of others; she would examine the sepulchre for herself. And her faithfulness received its due reward. She did not at first find Jesus; but she found Angels who instructed and comforted her;—messengers sent from God to do honor to His beloved Son, and to teach her that there was no gloom hereafter in the grave, no barrier that could not be broken through, no stone that could not be rolled from the door of the sepulchre. She saw them—for her eyes were now opened to perceive them—"sitting, the one at the head, and the other at the feet, where the body of Jesus had lain." As one has beautifully said: "His resting-place was between two Angels, like the mercy-seat of old. Even in His death He is found to have dwelt, as of old, between the cherubim."

If we, my beloved people, need comfort at the grave, we must find it, as Mary did, by looking into the sepulchre. We must not be satisfied to gaze upon the mound of earth which covers our dead, or to look upon the sepulchre which holds their bodies: but we must endeavor to look into it, and to study it for ourselves. We must not be afraid of looking Death in the face; nor of standing by the grave, and demanding its secrets. If we go there boldly in the

[1] Isaiah xxvi. 19.

name of Jesus, we too shall find angels to instruct and comfort us. We must not trust to others in a matter like this: we must search for ourselves. Death is too terrible an enemy for us to pass him by without contesting his claims to hold us in bondage. The grave is too dark a pit for us to lie in, passive and submissive, without endeavoring to throw light upon its darkness. And it rests now with ourselves to understand it all, through faith. If, instead of merely weeping at the sepulchre, we will pierce into it, we shall find prophets and Apostles and the Son of God Himself, — messengers from God, angels, and more than angels, — ready to enlighten us; full of hope, and full of comfort: shedding into its darkest recesses light and immortality. We ought never, in these days, to stand by the grave without the Bible in our hands. Instead of weeping there, we should read the story of Jesus at the grave of Lazarus. We should dwell upon his solemn words: "I am the Resurrection and the Life;" and we should elucidate them through these scenes which the Church illustrates to-day. The Gospels contain the utterances of *our* angels; and we should never look upon a grave without seeing them sitting there, and uttering to us the words of comfort and of hope. Poor creatures of sense that we are! because we do not see, we cannot believe. Because the grave does not open for us, and we do not *behold* the angels sitting there, we cannot take in the glorious truth that the dust of those we love is watched over by the eyes of Jesus, — is consecrated dust, waiting only for the signal from its ascended Redeemer to spring to life, immortal, glorious, spiritual! And yet these messengers of God tell us so; point us to the empty grave of Jesus; and sound in our ears what ought to be the words of the world's jubilee: "Because I live, ye shall live also!"[1] Oh that we could have faith but as a grain of mus-

[1] S. John xiv. 19.

tard seed! — how should we then rise above these darkest shadows of our life, Death and the Grave, and dwell in an atmosphere of hope, sorrowing over those we love, because they are separated from us, but yet rejoicing in the hope of everlasting life!

The question of the Angels to Mary when they saw her weeping at such a scene of wonder and of glory, was just such a question as Angels only would have asked: "Woman, why weepest thou?" Men would never have asked such a question, when they saw a woman weeping at a grave. They would have known too well its meaning. They would at once have understood, from what themselves had witnessed and experienced of life, the reason for her tears. She was standing near a sepulchre: that was enough for man. Tears and the grave had been ever associated in their minds. But when the angels saw her weeping, they only marvelled: for they had no knowledge of Death or of the grave. No such curse had ever fallen upon them. No such enemies had ever been known in Heaven among unfallen spirits. And what they now knew of death and of the grave, was associated with victory and triumph, — with the overthrow of him who had the power of death. They saw her weeping, when she should have been shouting for joy; lamenting, when she should have been singing *Alleluia* to Him who had put under His feet the cruellest enemies of her race. She found comfort, but no sympathy. They could not even comprehend her tears: "Woman, why weepest thou?" Heaven is glowing with one universal feeling of exultation. Its hosts are marshalling to welcome the Conqueror home; and thousands and ten thousands of Angels are tuning their harps to the refrain: "Lift up your heads, O ye gates; and be ye lift up, ye everlasting doors: and the King of glory shall come in. Who is this King of glory? the LORD strong and mighty, the LORD mighty in battle."[1] "Why weepest thou?" It was not for Angels that He died; it was for you. It was not for the unfallen hosts of Heaven that He was laid in this sepulchre; it was for you: and yet thou weepest at His victory! If they are tears of joy, we can comprehend them; but tears such as woman has shed in the past over the grave, have no place here. The sepulchre is henceforth the burial-place of grief. Woman is to find here, in the future, the source of all her hopes, — the fountain of a love which is to be undying!

And as the Angels asked this question of Mary, so may we, the messengers of this risen Saviour, ask it of every one of you who has a Christian hope. Weak as we are ourselves; trembling as we do before Death and the Grave; we feel, as the ambassadors of God, that we can yet ask you: "Why weepest thou?" I know that Love is strong as Death; that nature has a yearning which cannot be satisfied with words; but we have that here, in the incidents of this scene, which are much more than words. They are *acts*, — acts of the sublimest import, performed by the Son of God Himself; done for us his creatures; wielded against our bitterest and most cruel enemies. Weep not, woman, at least for to-day! Dry your tears, however full may be your heart, while standing with Mary at the sepulchre of Jesus! What the angels implied in their question to her, they implied for your sake. As old Bishop Andrewes said: "They mean, that she had no cause to weep. She weeps because she found the grave empty, which God forbid she should have found full! — for then Christ must have been dead still; and so, no Resurrection. And this case of Mary Magdalene is our case oftentimes: in the error of our conceit, to weep where we have no cause; to joy where we have as little. Where we have cause to joy, we weep;

[1] Psalm xxiv. 7, 8.

and where to weep, we joy. False joys and false sorrows, false hopes and false fears, this life of ours is full of. God help us ! "

And this, mourner, is one of the occasions upon which you are weeping, when you should be rejoicing ! You are indulging a false sorrow, if you be weeping over one that is asleep in Jesus. "He is not dead, but sleepeth." He is taking rest after the sharp battle of life, awaiting in hope the final resurrection. Jesus is guarding his dust, and the grave is sanctified by angels' presence, because it is sown with seeds of immortality. Strive to lay aside your spirit of heaviness, and to receive the oil of joy for mourning! Trust your dead to Him who Himself has died, and can sympathize with the dead far more than you. Leave their ashes with Him who Himself has lain for days in the grave, and knows far better than you what the departed spirit needs. The lesson we have to learn, and which we find it so hard to learn, is that a loving God is with us at all times and in all places: with us in life, with us in death, and with us when sleeping in the grave as well as when sleeping upon our beds. He never leaves us, nor forsakes us. He breathes into us the breath of life; He carries us in His arms when we are weak or sick; He guards us from perils and dangers, both of body and soul; He walks with us through the valley of the shadow of Death; He receives our spirits as we pass under the yoke of our last enemy; and He commands the earth to hold our dust until the last trump shall summon our bodies from this universal sepulchre. We are in no more danger in the grave than in our beds. God takes equal care of us in the one as in the other. "Woman, why weepest thou" at witnessing the scene which has produced all this? It is a false sorrow: not a pretended, but a *false* sorrow!

The answer of Mary showed that while her affection was

strong, her faith was weak. "She saith unto them, Because they have taken away my Lord, and I know not where they have laid him." She was thinking of the beloved Master for whom her heart yearned, and not of the rising again in three days which He had told them of. She seemed to have forgotten every thing in her grief, — His promises, His power over death, His Divinity, the signs and wonders which had accompanied His Death. Her woman's heart had driven out her remembrance of all these things, and her simple cry was, "The Body, the Body!" As Matthew Henry says: "Mary Magdalene is not diverted from her inquiries by the surprise of the vision, nor satisfied with the honor of it; but still she harps upon the same string: 'They have taken away my Lord.' A sight of Angels and their smiles will not suffice, without a sight of Christ, and God's smiles in him." He had been every thing to her, for it was she out of whom He had cast seven devils: and she had rather find his dead Body than hear of any thing else.

And as with Mary, so with us in our grief. We forget every thing in the intensity of our love. We crave the body which has been taken from us, and are impatient at any words which are used to divert us from our grief. Mary would scarcely listen to the Angels: and thus too, the grieved and smitten heart turns away, in the first bitterness of its grief, from the messages of comfort which are written for its balm in the Word of the Gospel. She grieved for Jesus, who had life in Himself, — who could lay it down and take it again. We grieve for those who can have no more life save in the power of His resurrection. Instead of seeking Him at once, and turning to Him, and clinging to Him for comfort: we cry out for the body, — the body that we loved! Oh slow of heart to believe! The body could not help you, for the spirit of *life* is gone. Christ alone can help you, who is the Resurrection and the Life, — who in the fullness of time will give you back that body, a new creation: changed, as S. Paul says, from corruption to incorruption, from weakness to power, from dishonor to glory, from a natural body to a spiritual body. How much better to wait upon the will of the Lord, and upon the appointed process of change, than to permit your private griefs to break through the bounds of His love and interfere with His gracious purposes! "In your patience possess ye your souls."[1] Patience has its work in grief, as well as in trial and temptation; and must be allowed to have her perfect work. If that Body for which Mary stood weeping had not been taken away, what should have become of her, and us, and all our race? For "if Christ be not risen, then is our preaching vain, and your faith is also vain."[1] And as with that body of our Lord, so likewise with those bodies after which we are craving. Unless they were taken from us, the order of the world could not go on; Christ could not make up the number of his elect; the fullness of the Gentiles could not come in; and the whole purpose of the economy of grace should be impeded, if not frustrated. Are we ready for these things? Should we not rather add our loved ones to the gathering crowd of the redeemed, than clog the chariot wheels of the Redeemer's triumphal march by our selfish wishes? Surely the glory that awaits those who die in Christ should help to satisfy our hearts!

During the time that the Congregational churches of the Eastern States were many of them insidiously passing into Unitarianism, and the ministers were leaving Christ and His atoning Blood out of their prayers and sermons, one of these ministers, as he came from a service in which his Saviour had been but little noticed or honored, met one of his old communicants weeping in the porch of his meeting-

[1] S. Luke xxi. 19. [2] 1 Cor. xv. 14.

house. He asked her the very question which the Angels asked of Mary: "Woman, why weepest thou?" And her answer was, like Mary's: "Because you have taken away my Lord, and I know not where you have laid Him." This, my hearer, should be indeed to you a sufficient cause for weeping, if indeed you should find that your Lord had been taken away from you, — taken away from you because you were not worthy of having Him; because you did not value His presence; because you set up idols in your heart which drove Him thence. Bitter cause have you for weeping, if this be your condition: for now are you weeping, not at the emptiness of the sepulchre, but at the desolation of your own heart: not at one loved object taken from you, but at the ashes and dust into which every thing has changed within you. Look to it lest your earthly grief produce this effect upon you, — lest the idolatry of your heart for the dead, drive Christ away from you!

The end of it was, that Christ rewarded her love by manifesting Himself unto her: "And when she had thus said, she turned herself back, and saw Jesus standing, and knew not that it was Jesus." As one has well said: "Before they had given her any answer, Christ steps in Himself to satisfy her inquiries; for God now speaketh to us by His Son: none but He Himself can direct us to Himself. Mary would fain know where her Lord is; and behold, He is at her right hand. Those that will be content with nothing short of a sight of Christ, shall be put off with nothing less. Is it Christ that thou wouldst have? Christ thou shalt have." He may hide Himself for a little moment, so that thou shalt not know Him: but nevertheless He is by thee, even though thou dost not for the moment recognize Him. He hid himself, that He might try Mary's love and faith: but they stood firm through every test; and she found, not a dead Body, but a living Saviour!

And so will it always be, my beloved people, with those who seek Christ in sincerity, with earnestness and love. They may not find Him at once: but they will surely find Him at last. Sense may be no judge of the presence of Christ. "Sometimes it pleases our Saviour to appear unto his, not like Himself: His holy disguises are our trials." But He is leading us on, often with tears in our eyes, among the graves: but always to light and joy. Be not afraid to follow Him: all will be right at the last.

We began with weeping, and end with joy. And thus are fulfilled those rich words of Scripture: "He that goeth forth and weepeth, bearing precious seed, shall doubtless come again with rejoicing, bringing his sheaves with him."[1] Mary went to the sepulchre, loving, but hopeless: she came back bearing the joyful tidings of Christ's resurrection. She went there rich in affection, but weak in faith: she returned, her faith having been changed into sight. And this is Life, if we use it aright. Begun in tears; spent weeping among graves: we may end it in the arms of a risen and glorified Saviour; asking, in the full assurance of hope: "O Death, where is thy sting? O Grave, where is thy victory?"

1866.

[1] Psalm cxxvi. 6.

Thirtieth Sermon.

And when the day of Pentecost was fully come, they were all with one accord in one place. And suddenly there came a sound from heaven as of a rushing mighty wind, and it filled all the house where they were sitting. And there appeared unto them cloven tongues like as of fire, and it sat upon each of them. And they were all filled with the Holy Ghost, and began to speak with other tongues, as the Spirit gave them utterance. — ACTS ii. 1–4.

THE fulfillment of the promise of the Father for which Christ had commanded His Apostles to wait at Jerusalem, found them all assembled upon the day of Pentecost, with one accord, in one place. "Behold, how good and how pleasant it is for brethren to dwell together in unity! It is like the precious ointment upon the head, that ran down upon the beard, even Aaron's beard: that went down to the skirts of his garments; as the dew of Hermon, and as the dew that descended upon the mountains of Zion: for there the Lord commanded the blessing, even life for evermore."[1] And not only is it like them, but it produces them: for lo! here upon these brethren, mingled together in love and prayer, descends the Holy Ghost, — the Antitype of that very sacred oil which consecrated Aaron to his priesthood, of that dew of Hermon which filled with life and beauty the mountains of Zion. May the eye of the Holy God, that Eye which searcheth the reins and the heart, perceive in us such charity, such faith, such unanimity, that at least a little of that oil may trickle upon us,

[1] Psalm cxxxiii.

who are as it were the skirts of the garment of our Aaron, —that something of the dew of Hermon may descend upon us, reviving us unto life everlasting. "Now is the accepted time,"[1] for "the day of Pentecost" is "fully come."

Every thing under the Old Testament was arranged for the more perfect covenant which was to be made in the latter days, — that covenant which was designated by the writing of the law upon the heart: the event that we celebrate to-day. Whatever was arranged by Moses was arranged after the pattern in the Mount, after the directions uttered by the mouth of Jehovah. Nothing was contrived by himself. When he spake to the Israelites, he was but the mouthpiece of their God; and that God, who saw the end of every thing from the beginning, took in, in his dispositions of the Old Testament ritual, that completer manifestation of the Godhead which was to be made when the fullness of time was come. It was by no chance, then, that the Holy Ghost came down upon the day of Pentecost. No! that was the day ordained, fixed upon, sealed, "from the beginning, or ever the earth was."[2] Its meaning was deep; and unless we read that meaning, much that is beautiful in the correspondency and harmony of things is lost.

The lamb that was slain at that first memorable Passover which the Israelites ate the night they were delivered from Egyptian bondage, was typical of that "Lamb slain from the foundation of the world,"[3] whose death the Church commemorates at a period correspondent with the Jewish Passover. Reckoning fifty days from that Passover, the Jews received the Law from Sinai, — received it on the day of Pentecost, a day forever memorable in their annals as linking them with Deity in the closest bonds of govern-

[1] 2 Cor. vi. 2. [2] Prov. viii. 23. [3] Rev. xiii. 8.

ment. Thenceforward their whole polity was theocratic; God lived in the midst of them, and was their King: so plainly such, that He said to Samuel, when that prophet mourned in vexation that the Israelites would have a king: "Hearken unto the voice of the people in all that they say unto thee: for they have not rejected thee, but they have rejected me, that I should not reign over them."[1]

Ever after that was He to be found over the mercy-seat, the place of His abode with the children of men.

It was in rich harmony, therefore, that upon the day of Pentecost the new Law, spoken of by the prophets, should be written in fire, by the finger of the Holy Ghost, upon the hearts of the Apostles. That which made the day illustrious under the Old Testament dispensation was to pass away; but not so the glory of the day: for even as the glory of the latter house was greater than the glory of the former house, because it enshrined Christ when incarnate; so does the day of Pentecost exceed in dignity and majesty its ancient renown, because upon it the Godhead removed from temples of wood and stone, and took up an abode in the hearts of the faithful. A new Law, and a new place of abode for the Godhead: but no new day. The day of Pentecost for both. God never changes that which needs no change. Moses' law must be changed into Christ's Law; the Covenant which gendered to bondage, into that which was full of liberty: but both must bear the same relation to the Death of the Lamb, to teach us that while they differ in their terms, they are the same in essence and in truth.

Another harmony is given us by S. Chrysostom, which is full of beauty and fitness. At the feast of Pentecost, under the law, was the sickle put into the corn, the first fruits of which had been offered up just fifty days before, at the feast

[1] 1 Sam. viii. 7.

of the Passover. Under the Gospel, it was gloriously correspondent that, at the same feast of Pentecost, the sickle should be put into the harvest of souls, Christ the first-fruits having offered Himself before the Lord just fifty days before, when He burst the grave and rose triumphant to His Father. The great spiritual harvest which began at this Feast, and which has ever since continued, is but the fulfillment, the reality, the substance, of that harvest which the Israelites yearly gathered in: they, like men, rejoicing over the weighty sheaves which filled their land with plenty; Jehovah, God-like, in the many souls that the love of the Son, and the power of the Spirit, were to gather into the Kingdom of Glory. How beautiful it is, thus to see the invisible in the visible, to lay over against the works of Nature and the operations of man, the works of Grace and the power of the Holy Ghost!

Upon this day of Pentecost, then, came down the Holy Ghost upon the Apostles. And as, upon the delivery of the Law at Mount Sinai, the Israelites saw the majesty of Jehovah in the Mount that burned with fire, and the lightnings and tempest that burst over its awful summit, and heard the voice of winds, and the sound of a trumpet: so, upon this day, was the new Law ushered in with a sound from Heaven as of a rushing mighty wind, and the presence of the Godhead made visible to them in tongues of fire resting upon their heads. They both were ushered in with fire: but one was the fire of wrath, the other the fire of mercy; the one indicated the consuming fire which God is, out of Christ, the other the purifying fire which God is, in the Holy Ghost. They both were accompanied by a sound. The sound of a trumpet — sad foreboding of the Archangel's trump, that shall summon the wicked to the mount of judgment — preceded the delivery of the Law: the sound of a mighty rushing Wind — that Wind which the prophet summoned to blow upon the dry bones in the Valley of Vision, which the Church prayed might breathe upon her to fit her for the presence of her Lord — announced the incoming of the Holy Ghost. May that gracious Wind blow upon us this day, filling us with the fullness of its grace! May the baptism of fire purge away our dross, that so the fires of hell may have nothing whereon to banquet!

How careful is the sacred writer to note that this sound as of a rushing mighty Wind came from Heaven! Ah, my hearers, there is many a wind which rushes by and through the Church, that is not from Heaven! Be not "carried about," says the Apostle, "with every wind of doctrine."[1] "Try the spirits," says another Apostle, "whether they are of God."[2] And nothing is there more important for us, than to determine this matter, — than to be skillful to discern whether the sounds and spirits that are about us and within us come from Heaven! Satan is skillful in deception, and will put on the garb of spiritual beauty to deceive. But there is one dress which he cannot assume, — one test which he cannot bear. He cannot put on holiness. He cannot abide the test of Scripture. He can be, by turns, every spirit save the spirit of holiness. He can withstand every formula of abjuration, but that which Christ employed against him: "It is written."[3] Let us measure every sound that comes into the Church by its results. Does it lead to holiness? Does it render Christians more humble, more meek, more like Jesus? Does it put them upon the searching of motives, upon the correcting of habit, upon the subjugation of passions? Does it fill them with good works? Then is it a sound from Heaven. Try every spirit by the Scriptures, whether it be a spirit in ourselves or in others, whether it be in our teachers or in those

[1] Eph. iv. 14. [2] 1 S. John iv. 1. [3] S. Matt. iv. 4.

we teach. Can it bear the scrutiny of the Bible? Can it harmonize with that Spirit which inspired the prophets and the Apostles? All that is written in the Scriptures is by inspiration of the Holy Ghost. There has He impressed Himself; there is His image. Place every spirit opposite that mirror, and it will certify you whether it be a spirit of purity or one of pollution. And let me pray you, my Christian friends, not only to know but to use these instruments for the detection of Satan. He is busy, awfully busy, within the Church and without the Church. Examine yourselves, whether ye be in the faith. Try every spirit, whether it come from Heaven.

When the Holy Ghost descended upon our Lord, He took the shape of a Dove, — the emblem of gentleness, of purity, of peace. Upon the Apostles He comes with the appearance of cloven tongues, like as of fire. And there was fitness in both these shapes. It was not meet that He should come upon Christ as fire; for He it was that the Baptist foretold as coming to baptize with fire and the Holy Ghost, not to be baptized therewith. Nor yet was it needful that He, who could speak with the tongues of men and of angels, should have His lips touched with a live coal from off the Altar. Upon Him must the Holy Ghost descend in that form which most expressed His distinctive Nature, his Spirit of Holiness: and what so fit as a dove, the only fowl that under the Law was clean, and allowed for sacrifice. But the Apostles required to be baptized, and upon them was poured out the Spirit foretold of Joel, in the manner prophesied of John: it was the baptism of fire and of the Holy Ghost, — of fire in the shape of tongues, that it might be diffused on every hand to enlighten and warm the nations into spiritual life. For the blessing of the nations, for the indication to the world that the sound of the Gospel was to go out into all lands, that the Holy Ghost was to be given to the Gentiles as well as to the Jews, was the curse of Babel turned into a blessing. *There*, God made every man to speak in a different tongue, so that each was severed from the rest: *here*, were "devout men, out of every nation under heaven," "Parthians, and Medes, and Elamites, and the dwellers in Mesopotamia, and in Judea, and Cappadocia, in Pontus, and Asia, Phrygia, and Pamphylia, in Egypt, and in the parts of Libya about Cyrene, and strangers of Rome, Jews and proselytes, Cretes and Arabians,"[1] hearing the Gospel preached every man in his own tongue wherein he was born. *There*, were the counsels of men discomfited, that they might not waste their pains in striving to escape God's wrath: *here* were they furthered, by rich powers from on high, that they might teach their fellow-men how to find God's mercy.

"God can send," says one of our old English writers, "from heaven no better thing, nor the devil from hell no worse thing, than the Tongue: 'the best member we have' saith the Psalmist; 'the worst member we have' saith the Apostle: both, as it is employed.

"The best, if it be of God's cleaving; if it be of His lightening with the fire of heaven; if it be one that will sit still, if cause be. The worst, if it come from the devil's hands. For he, as in many other, so in the sending of tongues, striveth to be like God; as knowing well they are every way as fit instruments to work mischief by, as to do good with. There be tongues of angels, mentioned in 1 Cor. xiii. 1: and if of good angels, I make no doubt but of evil; and so the devil hath his tongues.

"And he hath the art of cleaving. He showed it in the beginning, when he made the serpent 'a forked tongue,' to speak that which was contrary to his knowledge and meaning, 'they should not die;' and as he did the serpent's, so he can do others'."

[1] Acts ii. 5, 9–11.

All this, while quaint, is deeply true; so true, as to make us pray fervently to God that our tongues may not be set on fire of hell, but may be cloven of the Lord for the more apt and fervent speaking of His praise. Truly, says the Apostle, the tongue is a little member, but oh! how great a matter a little fire kindleth. Oh, that the Holy Ghost would this day sanctify our tongues! For "if any man offend not in word, the same is a perfect man," [1] says S. James.

And lo! another mark of the Holy Ghost: "It sat upon each of them." Its permanence was to be a sure token of its presence. "I will pray the Father, and he shall give you another Comforter," says Christ, "that he may abide with you forever." [2] Upon whomsoever the Spirit truly lights, there He abides. He enters into the heart, and makes it His temple, and fills it with peace and the graces of Christ, and becomes its indwelling Deity. Nothing more surely marks the absence of the Holy Ghost in any seeming work of grace or revival, than evanescence. It is not the Nature of the Holy Ghost to be here to-day, and there to-morrow. Where He visits, there He makes His rest. "He which hath begun a good work in you will perform it until the day of Jesus Christ," [3] saith the Apostle Paul to the Philippians. Eloquence may die away, and, with its tones of power or of sweetness, may vanish its impressions. Sympathy may wear itself away, and, with its decay of feelings, the chords which it has touched may lose their Christian harmony. Truth may again be overlaid with error, and, with the rising of the cloud, the knowledge which for a moment beamed in upon the soul may be obscured. But when the Holy Ghost enters, He abides forever. His touch scatters darkness, makes sin odious, manifests Christ Jesus, plants a love for holiness which it is almost impossible to

[1] S. James iii. 2. [2] S. John xiv. 16. [3] Philip. i. 6.

efface. The work of the Spirit in the individual is ordinarily a quiet, deep, abiding work. Jesus breathes upon the soul, and says, "Receive thou the Holy Ghost:" while this which we commemorate to-day was an extraordinary blast, sudden, public, overwhelming, accompanied with miracles, suitable to the first giving of the new Law needful to the interests of the rising Church.

The result of this heavenly visitation was twofold. The Apostles were filled with the Holy Ghost, and they spake with tongues. The fullness of the Holy Ghost may be participated in by all, and the utterance with tongues was peculiar to the few. But, like every thing in Nature, the most common of these gifts ranks, with the Apostle, as by far the most valuable: "Though I speak with the tongues of men and of angels, and have not Charity, I am become as sounding brass, or a tinkling cymbal."[1] "Yet show I unto you a more excellent way"[2] he said, when he had been discoursing of miracles, and gifts of healing, and tongues; and that "more excellent way," is the way we are led by the ordinary guidance of the Holy Ghost. There is no bosom, however humble, — and the more humble the better, — in which the Holy Ghost will not implant His fullness. Tongues have been vouchsafed but to a few, and we see how fatally some even of those few abused them; but the fullness of the Spirit hath been enjoyed from generation to generation, by the faithful of every age, each, in turn, witnessing to its power and its preciousness. Let us aim to be filled with this Spirit; not that we may speak with tongues, not that we may win men to admiration by our gifts and spiritual powers, but that we may imitate the meek and lowly Jesus, and walk humbly with our God. The fullness of the Spirit hath always the impress of graces which the world can scarcely understand, — graces which show themselves

[1] 1 Cor. xiii. 1.

[2] *Ibid.* xii. 31.

in an ever increasing holiness. That is the will of God, even our sanctification; and for that result will He fill us with His Spirit according to our desires.

It was when the Apostles were engaged in prayer that the Holy Ghost descended upon them: "And when they had prayed, the place was shaken where they were assembled together; and they were all filled with the Holy Ghost, and they spake the word of God with boldness."[1] It was while Peter preached that the Holy Ghost fell upon the Gentiles: "while Peter yet spake these words, the Holy Ghost fell on all them which heard the word."[2] It was when Christ ascended from the Waters of Baptism, that "the Heavens were opened unto him, and he saw the Spirit of God descending like a dove, and lighting upon him."[3] It was in Confirmation that the Holy Ghost came upon the disciples: "And when Paul had laid his hands upon them, the Holy Ghost came on them."[4] See then, brethren, the means which God has instituted in His Church for the procurance of the Holy Ghost: *Prayer*, *Preaching*, and the *Sacraments*. May we not with confidence look for His presence, if we use them faithfully and diligently? Nay, must we not be condemned, condemned in our own consciences, condemned in the eyes of each other, condemned in the view of spiritual men, and angels, if the Holy Ghost does not come upon us? What shall hinder it? Our Saviour Christ has led captivity captive, and offers gifts to men, and this His chiefest Gift. He has established His Church upon earth; and we worship in that Church, according to His own arrangements, — those arrangements which He has sanctified everlastingly by the Descent upon them of the Holy Ghost. What shall hinder His presence among us? *Faithlessness*, *indevotion*, *uncharitableness*, *impurity*. These shall deter Him from mingling His holiness

[1] Acts iv. 31. [2] *Ibid.* x. 44. [3] S. Matt. iii. 16. [4] Acts xix. 6.

with our assembly; and shall we prefer these guests to the Holy Dove? Oh no! Let us watch for His presence: and when He comes, let Him find the window of our Ark open to receive Him, our hands stretched out to take Him in.

1843.

Thirty-first Sermon.

Quench not the Spirit. — 1 THESSALONIANS V. 19.

WE do not enough realize that we are living, in these latter days, under the dispensation of the Spirit; — that the Holy Ghost, the Third Person of the adorable Trinity, is the active, life-giving Being, by whom and through whom all the operations of God upon the heart of man are carried on, whether those operations be individual and private, or stand connected with the visible Church and its public ordinances. We talk vaguely, and there is a great deal of vague preaching about the Spirit, — the Spirit of God, the Spirit of Christ, — not considering, or at least not keeping the consideration very clearly before the mind, that He is a Person of the Godhead, as real a Person as the Father or the Son; and that to Him is committed the work of operating upon the heart of man in such wise as to lead him to lay hold of the Salvation which is in and through Christ Jesus; or else put him to the terrible alternative of quenching the influences which are brought to bear upon his understanding, his affections, and his conscience.

We find in the Old Testament strong indications of a very material difference between the covenant under which the people of Israel were placed by Jehovah, and that which was to be manifested at some future time, to which the Jews were made to look forward as the period of promise and of hope: "Behold, the days come, saith the LORD, that I will make a new covenant with the house of Israel, and with the house of Judah: not according to the covenant that I made with their fathers in the day that I took them by the hand to bring them out of the land of Egypt; . . . . . but this shall be the covenant that I will make with the house of Israel; After those days, saith the LORD, I will put my law in their inward parts, and write it in their hearts; and will be their God, and they shall be my people."[1] And again, in Ezekiel, speaking of the same future: "Then will I sprinkle clean water upon you, and ye shall be clean: from all your filthiness, and from all your idols will I cleanse you. A new heart also will I give you, and a new spirit will I put within you: and I will take away the stony heart out of your flesh, and I will give you an heart of flesh. And I will put my Spirit within you, and cause you to walk in my statutes, and ye shall keep my judgments, and do them."[2] And in Joel more distinctly still: "And it shall come to pass afterward, that I will pour out my Spirit upon all flesh; and your sons and your daughters shall prophesy, your old men shall dream dreams, your young men shall see visions: and also upon the servants and upon the handmaids in those days will I pour out my Spirit."[3] And these prophetic promises plainly marked out a new dispensation, which was to be distinguished by two features: the first, a much more decided and universal operation of the Spirit of God upon the world; the second, an influence of that Spirit, which besides its extraordinary manifestations, was to be silent, inward, converting, so that the creature who received it might be said to have a new heart, — a heart changed from stone to flesh. During the earth-life of our Saviour we begin to see the development of this new covenant, — to see it however only in the reiteration of the promises which had been made in the Old Testa-

[1] Jer. xxxi. 31–33. [2] Ezek. xxxvi. 25–27. [3] Joel ii. 28, 29.

ment. Until His work was accomplished, the Holy Ghost could not be poured out; because it was the especial Gift which He was to obtain from His Father for the children of men. "I have a baptism to be baptized with," was His expression while fulfilling His work upon earth; "and how am I straitened until it be accomplished!"[1] His own part of the plan of redemption He could carry out triumphantly to its consummation. Every step in His onward progress was a victory over some one of the enemies of man: but until His final cry of triumph was heard from the Cross — that cry which rent in twain the vail of the Temple, which made the earth to quake, which opened the graves, which roused the dead from their corruption — the promise of the Father could not be fulfilled. His command, therefore, was laid upon His Apostles, "that they should not depart from Jerusalem, but wait for the promise of the Father, which, saith he, ye have heard of me. For John truly baptized with water; but ye shall be baptized with the Holy Ghost, not many days hence."[2] This promise of the Father was fulfilled upon the day of Pentecost, when the Holy Ghost descended upon the assembled Apostles, appearing in the form of cloven tongues, like as of fire, and filling them not only with the ordinary, but with the extraordinary gifts of the Spirit. This was the manifestation of the Holy Ghost, prophesied of in Joel; and was the indication to the world, that, the testator being dead, the New Covenant or Testament became of force, — that New Covenant which was sprinkled with the Blood that speaketh better things than that of Abel. But besides the miraculous exhibition of the giving of the Holy Ghost, which was the manifestation to the Apostles of their having come into the full fruition of the New Covenant, there was very soon after a marked indication that some new and divine influence was

[1] S. Luke xii. 50.

[2] Acts i. 4, 5.

working extraordinary changes in the hearts of those, who, until now, had exhibited an entire callousness to the divine words and miraculous works of Jesus of Nazareth. In the midst of Jerusalem, within view of the very spots where the infuriated multitudes had forced him through all the forms of suffering to which a mortal man could be subjected, the very people who had cried out "Crucify him, crucify him," were now pricked to the heart under the plain and pungent preaching of the Apostles, and were asking, "What shall we do to be saved?" were receiving baptism, and rejoicing in the Name of Jesus; were confessing His Cross, even unto martyrdom. Truly had the Saviour said, "I will not leave you comfortless: I will come to you."[1] And again: "Nevertheless I tell you the truth; It is expedient for you that I go away: for if I go not away, the Comforter will not come unto you; but if I depart, I will send him unto you. And when he is come, he will reprove the world of sin, and of righteousness, and of judgment. . . . . He shall glorify me: for he shall receive of mine, and shall show it unto you."[2]

As we proceed in the history of the Church, and reach the time when S. Paul began to write his Epistles to the Churches, we find a yet more distinct declaration of this peculiarity of the New Testament, — the peculiarity of its being distinctively the dispensation of the Spirit. In writing to the Corinthians, lest their false teachers should charge him with vain-glory, he runs a comparison between the ministers of the Law and of the Gospel: "Our sufficiency," writes he, "is of God; who also hath made us able ministers of the new testament; not of the letter, but of the spirit: for the letter killeth, but the spirit giveth life. But if the ministration of death, written and engraven in stones, was glorious, ... how shall not the

[1] S. John xiv. 18. [2] *Ibid.* xvi. 7, 8, 14.

ministration of the spirit be rather glorious?"[1] And again: "Wherefore I give you to understand, that no man speaking by the Spirit of God calleth Jesus accursed: and that no man can say that Jesus is the Lord, but by the Holy Ghost. Now there are diversities of gifts, but the same Spirit. . . . . And there are diversities of operations, but it is the same God which worketh all in all. But the manifestation of the Spirit is given to every man to profit withal. For to one is given by the Spirit the word of wisdom; to another the word of knowledge by the same Spirit; to another faith by the same Spirit;" and thus he runs through the various gifts of the Spirit, ordinary and extraordinary, concluding with the words: "But all these worketh that one and the self-same Spirit, dividing to every man severally as he will."[3] And in his Epistle to the Ephesians he runs through the catalogue of the officers and teachers in the Church, commencing with Apostles, and ending with Pastors, tracing them all up to the Ascension of Christ, and His giving unto men the gifts of the Spirit, which He depend your growth in grace and in the knowledge of the Lord; your spiritual wisdom and understanding, your comfort, and joy, and peace in believing. Just as no man can call Jesus Lord but by the Holy Ghost, so can no man move forward in the Christian life but through the divine influences which are appointed to flow down upon him through the Spirit: and therefore is it that, in the laying on of hands, the prayer is offered that the candidates may be "strengthened" with "the Holy Ghost, the Comforter;" that "the manifold gifts" of God's "grace" may be "daily increased" in them;—"the spirit of wisdom and understanding, the spirit of counsel and ghostly strength, the spirit of knowledge and true godliness," and lastly "the spirit of the Holy fear" of the Lord. How very interesting and important, then, does the rite of Confirmation become, when we consider that it distinctly and especially invokes upon the head of the candidate the very Spirit under whose dispensation we are living, and by whose gifts we are made more and more like Him who is first our Saviour, and then our Example!

Every step in the Christian life, moreover, is made to depend upon the Holy Ghost. The very first sense of sinfulness comes from Him: for "when he is come," says our Saviour, "he will reprove the world of sin."[1] The very faintest, as well as the most exalted, views of Christ come from Him: for, says our Saviour, "He shall glorify me; for he shall receive of mine, and shall show it unto you."[2] The growth in knowledge, in wisdom, in faith, all come from Him: "for to one is given," says the Apostle, "by the Spirit, the word of wisdom; to another, the word of knowledge by the same Spirit; to another, faith by the same Spirit."[3] The sense of adoption comes from Him: for "the Spirit itself beareth witness with our spirit, that

[1] S. John xvi. 8. [2] *Ibid.* 14. [3] 1 Cor. xii. 8, 9.

we are the children of God."[1] The security of our inheritance comes from Him: for "ye were sealed," says the Apostle to the Ephesians, with that Holy Spirit of promise, which is the earnest of our inheritance until the redemption of the purchased possession, unto the praise of his glory."[2] From the beginning to the ending, from the first faint sense of sin up to the full assurance of faith and hope, the Holy Ghost is the giver of all those graces which Christ has obtained for His people, — the dispenser of those unsearchable riches, which are laid up with God for the strength, the comfort, and the joy of all Christian hearts. How deeply important then, and how universally important, the exhortation of our text: "Quench not the Spirit:" — deeply important, because upon the life of that Spirit within the heart depends all personal religion; universally important, because the work of the Spirit extends over the whole length and breadth and height and depth of the Christian life. Nothing can be done at any point of the soul's history without the Spirit; and there is no point at which He may not be grieved and quenched if God's grace desert us. And it becomes still more a matter of awe, when we remember that terrible things are spoken in the Scripture respecting the Spirit, such as these: that "My Spirit shall not always strive with man;"[3] that "it is impossible for those who were once enlightened, and have tasted of the heavenly gift, and were made partakers of the Holy Ghost . . . if they shall fall away, to renew them again unto repentance; seeing they crucify to themselves the Son of God afresh, and put him to an open shame;"[4] that there is a sin against the Holy Ghost, which "shall not be forgiven, neither in this world, neither in the world to come."[5] How any one, — with the knowledge of our entire dependence

[1] Rom. viii. 16.
[2] Eph. i. 13, 14.
[3] Gen. vi. 3.
[4] Heb. vi. 4, 6.
[5] S. Matt. xii. 32.

upon this Spirit, with a proper sense of the exclusive authority with which every thing is committed to Him in the Church upon earth, with a remembrance of these solemn warnings resting upon his heart, — can venture to quench the Spirit, to trifle with such a Being, to vex Him, to grieve Him, to drive Him from His work in the soul; is past all comprehension: and yet, strange as it may seem, this awful work is going on busily in the world, and in the Church; sometimes visibly, so that man can see and trace the progress; sometimes secretly, so that it shall never be suspected until the secrets of all hearts shall be disclosed.

One would suppose that the last person in the world to quench the Spirit in a child would be a Christian parent, — one who had tasted the preciousness of Christ, the joy and peace in believing. And yet, unnatural and monstrous as it may seem, parents are often the very first; because to them is committed the spirit of the child, during its earliest years. They bring it to the baptismal font; they pray that the Holy Spirit may be poured out upon it, that it may be regenerate and born again of water and of the Spirit, that it may be made an heir of everlasting salvation; they hear the Minister declare that the "child is regenerate, and grafted into the body of Christ's Church:" and they go away, proving by their conduct that they have no faith in the ordinance or in the promises of God, because they forthwith conclude that the child cannot be and must not be religious until it shall have reached a certain undefined period of life, and has passed through a certain routine of worldly experience. How much early piety is thus extinguished! How many young spirits, yearning for a higher life, are bound down by low views like these to the earth and earthly things, when they should be soaring on the wings of faith and love into the presence of their God! How many heavenward aspirations are quenched in those of whom Christ said: "of such is the kingdom of God."[1] Why, Christian parents, are ye so doubtful and so afraid of early piety? Why cry out against such manifestations as indications of undue excitement, of artificial feeling, of affections that must die out? Is it so unnatural that a young soul should love its God? Is it so unaccountable that a warm-hearted child should feel its affections kindling at the tale of Christ's love and sacrifice for it? Are the promises of God to go for nothing, which command the young to remember their Creator in the days of their youth? which declare that those who seek Him early shall find Him? which ensure parents a reward for the training of their children in the nurture and admonition of the Lord? The Spirit of God deals with our children, my beloved people, at a very early age; nay, we have reason to hope, from the very moment when we dedicate them to God in baptism. Let it be our duty to guard and direct that influence, treating it as we should a tender and delicate plant, which is just pushing its feeble blade through the earth which nourishes and yet buries it.

Religion will not be in a child what it will be in an adult; and we must not expect it. It will be the piety of a child, — simple, trustful, guileless, mixed up with the frivolities of childhood: but still, piety with all the elements of genuine Christianity, — sorrow for sin, confession of sin, a looking to God for forgiveness through Christ, a determination to amend and do better for the future. Quench all this, either through indifference, or inadvertence, or harshness, and you are quenching a Spirit which may not work again within that heart for many a long and weary year which you may have spent in tears and sorrow over an impenitent and ungodly child. Cherish it, and it may grow up into a Christian character that shall give you

[1] S. Mark x. 14.

infinite comfort in this world; — that may illustrate the Church of Christ upon earth!

As the children of the Church advance in age, they pass from the parent's teaching under that of the ministering servants of the Lord; and they, too, must be very careful not to quench the Holy Spirit in the young. They, too, may fall into a like error with that noticed in parents, — of not expecting the young to devote themselves to Christ, of fearing to encourage their profession, lest they may prove unsteady, inconsistent, or may fall away from their profession. My own experience has rid me very much of this fear. It has been my lot as a minister to have been thrown very much with the young, and over the young; and in almost every instance of early profession, I have found a very great consistency of Christian character, a very great steadfastness in the love of the Church. And I say this for the encouragement of any young persons who may now be desirous of Confirmation in the Church of Christ, and may yet be hesitating and fearing to profess Christ before the world. "Quench not the Spirit." He is striving with you now, — calling you at a most impressive period of your life, when you have virgin hearts to offer to the Lord. Listen to the call. Be obedient to His voice of Love. Follow His holy and divine guidance. Meet Him — where He loves to dwell — in the Church, and at the Altar; and you will lay up for yourselves a rich fountain of happiness for your future life. And life, my youthful hearers, needs such a fountain. It has its joys: but they are intermingled with many sorrows. It has its sunshine, and may much of it rest upon your heads: but the days of darkness must come. Its path sometimes leads through green pastures and smiling landscapes: but much of it is a weary waste, in which the heart faints, and the strength fails. Flee at once to the dear secret fountain of joy, which Christ alone can plant within you; and quench not, for a single moment, even of thoughtless youth, the Spirit who is guiding you to your eternal peace!

It is a sad mistake into which men so often fall in regard to the Church of Christ, as if it were a place only for the perfect. Gracious Father of mercy, if this were true, which of us could claim our places within its sacred precincts? Which of us, from the highest in office to the humblest in feeling, could dare to kneel at its Altars? Oh, no! It is a sanctuary for all those who are penitent; who are believing, even while they tremble; who are fighting the good fight of faith; who are resting upon Jesus, in humility, for strength and for grace. To this sanctuary is the Spirit of God endeavoring to lead every one of you; and for this purpose is striving with your hearts to convince you of sin, to manifest Christ unto you, to unite you with Him through a means of grace which He has instituted in His Church. In whatever way the Spirit may be dealing with you, quench Him not! It may be that He is striving to lead you to Christ through a thankful and grateful heart, — thankful and grateful for mercies received. Oh! "quench not the Spirit," lest He afterwards say to you: "I spake unto thee in thy prosperity; but thou saidst, I will not hear."[1] It may be that He is plunging you into a sea of troubles, that you may sigh for rest, and find it upon the bosom of Jesus. Oh! "quench not the Spirit," lest the waters overflow thee, and thou perish out of the Ark of safety! It may be that He has snatched from you the pride of your heart, the delight of your eyes, and transferred them to Heaven, that your affections may soar thither and find reunion in Christ. Oh! "quench not the Spirit," for "O LORD, are not thine eyes upon the truth? thou hast stricken them, but they have not grieved; thou

[1] Jer. xxii. 21.

hast consumed them, but they have refused to receive correction: they have made their faces harder than a rock; they have refused to return. Therefore I said, Surely these are poor; they are foolish: for they know not the way of the LORD, nor the judgment of their God."[1] It may be that He is guiding you calmly along the path of life, opening gradually before you the things of Christ. Oh, "Quench not the Spirit;" yield to His gentle influences; be guided by His divine counsel: and soon shall you find your peace as a river, and your righteousness as the waves of the sea. Whatever may be your circumstances, or whatever your condition, whatever your age, whatever the influences under which the Holy Spirit may be leading you to Christ, Oh! "quench not the Spirit:" for, once quenched, He may never again cast the bright beams of His glory within your heart!

1865.

[1] Jer. v. 3, 4.

Thirty-second Sermon.

And God said, Let us make man in our image, after our likeness. — GENESIS i. 26.

Compared with

And Jesus, when he was baptized, went up straightway out of the water: and, lo, the heavens were opened unto him, and he saw the Spirit of God descending like a dove, and lighting upon him: and lo a voice from heaven, saying, This is my beloved Son, in whom I am well pleased. — S. MATTHEW iii. 16, 17.

[FIRST PART.]

IT is roundly asserted and generally believed that the doctrine of the Trinity is one of late introduction into the Christian system, and was neither known nor exacted as a matter of faith until the second or third century of the Christian era. And yet, in the very face of this declaration, the Lessons selected by the Church for Trinity Sunday are chosen, the one from the first chapter of Genesis, the other from the third chapter of S. Matthew's Gospel, as exhibiting, with peculiar distinctness, the Personality of the Godhead. How can a doctrine be of late introduction, which manifests itself thus distinctly upon the very opening scenes, the one of the world's economy, the other of the Christian dispensation? How can that be new, which is inscribed upon the very first page of the Revelation that God made of Himself to His creatures, and which, after a lapse of fourteen hundred years, during four hundred of which there was silence between Heaven and earth, God not speaking to the world, reappears at the very earliest moment of the renewal of intercourse? So far from its being a novel doctrine, it constitutes, in my view, the very foundation of the whole Christian scheme, and seems to have been arranged by God for a peculiar purpose, — so arranged, that while the Unity of the Godhead should be impressed upon the world, that world should not be permitted, even for a moment of time, to conceive of that Unity, save as embodying the divine mystery of Three Persons in that Unity. My reading of the Bible satisfies me that the doctrine of the Unity of the Godhead was not revealed an instant earlier than that of the Trinity; and that it was the harder one to force upon the world. When the inspired writers of the Old Testament reiterate the declaration, "Hear, O Israel, the Lord our God is one Lord."[1] When they press it home upon the gainsaying Israelites, and seem never to tire of its repetition, it was not against the Trinity that they were guarding and warning the chosen people of God, but it was against the corrupt tendency of human nature, which had developed itself all the world over, and was rife around them, to make Gods many and Lords many, and to people every mountain and valley and river and forest with deities. The doctrine of the Three Persons in the One Godhead, had it been taught apart from its mystery of oneness and coequality, would have been greedily caught at among the Pagans, for it would have fallen in with their natural sentiment of polytheism. It was the doctrine of the Unity of God which was strange; which was considered unnatural; which had to be forced upon the world, and then kept in it, by the separation and perpetual discipline of a people set apart for the very purpose; which was preserved, only by means like these, until such time as Christ became incarnate, and by the sacrifice of Himself introduced the Holy Spirit to the world, through whose agency and power over

[1] Deut. vi. 4.

the heart it finds belief and reception. Men of the present generation can scarcely conceive the true state of this question; can scarcely realize how much more unnatural the doctrine of the Unity of God is to man, than that of a plurality of Gods; how much more difficult it is to keep his affections fastened upon one object, than upon many. Because, after an education of six thousand years, and after the introduction into the world of the Holy Ghost, whose sublime office it is to keep religion pure in the heart, Man has learned at last to receive and worship God in His Unity, he imagines it to be a natural sentiment. Never was he more mistaken. Never was there a doctrine more distinctly a matter of education. And even now, wherever man is found without that religious training, there is found with him the belief and worship of a plurality of Gods; or, at the least, of a duality, the two antagonistic principles of good and evil, of light and darkness, of benevolence and malice.

There is no doubt that the word Trinity was not used as a distinctly theological word until after the coming of Christ: but it is not the word that is important, but the thing; it is not the term, but the *doctrine*. What has been revealed to us, upon this point, from the beginning? What has been the doctrine taught by the Scriptures? What has been the faith impressed upon the world? What has been embodied in the Creeds of the Church from the time when Creeds became necessary? These are the points to be settled, and not the time of the introduction of a word adopted and used, for convenience sake, to express compactly and forcibly a revealed and therefore existing truth. If any man tells me that he believes what is expressed by the word Trinity, I will not quarrel with him about the word Trinity. If he will say, in the language of our Article, — "There is but one living and true God, everlasting, without body, parts, or passions; of infinite power, wisdom, and goodness; the Maker and Preserver of all things both visible and invisible. And in Unity of this Godhead there be three Persons, of one substance, power, and eternity; the Father, the Son, and the Holy Ghost:"[1] — I shall not dispute with him about the *word*. The word is not a thing of Revelation, and therefore is not essential: the doctrine is a thing of Revelation, and therefore is essential. To dispute, consequently, about the mere word, is to cavil against that which is not the material thing. Supposing the term "Trinity" to be given up, the doctrine of the Trinity still stands, as it is believed and explained by the Church, and will forever stand, until the Word of God shall be of none effect among men. Nothing is gained, then, by warfare against the term, more than the getting rid of a convenient word which expresses briefly what is taught diffusely and at intervals. All this is beside the mark, is unworthy of a sensible controversialist, is making a point of that which has really nothing to do with the question. The true and earnest matter is: "What has God declared from the beginning of His Revelation to be His mode of existence? And I answer emphatically, and without all fear of contradiction: "Three Persons, the Father, the Son, and the Holy Ghost, of one substance, power and eternity, subsisting in the Unity of the Godhead."[2]

We have no right, in the examination of any Christian doctrine, to separate the Old and New Testaments from each other. They together constitute one *Revelation;* and I am bold to assert that if the one is not a Revelation from God, neither is the other. They stand or fall together. The one is the complement of the other: and if it be necessary at times to interpret the expressions of the older dispensation through the disclosures of the new, it is essential

[1] Article I.

[2] *Ibid.*

to the newer dispensation to have the older to rest upon for its defence against the assaults of infidelity and false philosophy. Unless I had the New Testament to explain the Old, I might often err in my inferences; but unless I had the Old Testament to defend the New, I should find it very hard to resist the sophistry of Mr. Hume, or the rationalism of the Neologists. It is because I have *both* that I feel invincible, — that I am sure I can do every thing and any thing which the reason may demand, or the intellect call for; — that I can wield from the treasury of the Bible an array of argument that can do every thing, except convert the heart of the creature and make it submissive.

Let us then, with this preliminary assertion, with this postulate (without which I should think it useless to argue at all), examine this very first chapter of Genesis, — this very first page in the Revelation of God, — and see what it asserts. Its very first words are: "In the beginning God created the heaven and the earth." That is the very first teaching man gets, — the first idea which is given him of God, the Creator of heaven and earth. Until this revelation, he knows nothing. God! what then is God? That is the idea to be developed. Man knows nothing of Him before Revelation, — knows not whether He is one or many; knows not His mode of existence; knows nothing of His intentions or purposes. He is altogether at large. His mind is a blank, upon which is to be written the disclosures of the Deity. He has no prejudications one way or the other. He confesses, like Confucius, a profound ignorance upon the subject. Can he, by searching, find out God? It is high as Heaven, what can he do? deeper than Hell, what can he know? He holds the attitude of one receiving knowledge, and not disputing about it. God! who and what is He? And he is obliged to wait for new disclosures. And the very next verse helps him: "And the earth was without form, and void; and darkness was upon the face of the deep. And the Spirit of God moved upon the face of the waters." "The Spirit of God:" what is that? Is it a quality? is it an emanation? is it a something subsisting in God, or distinct from God? This is certainly a fresh idea. Everywhere else, except in this passage, up to the 26th verse of the chapter, the language is, "God created," "God said," "God called;" here it is the "Spirit of God moved upon the face of the waters." This fresh idea must therefore be reserved for consideration, — must be kept weighed in the mind for further development until such time as new revelations shall make it more plain. Should it not be rash in a creature, when he knew that he was the recipient of a Revelation which was to be progressive, to decide hastily upon any point which had not been entirely unfolded, — to say at once, and presumptuously, that this Spirit of God was a mere quality, emanating from God and returning to God, having no personality nor separate existence? Certainly it should. His only proper attitude is that of cautious reserve, until he shall hear more of this God; until the Revelation shall more clearly explain itself. He is a learner and not a guesser; an humble disciple to whom things are unfolding themselves, and not a critic. He must wait upon the will of God, in patience and humility.

The 25th verse of this first chapter of Genesis closes the narrative of the creation of all animal life save the highest earthly being — Man. The 26th verse introduces that most important act, — introduces it with great solemnity, and with an entire change of phraseology. In all the previous exertions of creative power, the language is, "God said, Let such and such things be created." The 26th verse opens in a very different and much more striking way. The first indicates a mere exercise of will; this indicates consultation among Persons not yet known to us. "And God said, Let us make man in our image, after our likeness:"—a very remarkable change of phraseology, one which may mean nothing, or which may mean a great deal; which may be a mere Oriental and regal mode of address, or may embody a deep mysterious truth. Now I do not ask you to admit that this teaches the Trinity; that will depend upon circumstances: but does it not call upon an humble enquirer into truth, upon one who knows nothing (except what he may be taught) about the mode of Divine existence, to pause and reflect, before he concludes any thing rashly?—to keep his mind in a state of suspense until further light shall be cast upon it from the Fountain of light? Once before, in the same chapter, has the narrative passed rapidly from God to the Spirit of God; and here again it has passed, at a most critical moment too, just when God is about to perform His greatest act of creation, from the singular to the plural form of expression: "Let *us* make man in *our* image, after *our* likeness." Who are included under this term "us"? To whom is God speaking? With whom is God consulting? It may be nothing, but are you sure that it is nothing? Are you so sure that it is nothing, that you can say that there is *no* evidence of Persons in the Godhead in the Old Testament? It seems to me that the phraseology of this chapter leaves the door open for much expectation; that at the close of this narrative, while I am well informed that God is the creator of heaven and earth, I am not at all sure what sort of Being that God is, what is His mode of existence, whether as an unit, or as more than one, or as several in one. I say that, from this chapter, the thing is left quite open, and beyond any man to say how it will be developed as the Revelation unfolds itself.

Now as we float along with the Revelation as it is developed from time to time, we discover very distinctly that there are not more Gods than one. This is very clear, for the expressions are frequent and impressive: "There is but one God," — "There is no other God but me," — "There is not any God besides me," with a thousand assertions like these, which settle that question. But because there is only one God, it decides nothing about the mode of existence of that one God. The believers in the doctrine of the Trinity do not say that there are more Gods than one; nay, they deny it most stoutly, as a misrepresentation of their belief: their position is that there is but one God, but that in the unity of that Godhead there are three Persons, Father, Son, and Holy Ghost. This is a very different position, one which does not in the least meet its denial in any of the texts of Scripture which affirm God to be one God, but which must look for its fulfillment in quite a distinct mode of investigation.

While we find, then, in following the stream of Revelation, that there is a clear denial of more Gods than one, there is, all along, an intimation of Persons who are to have a most wonderful influence upon the history and development of religion. Besides this "Spirit of God" who moved upon the face of the waters, we read of "a Seed of the Woman who is to crush the serpent's head;" of "a King who is to reign in righteousness;" of "a son to be born, of a child to be given;" of "a Being who was to be the fellow of Jehovah:" and most wonderful appellations are given to this Being, — appellations which can rightfully belong to no human creature. All this keeps the mind suspended as to God's mode of existence; — all this leaves it yet uncertain how the Godhead will be developed, when the Revelation shall have been fully made. Enough is seen to satisfy us that there is an unsolved mystery, that Beings are unfolding behind the veil who are one day to occupy a most essential place in the economy of grace: but what place, and in what precise relation to the Godhead, it is not yet possible for man to decide.

But so soon as the fullness of time was come, when God's plan of salvation was to be fully disclosed, the whole mystery is made plain, and throws a flood of light back upon all the dark passages of the Old Testament, and especially upon this first chapter of Genesis. Let us now turn to the second Lesson of the day, the third chapter of S. Matthew's Gospel, and see how that illuminates and glorifies the first of Genesis. We there see a person called Jesus of Nazareth coming out of Galilee to Jordan unto John, to be baptized of him. "But John forbade him, saying, I have need to be baptized of thee, and comest thou to me?" Why did John forbid Him? He had forbidden nobody else. He had baptized all the leading people of the Jews, soldiers, scribes, Pharisees, Sadducees: why forbid this Man? He, John, was by very far the greatest of all the Prophets; was heralded beforehand by prophecy itself, which no other man had ever been; had been conceived and born miraculously, and then trained in a school of surprising austerity. Who then was this to whom he said: "I have need to be baptized of thee, and comest thou to me?"

Let us see what the simple narrative says: — "And Jesus answering said unto him, Suffer it to be so now: for thus it becometh us to fulfill all righteousness. Then he suffered him. And Jesus, when he was baptized, went up straightway out of the water: and lo, the heavens were opened unto him, and he saw the Spirit of God descending like a dove, and lighting upon him: and lo a voice from heaven saying, This is my beloved Son, in whom I am well pleased." Here are evidently three distinct agents: A voice from heaven, as the voice of a Father; a being in the form of Man, addressed from heaven as "my beloved Son;"

and that same Spirit of God which we encountered in the first chapter of Genesis brooding over Chaos, and now assuming the form of a Dove. This is, at the very first glance, very striking, occurring, as it does, at the opening of the Christian dispensation; but it becomes infinitely more so, when we turn to other portions of the New Testament, and compare them with the Old. Who is this beloved Son? — and now that we find him announced from Heaven so publicly, we remember that the Psalmist said, a thousand years before: — "Yet have I set my King upon my holy hill of Zion. I will declare the decree: the LORD hath said unto me, Thou art my Son; this day have I begotten thee. Be wise now therefore, O ye kings: be instructed, ye judges of the earth. Kiss the Son, lest he be angry, and ye perish from the way, when his wrath is kindled but a little."[1] We remember what Isaiah said: "For unto us a child is born, unto us a Son is given: and the government shall be upon his shoulder: and his name shall be called Wonderful, Counsellor, The mighty God, The Everlasting Father, The Prince of Peace."[1] With these striking passages of the Old Testament recurring to us, and with the recollection of that remarkable phraseology of the first chapter of Genesis, "Let us make man in our image," we open the New Testament at the first chapter of S. John's Gospel, — the Gospel of that Apostle whom Jesus was most familiar with, — and we read: "In the beginning (the very time, you will notice, of the Creation, for that also was "in the beginning;" *when*, we do not know, ages ago, perchance, as science teaches us) was the Word, and the Word was with God, and the Word was God. The same was in the beginning with God. All things were made by him; and without him was not any thing made that was made." If this "Word" can be shown to be a Person, we have at last an

[1] Psalm ii. 6, 7, 10, 12.

[2] Isaiah ix. 6.

explanation of the words of the Old Testament, "Let us make man in our image;" and what do we find in the 14th verse of this first chapter of S. John?—"And the Word was made flesh, and dwelt among us, (and we beheld his glory, the glory as of the only-begotten of the Father,) full of grace and truth." This "Word" then, who was with God in the beginning, who was God, without whom nothing was made that was made, is the person, Jesus Christ, who was pronounced at his baptism by a voice from the Father, saying, "This is my beloved Son," who is called elsewhere, "the only-begotten Son of God,"[1] "the brightness of his glory and the express image of his person,"[2] "Alpha and Omega, the beginning and the ending, which is, and which was, and which is to come, the Almighty."[3] Is this a second God? No! for the Bible tells us, "I am God, and there is none else."[4] Is this God the Father in human flesh? No! for God the Father says of Him, "This is my beloved Son, in whom I am well pleased." What is He then? for He is called in Zechariah, "The fellow of Jehovah;" in Isaiah, "Wonderful Counsellor (mark that word, and remember "Let us make man in our image"), The mighty God;" in S. John absolutely, "God,"—"The word was God;" by S. Paul, in Colossians, "The image of the invisible God," by whom "were all things created, that are in heaven, and that are in earth, visible and invisible, whether they be thrones, or dominions, or principalities, or powers;"[5] and He Himself saith, "All things that the Father hath are mine,"[6] "I and my Father are one."[7] He is precisely what the Creeds of the Church describe Him to you: "And I believe in one Lord Jesus Christ, the only-begotten Son of God, Begotten of his Father before all worlds; God of God, Light of Light, very God of very God,

[1] S. John iii. 18. [2] Heb. i. 3. [3] Rev. i. 8. [4] Isaiah xlv. 22.
[5] Coloss. i. 15, 16. [6] S. John xvi. 15. [7] S. John x. 30.

Begotten not made, Being of one substance with the Father; By whom all things were made:" and this Person we call, in the language of theology, the Second Person of the adorable Trinity.

1866.

Thirty-third Sermon.

And God said, Let us make man in our image, after our likeness.— GENESIS i. 26.

Compared with

And Jesus, when he was baptized, went up straightway out of the water: and, lo, the heavens were opened unto him, and he saw the Spirit of God descending like a dove, and lighting upon him: And lo a voice from heaven, saying, This is my beloved Son, in whom I am well pleased.— S. MATTHEW iii. 16, 17.

[SECOND PART.]

IN pursuance of the subject begun this morning, I would now draw your attention to the fact, that in the first chapter of Genesis we were informed that the "Spirit of God" moved upon the face of the waters; and our interest was excited by it at the moment. Since we have found, in the New Testament, so much light thrown upon the phrase "Let us make man in our image," we feel inclined to trace that expression, "the Spirit of God," and see to what it will lead us.

We now perceive very clearly that Holy Scripture embraces a scheme which is unfolded gradually; — that, while it wraps up in the very first moment of its enunciation the richest and most precious truths, it is a long time ere they are fully developed. Why this is so, it would occupy far more time than I have at my disposal to declare unto you; suffice it to say, that every doctrine of our holy religion presents a like feature, and that it is in strict analogy with the other arrangements of God, which all seem to be progressive, unfolding and maturing from time to time: not developing in any way like that advanced in the La Marckian system; but all perfect from the beginning, in the germ, though only displayed to man when the fitting time was come, and when he was able, through his previous discipline and education, to receive and cherish it. Man himself, the being whom all this most concerns, has to pass, himself, through his various stages of embryo, of birth, of infancy, of youth, of manhood. How much time is occupied with all this! Fully as much of his life is expended in mere preparation for maturity, as afterwards in the exercise of his faculties: — quite as much, in proportion, as the unfolding of Christianity has occupied of the world's duration. It is not, therefore, at all strange that a Revelation from God should exhibit this feature: nay, it should be unlike any thing else in creation, if it did not exhibit it. Language has been progressive; Law has been progressive; Government has been progressive; Civilization has been progressive: why not Religion? It is only of a piece with every thing else.

To return, however, to our point. We read in the first chapter of Genesis, that "the Spirit of God moved upon the face of the waters;" and we perceive, as I said this morning, that it is a change, and has a meaning. What and who is this "Spirit of God?" Is it a quality? Is it an emanation? Or is it a distinct Person in the Godhead? This we can determine only by an examination of the further records of Revelation. Just as we traced out the Son, and found Him to be a Person coequal with the Father, must we trace out this Spirit of God, and perfect the scheme of the Almighty. We have nothing to do with the explanation or elucidation of all this: we have only to show you that it is contained in the Revelation, and that, being contained there, it is not a late invention drawn from Platonism, or from Christian philosophy; but that its germs are as much contained in the very earliest books of the Bible, as the germs of any other doctrine. When this shall have been done, I must leave it with you: with you must rest the responsibility of receiving or rejecting God's Revelation of His own mode of existence. As I told you this morning, one is supposed to come to this inquiry knowing nothing; — utterly ignorant of who God is, or what He is, prepared to receive whatever He may reveal. When I shall have shown you, as plainly and as fairly as I can, what that Revelation announces, my task will be finished. It is for you to receive it, and take it to your heart: or to reject it, and disbelieve it. That is your probation. The contest will lie between what the world erroneously calls reason, and what the Bible calls faith. For myself, I cannot see the difficulty which some men pretend to: for the simple reason that one mode of Divine existence is just as possible as another, before Revelation; and therefore, after Revelation, should be received as truth under whatever aspect it may be presented unto us.

We find in the third chapter of S. Matthew, — to which we now turn in our investigation of this topic, — this Spirit of God reintroduced in a personal shape: "And Jesus, when he was baptized, went up straightway out of the water: and, lo! the heavens were opened unto him, and he saw the Spirit of God descending like a dove, and lighting upon him." The sacred writer does not say that it was a material dove; but "descending like a dove." Here was the Son just ascending from the waters of baptism; the Father uttering His voice from heaven, saying, "This is my beloved Son, in whom I am well pleased;" and at the same moment, the Spirit of God, appearing from out the riven heavens, descending "like a dove:" three agents, most distinctly. And if we pursue the inquiry respecting the Spirit, as we did respecting the Son, we shall arrive at the same results: the results of Personality and Divinity.

The "Spirit of God," being that Person of the Godhead who was to be made manifest to man latest in the order of time; who, although operating from the beginning in various ways, — moving upon the face of the waters in Creation, speaking by the Prophets, inspiring the holy men of old, — was not to be fully developed until Christ's departure from the world: is brought before us clearly, just before our Lord's Crucifixion. In the closing chapters of S. John's Gospel, He is promised by Christ, and promised as a Person: "But the Comforter, which is the Holy Ghost, whom the Father will send in my name, he shall teach you all things."[1] "He shall testify of me."[2] "He will reprove the world of sin, of righteousness, and of judgment."[3] "He will guide you into all truth."[4] And surely that which teaches, and testifies, and reproves, and guides, must be what we call a Person. These powers must subsist in some substance; for a quality cannot do these things, nor an emanation: and wherever they do subsist, that is the Holy Ghost.

As we proceed in the history of the Church, we find the care of the Church committed to this Personal agent. Jesus Christ, whom we showed you this morning to be the second Person in the Godhead, is now ascended into Heaven; is acting there as Advocate and Intercessor; is pleading for man with God. The Holy Spirit has taken His place on earth, and is speaking, acting, directing as a Person: "The Spirit said unto" Peter, "Behold, three men seek thee."[5] "The Holy Ghost said, Separate me Barnabas and Saul for the work whereunto I have called them."[6] "Take heed therefore unto yourselves, and to all

[1] S. John xiv. 26. [2] *Ibid.* xv. 26. [3] *Ibid.* xvi. 8.
[4] *Ibid.* xvi. 13. [5] Acts x. 19. [6] *Ibid.* xiii. 2.

the flock," says S. Paul to the elders of Ephesus, "over the which the Holy Ghost hath made you overseers."[1] And whosoever speaketh, acteth, ordaineth, must needs have with him Personality.

But this Spirit of God, when we come to investigate His claims, is more than a Person: He is a Divine Person. For we find our Lord Jesus Christ thus speaking of Him: "Wherefore I say unto you, All manner of sin and blasphemy shall be forgiven unto men: but the blasphemy against the Holy Ghost shall not be forgiven unto men. And whosoever speaketh a word against the Son of Man, it shall be forgiven him: but whosoever speaketh against the Holy Ghost, it shall not be forgiven him, neither in this world, neither in the world to come."[2] How could a distinction be made in blasphemy against the Son and blasphemy against the Holy Ghost unless they were distinct Persons? Could sin and blasphemy against a quality, or an emanation, be unpardonable, while sin and blasphemy against the Substance upholding that quality is pardonable? But again, in another place: "The word of wisdom," "the word of knowledge," "faith," "gifts of healing," "miracles," "prophecy," "discerning of spirits," "tongues," "the interpretation of tongues:" "all these worketh that one and the self-same Spirit [the Holy Ghost] dividing to every man severally as he will."[3] Would all these mightiest operations of Divinity be entrusted to a creature? No! if there be any thing in the Scripture that proves Divinity, it is ascriptions such as these, which we find at every step laid upon the Holy Ghost.

And in pursuing this investigation we can proceed yet a step further. We can show that this Spirit, which was found in the first chapter of Genesis moving upon the face of the waters, is of one substance, majesty, and glory with

[1] Acts xx. 28. [2] S. Matthew xii. 31, 32. [3] 1 Cor. xii. 8–11.

the Father and the Son, is very and eternal God. Let us pursue this.

Whatever we find ascribed to the Father and the Son, we find also ascribed to the "Spirit of God." He is not left in shadow and obscurity. He comes out into bold relief, so soon as the moment arrives when His work is to be performed. "In the beginning," says our first chapter of Genesis, "God created the heaven and the earth." "In the beginning," says S. John in his Gospel, "was the Word, and the Word was with God, and the Word was God. All things were made by him; and without him was not any thing made that was made."[1] The Psalmist beautifully describes the rapidity of creation: "Thou sendest forth thy Spirit, they are created."[2] How is this? — three Creators? No! for there is but one God. How then? Three Persons in the Unity of the Godhead, acting in harmony. This is the only explanation which can make the Scriptures consistent: and therefore is it the Creed of the Church.

But again: "I the Lord," says God of Himself in Jeremiah, "search the heart, I try the reins."[3] But Christ says, in Revelation: "All the Churches shall know that I am he which searcheth the reins and hearts."[4] But S. Paul places alongside of these the pretensions of the Spirit: "The Spirit searcheth all things, yea, the deep things of God."[5] Are there three claimants to this divine prerogative of searching into the deep things of man and God? No! this power belongs only to God; and if three exercise it, then are they Persons of the one Godhead, acting in fulfillment of the inherent privileges which belong to each and all. There can be no other solution. They are all Persons; they are all *Divine* Persons; they are all, as it

[1] S. John i. 1, 3. [2] Psalm civ. 30. [3] Jeremiah xvii. 10.
[4] Rev. ii. 23. [5] 1 Cor. ii. 10.

seems, possessed of equal powers: and yet there is but one "God;" there "is none else." What is the necessary solution? It can be but that which our Article gives: "that in the unity of this Godhead there be three Persons, of one substance, power, and eternity; the Father, the Son, and the Holy Ghost."[1]

This is the result to which we are brought, when we take hold of that phrase, "the Spirit of God moved upon the face of the waters," and run it up to its entire development. It introduces us to a Person, to a Divine Person, to a Person having like attributes, faculties, powers, with the Son and with the Father. Is there nothing, then, in that phrase, "Let us make man in our image"? I trow, I have shown you that there was a great deal; that it was a most pregnant phrase; that while, in the germ, it seemed as if it might mean something or nothing: in the maturity, it was the Power of God and the Wisdom of God unto salvation. How it has expanded! How it has thrown out leaf, and flower, and fruit, on every hand, until it has waxed into a growth overshadowing the whole earth and bringing healing to the nations! How the patient humble inquirer has been rewarded for his long waiting! What before was mysterious, has been made plain for him; what hung in suspense, has become settled and assured. The word "God," which was his first introduction to the idea of the Divine existence, has been explained to him; and he now rests his spirit, with folded wings and in peace, upon the wonderful truths of Revelation. He is no longer stumbling in ignorance and darkness. The whole truth has been placed for him in bold relief by the Church of God: and God is with him, one God; yet related to him through the blessed names of Father, Son, and Holy Ghost.

[1] Article I.

But it is said that the Jews never held the doctrine of the Trinity, and that it is strange that they should not have perceived it, if it was clearly writ upon the Old Testament. But I have not said that it was clearly written there. I have only said, what is strictly true, that its germs were all there; that the truths were infolded in such passages as I have been commenting upon this day; and that, when the fullness of times had come, they would manifest themselves to the world. It would be contradicting myself to say, that those truths were clearly written there: because I have already said that the Christian scheme was progressive; was a thing of steps and stages; had its infancy, its childhood, its maturity; and, while "the child is father of the man," no one will pretend that he can clearly foresee in the traits of the child the future development of the man. All that it is necessary for me to show, is, that it was as distinctly there as any of the other most essential doctrines of Christianity; and that, if the Jews did not hold it, they treated it no worse than any of the other truths committed to their keeping.

If there was one doctrine more than another upon which the Jews rested all their hope and expectation, it was the coming of the Messiah. This involved not only their individual, but their national anticipations. It was not only salvation they looked for through him, but greatness upon earth, endurance as a nation, and supremacy. Let us then turn back to Genesis (the third chapter this time) and note the very obscure form in which that Messiah was first promised to them. In the curse laid upon the serpent, God says: "And I will put enmity between thee and the woman, and between thy seed and her seed; it shall bruise thy head, and thou shalt bruise his heel."[1] That is all. Is the doctrine of the Trinity any more obscurely taught than

[1] Gen. iii. 15.

that of the Messiah in its beginning? Has not that to be developed, step by step, just as the other doctrine was unfolded? It rested in that single expression until the time of Abraham, when one leaf expanded itself, on which was written: "In thy seed shall all the nations of the earth be blessed."[1] And after that, it was not until Jacob lay upon his dying bed that another ray stole in to cheer him and his family, and open the mystery more distinctly and graciously: "The sceptre shall not depart from Judah, nor a lawgiver from between his feet, until Shiloh come."[2] And then another long pause, until the days of Moses, — although the characteristics of the Messiah were, all the time, being written upon the sacrificial arrangements of the Jews, — when it was promised: "The Lord thy God will raise up unto thee a Prophet from the midst of thee, of thy brethren, like unto me; unto him ye shall hearken."[3] This is all the progress that the doctrine of the Messiah had made in five and twenty hundred years. He was to be born of a woman, and in some mysterious manner to be her seed; He was to descend from Abraham, and be a blessing to the whole earth; He was to come of the tribe of Judah before the sceptre should depart from that tribe; and He was to be a Prophet like unto Moses, and was to arise among the Israelites. Was that any faster than the unfolding of the doctrine of the Trinity, especially when we consider that the coming of the Messiah was a necessary antecedent to the unfolding of the doctrine of the Trinity? And it took fifteen hundred years from the days of Moses to develop that Messiah in all His characteristics, so that He should be known and recognized when He did come! And who received him after he came? "He came unto his own, and his own received him not."[4] So soon as the Persons of the Trinity were made manifest every one who acknowledged Christ

[1] Gen. xxii. 18. [2] *Ibid.* xlix. 10. [3] Deut. xviii. 15. [4] S. John i. 11.

acknowledged the Divinity of Christ, whether Jew or Gentile. "Dost thou believe on the Son of God?" "Lord, I believe."[1] This was the confession exacted from all; and they received it one and all, simultaneously with their belief that Jesus of Nazareth was the Messiah.

If we are to receive a doctrine only when the Jews believe in it, we shall strip Christianity very bare! Who of them seemed to understand the Scriptural doctrine of the Messiah, at the time when our Lord became incarnate? Only two, that I read of in the Scriptures, were waiting for the consolation of Israel, Simeon and Anna; together with those "that looked for redemption in Jerusalem." At the close of our Lord's ministry, when He had been, for three years, instructing the Jews by every means, both in the nature of His office and in His identity with the Messiah: a mere handful acknowledged Him. And why? Because they had taken up wrong notions of the Messiah; because they were expecting God to come in temporal power; because they were looking for an earthly monarch, to lead them to earthly dominion. And because they did not understand the Messiah, are we to reject Him? Because they in their blindness and madness cried, "Away with this man,"[2] "We will not have this man to reign over us,"[3] are *we* to reject Him? Certainly not. We have received the light which they refused. We have learned through the teachings of the Holy Ghost, that Jesus of Nazareth agrees exactly with the requirements of the Prophets. The Jews did not see it, because of their prejudices; but the Gentiles, of whom we are a part, saw and flocked to the brightness of His rising. And if we do not reject Christ as the Messiah because they did not understand the doctrines respecting Him: why should we say that the doctrine of the Trinity is not a Scriptural doctrine, because

[1] S. John ix. 35, 38. [2] S. Luke xxiii. 18. [3] *Ibid.* xix. 14.

they did not hold it? It was of much greater difficulty to them than the other; it was of much less necessity. In the order of the divine manifestations, it could not be fully unfolded until the Holy Ghost was given; and He did not come until after the Ascension of our Lord. Enough for us is it, that the teachings of the Old Testament exhibit its truth all wrapped up there, and give intimations, as they ripen into the fullness of time, that there were Beings in the Unity of the Godhead, who were to illustrate the Christian economy.

It would be as unwise, my beloved hearers, for us to be regulated in our belief by the Jews, as for a man to be directed or controlled by a child. "The Prophets," says S. Peter, "prophesied of the grace that should come unto you: searching what, or what manner of time the Spirit of Christ which was in them did signify, when it testified beforehand the sufferings of Christ, and the glory that should follow. Unto whom it was revealed, that not unto themselves, but unto us they did minister the things, which are now reported unto you by them that have preached the Gospel unto you with the Holy Ghost sent down from heaven; which things the angels desire to look into."[1] That is our position, — the highest in the scale of advancement. All that have come before us, Patriarchs, Prophets, Apostles, the incarnate Son of God Himself, have ministered unto us. The truths which have been revealed to us, Angels desire to look into. There is nothing more to be revealed. The Book of Prophecy and of Truth is "closed up and sealed till the time of the end."[2] We shall receive no more voices from between the cherubim, nor from out that higher sanctuary not made with hands, eternal in the Heavens. The whole record of God's will is before us. The Holy Spirit, that Spirit which moved upon

[1] 1 S. Pet. i. 10–12. [2] Daniel xii. 9.

the face of the waters and brought order out of chaos, must move for us over the face of this Revelation, and make it harmony and peace for us: harmony in its truths, peace in its fruits. He can make every thing clear to you, can illumine all that is dark, and raise up all that is low. Let us humble ourselves before Him, and cry for knowledge; let us utter the words which are suitable to our condition, and say:

> Eternal Spirit, by whose breath
> The soul is raised from sin and death,
> Before Thy Throne we sinners bend;
> To us Thy quickening power extend.

1866.

Thirty-fourth Sermon.

They are of the world: therefore speak they of the world, and the world heareth them. We are of God. He that knoweth God, heareth us; he that is not of God, heareth not us. Hereby know we the spirit of truth, and the spirit of error. — 1 S. John iv. 5, 6.

THE Church, having led her children through all her circle of joy and of sorrow, from the Sundays which proclaimed the Advent of her Lord up to the moment when she wrapped up every thing in the glory of the eternal Trinity, begins to-day her lessons of practical piety, the true and genuine fruits of her doctrine; and continues them through many successive Sundays, until she has exhausted the topics which make up the harmonious Christian character. The facts of our Saviour's life, and the great consequences of it, lay the foundation of the Christian scheme: the life which is expected to grow out of those facts through the working of the Holy Ghost, constitutes its superstructure and perfectness. Until, therefore, the whole scheme was placed before us, and each Person of the adorable Trinity was announced and unfolded and His part in the economy of grace was distinctly set forth, the Church could not logically press good works upon her children, because they were the fruits of Beings and of Agents not yet clearly made known to the world. These good works are called, in the Scriptures, the fruits of the Spirit; and are thus shown to be dependent upon the "Spirit of God" of whom we treated in full on the last Lord's day. But now, having developed fully the whole earth-life of our Saviour, and having commemorated the descent of the Holy Ghost, and taught us that all Church work has been vested in Him, so that we are said to be living under the dispensation of the Spirit: she begins to-day with a general proposition,—how we may distinguish between a spirit of error and a spirit of truth. This distinction is of the most important kind, and precedes all personal action: for until we can be certain that we are right, we will not press forward with that zeal and devotion which are becoming to the Christian character.

We must not suppose that when the work of Christ was consummated, and His Church established in the world through the operation of the Holy Ghost, and inspired men wrote as they were moved by the Spirit of God and committed those writings to the care of the Church, that all opposition ceased to truth and godliness. The Devil, 't is true, had been vanquished by Christ in all the conflicts they had waged; Death and the grave had been conquered; sin had been made powerless against all who procured for themselves the strength of Christ: but the Church was yet militant upon earth, and each individual had yet his probation to pass through on his passage to Heaven. 'T is true, for the comfort of us who are undergoing this probation, that "greater is He that is in us, than He that is in the world:"[1] but nevertheless the Devil is still permitted to rage, and "to contend against that which he cannot overthrow; to corrupt what is good, to pervert what is true, to disseminate error, to disfigure the fair beauty of the Gospel. Lord, didst Thou not sow good seed in Thy field? From whence, then, hath it tares? . . . An enemy hath done this."

It is this enemy that fills the world with spirits of error, who mislead those whom they profess to guide. And these

[1] 1 S. John iv. 4.

spirits of error assume a thousand shapes,—from the grossest licentiousness and ungodliness, up to angels of light, so as to deceive, if it were possible, the very elect. It is a great mistake to suppose that error is always hideous. Far from it: it is often very attractive, because it is made to harmonize with the affections and feelings of human nature; to captivate the imagination; to charm the fancy; to satisfy the lusts; to counterfeit truth; and so to disguise itself as to require a keen spiritual discernment to detect the cheat. Nor is it confined to the world. It creeps into the Church, fomenting divisions, corrupting the spirituality of the faith, overlaying the plain word of Scripture with traditions, bringing into the sanctuary the meretricious accessories which distinguished Paganism, and giving power to unbelief by hiding the simple truth as it is in Jesus. And all this is going on perpetually. It never ceases. When driven away out of the Church under one form, it creeps back very soon under another; so that no age and no individual is exempt from the trial. All along the history of the Church, are spread out the various heresies which have disfigured and perverted the Truth. Her whole pilgrimage, from Calvary until these latter days, is strewed with the victims of the deluding spirit of error; and in nothing is Church History more interesting and more important, than in its faithful delineation and its graphic exposure of this innumerable spawn of error. Thick as locusts have they lighted down upon the fair fields of the Church, and eaten up the good seed which has been sown, or else so intermingled the seeds of untruth that the harvest has been meagre and unwholesome. How important, then, that the beloved disciple should, ere he left the world, have warned—in his own loving words, with his own loving heart—those who were to follow him,—"Beloved, believe not every spirit, but try the spirits whether they are of God:"[1] and should have left to us in his inspired word the means of separation between truth and error.

Every age has, of course, its own peculiar temptations; and S. John, in the beginning of the chapter from which we preach, is guarding his contemporaries against a particular form of heresy, connected with the personality of Christ, which was rife at that time: but as he proceeds, he generalizes his subject; and it is from that generalization that I preach to-day, and warn you against the spirit of error, which — as I said before — is always rife, and very much so in our times and in our country. And in that generalization he makes these distinctions: "They are of the world:" "We are of God." "They speak of the world, and the world heareth them:" "We speak from God; he that knoweth God, heareth us. He that is not of God, heareth not us. Hereby know we the spirit of Truth and the spirit of error."

The great distinction between truth and error which is made in this place, is that the one is only acceptable and listened to by those who are of God, while the other is listened to by those who are of the world. The world refuses to listen to any doctrine which requires a departure from the ways of the world, or which proceeds upon principles antagonistic to those of the world. If Christianity calls for faith, the world rejects it: because that proceeds upon sight and sense. If it demands its acceptance because revealed by the Spirit of God, the world will not hear it: because that rests its conclusions upon reasoning and induction. If it requires self-denial and self-discipline, the world turns away from it: because that loves ease and indulgence. If it proclaims the heinousness and punishment of sin, the world repudiates it: because it cannot see

[1] 1 S. John iv. 1.

the odiousness of sin; nor how what it considers a slight offense can deserve such penal infliction. If it call for remission of sin through the shedding of blood, the world flings it away with abhorrence: because that declares repentance and amendment of life to be all-sufficient. If it teaches the coming and presence of the Holy Ghost, the world expresses disgust at such fanaticism: because that deems the light of nature, of reason, and of conscience, to be enough for man, in time and in eternity. If it points to the Church and her ordinances and sacraments as necessary to salvation, the world consents to it as an institution of civilization and morality, but will go no further: because that thinks such an institution is not necessary for man's salvation.

And thus, from Alpha to Omega, from the very first doctrine of Christianity to that Church which is the pillar and ground of the Truth, the world is opposed to the whole spirit of Christianity, to all the doctrines which make its distinctiveness, and to all the practices which are its ornament and its power. And as it has been in the past, so will it ever be to the end. And thus is furnished a test between truth and error. For all this which the world rejects and repudiates, the child of God receives and appropriates and lives upon. It is the very foundation of his hope; the very anchor of his soul; the very life of his spirit; the very comfort of the present, and the hope of the future; the confidence which he has, that he shall be able to stand in the day of final account. What one rejects, the other hugs to his bosom; what one considers as the wisdom of God and the power of God unto salvation, the other deems foolishness; what one makes the rule of his life, the other counts unnatural and ascetic. And so they stand, hostile at every point; in doctrine, in worship, in discipline, in life: and so they afford a striking and pregnant standard for the decision of truth and of error, that is, of truth in accordance and sympathy with the Christian Revelation; of error, in antagonism and antipathy to it. If one wishes to try the spirit that is tempting him, let him see whether that spirit is accepted by the world and is popular with it, or whether it is in harmony with the Church, and is welcomed by the children of God. Each has its own instinct, its rapid power of perception and decision. Each knows its own, and rushes to its embrace. Those who are of the world drink in the teachings of the spirits of error, and get drunk over them. Those who are of God shrink from them, as a maiden from impurity, or an honorable man from shame. When a spirit is not accepted by the children of God, beware of it! When it does not harmonize with the doctrinal teachings of the Church, turn away from it! It is false, and will run rapidly into error.

This is one test of truth. But there is yet another, quite as important, which must be kept before the mind; and that is, that any doctrine is necessarily error, which strikes at the Divinity of our Lord Jesus Christ, or which elevates any thing above Him in reverence and in worship. It is His Divinity, which is the special object of hatred on the part of the Devil. His Divinity it was, which drove him headlong, "with hideous ruin and combustion dire," from the precincts of God's holy habitation; it was His Divinity, which baffled all his designs against man; it is His Divinity, which holds him in a grasp of iron, and will one day bind him in fetters of adamant in that bottomless pit which is prepared for him and his angels. That Divinity he therefore hates with all the intensity of his devilish malice, and against it he hurls all the instruments which he can wield through Nature and through man. Around that Divinity has his fury always raged, and — sad to say — he finds in the world those who are ready to assist him, and ready to coöperate with him, against Him who came to earth to redeem and to save a fallen race. He stirs up some to deny the reality of His personality, as in S. John's day; others to deny his Divinity, as in our day. He incites some to lower His dignity and make Him no more than a created being; others to give Him Divinity, but to refuse to acknowledge his coëquality with the Father. In our day this hatred is running into terrible excess, and Christ is assaulted, in every form and shape, if so be that He may be degraded in the eyes of the world, and men be led to look elsewhere than to Him for salvation. He is denounced as a myth. His miracles are all denied and attempted to be explained by what are called — idly enough — rational solutions. His Atonement is ridiculed as absurd. His power to save is confined to His influence as a man of wisdom and of goodness. His teachings are derided as below the wisdom of the current times; His philosophy as too shallow for such an age of progress and advancement. This is the current language of the world. And while these taunts and reproaches are hurled upon Him from the one side, on the other hand one of the oldest branches of the Church is divesting Him of His honors and His offices in favor of the Virgin Mary, whom they think thus to honor by the degradation of her Son. It is horrible to read the language which is used, upon this head, in the practical working of the Roman Church. A few of these expressions will I quote, using as my authority no less a divine and scholar than Dr. Pusey, — a man never considered an enemy to Rome, but who says, in his late work, *The Eirenicon*, that he is kept from any further advance towards Rome by expressions such as these: —

"Her intercession (*i. e.* the intercession of the Virgin Mary) is held to be coextensive with His 'who ever liveth to make intercession for us' — our divine Lord, and to be the access to His intercession. And this is taught, not as the glowing expression of Southern feeling, but as the deliberate mind of the present Roman Church." "God," it is conceded, "could grant His graces without the intercession of Mary," but it is asserted that He will not. It is one of their most learned writers who says: "It is the universal sentiment of the [Roman] Church, that the intercession of Mary is not only useful, but necessary, with a moral necessity; because the Church seems to think that God has determined to give us no grace except through the hands of Mary." So, then, it is taught in authorized books, that "it is morally impossible for those to be saved who neglect the devotion to the blessed Virgin;" that "it is the will of God that all graces should pass through her hands;" that Jesus has in fact said: "No one shall be partaker of My Blood, unless through the intercession of My Mother;" that "our salvation is in her hands;" that "whom the justice of God saves not, the infinite mercy of Mary saves, by her intercession;" that "God is subject to the command of Mary;" that "God has resigned into her hands His omnipotence in the sphere of grace;" that "it is safer to seek salvation through her, than directly from Jesus;" that "God retaineth justice unto Himself, and granted mercy to her;" that "she is the Throne of Grace, whereof the Apostle speaketh;" that "she appeaseth the just anger of her Son;" that "she is the only Refuge of those who have incurred the Divine indignation." And, to show you the impression which this *cultus* of the Virgin Mary is making upon heathen lands, Dr. Pusey states that "In southern India and Ceylon, our churches are called by the natives, 'Jesus Churches;' the Roman Catholic Churches, 'Mary Churches.'"

Does it not seem wonderful? And does it not make us

tremble at the power of Satan, and at his ability of placing error in the room of truth, that a system of teaching like this can be tolerated by people having the Holy Scriptures in their keeping? And yet it is not only tolerated, but perverts are making to it in England and this country,—perverts among the intelligent and the learned. For these things, which I have quoted, are not accusations made in a corner, but have been published in the face of the world by one of the profoundest theologians of the day, and challenge confutation. It teaches us how we are all liable to be deceived and blinded;—how the same spirit of error can exhibit itself in the boldest rationalism on the one side, and in the most extreme Church worship on the other hand: how Christ may be degraded by a denial of His Divinity; and still so much degraded by such an exaltation of the blessed being from whom He was born after the flesh, as to place the dispensation of His grace at her command. The same result is produced by either process; and each is alike welcome to the world and the Devil.

Let us pause here, and furnish you with a second test for distinguishing truth and error in Christianity. The first was by noticing how any doctrine or practice was received by the world and the Church respectively: the second is to observe how any doctrine or practice which may come upon you, deals with the character and offices of our Lord Jesus Christ. For the whole purpose of Christianity is to exalt Jesus Christ; is to teach that salvation comes only through His Name; is to place Him above all created beings which are in heaven and which are upon earth; is to glorify Him up to an equality with the Father in the one eternal Godhead; is to place every thing of mercy, of grace, and of glory, within His gift; is to crown Him Lord of lords and King of kings. To divest Him of any of these prerogatives, or to place any one above Him, is to teach what is discordant with the whole scope and tenor of Scripture; is to indicate at once a spirit of error pervading the teachings whether of individual or Church. It is an infallible rule, one which I leave with you without any fear of abuse. Christ Jesus, the only-begotten Son of the Father, must stand in Christianity preëminent as its central Image: crowned with thorns in this world; but, in the hereafter, crowned with the glory of all the hierarchy of Heaven and all the redeemed of earth casting their crowns at His feet, and crying: "Blessing and honor, and glory, and power, be unto him that sitteth upon the throne, and unto the Lamb, forever and ever."[1]

These are the two tests which arise naturally out of our text, and should be used freely and fearlessly in the determination of the spirit of truth and the spirit of error. Men often hide themselves from their convictions by affirming that they cannot distinguish between truth and error. In this are they mistaken, for in Christianity they are separated by very marked lines. The world points them out to every honest, sincere mind; the Church points them out; the children of God point them out. All these have their fingers pointed directly, the one to truth, the other to error, just as fixedly as the needle points to the star. What is wanted by man is, not the power to distinguish truth from error: it is the *will*. His own nature, in its state of corruption from the fall, is against the truth. He is glad to be blinded; and so the god of this world blinds him, now by pride of reason, now by the deceitfulness of riches, now by the lusts and cares of the current life, now by the evil heart of unbelief. Truth and error are before him: and others — those who have submitted to be guided by the Spirit of God — clearly distinguish between them. He cannot, because he must guide himself; because he places

[1] Rev. v. 13.

reason above faith; Nature above Revelation; the delusions and vanities of the world above truth and the reality of life. The words of Scripture point out the way, — "I am the way," says Christ; point out the truth, — "I am the truth," says Christ; indicate the proper frame of mind to attain it, — "Be not wise in thine own eyes: fear the LORD, and depart from evil;"[1] and crown all with the glorious reward: "To him that overcometh will I grant to sit with me in my Throne, even as I also overcame, and am set down with my Father in His Throne."[2]

1866.

[1] Prov. iii. 7.

[2] Rev. iii. 21.

Thirty-fifth Sermon.

These all died in faith, not having received the promises, but having seen them afar off, and were persuaded of them, and embraced them, and confessed that they were strangers and pilgrims on the earth. For they that say such things declare plainly that they seek a country. — HEBREWS xi. 13, 14.

CHRISTIANITY has its rolls of fame, as well as the world; — its catalogue of wise and heroic men, who have illustrated its annals and glorified the name of Jesus upon earth. And these stretch back to a period coëval with the creation, — before whose antiquity all the records of existing nations fade into utter insignificance. What is the roll of Battle Abbey, what the lineage of the Cæsars, what the song of Troy, what even the cylinders of Assyria or the obelisks of the Nile, compared with a monument like that of the Bible, embracing the undying actions of such beings as Abraham, and Noah, and Enoch, and Abel? Those are but of yesterday: these, the deeds which were performed when the world lay in its primeval glory, — the Golden Age, ere yet man had defaced its beauties with his hand of ruthless violence. And although they tell not of conquered nations and devastated countries; although their note of triumph is not swelled with the groans of the dying and the curses of the slaughtered; although no earthly pyramids nor colossal piles mark the spots where they died — a holy band of martyrs: still are they memorials of the highest heroism the world has ever known! These heroes did not conquer man, but they subdued within themselves *the fear* of man; they did not trample upon the necks of prostrate kings, but they put under their feet *the world* and the *love of the world;* they did not found dynasties and establish nations, but they planted in the earth the seed of Faith, confident that it would, in God's own time, become the salvation of the world! Theirs was the heroism of self-denial, — of conquest over things present, of martyrdom for despised truth. Theirs was the glory of seeing the end from the beginning; of heralding, before even the gray dawn of morning, — by starlight, as it were,[1] — the rising of the Sun of Righteousness: theirs the divine privilege of living — before the example of Christ's life was exhibited upon the earth — as men should live, who are "born, not of blood, nor of the will of the flesh, nor of the will of man, but of God."[2] Their memorial has been cast out by profane history, but it has been preserved by holy men of old, speaking as they were moved by the Holy Ghost. Their names have found no record among the lyric songs of the Pierian spring; but lips touched with a live coal from off the Altar, have embalmed them in undying prophecy. They have received no glory here, but they stand among the four-and-twenty elders, around the throne of God, with their crowns, and with their harps, singing forever the "new song" of the Redeemed.

Such men, and it is of these we preach to-day, were men of like corruption and like infirmities with ourselves, and yet have now their places upon this record of inspired fame. And this, too, under enormous disadvantages. Like us — for all the just must live by faith — they were required not only to live by faith, but to die in faith; and that faith resting only upon promises! Verily may we blush when we read their deeds of spiritual power, and remember the wide difference between the promises in which they rested, and

[1] 2 S. Pet. i. 19.

[2] S. John i. 13.

the full light of Gospel fulfillment which shines upon us. If they were faithful unto death, only seeing the promises afar off: how shall we escape, if we neglect so great salvation? If they confessed that they were pilgrims and strangers upon the earth, with nothing to support them but a persuasion that what God promised He would perform: how ought we to live, when our faith rests upon a covenant spoken by the Lord Jesus Himself in person, confirmed unto us by them that heard Him, God also bearing them witness both with signs and wonders and with divers miracles and gifts of the Holy Ghost? Let us to-day examine their faith, and our unbelief!

Earth seems, to the eye of sense, to be man's home. It is the only substantial thing which meets his eye, amid things unsubstantial. The sea, the air, the heavens, are all restless and unstable, unfitted for his resting-place. He can use them for his purposes, but it is always at his peril; and his feeling of security returns to him only when he finds himself once more upon the bosom of his Mother Earth. 'Tis there he builds, and plants, and reaps; 'tis there his plans are carried out; his feelings are all bound up with it, his associations and his affections are twined around it. Upon it, shall all he really knows of life be spent; and when that life is done, he will commit his body to its keeping, and leave his children, his treasures, his works, still to endure upon it. He has no real bodily connection with any thing else; and although his mind can soar into regions of abstraction, and create unsubstantial images: it is forced quickly to return to the earth, and attend to the necessities of its daily life. The beings like himself who inhabit its surface are those with whom his comfort and his happiness are inseparably bound up. To agree with them in opinions and interest, is to be at peace: to differ from them, and to be peculiar, is to be in a state of warfare. Contempt and ridicule are his portion when his aims and purposes are contrary to the current views of his fellows; and persecution and martyrdom, when he dares to correct their errors, or himself pursue a better course of life. This is man's connection with the earth. Every thing entices him to make it his rest; and strong indeed must be the motive which should induce him to rise in rebellion against its allurements, and walk, an independent being, in an atmosphere above that which all around him breathe.

Well, this was just what these men of whom I preach to-day, dared to do. Not only were they bold to live upon this earth, such as I have described it, as strangers and pilgrims; but they were willing to confess it. They were not ashamed to acknowledge before an earth-loving generation, — in the face of men who were adding field to field and joining house to house, — that they had more confidence in the Word of God, than in the sight of their eyes and the experience of their fellows. They were ready, not only to give up what of comfort and of happiness there was in earthly permanency and earthly influence, but also to bear reproach and ridicule for their conduct. They had nothing to rest upon but the *bare word* of God: and yet, for it, they were prepared to yield up every thing which their eye told them was fair and pleasant, and to act contrary to what every appearance in Nature seemed to warrant. All of you who know any thing of human life, know how hard this is to bear; but it will be still more apparent when I shall have selected two of the individuals named in the catalogue which precedes my text, and shown you, in their cases, what was meant by being strangers and pilgrims on the earth.

If we attempt to reproduce the earth in the days of Noah, we shall find it full of unbelief and vile corruption.

The touches of the Bible are few, but vigorous. It tells of the intermarriage of the sons of God with the daughters of men, intimating in an obscure way the yielding of the righteous to temptation and to sin. It tells of the wanton disregard of the Spirit of God, so that it "should not always strive with man."[1] It speaks of giants in the earth, and mighty men, men of renown; and coupling this with the succeeding verse, that "God saw that the wickedness of man was great in the earth," we shall not be far wrong in conceiving these men to have been lawless and reckless, having neither the fear of God nor of man before their eyes. And when to these is added the conclusion to which a survey of the world brought a gracious and long-suffering God, "And it repented the LORD that he had made man on the earth, and it grieved him at his heart. And the LORD said, I will destroy man whom I have created from the face of the earth:"[2] we may fairly conclude that it was full of the most hardened infidelity, and the most abandoned licentiousness. Now imagine in the midst of such a world — surrounded by such giants in vice and unbelief — a single individual setting his face against this torrent of wickedness, and living in their daily intercourse a peculiar life of belief, and setting an example of conduct which was a constant reproach to them. And when, after denouncing upon them the indignation and wrath of God, he commenced building an enormous vessel, such as had never been seen upon the earth before, — building it, too, at a distance from any water which could ever float it, — their ridicule upon him must have been immeasurable. And when he told them its purpose — that it was to shelter him and his family and the beasts of the earth from a deluge which was to sweep off all living things — how they must have taunted him, as year after year rolled away and no

[1] Gen. vi. 3 [2] *Ibid.* vi. 6, 7.

clouds gathered wrath over them, and the windows of heaven were not opened, and the fountains of the great deep were not broken up, and they were permitted to revel on in sensuality and lust! And what a trial of his own faith, as he toiled through day and week and month and year upon this huge structure, while yet the long-suffering of God endured! How his heart — for he was just such a man as we are — must have ofttimes fainted within him, as he measured the toil that was before him, and writhed under the settled reproach of all his fellow-creatures, and saw nothing which looked like any change in Nature! How often must he have felt doubts arise within himself, and temptations to unbelief assail him, and weariness in well-doing steal over him! How he must gradually have weaned himself, and his, from all attachment to the earth, and torn his heart from its associations with places and with things, — the pleasant fields of the young earth in which he had labored; the home of his love and of his pride; the green pastures in which he had fed his flocks, and the still waters beside which he had made them to repose: and looked upon them all as doomed to an impending and awful destruction! And as he glanced from the firm earth on which he stood, from its rocks, and the strong foundations of its everlasting hills, to the Ark in which he and all that he loved were to be embarked upon a tumultuous sea — a sea of wrath and of destruction — the trial of his manhood must have been sore indeed! He realized what it was to be a stranger and a pilgrim upon the earth, to be on it but not of it, a traveller without a home, a resident without a friend!

In Abraham's days the world had renewed its prosperity and its wickedness. It was now well peopled since the Flood, and civilized and well-ordered communities — communities abounding in wealth and in power — had overspread its surface. Among its countries, none was more fertile, none more lovely, than the plains of Chaldea. Luxuriant grain waved its golden tresses over the land, and herds and flocks innumerable revelled in its fatness. The pastoral life — the pleasantest upon earth in a land of sunny climes and watered valleys — regulated by the gentle rule of the Patriarch (such a life as Theocritus loved to paint), was that which diffused comfort and happiness among its people. Plenty was there; peace was there; love was there. Into this land of earthly joy came the word of the Lord, and summoned from its pleasant homes a single individual: "Get thee out of thy country, and from thy kindred, and from thy father's house, unto a land that I will show thee: and I will make of thee a great nation, and I will bless thee, and make thy name great; and in thee shall all the families of the earth be blessed."[1] Every thing present was to be abandoned. The ties of a whole lifetime were to be rudely snapped asunder. Country, kindred, his father's house, were all to be left forever. His wife, and his household, and his goods were all to be dragged into a country of which he knew nothing, and there were they to dwell, in tents and in tabernacles, pilgrims in every sense of the word, strangers among a people strange in manners, strange in customs, strange in language, strange in their idolatry. And all this was to be done openly and avowedly upon a bare promise of God, to be fulfilled in the distant future. No language can describe it more forcibly than the language of Scripture: "By faith Abraham, when he was called to go out into a place which he should after receive for an inheritance, obeyed; and he went out, not knowing whither he went. By faith he sojourned in the land of promise, as in a strange country, dwelling in tabernacles with Isaac and Jacob, the heirs

[1] Gen. xii. 1-3.

with him of the same promise:"[1] and we can imagine the earnest persuasions, the affectionate entreaties, the sad forebodings, the dogged unbelief, with which his intention was received by the kindred and the companions he was leaving. As it would be now, so was it then. Just as the Missionary spirit is sneered at and ridiculed now; just as the whole unbelief of the world is brought to bear upon any one who determines to give up country, and kindred, and his father's house, for the work of the Lord in strange lands: so was it when Abraham determined to abandon all that man deemed valuable upon earth, and confess the life of a pilgrim and a stranger. Instead of his father's house, he was henceforth to have no fixed habitation, wandering, as the Lord commanded, until his set time was come. Instead of fields and estates, which he might name after himself, and hand down to his posterity, he was to possess not so much as a foot of earth which he might call his own. Instead of becoming a mighty man among the Chaldeans, surrounded with the riches of his time, — a numerous posterity, a devoted household, a band of bold retainers, — he was to be unknown and unnoticed, fleeing hither and thither, without a child to cheer his home or reässure his faith, yielding up every thing — if so be that he might be obedient to the Lord. And oh! how his faith must have been tried, when through long and weary years he saw no sign of the nation that was to issue from his loins, no approach to the possession of the country which he had been called to inherit, no token that he should ever become a blessing to the nations! And when we follow him as he traversed the country to which the Lord had called him, weaned from all earthly ties, bound to no local habitation, having no communion with the idolatry that was about him: we can understand that he, like Noah, was a pilgrim and a stranger in the earth!

[1] Heb. xi. 8, 9.

It was by actions like these that Noah and Abraham confessed themselves to be strangers and pilgrims on the earth. And what was the impelling power? What was strong enough to induce them to despise the earth and earthly things, and to separate themselves by a line so marked from the rest of the world? It was faith, — faith of the highest and purest kind; trust in the word of God; belief that what He said, He would do; that what He promised, He would perform. They had nothing else to go upon. Sight was all against them. The appearances of things foreboded, in Noah's case, no unusual disaster to the stable world; in Abraham's case, no likelihood that a man without a child should ever displace by his posterity the nations of Canaan, or become a blessing to the world. Experience cried out against it with her utilitarian voice, for the world had continued as it was from the foundation of things. It was simply that they were persuaded of these promises, and embraced them, because *God* had made them. They knew in whom they trusted; and were satisfied not only to live by faith, but to die in faith!

Living by faith, my hearers, is the hardest thing which man is called upon to do: but to die in faith is the crowning glory of the saint. To endure through a whole lifetime; to be patient unto the end; never to faint nor grow weary; to lose no confidence by the way, and, when the end comes, to trust in an unseen God; to believe that all things are working for your good, when every thing seems to the contrary; to commit yourself to His care, who is at the very moment permitting Death to overcome you: these are triumphs which place the Christian in the roll of spiritual fame! And this was what these men achieved. They all died in faith, and by this declared plainly that they sought a country. Theirs was not a faith which expected any rewards here, — which hoped, when it had been tried, that it would be permitted to enjoy its recompense in this world. They died in it, confessing that they looked for nothing upon earth, but that they trusted in God for that rest which remaineth for His people. It is a beautiful expression, full of deepest meaning, conveying the idea of martyrdom for the sake of divine truth. A man may be a martyr, who never sees the stake, — a martyr in the crucifixion of his natural passions; a martyr through a casting down of high imaginations; a martyr in bearing, unto death, reproach and contempt. Fire is not the cruellest instrument of man's torture: a daily humiliation is keener anguish to a high-toned spirit; a life long-struggle with unbelief, a heavier cross to a faithful soul. And then this glorious consummation, "These all died in faith," conjures up, beyond the grave, that hope which never dies, that country where there is no curse, that inheritance incorruptible, undefiled, and which fadeth not away. So long as they were only *living* by faith, they might have returned to that country whence they came out; but when it could be said that they *died in faith*, the fight was fought, the victory won!

And now, my beloved hearers, how many of us are living this life of faith? How many of us are acting as though we were strangers and pilgrims upon earth, and confessing it before men? The command may not have been laid upon us to manifest our faith in the same striking way as it was exhibited by these Patriarchs, but the Apostles of our Lord have told us, under the inspiration of the Holy Ghost, that we must be a *peculiar people*, and in that peculiarity is to consist our confession. And by this peculiarity is not meant eccentricity, or rudeness, or moroseness, or singularity in dress or voice, or any thing of that outward sort: but a Christian firmness in opinion, and feeling, and conduct, towards man and God. God has spoken to us as plainly as He spoke to Noah and Abraham; for they saw not

His form, but only heard a voice: and He has instructed us how to live, in view of His purposes for the present and for the future. He has warned us against setting our affections upon the things of this world, and commanded us to fix them where Christ sitteth at the right hand of God. He has prayed for us to His Father, that, while we should not be taken out of the world, we should be kept from the evil. It is this being kept from the evil which is to be our peculiarity, — the evil of a worldly life, the evil of covetousness, the evil of ambition, the evil of following a multitude into sin, the evil of being and doing as others because it is the custom, or fashion, or the popular whim, of the moment. And while we are not called upon to be offensive in our language or harsh in our conduct, it is our bounden duty to confess our own Christian life before the world; to act as becomes us; and to say, if need be, that we so act because we are Christians. Noah is called, in the Second Epistle of S. Peter, a preacher of righteousness, although we have no evidence that he went about exhorting and warning the world before the flood. He preached by his actions. The building of the ark was his sermon; and by it he condemned the world. It was the exhibition of his faith, and their unbelief. And so to-day: every truly consistent Christian is a preacher of righteousness, and is a condemnation to all who live ungodly. He may not say a word, — he may not utter a rebuke or a reproach: but his life is a standing rebuke, being his confession that he is a pilgrim and a stranger, — *in the world*, but not *of the world*.

But we must not only live by faith: we must die in faith. It is not enough that we begin to run well; we must persevere unto the end! "O foolish Galatians," was the expression of the Apostle, when he found that they had been tempted to turn away from their faith in Jesus, — the faith in which they had first walked, — "who hath bewitched you?"[1] What folly is this, that when you have been taught of God, you should turn again to the beggarly elements of the world? Is this folly the folly of any of *you?* Having begun in the Spirit, are ye going to end in the flesh? Your faith will avail you nothing, except you die in it. "These all died in faith:" that was their praise. They not only performed some splendid act of faith, but they lived day by day through temptation, through trial, through care, through reproach, through ridicule, and never faltered. Let this be our example. Let us, like them, live upon the promises, and steer by faith a steady course,

"Through ruffling storms and swelling seas,
O'ercome the world, keep down our fear,
And still possess our souls in peace."

1860–3.

[1] Gal. iii. 1.

Thirty-sixth Sermon.

Not every one that saith unto me, Lord, Lord, shall enter into the kingdom of heaven; but he that doeth the will of my Father which is in heaven. Many will say to me in that day, Lord, Lord, have we not prophesied in thy name? and in thy name have cast out devils? and in thy name done many wonderful works? And then will I profess unto them, I never knew you: depart from me, ye that work iniquity. — S. MATTHEW vii. 21–23.

THE judgment of God upon our daily life, and upon that character which is to entitle us to the Kingdom of Heaven, is very different from the judgment of man. In nothing are we more astonished in this world, than in the dealings of God with His creatures; and we shall be still more amazed, when, at His Judgment, we shall hear Him unmask hypocrisy, and expose deceit, and strip pretension bare, and bring pride and presumption to the dust. Truth will be made terrible in that day, and many of man's judgments will be dreadfully reversed. So struck was S. Paul with this certain aspect of things, that he said: "Therefore judge nothing before the time, until the Lord come, who both will bring to light the hidden things of darkness, and will make manifest the counsels of the hearts: and then shall every man have praise of God."[1] It is these hidden things of darkness which man cannot see, and these counsels of the heart into which he cannot pierce, that make all the difference between sincerity and untruth, between purity and iniquity, between man's estimate of man

[1] 1 Cor. iv. 5.

and God's record in the Book of Judgment. We can judge only by the appearance: God judges by the reality; and it is reality which is so rare and precious. Among ourselves, we value it above every thing. When we find it in man or woman, we prize it, and trust to it, and rest upon it as upon a rock, giving it various names according to its use, but all running into and concentrating upon that one word *reality*. Sometimes we call it honesty, sometimes sincerity, sometimes truthfulness, sometimes guilelessness, sometimes simplicity; but under all these diverse appellations we value the thing, as something the opposite of man's general characteristics, and as higher than the tone of the world. We do not always admire the persons in whom this reality is found, for it puts to shame very often our own artificialness, and uncovers by its frankness our own insincerity: but we nevertheless value it, and turn to it in the day of trouble, and find in it the counsel which we need, and the support which will sustain us. No quality in man or woman grows so much as this of reality; and, however unpopular it may make its possessor at the first, it ends in placing him high in the esteem of all good and virtuous people. And as with man, so with God. That which we value in the experience and working of life, and which we ultimately find to be a necessity for us, God values above all things; and reckons it as the test of profession, and the touchstone of words and of actions. We cannot put Him off with outward show, with boisterous words, with long-faced pretensions. He is beyond all that; and while He often permits it to prosper in this world, for His own wise purposes, it never passes beyond the grave, except to be exposed in the sight of all men, and to be sent to its own place with scorn and everlasting contempt.

Not only to us, who openly profess Christianity, is the rule of God's judgment most important, but also to every man who expects to be held accountable in the future. It is the rule of common sense, — a rule piercing down into the motives and counsels of the heart, and touching the very bottom of every thing which it pretends to judge. It commends itself to the approval of every man of right feeling, whether he may expect to be judged according to the principles of Christianity, or according to some criterion of his own, independent of revelation. If he be a true man, what he would ask for would be honest judgment, — judgment getting at the truth of every thing. And we will perceive, by examining our text, that such is its purport, — that it puts aside every thing of mere outside show; and that nothing can stand before it, but what is capable of bearing the scrutiny of an Eye that cannot be deceived, and of a Judgment that cannot be perverted. Any man who is prepared for this judgment must approve it: for it separates truth from falsehood, pretension from reality, with a sternness which none can seduce, and with a justice which cannot be gainsaid.

Our text brings under consideration two classes of professors, which comprise nearly all of those who presume upon that title: those who profess loudly, and do not the works of God; and those who do many things in the Name of Jesus, and yet have not the spirit and mind of Him whom they pretend to serve.

Christianity, as expounded to us in the New Testament and in the life and character of Christ, is made up of a mixture of feeling and of action. If the one exists without the other, the harmony is not complete; and the judgment of Christ will bear hard upon the character. And we see this lack of harmony exemplified everywhere in the Christian Church, making us tremble for those we love, when they shall come to stand at that bar of final Judgment. Let us to-day look into this matter, and see whether a judgment made here on earth, and in the Church, may not arouse our living, active Christians, and prepare them for that final Judgment in which there is no reversal, and from which there is no escape.

"Not every one that saith unto me, Lord, Lord, shall enter into the kingdom of heaven; but he that doeth the will of my Father which is in heaven." This is the first rule of judgment, which comes out of our text, and takes to pieces a great many professors of religion, analyzing them and stripping off that in which they are trusting.

They are crying, "Lord, Lord;" they are making an open show of their devotion to the service of the Lord; they are attending upon the services of the Church; they are communing at the Lord's Table; their names stand upon the Church's record: but what are they doing for Christ? All these Church observances are to benefit themselves. But besides this aspect of Christianity, there is another. There is a side which turns away from self, and looks toward God, — to the advancement of the Kingdom of Christ, to the edification of His Church upon earth, to the vindication of His Name and glory, to the doing of what is called in my text the will of the Father which is in Heaven. They are fulfilling the one side of the requisition of judgment, — crying "Lord, Lord:" but are they fulfilling the other side? This is the question to be settled, and therefore the question to be examined. We will do it plainly and fearlessly, and each one's conscience must answer for itself.

There is nothing more common in the Church than an empty profession, — a profession that begins and ends in talk. And this takes shape according to the forms of religion in which they may have been bred and trained. With those in whose practical systems there is much excitement, it develops itself in a great parade of religious feeling, and a great deal of talk about frames and affections; but disappears when they are called upon to put their hands in their pockets, and advance the kingdom of Christ upon earth. They will attend any number of services; do any amount of religious exercises; talk, and groan, and shout: at the same time that they are worshipping God in buildings in which they would be ashamed to live themselves; are starving His ministers, and are utterly refusing to contribute any thing to the Missionary cause. With others again, of a more quiet stamp, there is an exterior sanctity that is truly edifying; a carrying of religion everywhere upon their persons and their faces; a loud talking about philanthropy, and human progress: but, accompanying it, a very careful observance of their own interests, and not much scruple about the nicety of morals which may regulate their conduct. Again, there are those brought up under still quieter systems, who simply consider themselves as doing their duty when they condescend to worship God at all; and suppose that their acknowledgment of Him before the world, — their crying, "Lord, Lord," — will be quite enough for their future welfare. They do not any thing which offends society, or defrauds man, or disgraces the Church: they simply do nothing for God; nothing for Christ; nothing for the advancement of Christianity. If it depended upon them, the Church would make no progress at all. They sustain it, for themselves; but care not for its extension to anybody else. They have none of the feeling which actuated the early Christians, who, for Christ's sake, sold their possessions, and laid the price at the Apostles' feet, and lived in common with the disciples of Christ. All these classes of Christians, no matter how diversely the effect shows itself, are under the same delusion, imagining that the mere cry of "Lord, Lord," will answer the requisitions of the Gospel of Christ; — the requisitions of that

Gospel which demands self-denial, self-devotion, almsgiving, and above all the Missionary spirit, to make it at all responsive to the will of the Father. And yet how many go on just in this manner, never once enquiring what is the will of that Father, or what duties and responsibilities belong to them as Christians! If they can save themselves, it is all that they care for: thus proving that selfishness, to which the Christian spirit is most diametrically opposed, is ruling over them. What a Christian is to look to in being a Christian, is, that he should no longer work his own will upon earth, but the will of the Father, whose love it is that has led to his redemption through the Sacrifice of His Son. If that is not considered, there can be no Christianity in the matter. If, when considered, it is not followed, there can be no hope of any place in the Kingdom of Heaven. And that will is so clearly marked out in the Mission of His Son, that every one that runneth may read. Even as early as Isaiah, the Divine Mission of the Saviour was pointed out, that Mission of which He said: "I seek not mine own will, but the will of the Father which hath sent me."[1] "The Spirit of the Lord God is upon me; because the Lord hath anointed me to preach good tidings unto the meek; he hath sent me to bind up the broken-hearted; . . . . to appoint unto them that mourn in Zion, to give unto them beauty for ashes, the oil of joy for mourning, the garment of praise for the spirit of heaviness."[2] And what was the will of the Father as manifested in the Son, is the will of the Father as manifested in the disciples: for "every one that is perfect shall be as his master."[3] How can any one, who studies the life of Christ, expect to attain the Kingdom of Heaven, without treading somewhat, at least, in His footsteps? Believe me, there never was a truer line in the Gospel than that uttered in my text:

[1] S. John v. 30. [2] Isaiah lxi. 1, 3. [3] S. Luke vi. 40.

"Not every one that saith unto me, Lord, Lord, shall enter into the kingdom of heaven; but he that doeth the will of my Father which is in heaven."

Let us pause at this point, and consider the position: "Not every one that saith unto me, Lord, Lord, shall enter into the kingdom of heaven." Who then shall enter it? No one but "he that doeth the will of my Father which is in heaven." The question, then, meets every one of us, full in the face: "Am I doing that will?" I know that I am doing a part of it, in having become a professor of religion; in having made a public acknowledgment of His Name; in having enrolled myself among His servants and soldiers. So far, well! But am I now doing any thing, as a servant and a soldier? Mere engaging to serve does not make a good and faithful servant; mere enrolling as a soldier does not entitle one to honor or reward. The servant, to be faithful, must do the will of his master. The soldier, to deserve the name, must fight his master's battles, and strive against his Lord's enemies. Inaction will do in neither. And so with the Christian. He must show his service; his record must be clear of supineness and indifference; the scars of honorable battle must show themselves upon his person. Are these things so with us, my fellow Christians? Think well; examine yourselves; reckon up what you have done for God, in return for what He has done for you; consider in what respect you have advanced Christ's Kingdom upon earth. Upon your treatment of this subject may depend your title to Heaven; for "Not every one that saith unto me, Lord, Lord," shall enter that Kingdom!

But our text does not stop here. It goes very much further, and arraigns another class of Christians, who seem to stand upon a much higher ground than the inactive drones we have been considering: "Many will say to me in that day, Lord, Lord, have we not prophesied in thy name? and in thy name have cast out devils? and in thy name done many wonderful works?" High pretensions, you perceive; practising not only the ordinary duties of Christ's prophets, but the extraordinary gifts of what would seem to proceed from the Spirit of God; and pleading these things as if they had done them in good faith, themselves believing them to be acceptable with God; — doing them in Christ's Name, and under His banner. And yet, what is the awful reply? "And then will I profess unto them, I never knew you: depart from me, ye that work iniquity."

And what is very striking in this passage is, that "many" will speak these words to Christ. It will not be one here and there, but many: as if such false prophets should abound; men deceived and deceiving; blinded by the spirit of evil, and blinding others. It is a very dreadful view of things; and yet one that we can very well understand! The world abounds with such now. Society is pestered with them; the Church is hindered in her work by them; the Kingdom of Christ is impeded in its progress. But for these, and the Gospel would have free course and be glorified. But such as these are what Christ calls them: "workers of iniquity;" — men who have used His Name, but have never known His Spirit: who have abused His Name, speaking lies and hypocrisy. And yet, by such are men deceived: good men, sober men, worldly-wise men; men with a Book in their hands which confutes all their teachings; with the life of Christ before their eyes, which dazzles with its brightness and majesty all their falsehood. Sad illustration of the corruption of the Fall, — that good can be so easily perverted, and the aliment of the soul be changed into destructive poison!

How watchful does this sentence of Christ call upon us to be, over ourselves! Which of us is the true servant of Christ? Who amongst us is illustrating the spirit of the Gospel? is living with God the true life of Christianity? We are all professing: which of us is working up to our duty and our responsibility; working, I mean, in the Spirit and with the Mind of Christ? The world is rushing on around us, and I fear that it has the most of our thoughts and feelings. Life is vanishing like a dream; and those we love are perishing, one after another: and yet we seem to forget that Judgment seat, at which the very broadest distinction is to be made between those who cry "Lord, Lord," and those who do the will of their Father in Heaven. How few can tell what that will is; and how much fewer really know what it is! Christ our Lord came to do that will: and you see what His life was. The will of God is the same to us, as it was to Him, however different the acts required of us may be. His will is the salvation of lost man, is the making the kingdoms of this world to become the kingdoms of Christ; is that the Church should shine as a light in the darkness, filling the earth with joy and peace and comfort. Our Saviour shed His Blood to work out those results, — gave Himself a sacrifice that He might "purify unto himself a peculiar people, zealous of good works."[1] We are not called upon to shed our blood, perhaps: but we are called upon to be a part of that peculiar people zealous of good works, who are by those works to help to bring in the glorious Kingdom of Christ. Are we doing it? Are we at work about it? Or are we satisfied with receiving the blessings of the Church and of the Gospel, without making any effort to extend them to others? These are grave questions, and we should answer them to our consciences. Are we not getting weary in well doing? are not the sadness and depression of the times operating upon our Christian characters, and making

[1] Titus ii. 14.

us listless, and careless, and indifferent! The dealings of God with us are sent to try our faith, to enlarge our charity, to purify our purposes: and not to paralyze our Christian efforts. By showing us the vanity of earthly affairs, His purpose is to fix our affections upon heavenly things, and make us more earnest in their advancement. By showing us how little dependence we can place on man, or on society, His aim is to turn our thoughts more singly to that Kingdom, which shall never end; to that home, eternal in the Heavens, from which is banished all change and all disappointment. We misuse adversity, unless we turn it to spiritual account, and use it for a blessing to ourselves and to others.

The great moral lesson, however, which the words of my text teach us, is, that we shall be judged and dealt with for exactly what we are, and not for what we seem to be. We ourselves are conscious of many sins and infirmities, of which the world knows nothing; of many omissions of duty, of which our dearest relations are ignorant; of many shortcomings, which would be looked upon as guilt only by an all-holy God: of how many more must an all-seeing God be conscious, when He searcheth the hearts and trieth the reins of the children of men! All these things will He bring unto judgment, — our secret thoughts, our hidden desires, our coldness in prayer, our lukewarmness in service, our self-indulgence: and the appearance which we wore to the people around us, will be as nothing in His eyes. Reality, truth, will then come to the surface. Our Christian graces will then be weighed. Our faith in the efficacy of the Blood of Christ, in the power of the Holy Ghost to overcome sin and to bring man to repentance, will be exhibited to all, especially to ourselves. Our self-denial for the good of others, our willingness to endure hardship for Christ's sake, our rejection of the allurements of ease and indulgence, will be cast into the balances, and be valued at their true worth. Our charity for the infirmities of others, our long suffering for injuries received, our kindness to those who are in error, our efforts for the restoration of the fallen, will all receive their real estimate, and will be brought home to our confusion in that day of awful account. There will be no deception there, no glossing over of false and artificial pretension. No prophetical office will screen us in that day; no wonder-working acts at which men have gazed in amazement and at which devils have laughed, will cause any deviation from the straight line of justice. Every one of us, no matter what our positions in life, what our pretensions as Christians, will be stripped of every thing false, and be judged according to the inexorable rule of right and wrong. God grant that we may not hear the terrible words which "many" are to hear: "I never knew you: depart from me, ye that work iniquity."

We have, my beloved hearers, but one Refuge, — the love and mercy of Christ. We can hide ourselves in Him, and He will be our hiding-place in the tempest. His Blood can atone for all our sins; His righteousness can cover all our unholiness. In Him can we find wisdom, and righteousness, and sanctification, and redemption. Remember that it is what we are, and not what we do, that is to be the question. And while it is a terrible ordeal, this reduction to stern reality, it is likewise, if properly understood, a wondrous comfort. To know that God will judge us, not by our feeble efforts, not by our limited performances, not according to our manifold infirmities; but by what He can see, — our love for Him, our devotion to Christ, our earnest desire for the advancement of the Kingdom of grace: is indeed a solace past all reckoning! Let us cling to that, and we shall be saved. Let us say with S. Paul, "By the grace of God I am what I am:"[1] and if we can say it sincerely, in the consciousness that we have trusted to that grace, and cherished it in our hearts, and rested upon it in faith and hope, we shall never hear the words: "I never knew you: depart from me, ye that work iniquity."

1866.

[1] 1 Cor. xv. 10.

Thirty-seventh Sermon.

Then said one unto him, Lord, are there few that be saved? And he said unto them, Strive to enter in at the strait gate: for many, I say unto you, will seek to enter in, and shall not be able. — S. LUKE xiii. 23, 24.

THROUGH all the intercourse which our Lord held with His followers, it was His persistent aim to turn their thoughts in upon themselves. He never gave the smallest encouragement to any thing like inquisitiveness into secret things, or to speculations which did not concern their personal salvation. Life was too short, and the work of religion upon the heart too solemn, for any time to be wasted in mere questioning. If an enquiry looked to practical personal religion, nobody was more prompt to explain, to satisfy, to guide, to bless: but if it was asked merely for the gratification of an idle curiosity, or the feeling of a prurient fancy, it was at once turned upon the enquirer, and changed into a lesson of truth for all time to come. Witness His reply to those, who told Him of the Galileans whose blood Pilate had mingled with their sacrifices, with the evident desire of drawing out His opinion respecting the degree of their sinfulness. "Suppose ye that these Galileans were sinners above all the Galileans, because they suffered such things? I tell you, Nay; but except ye repent, ye shall all likewise perish."[1] Witness His answer to S. Peter, when he asked Him of John's future career: "If I will that he tarry till I come, what is that to thee? Follow thou me."[2] And in our text we perceive the like un-

[1] S. Luke xiii. 2, 3.

[2] S. John xxi. 22.

willingness on the part of Christ to answer a question which could lead to no practical result. "Lord, are there few that be saved? And he said unto them, Strive to enter in at the strait gate: for many, I say unto you, will seek to enter in, and shall not be able."

An awful question, my hearers: and a still more awful answer! The question involving that which is most truly important to a responsible creature: the answer implying difficulty at every point of man's efforts. The question rendering one almost breathless with anxiety to hear the reply of such a Being as Christ: the answer making him feel that, while it is evaded, enough of light is thrown upon it to render every man certain that he must work out his salvation with fear and trembling. If the gate be strait,—that is, narrow: if strenuous effort be necessary to pass through it into life eternal; if many shall seek to enter in, and shall not be able: well may every man feel that the mere cry of "Lord, Lord," will not be sufficient in that hour of necessity, and that he must begin, betimes, to prepare himself for that hour when the question of admission or exclusion is to be finally settled.

Our Lord answered this question, as He did every other, in the very wisest manner. It is really of not the least practical importance to us whether many or few are to be saved; and yet if our Saviour had answered it either way, it might have worked very evil effects upon men. Had He said that but few were to be saved: despair might have taken the place of hope, and men might have run into "desperation, or into wretchlessness of most unclean living." If, on the other hand, He had opened the door to every one who claimed to enter, a flood of carelessness and ungodliness might have rushed in upon the Church. His answer was liable to neither objection. It left the question unsettled,—except in this, that personal effort would be necessary for each man's own salvation; — that whether many or few were to be saved, no one need expect it in his own individual case, who did not strive after it earnestly and sincerely.

How continually do we see persons trifling away their precious time upon questions just as unimportant as this one of the disciples! Instead of looking their own salvation directly in the face, and being in earnest about it, they are worrying themselves about points, which, even if they could be settled, would have no bearing at all upon their individual condition. Of what importance is the question which is so often made about the origin of evil? We know every thing that is important *to us.* We are satisfied that moral evil does exist; that it has spread through the world, and corrupted human nature; that its poison is circulating in our veins; and that, unless an antidote can be provided against it, we must perish. Suppose under these circumstances that it could be determined what was the origin of evil, of what advantage should it be to us? Should it help our individual case at all? Should it render our duty any the more imperative, or our work any the more easy? Should we not have the same strait gate to enter; the same conflicts to pass through; the same necessity for earnestness and vigor? When our minds had been satisfied upon this very deep question, — one of the secret things which belong to God, — should our hearts be any the more purified? We do not act so in things pertaining to our physical welfare. When I am smitten by a sore disease, I do not say that I will use none of the remedies which are prescribed for me until I can be satisfied how I took the disease, or where it originated? If my physician was impertinent enough to pause over such questions as these, I should say to him, "For mercy's sake cure me first, and then afterwards you may discuss such matters to your heart's content: but do not leave me to perish, while you are settling a matter of not the least practical importance." This would be the impulse of any one who was in serious danger from disease; and yet, in spiritual matters, in the fearful disease which perils the soul, a trifling—the very reverse of this earnestness—is indulged in. Question after question is started, if by any means the real, practical one of personal salvation may be avoided;—if the probe may be kept from the seat of the disease. Such a course always satisfies me that there is no real earnestness, no conviction of sin, no desire for a change of things, no faith in the awful matters of which Christ is the Centre and the Arbiter. These questions are started merely to get rid, in a polite way, of any thing closer or more personal; to evade, if possible, the struggle which has to be entered upon, the moment the real point of one's own salvation is grappled with.

And as it is with this question of the origin of evil, so likewise with all the other speculative questions which may meet us as we approach the truly earnest one of our own condition. They are strewn all along; meet us at every point; are suggested at the most critical moments of our religious life; rise up, one after the other, under the influence of the Devil, and mock us every step we take towards salvation. We quell one, only to find another springing up before us; and it is not until we have the firmness to press forward boldly, that they vanish from our path. They are like the grotesque images which a dim, uncertain twilight casts upon the path of the traveller. Were he to pause upon his journey to examine each one of them, and ascertain its origin and its insubstantialness: darkness should come upon him, and his feet should stumble on the dark mountains. His safety consists in pressing forward for the home which is before him, looking neither to the right hand nor to the left: trusting that the path of duty is the path of safety, and that the lions in the way will be found either chained or having no existence save in the play of the light and the shadow.

When one is ready to leave all this idle questioning and come to the point, the real distinction which will be found in this answer of our Saviour is, that many "seek," while only a very few "strive." Our Saviour did not mean to teach that any who really strive, should not be able to enter; but that vast multitudes would confound a listless *seeking*, with such a strife as is necessary for *finding* Christ. Flatter ourselves as we please, Heaven is not to be won as easily as we imagine. Let us select a passage here and there from the Bible, and in that way come to an understanding of what is required of us for success in this matter of salvation. I will take a few verses from Proverbs, to begin with, and they will throw some light upon the matter.

"My son," says Solomon, "if thou seekest her as silver, and searchest for her as for hid treasures; then shalt thou understand the fear of the LORD, and find the knowledge of God."[1] Now mark the comparison, and then bring before your mind's eye men seeking for silver and searching for hid treasures. What earnestness! What greediness! What unceasing labor, day and night! What indifference about heat or cold, about hunger or thirst? What following up of every indication that seems to give promise of success! Oh! those restless, unquiet diggers, how they keep every thought, every look, every stroke of the pick concentrated upon the one object of their pursuit! Let a mineralogist light among them and begin to speculate upon the origin of gold, upon its matrix, upon the mode in which the auriferous veins were molten: and they will tell him that they have no time to listen to his speculations. If he will take a tool and help them in their search, they will

[1] Prov. ii. 4, 5.

thank him; if he will not, they cannot be disturbed by his unprofitable talk. Work, work, is what they are engaged in; and they have no leisure for any thing else. This is *striving*. This is what our Lord means when He draws this distinction, — the difference between a man peering about and talking, and striking a stroke now and then: and another man putting forth all his effort and all his strength to gain His treasure! Let us take another passage, and this time from the New Testament, to show the difference here intended by our Lord. "Know ye not," says S. Paul, in his First Epistle to the Corinthians, "that they which run in a race, run all, but one receiveth the prize? So run, that ye may obtain. And every man that striveth for the mastery is temperate in all things. Now they do it to obtain a corruptible crown; but we an incorruptible. I therefore so run, not as uncertainly; so fight I, not as one that beateth the air: but I keep under my body, and bring it into subjection."[1] The figure is changed: but the lesson is the same. The Olympic race takes the place of the mining for hid treasures: but when we bring our memory and our conception to bear upon the simile, we perceive the like earnestness, the like hard training, the like unceasing effort, the whole soul cast into the struggle. That corruptible crown put every candidate to his utmost strain; no time for trifling then; no space for theory; it was all stern work. And thus again we have the difference between striving and seeking; — between a real struggle for the prize, and a mere desire accompanied by a few, faint, irregular efforts.

This is the meaning of Christ, that mere seeking will not do. Many shall seek, but shall not be able to enter in. The mere wish of Balaam, "Let me die the death of the righteous, and let my last end be like his!"[2] is not *striving*.

[1] 1 Cor. ix. 24–27.

[2] Num. xxiii. 10.

The mere question of the young man in the Gospel, "What shall I do to inherit eternal life?" is not striving. The mere hearing the Word of God, as we find it illustrated in the parable of the sower, is not striving. The mere coming to be baptized and confirmed, as in the case of Simon,[1] is not striving. And it is such as these, who think Heaven worth such effort, but not a steady persistent struggle, that Christ means, when he says that "many will seek to enter in, and shall not be able." His remark is not directed against the earnest, against the humble, against the sincere, against those who hunger and thirst after righteousness, however feeble and infirm they may be. It is against the unstable, who wish to-day, and forget to-morrow; who make vows in times of calamity, and break them as soon as the storm of trouble blows over. It is against the fickle, who are zealous to-day, and to-morrow are driven from Christ by some hard saying which cannot be swallowed. It is against the loaves-and-fishes converts, who follow the Saviour in sunshine and favor, but fall away when affliction and persecution come for righteousness' sake. Christ said, "Seek, and ye shall find:" but it was seek in the sense of *strive,* — seeking as for hid treasures, seeking as for victory in a race!

But not only must we strive instead of seeking, but we must strive in the right way. "Strive to enter in at the strait gate," implies that there may be a striving, and yet it shall come to naught because it is in a wrong direction. It cannot too often be pressed upon the world, "that there is none other Name given among men, whereby we must be saved,"[2] than the Name of Jesus Christ of Nazareth. Men are apt to imagine that there are many ways to Heaven. Christ, *our Lord,* says emphatically, "I am the way: no man can come unto the Father but by me."[3]

[1] Acts viii. 17. [2] *Ibid.* iv. 12. [3] S. John xiv. 6.

Men are apt to suppose that if their lives are right in the sight of their fellow-men, they cannot fail to enter the Kingdom of Heaven. Christ, our Lord, says distinctly: "Except a man be born of water and of the Spirit, he cannot enter into the Kingdom of God."[1] Men assert that all that is necessary to secure salvation is, that they should repent and amend their lives. The inspiration of God says distinctly: "Without shedding of blood is no remission."[2] Men claim that God is a God of love, and that they may safely rest themselves upon His mercy. The Bible affirms that, out of Christ, "God is a consuming fire." It is these declarations of the inspired Word of God which make the gate of salvation so strait a gate; — strait, not in the sense of its being hid from any humble, holy child of God, who rests in the mercy of Christ: but strait, because it binds human nature down to the will of God; because it forces every soul to bow the knee to Jesus Christ; because it demands of him who would be saved a stern antagonism to the world, the flesh, and the devil. And these are the things which a proud heart rebels against. It loves nothing so well as its own will; it revolts at nothing more determinedly than a restriction to one plan of salvation, and that a plan wherein it can claim no merit to itself. It loathes nothing more hatefully than the scheme of life which places it as a pilgrim, passing through an enemy's country, and overcoming as it advances the seductions and allurements of the world. All this makes the gate very strait; — hard to find, and difficult to enter. How many turn aside at some point or other of the way, and perish! How many are tempted, and destroyed! How many put their hand to the plough, and turn back! How many wander into the broad path of ease and lukewarmness, and go down to hell! And all these were seekers, — persons

[1] S. John iii. 5. [2] Heb. ix. 22.

who at one period or another of their lives, seemed to be in earnest; did begin to run well: and yet are not found when Christ maketh up His jewels. We see it verified every day in the Church upon earth, as it will be more strikingly exhibited in the Church triumphant: "Many shall seek to enter in, and shall not be able."

And this in spite of our dear Lord's proclamations of mercy. He says, "I am the door:" and has unceasingly called upon sinful man to enter in and be saved. While we listen to the words which He put, by His Spirit, into the mouths of His servants, we cannot doubt but that the straitness of the gate is due to our unwillingness, and not to His want of compassion. When we remember the gracious words of His prophet, calling the Gospel an highway of holiness, and telling us that the wayfaring man, though a fool, should not err therein; when we catch the echo of their words reaching to us over an interval of three thousand years, saying even then, "Ho, every one that thirsteth, come ye to the waters;" when we bring to our mind's eye the gracious Saviour standing on that last day, the great day of the feast, and crying aloud in the hearing of the multitudes: "If any man thirst, let him come unto me and drink;" when we linger about the departing spirit of the last of the Apostles,—that beloved disciple who leaned in deep affection upon his Master's bosom, if so he might shield Him from the Cross,—and hear his last notes, sweeter, like those of the swan, because they were his dying notes, sounding to a sinful world the cheering music of free, unconditioned grace: "And the Spirit and the Bride say, Come. And let him that heareth say, Come. And let him that is athirst come. And whosoever will, let him take the water of life freely:"[1] we cannot think of the gate of entrance as strait. Our spirits rise at the remembrance;

[1] Rev. xxii. 17.

and we feel, with the Psalmist: "For as the heaven is high above the earth, so great is His mercy toward them that fear him. Like as a Father pitieth his children, so the Lord pitieth them that fear him."[1] It is only when we consider ourselves and our kind, — when we trace the records of our race and see its hardness of heart, its perverseness, its willful ignorance, its scorn of the meek and lowly Jesus, its unwillingness to sit humbly at the feet of Jesus and learn, its perversions of His Gospel, that we can understand that the gate is strait, and that man himself makes it so. As one has strikingly said: "When I look at men, my wonder is that any are saved; when I look at Christ and hear the Gospel, my wonder is, that any one is lost."

If you will only strive, my beloved hearers, you cannot conceive how much help you will receive. It will come flowing in upon you from the Church, from the Scriptures, from the influences of the Holy Spirit. The worldly maxim "that God helps those who help themselves" is in nothing more true than in spiritual things. If you sit, waiting for the coming of the impulses which are to lead you onward to Heaven, you shall be very apt to sit unmoved forever. It is "the soul of the diligent" that "shall be made fat."[2] It is he who seeketh everywhere for his Beloved, that shall find Him. The difficulty in Christianity is most often in the very first step, — in saying, "I will arise, and go to my Father." While that resolution is forming, Satan piles up mountains of difficulty in the way of the sinner: but faith scatters them all as clouds before the sun. Let him but persevere, and he will find his faith tried: but in that trial he will get knowledge, patience, godliness, charity. He will have to struggle: but his path will shine brighter and brighter; and when his sun is about to set, the clouds of

[1] Psalm ciii. 11, 13. [2] Prov. xiii. 4.

doubt, of diffidence, of faithlessness, which may have followed him to his rest, will suddenly be lighted up with the love of Christ, and be changed into a retinue of glory ushering him in triumph to his Heavenly home!

Thirty-eighth Sermon.

I will arise and go to my father, and will say unto him, Father, I have sinned against heaven, and before thee, and am no more worthy to be called thy son: make me as one of thy hired servants. — S. Luke xv. 18, 19.

HOW to become religious is quite as important a question as what Religion is; and as much more interesting to us, as how to acquire an estate is more absorbing than a mere description of it. Christianity is of moment to us just in proportion to its being attainable; and if we were persuaded that it was out of our reach, it would at once cease to excite any emotion in us. Formal, didactic instruction about religion, or naked descriptions of its beauty, however eloquent, are of very little concern to intelligent minds. They already know all that. Their taste or their reading has satisfied them upon those points. They consent at once to the purity of its morals, to the Divinity of Christ's character, to the sublimity of His promises. They come to Church, not to hear such abstract questions discussed, but to be told how they themselves, as individuals, may reap the benefit of this mercy, and may attain the hope of everlasting life which is held out in the Gospel. They want Christianity brought home to themselves; and even though they be not ready to embrace it, they desire to be persuaded that it can be laid hold of whenever they may be prepared to make the effort. A busy man has not much time to give to any matter treated in an unpractical way, nor does he put much faith in rhetoric.

He is accustomed to look at every subject in a business point of view; and his mind gets to be so trained in that way, that he is impatient unless one dealing with him, even about spiritual things, comes directly to the point. He wants no descriptions; he calls for reasoning. He turns away from the imagination; but is very ready to listen to common sense. "All this," says he, "is very fine; but the interesting question for me is, Can I obtain this religion? If I can, how shall I set about it? Trace out for me the steps which I am to take, to lead me to salvation. I do not promise you to follow your instructions; but I should be glad to understand my logical position, — if I may use such a term, — and to know what is the first move in this sublime matter of salvation."

It is very striking how exactly the sacred writers meet these wants. Our Saviour was the most practical teacher that ever lived. He came always directly to the point, and never wasted a word or a moment upon any thing that was abstract or rhetorical. And this is the reason why all the greatest topics which can interest man for time or for eternity are discussed and settled within a space incredibly small. The life of Christ, and the teachings of Christ, are included in the compass of what would be considered, nowadays, a very moderate pamphlet: for we must remember that the same story and the same teachings are given by the several Evangelists, and S. John is the only one who introduces much new matter into his narrative. A tract, therefore, equal in size to two of the Evangelists, would embrace every thing which He thought it necessary to utter upon such topics as morals, and Religion, and the true philosophy of life. And in that same tract would be found, besides, the whole story of His divine example, from His conception to His resurrection. This assures us that there is nothing superfluous; nothing that could be omitted with safety to the soul or its interests: and it leaves the busiest man without excuse, when it asks of him the study of a Book so small that it might be read over every day without the slightest interference with any of his duties.

The peculiar feature of our Saviour's teaching, as preserved for us in the Gospels, consists in His constant use of parables and similitudes. "If we take any portion of our Saviour's discourses in the first three Gospels," says a beautiful writer of our day, "we are struck at once with the richness of its texture. It is like a beautiful piece of tesselated work, composed of rich designs of imagery, each of which is beautiful in itself, but runs into the next; while perhaps, in the midst, to continue our image, comes a fuller and more finished picture, set as in a rich border. There is scarcely a sentence that descends to what we should call prose. Every thought is conveyed in a sententious, proverbial, and easily remembered form: or it is a beautiful and perfect simile; or it is a more formal and complete allegory, corresponding point by point with a more solemn lesson. Now to every one of these forms of speech the term parable is applied; therefore the Scripture is literally true: "All these things spake Jesus unto the multitude in parables; and without a parable spake he not unto them."[1] It is this solemn lesson, deduced from one of these allegories, that I shall use to-day as the reply to your practical questions.

There is no portion of Scripture which answers more cheeringly your question, "Can I obtain this religion?" than the parable of the Prodigal Son. It combines the things which seem to stand at the extremest distance,—the holiness of God, and the reckless sinfulness of man; and teaches us how they can be reconciled. No one need despair when he shall have studied this allegory; for no

[1] S. Matt. xiii. 34.

one can have plunged himself into deeper sin or viler degradation. Ingratitude, forgetfulness, lust, bestiality, loathesome vulgarity, were all united in him: and all found mercy and generous forgiveness. He learned, — when he had come to himself, when he used the proper means for restoration, — that his Father's love had never been extinguished; that his own wickedness had alone separated them so long. For filthy rags, he received at once and unconditionally the very best robe. Instead of rebuke, he was met with the most joyous affection; and every thing was done which love could dictate, to do him honor and give him assurance of unreserved forgiveness.

The verses from which I preach occur in that portion of the parable, in which the Prodigal occupies the very standpoint you do when you ask what is your logical position, and what is first to be done in this great work of salvation. You may not have reached the depth of misery and humiliation to which he had sunk. That feature of his condition is immaterial, it being an extreme case, used to manifest the great love and mercy of God: but, like him, you find it necessary to move towards God. What, according to the scheme of the Gospel, is the order of things? Must I approach God? or shall I wait until He approaches me?

This is, you perceive, a practical question: and we must therefore avoid all the metaphysics which may be made to play around it. Innumerable points connected with the Will might be discussed, which could only darken counsel by words without knowledge; but they are unnecessary here, for Christ in His peculiar way, has passed them all by; and has made the Prodigal, out of the depths of his misery, say, "I will arise and go to my Father." No discussions about liberty, or necessity, — no cavillings about the motives which influence the Will, — no question about power or impotence! The Gordian knot is cut at once by the common sense of a stern misery; and he determines to do that which he feels he can do, — arise and go to his father.

This is the answer to your question. The first move is required on *your* part, because "God so loved the world, that he gave his only-begotten Son"[1] to die for its salvation. This sacrifice of His Son has reconciled Him to all sinners conditionally, and has made it altogether suitable with His character to receive any who will arise, and come to Him, and humble themselves before Him. His position is that of the father in the parable, who simply waits until his son will arise and come to him. God's love has known no cessation; His feeling has been one of grief and compassion; and He has authorized His messengers to proclaim that, to every one of you. The office of us who preach to you is called "the ministry of reconciliation; to wit, that God was in Christ, reconciling the world unto himself." "Now then," says the Apostle Paul, speaking for all of us, "we are ambassadors for Christ, as though God did beseech you by us: we pray you in Christ's stead, be ye reconciled to God."[2] In this, you perceive, the reality of the Gospel exceeds the imagination of the parable. In that, the son makes up his determination without any entreaty on the part of his father; it arises simply out of his misery. With you, there is added the earnest message, sent by God through His Ministry beseeching you to come, — so earnest that the Apostle calls it a *prayer*. What more can He do? He has given His only-beloved Son to death (as you see commemorated before you to-day), that He may be enabled to occupy this position. He has accepted the Sacrifice, and pronounced it sufficient; He has instituted a Church in which to welcome, strengthen, and comfort all who may come; and in that Church has organized a Ministry as His ambassadors to *pray* you, —

[1] S. John iii. 16.

[2] 2 Cor. v. 18–20.

that is the term, — to be reconciled to Him. And with that Church and with that Ministry has Christ promised through the Holy Spirit to be, always, unto the end of the world.

The first step, after all this, is on *your* part. God is reconciled to you, and is ready to welcome you. He waits now upon your determination. And it is just here that the office of the Minister as a preacher comes in. He addresses you Sunday after Sunday, urging you to do — what? To determine to arise and come to God! He sometimes appeals to you by one motive, and sometimes by another. In one sermon, your excuses for not coming are examined; in another, the temptations to keep from God are laid open before you. Now your fears are assailed; and then the allurements of the Gospel are presented to you. But whatever form these addresses may take, they all look to that single point, — to lead you to say, "I will arise and go to my Father." If you will only say *that* from the heart, you are safe; for He has said, "Him that cometh to me, I will in no wise cast out."[1] And until you say *that*, nothing more can be done: for God cannot have mercy upon a proud, impenitent, sullen sinner. He may love you, as one of His creatures; He may pity you, as one bent upon everlasting destruction: but He will not permit either that love or that pity to make Him swerve one hair's breadth from His covenant of salvation. He cannot do it: because it was a solemn covenant made with His Son, — a covenant requiring the humiliation and death of that Son; and should He change its terms for you, or me, or the whole world, he should acknowledge to the Universe that He had made a needless sacrifice of His Son. That Son gave Himself to the Cross, because man's sin could no otherwise be forgiven; and when you imagine that it

[1] S. John vi. 37.

can be set aside for you, it plainly shows that you have no proper conception of the mysterious awfulness of that Crucifixion.

Nor is this demand upon you to arise and go to your Father any interference with the sovereign grace of God. 'T is true our Saviour said, "No man can come to me, except the Father which hath sent me draw him:"[1] but what is meant by this "drawing?" How was the Prodigal drawn? By his misery. His father permitted him to suffer, until his sufferings could no more be borne: and *then* he said, "I will arise and go to my Father." And how was the Canaanitish woman drawn? By the misery of her child. And how were the multitudes who turned in the days of the Apostles drawn? By the preaching of the Word. And how were the Bereans drawn? By searching the Scriptures daily. And how was Timothy drawn? By the Christian instruction of his mother and grandmother. So that this drawing is, you perceive, as various as the circumstances of the individuals, the Holy Spirit working in and through them all. No matter what, then, may be the motive which draws you to God, provided it be a good one, the Holy Ghost is probably using it to bring you to a decision. It may be affliction; it may be gratitude; it may be a feeling of satiety with the world, or perchance a heart overflowing with love; it may be sickness; it may be the fear of death. No matter what,—if it make you ready to cast yourselves into the open arms of your Father,—listen to it; quench not the Spirit; be not tempted away by any fear or distrust. It is a Father who invites you; who prays you to be reconciled to Him; who offers you in exchange for your submission the noblest treasures of His house and the richest graces of His own divine Nature.

And do not delay because you are not fit to come. Look

[1] S. John vi. 44.

at the condition of the Prodigal Son, when he said, "I will arise and go to my Father." Look at his plight when he reached that forsaken home. He rose right up from company with the swine, and went just as he was. He did not try to deceive his Father by assuming a better appearance than he was rightfully entitled to. He did not think that he would fare better for being "decent." Common sense told him that a loving Father's heart would be more moved by his misery and woful appearance than by any thing else; and he went, just as he was. And so with you. You are many of you waiting until you can approach God more acceptably. And this you think meritorious; when it is all a device of the Devil. He is anxious to keep you from your Father, and he whispers to you, as if in honor of that Father: "Certainly you are not going as you are, to that great and Holy God (mark you, how he keeps from you the tender epithet of "Father"). He will not receive you, miserable sinner as you are! Amend your ways a little more, before you press into His presence." Listen not to any such advice. I am God's ambassador, knowing God's will much better than the Devil does; and I pray you, in Christ's stead, "Be ye reconciled to God." The Spirit and the Bride say, *Come!*

When you have made this resolution — "I will arise and go to my Father" — you have included in the act the two conditions of salvation. You have repented and believed: — repented, in that you are sorry for having wandered away from God; believed, in that you have trusted the love of God in Christ, and have cast yourself upon His mercy. And this view may relieve you of some of the difficulties which are made to surround the doctrines of Repentance and Faith. They can be involved in much intricacy, and made to perplex an anxious soul; but here is our Lord's solution of them. With this Prodigal, repentance is made to be a turning away from a course of evil, and a turning unto God. No measures of repentance are described: no degree of sorrow or of tears is fixed upon. It is simply a determination to change from the world to God. Sorrow for sin may accompany it, and certainly will be produced by it in the end; for the more we see of the holiness of God, the more shall we mourn over our own corruption: but it may not be very intense in the beginning of the Christian life. Our whole change is produced by the Spirit of God: and the degree of our compunction will be regulated by Him. He may choose to work no further upon you at first, than to lead you to determine to arise and go to your Father. That is for Him to decide, and not for you; and if you have made up your mind sincerely to go to God, that is enough. Leave the divine Spirit to deal with you as He thinks best, touching the degree of sorrow you may feel. And as with repentance, so with faith. It is made, in the analogy of this parable, to consist in casting one's self upon the love and mercy of God. It is independent of all frames and feelings; and is simply *trust in God:* such a belief in His abounding compassion in and through Christ, as shall lead you to go to Him exactly as you are, trusting that He will make all the necessary changes within you.

Your next step is confession — confession to God, and not to man. "Father, I have sinned against heaven, and before thee, and am no more worthy to be called thy son:" — that is, "I have sinned against Thee, my Father in Heaven." When you will do this, my hearer, you are fast making your peace with God; because you have at last recognized the real evil of sin to be its offence against God. That is striking at the root of sin, when you see it in this light. "For," as one has well expressed it, "we may injure ourselves by our evil, we may wrong our neighbor, but strictly speaking, we can sin only against God; and the recognition of our evil as first and chiefly an offence against Him, is of the essence of all true repentance, and distinguishes it broadly from many other kinds of sorrow which may follow on evil deeds." The error the world makes is precisely the contrary of this: it reckons sin to be heinous exactly in proportion to its interference with the security of life and property. It never considers the offence against God, and therefore it is that we see Society and the Church at such issues about sin. Many whom the Church condemns, the world upholds; because their crimes are crimes only in the eyes of religious people. Many on the other hand whom the world condemns, the Church upholds; because the world is persecuting them for Christian graces, for meekness, for forbearance, for humility. When a confession therefore, such as this, falls from the lips of a man, it is a sure sign of grace, — a token that he has been moved by the Holy Ghost to arise and go to his Father.

And this confession no *man* has a right to call upon you to make to *him*. There is no more flagrant usurpation over the conscience than the auricular confession of Rome, — no greater engine of tyranny in the whole armory of its despotism. It puts everybody into the power of the priesthood. It gives the priesthood dominion over the individual, the family, and the nation. For there is no human heart which has not its weakness; no human family which has not its secrets dearer to it than life. And when these are all sucked into the confessional, and motives, and desires, and imaginations, and weaknesses are all probed, and the web of superstition is woven around them, how can such a power be resisted? And it has no warrant of Scripture. S. James exhorts Christians to confess their faults one to another, and pray one for another: but this is altogether a voluntary matter. Our own Church goes as far as recommendation, in peculiar cases, of confession. It is contained in the close of the exhortation immediately following the Prayer for the Church Militant in the Communion Office, in these words: "And because it is requisite that no man should come to the Holy Communion, but with a full trust in God's mercy, and with a quiet conscience; therefore, if there be any of you, who by these means cannot quiet his own conscience herein, but requireth further comfort or counsel, let him come to me, or to some other Minister of God's Word, and open his grief; that he may receive such godly counsel and advice, as may tend to the quieting of his conscience, and the removing of all scruple and doubtfulness." But this is very different from compulsory confession. This is very little more than asking the advice of a pastor. But to require confession under penalty of an anathema is to usurp the place of God, who has told us to come boldly ourselves to the throne of grace, because we have an High Priest there who can be touched with a feeling of our infirmities.

The last grace which is developed in these verses, is that sweet grace of humility: "Make me as one of thy *hired* servants." "I do not come to thee, O Father, that I may have honor, or favor, or ease: I am not worthy to be thy son. Put me in the very lowest place, as one of thy *hired* servants. I come to thee in repentance and faith and love. Do with me as Thou pleasest: only give me Thy mercy. I do not claim the honor of a son. I do not ask even for the place of a slave born in thy house, or bought with thy money: because they can claim thine attachment, and thou art bound to them by ties of interest and obligation and feeling. But make me as one of thy hired servants, between whom and Thee there is no necessary tie; — from whom Thou mayest separate Thyself at any moment without a pang. Even this place I will be satisfied with, if so be Thou wilt only admit me into Thine house." This is true humility, — the very spirit of David, when he said, "I would rather be a doorkeeper in the house of my God, than to dwell in the tents of ungodliness:"[1] — any place, O Father, even the lowest, so I may dwell in Thy Presence, and bask in the beams of Thy Love.

These are your steps: Repentance, Faith, Confession, Humility. I trust that I have made them plain to you. May God give you grace, while you have time and opportunity, to say out of an earnest and sincere heart: "I will arise and go to my Father."

[1] Psalm lxxxiv. 10.

Thirty-ninth Sermon.

The heart knoweth his own bitterness; and a stranger doth not intermeddle with his joy. — PROVERBS xiv. 10.

HOW much we live to ourselves in this life, even though we are perpetually surrounded by beings like ourselves, many of them most closely united to us by the strongest and sweetest ties of sympathy and love! We dwell together in the same house; we eat together at the same table; we meet each other and interchange thoughts and opinions at all hours of the day; we mingle together in the same pursuits, and think that we know each other intimately: and yet each one has a life of his own, an inward life, entirely distinct from every other, and known only to God and himself. Every heart has its own sorrows and its own joys, independent of those which are permitted to mingle in the current of our ordinary life. Every spirit has its own sanctuary, in which are cherished memories, often of bitterness, dreams, hopes, fancies, never to be disclosed to any human eye. The outer life is carried on in the sight of all men, while the inner life, that which shapes and colors it all, is as much hidden as a stream running through the bowels of the earth. We think we know each other; and thinking so, we judge and freely criticise each other: when, if the truth were really known to us, we should be amazed at our utter misconception of character, and ashamed at our false and cruel judgments. Beneath the smiling face the heart is often kept from breaking only by the comfort of God; and beneath a grave and saddened aspect there is just as often a wellspring of joy swelling and bubbling, which, were it seen and understood, would be the envy of the world. When our blessed Saviour said, "Judge not according to the appearance, but judge righteous judgment,"[1] He appointed His disciples one of the most difficult of all tasks: and for this very reason, that we do know and can know so little of one another; that we see each other's actions but cannot know each other's motives; that all the springs of life are hidden from us; that the sanctuary is not open to us; that a veil hangs before our holy of holies, into which none can enter save He who "may be touched with a feeling of our infirmities." What caution should this teach us to use, in forming our estimate of each other's life and character! We never know the real influences which are at work within, — the private feelings which lie behind the conduct that we do rest our judgments upon. Happiness and grief, smiles and tears, hope and despair, are alike hidden from the public eye; and man lives an inner life within himself, baffling the judgment of man, and ofttimes rejoicing in the judgment of God.

It is not strange that we should thus be appointed to live alone, when we consider that we shall have to die alone. Our last great conflict can be known to none save God. Our friends may stand in numbers around our dying bed; those who love us more than they love themselves may pour out their hearts in anguish and in supplication over our struggling spirit: but they cannot help us; the battle must be within ourselves. We are in that moment alone with God's Holy Spirit. He only knows the bitterness of our heart in that moment of awful sorrow; he only knows its joys, when life is ebbing away, and heavenly visions are rising upon us, and mingling themselves with the closing

[1] S. John vii. 24.

scenes of earth. We are dying alone, just as we have lived alone; and our heart-life is all that is important to us. Actions tell but little, either in life or in death; words still less: it is the heart which is the only reality; and none see that, save the Eye which can look into it, and search it, and try it. And thus we end as we begin, nobody knowing us, save God; nobody really helping us, save God; nobody able to comfort us, save God. In Him we live, and move, and have our being in its truest sense: for our heart-life is our real life, and that which alone can give us any true happiness either in life or in death. It is but of little matter to ourselves what the world may think of us and say of us. If we have the springs of true joy within ourselves, no stranger can intermeddle with it; and all his flattery and adulation cannot take away the bitterness which may have cleaved to the heart. Self-consciousness clings closer to us than any judgment of the world; and man has no power to intermeddle with that joy which cometh from the fountain of love and of peace.

It is wonderful that man does not think of this when he is endeavoring, as he often is in life, to flee away from himself. He must die alone, — alone with God. He cannot escape that terrible loneliness. However much he may succeed in drowning his own true life in pleasures or in cares while God allots him the privilege of living, he must meet the reality at last. If he will not be alone with himself in life, he must be alone with God in death! There is no discharge in that war. However he may strive to escape from the bitterness of his own heart in life, — a bitterness which God perhaps has sent to turn him to Himself, — he must meet it at the last. God cannot be gotten rid of. He fills the spiritual world, pervading it with His presence and His power; and it is the spiritual world into which the dying man is about to enter. His inner life is being laid bare, and that bitterness which only his heart was conscious of, and that joy with which no stranger ever intermeddled, are alike unveiled. He to whom all hearts are open, all desires known and from whom no secrets are hid, is looking into that heart and searching it to its depths. By His judgment must man stand or fall, entirely independent of all outward influences of friends or enemies, of nature or the world.

And how kind and gracious it is in our heavenly Father that we should be thus known only to ourselves and to Him! How blessed is it for us that, in our condition of corruption, we should not be unveiled to each other! How much there is in every one's life that is better hidden from every eye, save that of God, — how much of feeling, and imagination, and motive, and purpose! The bitterness of the heart would be made tenfold more bitter by being perceived in an unsympathizing world; and its joys might only bring down upon it, were they disclosed, ridicule and envy. We are never permitted, in this world, to forget that we are living under the curse, and that temptation and sin are forever besetting us. Those pleasures which will make up the felicity of Heaven, — the undisguised heart; the unrestrained feelings; the pure and perfect love; the unfettered affections, — cannot be indulged in here. Too much impurity cleaves to us to permit such intercourse on earth. The heart must be very much shut up within itself, and its bitterness and its joys must many of them be hidden within itself. And well is it that it is so; otherwise there would be endless strife, and confusion immeasurable. Even truth, were it universally spoken, would, in a world like ours, produce disgust, and stir up the fiercest feelings. How much more then were every heart unveiled, and we were permitted to read each other in all the stern reality of life, without any disguise or any palliatives! It would set the world on fire, and kindle such flames as only death could extinguish! The disclosure of the bitterness of one heart would ofttimes steep another in gall; and the hidden joys which are now clothing the path of some poor weary pilgrim with beauty and fragrance, would be withered in a moment, if they were brought to the light and made the criticism of the world. No! we are doomed to live our inner life alone; to carry our joys and sorrows in company only with Christ. Even such an imperfect agency as the confessional has to be kept under the sacred seal of inviolate secresy, because the heart's life is there pretended to be disclosed. There love, jealousy, hatred, remorse, are all whispered into priestly ears; and, though imperfectly, unfold a fearful view of earthly unhappiness: unhappiness which can be remedied only by the Spirit of a Holy God. Man can exhort his fellow to bear and to suffer; to pray, and to strive; to endure and to trust: but he can do no more. Even in this, man's struggles must all be alone: and to get even peace in this world, he must commune alone with God, and roll his burdens and his cares upon Him who has "borne our griefs and carried our sorrows."

And this, my beloved people, is the great consolation of our present existence, that we are not quite alone; that we have a Friend, human in form but Divine in Spirit, who has condescended to call us brother, and to whom our bitterness and our joys may alike be carried. O the terribleness of suffering alone, — of carrying a laden, smitten, bursting heart, without daring to ask for sympathy or for help, — of smothering all our sorrows, of beating back upon the heart its yearning desire for utterance and for consolation! One must know this loneliness to know the precious comfort of a human Saviour, — of a Being coming to us with love and the soothing balm of mercy dripping upon us from His lips. "Come unto me, all ye that labor and are heavy laden, and

I will give you rest,"[1] are the gracious words which He has proclaimed to all who are feeling their need of a bosom to lean upon, and a heart to beat in unison with their own. No longer is it the fate of any of us to suffer alone: all have the blessedness offered them of friendship and of sympathy; and of more than these, of mercy, pardon, and peace. We have not merely a priest to make our confession unto; a priest who cannot tell whether we speak truth or not; who may be deceived by a half-told tale; who can give us only that absolution which may be rendered void because given upon unsound confession: but we have a High Priest, one who has been tempted in all points like as we are, yet without sin; one who cannot be deceived, but looks into the heart, and when He gives us peace, gives it to us with a full knowledge of our condition, and with a divine power of making it good in the courts of Heaven. "Let us therefore come boldly unto the throne of grace," are the concluding words of the Apostle, "that we may obtain mercy, and find grace to help in time of need."[1]

And as with the bitterness of the heart, so with its joys. How much are they increased, when they can be partaken of with one who feels with us, and is in harmony with our spirit! This makes up all the endearment of family relationship: but in this world, even at the very best, where there is true love and genuine affection, there is much, in the very current of life, to interrupt the joys even of the purest kind. The curse stains every thing; its slime is upon every state of life; and strangers can intermeddle even with the highest condition of human happiness, unless it be that hidden joy which can exist between God and the soul. That alone gives unalloyed pleasure. Every other tie may be tampered with; every other relationship of life may be marred by scandal and calumny and jealousy

[1] S. Matt. xi. 28.

[1] Heb. iv. 16.

and intermeddling: but no one can come where the true joy of divine love is, and do us any mischief. Those joys raise us above the earth, and make us independent of man and the world. As one of our Hymns[1] beautifully expresses it: —

> A bleeding Saviour, seen by faith,
> A sense of pardoning love,
> A hope that triumphs over death,
> Give joys like those above.

How many lessons we are called upon to learn, my beloved people, from this condition of loneliness under which the curse has necessarily placed us! And one of the most important is a lesson of charity towards our fellow-creatures. How little do we know of any one's real trials and sufferings! How little are we prepared to enter into any one's position in the world. We walk among men in total ignorance of them. We judge them by appearances. We condemn them, knowing nothing of their temptations. We solace ourselves with thinking how much better we are than they; when alas! their bitterness, which is known to God and against which they may have struggled long and manfully, may place them far above us, who have had no struggle and but little temptation. It is said of a clergyman of some notoriety who did not always control his temper, that upon one occasion, when reproved by a friend for an ebullition of this kind, his answer was: "Sir, I thank you for your reproof; but I have conquered more temper than you ever had." This man knew and felt the bitterness of his heart, and God may have seen in him a struggle which was manful and true, and which placed him far above one who judged him while he had had no struggle at all. How Christ struck directly at this tendency of human nature! "Judge not, and ye shall not be judged: condemn not, and ye shall not be condemned."[2] It was one of the

[1] Hymn 148.

[2] S. Luke vi. 37.

first lessons He taught His disciples; and it is one of the first lessons that every Christian should learn. We are too short-sighted and too prejudiced to sit in judgment, even though we were certain that we knew perfectly the facts upon which we formed our judgments: but when we really are so ignorant of every one's inner life, of his troubles and trials, his temptations and embarrassments, we should shrink from all judgment, and cover over with the mantle of charity those things which may strike us as strange and improper. As one has beautifully said: "God has been kind enough to veil our infirmities from others; let us be equally careful to veil the infirmities of our brethren from every human eye."

Another lesson which it teaches us is, that we should deal gently with our fellow-creatures, and banish harshness, as entirely as we can, from our manners and our language. We know not the bitterness that may be resting upon the heart of any creature we may chance to meet or be concerned with. Kind words, a cheering smile, tender sympathy, a gentle tone, may often produce effects upon the human heart far beyond what might be reckoned as their real value, and do good not only for time but for eternity. We should always keep resting on our memories the many, many moments when a kind word would have cheered us; when a tone of sympathy would have sunk deep down into our hearts; when encouragement would have sustained us, and harshness have driven us to despair. The course of life is hard and harsh enough without our adding any thing to its roughness. The evils of life are too many and too heart-rending for us to accumulate them either in number or in sharpness. Our task should be to imitate Jesus in His love and gentleness; to go about doing good; to give to the world beauty for ashes, the oil of joy for mourning; the garment of praise for the spirit of heaviness. Leave harshness and severe judgment to the world. Let the Church, and those who call themselves the children of God, utter words of hope and peace for the worn and weary children of sin and unrest. "Good will towards men," was a part of the Angels' song when they announced the birth of Jesus; and let us keep the motto upon our hearts, and illustrate it in our lives and conversation.

Another lesson of our text comes nearer home, and should be learned for our own comfort in life. "The heart," says our text, "knoweth his own bitterness, and a stranger doth not intermeddle with his joy." We may have to live very much alone in this world, and some of you may have bitterness almost more than you can bear. Remember Christ. Do not attempt to carry your sorrows or your joys alone. If you do, Satan will most certainly tempt you in some shape or other. He will stir up discontent with your lot in your heart; or he will incite you to harshness and ill will against the world; or he may drive you to despair and hopelessness. Or, on the other hand, that joy with which a stranger doth not intermeddle may make you selfish and egoistic; may seduce you to morbidness and neglect of duty. However your bitterness or your joy may be or must be necessarily secret from the world, let it not be partaken of without the constant presence of Christ. His participation of it will very much relieve your own burden, or increase your own happiness; and will preserve it from impurity or excess. Either bitterness or joy which is obliged to be kept hidden from the world is dangerous to the spirit; and you must place it in Christ's hands for regulation. He knows all through His divine Spirit; but He will not interfere, unless you show your confidence in Him, and come boldly to the throne of grace. Be not afraid of Him. He is not come to judge the world, but to save the world. Although He knows all, yet may we say, in the tender words of Keble: —

> "Thou know'st our bitterness: our joys are thine:
> No stranger Thou to all our wanderings wild:
> Nor could we bear to think, how every line
> Of us, Thy darkened likeness and defiled,
> Stands in full sunshine of Thy piercing eye,
> But that Thou call'st us Brethren. Sweet repose
> Is in that word. The Lord who dwells on high
> Knows all, yet loves us better than He knows."

1865.

Fortieth Sermon.

Have I been a wilderness unto Israel? a land of darkness?—JEREMIAH ii. 31.

WHY is it, my beloved people, that Christianity is not more willingly embraced by the intelligent and refined men of our congregations, and enjoyed as one of the richest blessings of God's mercy? Why is it, that so many of our very best people, looking at them as citizens, should keep so entirely aloof from the ordinances of the Church of Christ? One would think, reasoning *a priori* and before considering any thing contained in the Revelation itself, that they would be the very earliest disciples of a system so clearly intended to elevate man and exalt the standard of social life; that they would be the most earnest advocates of a philosophy which inculcated the practice of whatsoever things are true, whatsoever things are honest, whatsoever things are just, whatsoever things are pure, whatsoever things are lovely, whatsoever things are of good report. And our reasoning would be right, if the Revelation of God ended with that philosophy. It fails because, over and above its morals and its social blessings, it contains a doctrine of spiritual life which demands a regulation of the inner as well as of the outer man; and makes us acquainted with supernatural influences coming to us through Persons of the Godhead, of whom the religion of Nature and of Reason knows nothing. It is this part of Christianity which the wise and the learned and the noble find it so hard to receive, and which the Apostles of our Lord foretold would prove their great difficulty. Every thing relating to domestic welfare and social happiness they could receive and value; but when it turned to spiritual things, to the sublime topics which alone render it of any eternal value, they ask with Nicodemus: "How can these things be?" and they reckon it as foolishness. And they do this, not because they do not appreciate the influence of morals and even of religion,—for they know well enough what a mighty instrument even superstition is, when it is wielded by society,—nor because they would not desire for themselves the possession of an interest with God, provided they could attain it by any rational process: but because they are, to say the least, doubtful about the truth of Revelation. They believe in God as their Creator and moral governor (none but a fool says in his heart, "There is no God"); they believe, for the most part, in the immortality of the soul and in a future state of rewards and punishments: but they have not yet come to any decision upon the Revelation of God. They are not willing entirely to reject the Scriptures, for the teachings of their childhood, and the sacred memory of a father's love and a mother's tenderness, are forever associated with them: and yet they are not prepared to subscribe to those doctrines of Atonement and Regeneration and spiritual influences which stand connected with the Persons of the Son and of the Holy Ghost. They are not willing to admit that they have rejected these truths of Revelation. They still acknowledge them, in a sort of Ecclesiastical way, and use every Sunday a Service which affirms and teaches them; but they are not ready to take any step which would place themselves in close spiritual connection with them. They are feeling their way, many of them, cautiously towards Christianity, and are watching to see whether there is sufficient ground for them to rest their feet upon in any movement towards the Altar of God.

They scorn hypocrisy, and have no desire to place themselves among the mere pretenders to spiritual illumination. They love reality; and, when they profess, they wish to take hold of Christ and His religion with an earnest grasp, which will admit no doubt, either with themselves or with others, that they are Christians indeed.

It is a great error for Christians to entertain the opinion, which is too frequent among them, that men who seem careless and indifferent about Christianity have no secret moments of reflection and religious effort. They have a great many; and they are looking out much more keenly than Christians think, for grounds upon which to form their judgments respecting the scheme of Christianity. The external proofs of its being a Revelation from God they admit to be very strong; and those proofs cast a very unpleasant doubtfulness around any conclusions they may come to against it. They cannot satisfy themselves that it is an imposture; and yet they cannot reconcile themselves to what they call the mysterious spiritual doctrines of the Revelation. They have never experienced any of them; and they are doubtful whether anybody else has. They reason, and they reason correctly, that such a doctrine as that of Christ should have a most vivid effect upon the affections of those who profess it. Its declaration is, that its aim is at the heart; that, leaving every thing else to be worked upon through the Spirit from this central point, its object is to bring man's spirit at once into subjection to the Spirit of God, to fill it with faith in God, — a faith which shall afterwards work by love, and renovate the whole nature. This is the true Christian hypothesis; and every one who names the Name of Christ receives Him upon this foot, or else does not receive Him rightly. Unless this is professed, the Christian has not taken hold of that which is the distinct spiritual teaching of the New Testament, and which the natural man calls foolishness. And, — whatever these keen observers and critics may themselves do afterwards when they become Christians, — for the present, they hold those who do profess Christianity to a strict account upon this very point. They say that Christ Himself has taught that "where the treasure is, there will the heart be also;" and that surely there is no greater treasure than the love of God in Christ, and the hope of everlasting bliss in a future world. They look to see, therefore, whether the profession is one which bears out this very just reasoning; whether the heart seems to be really concerned in the work; whether the affections are fixed upon those eternal interests which are wrapped up in Christ. And they have a right, my beloved people, to judge us by this criterion; for it is a Scriptural rule of judgment, and one of which we should be enabled to bear the test. The world has a right to expect to see Christians deeply interested in religious things, to find them earnest in all that concerns the advancement of the kingdom of Christ; nay more, to find religion filling their hearts as a satisfying portion, giving them comfort in affliction, contentment under adverse circumstances, peace in the midst of perils, hope when thick darkness covers the people. They may well ask how the life accords with the profession, how the effect harmonizes with the promise, when they perceive Christians evidently considering their profession a yoke of bondage, its requirements a burden, its fruits a mere myth, its hold upon the affections subservient to every thing else. The bright promise of Christianity for this life is, that it furnishes that which will satisfy an undying soul and immortal lives; that it gives, what the world cannot and does not profess to give, quiet and rest; that it supplies a want which man universally feels, yet the satisfaction of which he cannot find. And if this promise is not fulfilled in

Christians, how can men of the world be expected to be attracted towards it? What have they to gain in giving up the world, if they are not to receive in return some treasure for the heart and the affections? Man does not live long before he finds out that happiness consists in employing the mind and absorbing the affections; and therefore is it that we meet him, at every turn, pursuing some one idea to the exclusion of every other, filling his heart and his soul with it, and sacrificing every thing in its pursuit. No matter whether it be an object which the world counts honorable, as glory; or mean, as avarice; or trifling, as pleasure: the principle which lies at the bottom is the same. It is, to fill the soul with something; to give zest to life, which would otherwise stagnate; to give employment to the mind, which would else gnaw upon itself; to give play to the affections, which must make an idol of something. If he could be convinced that religion could give him a satisfying portion of the soul, there is many a man who is now recklessly plunging through life, caressing objects which he despises, solicitous only to get rid of it, who might pause and seek after something more worthy the absorption of infinite affections. But every thing conpires to make him despair: his own heart of unbelief, the unwearying delusions of the Devil, and — last though by no means least — the dishonor which Christians do their Master's cause, by permitting the world to perceive that their Christian profession gives their hearts no ease, and their spirits no contentment. How many who grieve over irreligious fathers, husbands, brothers, sons, seem to be unaware that they are helping on that unbelief, and riveting upon the soul the motions of infidelity and the temptations of the Devil!

Truly may God ask of Christians what He asked of His people of old, through his prophet Jeremiah: "Have I been a wilderness unto Israel? a land of darkness?" Have My redeemed people found no joy in Me, no light in My presence? Have there been no flowers along the path by which I have led them, no green pastures, no still waters? During the toil and wearisomeness of life, has there been no bright sunshine upon the landscape, no sound of music by the way? When care or trouble or sorrow has pressed upon you, has no ministering spirit been near you to lighten your burden and alleviate your pain? When sickness has brought you nigh to the gates of death, has there been no spiritual Physician to soothe the soul, and to give it peace? When the days of darkness have brooded over the soul, and there was no comfort in man or the son of man, has no Comforter come to thee from Him who promised, "I will not leave thee comfortless, I will come to thee"? Has no fresh glory come from Me, making the grave radiant with the presence of Angels, and forever rolling away the great stone from the door of the sepulchre? And are ye now weary of Me? And are ye saying to the world, by actions if not by word, "The way of the Lord is a wilderness; the land of the Lord is a land of darkness"? "Be astonished, O ye heavens, at this, and be horribly afraid . . . . For my people have committed two evils; they have forsaken me the fountain of living waters, and hewed them out cisterns, broken cisterns, that can hold no water."[1]

You do not realize, my beloved people, how much dishonor you cast upon your Lord, how much suspicion you bring upon yourselves, by finding no joy in your Christian profession, no happiness in the exercise of the Christian life. David's declaration was: "All my fresh springs shall be in thee."[2] His fresh springs, — the water that was to satisfy his loving heart, that was to quench his immortal thirst, that was to refresh him when he was weary, that was to

[1] Jer. ii. 12, 13.

[2] Psalm lxxxvii. 7.

give him new life when he was spent, — all flowed from God. The world and its waters he left to those who knew not his God; but he could not find any comfort in them. And when we put on Christ, my beloved people, this is our declaration: that He is the source of all our true joy, that all our springs are in Him, and from Him all our streams flow. Why then should our practice be so different from our profession? Have we been deceived? Has Christ and His love been a wilderness unto us? a land of darkness? God forbid! We may not have enjoyed religion as we should; we may have permitted pressing temptation to steal away our hearts from Christ for a little while; we may have been overwhelmed with cares or afflictions, and so the deep waters may have gone even over our souls: but I know that if the choice were given you now, — a final choice, a choice which you should never be enabled to alter, between Christ and the world, — that you would flee to Christ, and hide yourselves in Him. Present temptation must not be confounded with permanent decision, — a temporary coldness of heart, with the declaration that Christ's service is a yoke which galls and frets the wearer!

And yet, hopeful as I trust that I may be, I must warn you against the very appearance of evil. When a Christian is perceived to be lukewarm in all that concerns religion, and yet earnest and busy about every thing else; inattentive to the public duties of the Church save when it is entirely convenient or agreeable, yet ready to be present at every occasion of civil interest; finding no time to read his Bible or say his prayers, yet finding abundant leisure for novels or newspapers or magazines; asking nothing about the warfare which is waging in heathen lands against the enemies of Christ's kingdom, yet, like the Athenians, seeking everywhere for some new thing concerning the warfare which is waging nearer home: to such an one I must put the question, on God's part: "Have I been a wilderness unto Israel? a land of darkness?" Is there nothing to interest an immortal creature, in spiritual things? nothing to occupy the attention of a Christian pilgrim, in the wondrous things of God's Law? Must he run to the world for all his pleasures, and come to Christ only on Sundays, and even then only when he can find no excuse to keep away? Is there no life in Christianity for you, no reality of joy, of hope, of divine meditation? Beware, my hearer, lest you not only wreck yourself, but become the cause by which others shall be kept from Christ and His salvation! The judgment which has been recorded against a lukewarm Church, is recorded likewise against a lukewarm Christian: "Because thou art lukewarm, and neither cold nor hot, I will spue thee out of my mouth."[1] What utter loathing this expresses upon the part of Christ! What danger it insinuates upon yours! To be spued out of Christ's mouth, and that for no striking or positive sin, for no flagrant act of irreligion, but simply for being lukewarm, indifferent about spiritual things! How many there are who think no harm of this; who satisfy themselves with the position that they are doing nothing to disgrace their Christianity, even while they are doing nothing to manifest it! A more hateful state of feeling there is not in the whole circle of Christian experience, for it argues the absence of almost every Christian grace. There can be no faith, where there is such a spirit; no humility, no hope. It presents one flat expanse of utter indifference. Any thing is better than it; — heat or cold, burning zeal or utter deadness: but this dilettanteism Christ utterly repudiates. Its basis is selfishness; its superstructure is conceit.

Oh, my people, let me beseech you to rid yourselves of this reproach. Let it not be said of you, "God has been

[1] Rev. iii. 16.

a wilderness to this people, a land of darkness." God in Christ, a wilderness? what an utter contradiction of all the promises of the Bible, of all the experience of God's saints! Long before Christ came, the Prophets were heralding His coming, upon the very ground that He would make the wilderness of the world (for in the Bible it is the world that is the wilderness) a place of gladness. One of them announced it as a new and wonderful thing: "Behold, I will do a new thing," saith the Lord; "now it shall spring forth; . . . . I will even make a way in the wilderness, and rivers in the desert. The beast of the field shall honor me, the dragons and the owls: because I give waters in the wilderness, and rivers in the desert, to give drink to my people, my chosen."[1] And the effects of that new thing were to be, that "The wilderness and the solitary place shall be glad for them; and the desert shall rejoice, and blossom as the rose. It shall blossom abundantly, and rejoice even with joy and singing."[2] And when the Lord would comfort His people, this was to be their comfort: "For the LORD shall comfort Zion: he will comfort all her waste places; and he will make her wilderness like Eden, and her desert like the garden of the LORD; joy and gladness shall be found therein, thanksgiving, and the voice of melody."[3] Ah! my people, if you find God a wilderness, then is there no hope for you, for you shall have turned the source of all earthly consolation into bitterness and a curse! The glory of Christ was to be, that "a man shall be as an hiding place from the wind, and a covert from the tempest; as rivers of water in a dry place, as the shadow of a great rock in a weary land:"[4] and *you* find Him a wilderness? I fear me that you know not the spirit you are of; and that you have a name to live, while you are dead!

[1] Isaiah xliii. 19, 20.
[2] *Ibid.* xxxv. 1, 2.
[3] *Ibid.* li. 3.
[4] *Ibid.* xxxii. 2.

How sad that it should ever be intimated of any people, that God was a land of darkness unto them! Why, the very object of coming to Christ was to get into a land of light. "If therefore the light that is in thee be darkness, how great is that darkness!"[1] Light is everywhere, in the Bible, the effect of God's presence, the glory of Christ's Advent. In the beginning God said: "Let there be light: and there was light."[2] In the fullness of times He said again, "Let there be light:" and Christ rose upon the nations as the Light of the world. And when He was come to scatter the gross darkness which covered the people, almost the very first utterance which He made to His disciples was: "Ye are the light of the world." The light of the world, and yet a darkness unto yourselves! What a contradiction in terms! Our profession is, and the world knows it, — for the Devil makes the world read the Bible, when that reading is done in an evil spirit, — "For God, who commanded the light to shine out of darkness, hath shined in our hearts, to give the light of the knowledge of the glory of God in the face of Jesus Christ."[3] Can this be true, and yet no light flow out from you upon the world? no light kindle within you to cheer yourself?

How terrible it is, as Job says, to "meet with darkness in the daytime, and grope in the noon-day as in the night."[4] We hoped for thee that even the sun was no more thy light by day, but that the Lord was "unto thee an everlasting light, and thy God thy glory:"[5] but, instead of this, the world sees you groping "for the wall like the blind," and groping as if you "had no eyes": stumbling "at noon-day as in the night."[6] And you were forewarned of all this by Prophets and Apostles. Jeremiah said, in tones of deep warning: "Give glory to the LORD your God, before he

[1] S. Matthew vi. 23. [2] Gen. i. 3. [3] 2 Cor. iv. 6.
[4] Job v. 14. [5] Isaiah lxi. 19. [6] *Ibid.* lix. 10.

cause darkness, and before your feet stumble upon the dark mountains, and, while ye look for light, he turn it into the shadow of death, and make it gross darkness."[1] And S. John reëchoed the warning: "Then Jesus said unto them, Yet a little while is the light with you. Walk while ye have the light, lest darkness come upon you. . . . While ye have light, believe in the light, that ye may be the children of light."[2] Christ's people have nothing to do with wildernesses and with darkness. Their profession is one of rich rejoicing. Their path is to shine "more and more unto the perfect day."[3]

Art thou in the wilderness, my heart? Fear not, even there; for, if you search, you may find God. It is there that God sometimes leads His people, to plead with them. "And I will bring you into the wilderness of the people, and there will I plead with you face to face."[4] Do you feel dissatisfied with your spiritual state, even while you mingle with the world? It is God pleading with you face to face. Are you harassed and careworn in your service of the world? It is God pleading with you face to face. Do you find no satisfaction in life, even after you have reached the summit of your wishes? It is God pleading with you face to face. Are you afflicted in the land of your captivity? It is God pleading with you face to face. He is asking you: "Have I been a wilderness unto Israel? a land of darkness?" Hear Him when He pleads! God will not be trifled with by His covenant people. "And that which cometh into your mind shall not be at all, that ye say, We will be as the heathen, as the families of the countries, to serve wood and stone. As I live, saith the Lord GOD, surely with a mighty hand, and with a stretched-out arm, and with fury poured out, will I rule over you. . . . And I will cause

[1] Jeremiah xiii. 16.
[2] S. John xii. 35, 36.
[3] Prov. iv. 18.
[4] Ezek. xx. 35.

you to pass under the rod, and I will bring you into the bond of the covenant."[1] Beware of that rod! It is a fearful thing to fall into the hands of the living God! "And if thou say in thine heart, Wherefore come these things upon me?" the answer will be, unless you repent and turn from the error of your ways: "This is thy lot, the portion of thy measures from me, saith the LORD; because thou hast forgotten me, and trusted in falsehood."[2]

JUNE 16, 1861.

[1] Ezek. xx. 32, 33, 37.

[2] Jer. xiii. 22, 25.

Forty-first Sermon.

God is love; and he that dwelleth in love dwelleth in God, and God in him. —1 S. JOHN iv. 16.

WHENEVER the Ministers of Christ turn aside from the rich promises and glorious hopes of the Gospel, to speak of the awful threatenings which overhang its rejection, and the severe penalties which await those who despise its mercy, the benevolent and the sentimental and the impenitent and the unbelieving at once take shelter, all of them, however much they may differ from each other in various particulars, under the declaration of our text, that "God is love:" without any analysis of what love is, in the sense in which it is used in the Scriptures; without any comparison of this naked phrase with other declarations of the Bible, which must limit and restrain it, being of equal authority with it; without any consideration that the proposition may be literally true in its most unlimited extent, and yet not true at all in the sense in which they interpret it. They all deem it a sufficient answer to any appeals which may be made to them upon the scope of God's present anger and of His impending wrath. How far these parties may put any real trust in this position, it is not for me to determine. So long as it is advanced and made a refuge against the terrors of the world to come, it must be treated as if it was believed and trusted in; and must be met with such a reply as shall at least satisfy the ambassador for Christ that he has declared the whole counsel of God, and delivered his own soul. More than this it is not in his power to do. The hearing ear and the understanding heart must come from a higher source. Paul can plant, and Apollos can water: but God alone can give the increase.

In discussing a point like this, every fair mind must at once perceive that the argument must proceed upon things as we find them. The character of God must be determined from what we can learn of it in the workings of the world, and from what has been revealed to us in His inspired Word, — that Word which contains the proposition "God is love," on which their hope is based. These are the only sources from which we can know any thing of God. If we cannot find His character in these, we have no right to say that "God is love," or that "God is not love." In that case we can only with honesty say, "I know nothing of the Gods or of their character: they have not spoken to me." To say, therefore, that this or that is the character of God, because, in your opinion, such ought to be His character, is to substitute your ideal in the place of truth; is to make your hopes and your desires the standard of God's revelation of Himself. In this matter, if in any, you should subject your reasoning to the severest scrutiny; for a mistake in it is of vital, because everlasting, importance. When you hide yourself, my hearer, under the wings of God's mercy, crying out that "God is love," you should be, above all things, certain that you are not abusing the most precious and glorious of His attributes.

We all agree in the proposition which forms the text, that "God is love," because with you it is the foundation of your hopes; with me, it is a truth of Revelation. The point for discussion between us is, "What is the meaning of the expression?" How far does it permit you to rely upon it as a ground of safety irrespective of the conditions of the Gospel? This is the question which should be determined; and determined not according to your fancy or your desire, but according to the truth of things as they are, and as they shall be. Only upon such a determination of this question should a man of sense permit himself to be at ease; for the time must inevitably come when nothing but truth can stand, — when all refuges of lies must be swept away before the clear exhibition of the character of God in the day of His manifestation. "To the law," then, "and to the testimony."

The first thing which strikes us in considering the character of God as shown to us from the sources whence alone we can derive our knowledge of Him, is, that His "love is never synonymous with weakness." Through whatever channel it may be manifested, it is invariably connected with a strict regard to justice and holiness. In the constitution and course of Nature we see this as plainly manifested as in the Book of Revelation. Very much around us and within us speaks to us of the love of God; but at the same time there is mingled with those accents of Divine affection, a stern adherence to the laws of an immutable morality, which indicates that it is the love, not of a weak, but of a wise, and therefore of a firm Parent. Vice, imprudence, folly, are permitted by this God of love to work out their inevitable consequences; and His creatures never find in Him, under His visible government of man in society, any such weakness as shall tempt them to a repetition of their sins through any vain dependence upon His forgiving love. They may and often do repeat them, — just as a poor silly moth may fly a second time into the flame that has already singed its wings; but with the sure consciousness that their sin or their folly will find them out. No Divine intervention ever comes, that we can see, between God's creatures and their violation of His moral law; those creatures for whom He has so lovingly decked this beautiful creation, and upon whom he has lavished so much of exquisite ornament that was not absolutely necessary for the purposes of life. We must be willfully blind not to perceive how very much of consistent and unswerving law is mingled with the love which governs the world; how entirely the Divine Benevolence is made dependent, in a natural way, upon the character of our own lives: nay more, that no sentiment of love, on the part of God, ever intervenes to check the course of the moral law, even though it descend upon children and children's children until it has worked out its natural, and therefore Divine, punishment. So far from there being any countenance, under God's natural government of the world, to the proposition that "God is love," in the sense of a Being who is too kind and benevolent to punish: nothing seems to me to give a more terrible and alarming idea of the nature of that love, than what we see of it in our experience of life. If we would only remember that the moral government of the world is under the guidance and direction of this "God," who as we say, and say truly, "is love," and then observe thoughtfully the working of that moral government, we should very soon be satisfied that the love of God is a very different thing from what men vainly fancy it to be; nay, that it had in it elements very different from the passion which leads us so continually to overwhelm with its burning and reckless torrent all justice and all principle.

If we turn from a consideration of the love of God as developed in the world around us, to that image of it which we find reflected in our own natures, we are brought to the same conclusion. We ourselves make a broad distinction, in the judgments which we pass upon others, between love and weakness; and thus vindicate the true character of God. We speak, every day, of the foolish affection of parents, of the improper indulgences in which they allow their children, of the weakness which they display in overlooking and forgiving their faults; and foretell, with sure certainty, the consequences of such conduct. We discriminate very clearly, especially when the case is not our own, between that which is truly love and that which is merely passion. And yet what we condemn through our natural sense of propriety in our fellow-creatures, because we perceive its present foolishness and its inevitable consequences, we transfer without any scruple to God, as His characteristic, and depend upon it for our future destiny. The love which we acknowledge to be of all things the most injurious to those upon whom it is lavished, which our experience tells us ends almost invariably in the moral destruction of its victims, we conclude to be the love which the all-wise God has selected as His chief attribute, and which He wields as the moral Governor of the universe. We make God as weak as the most foolish and indulgent mother, just because it suits our sentiment or our necessity; and are not ashamed, as men of sense, to look such an argument in the face. How absurd, as if any government could be carried on upon such a system, much less the government of an Universe!

Let us now pass on to the dealings of this God with His Old Testament Saints and with His elect People, and learn whether there is any more indication of a love which has no firmness in His dealings with them, than we have found elsewhere. We cannot read the truthful narrative which we find in the Old Testament without observing the unchanging love which God had for them; the miracles which He worked in their behalf; the tenderness with which He watched over them; the fury with which He turned upon their enemies: nor, at the same time, without likewise observing the undeviating rigor with which He insisted upon obedience and faithfulness, and the unsparing rod with which He chastised their waywardness. They were the people of His love; but that love had in it no signs of weakness. And as with the Nation, so with the individual Saints. Those most honored and favored with His love never found that love blinding Him to their faults, nor passing over their delinquencies. The Moses, whom He spake with face to face, whom He considered as the Prophet next in honor to His own Son, He would not permit to enter the promised land, because he had committed what we should be apt to call a very trivial offence. David, the man after His own heart, whom He had raised from the sheep-cote to the throne, He punished with a most terrible succession of chastisements, so soon as he sinned against His law. Love we find everywhere; but always bearing the like characteristics of firmness and principle, of adherence to justice and holiness.

Let us come now to the New Testament, and examine the character of God's love as displayed in the great mystery of godliness. According to Revelation, the second Person of the adorable Trinity was the Only-begotten Son of His Father, the brightness of His glory and the express image of His Person. This Son covenanted to take upon Him the sins of men; to be the Lamb that should be offered up in sacrifice for those sins. In such a case as this, how did God's love manifest itself? — the love of this God from whom you are expecting a free pardon because of the tenderness of His Nature. Precisely as it manifested itself in all the examples we have given you of it. He accepted the Sacrifice, as you see before you this morning:[1] but did not abate one jot or one tittle of the full demands of justice; did not relieve His own Son from any of the punishment of sin; but passed Him through all the humil-

[1] Referring to the Holy Communion, for which the Altar was spread.

iation and shame and suffering which belonged to the place He had assumed. Although that Son appealed to Him: "Father, if it be possible, let this cup pass from me"; although He cried in the depth of His anguish, as His Father hid His face from Him: "My God, my God, why hast thou forsaken me?" He was unmoved until the last farthing which man owed for sin was paid! Here was love, — love for the human family, love for His Only-begotten Son: but still that same unyielding firmness which recognized not that love unless it harmonized with the other attributes of His Divine character; unless it cast no shadow over the glory of His perfectness.

The next feature in this love of God as we see it in all its manifestations, is, that it never winks at sin. This has been, in some measure, mingled with the point we have just discussed, but deserves nevertheless a separate consideration. When you trust to the declaration that "God is love," your meaning evidently is, that He is so tender and merciful that He will overlook sin: for you cannot mean, of course, that you have never sinned. But you have no more reason for this idea than for the one which confounded love with weakness. The way of transgressors is hard, even in a world where there is a fellow-feeling for them; and disease and pain and death and an evil conscience all bear witness that the love of God is no impediment to the natural punishment of sin. In the world there is sin unspeakable and all-devouring; and there is, along with it, a horrid train of evil which proves that God hates it and perpetually punishes it. Besides the common and ordinary mischiefs which sin has introduced, — so common and ordinary that we forget, in their universality and regularity, that they are punishments, — there are others, such as war, pestilence, famine, oppression, which sweep the earth with their train of horrors: punishments for sin, — God's voices in the earth, proclaiming that His love for man can never blind Him to the justice which glorifies His character. And although He loved the world so much that He gave His Only-begotten Son to die for it, He did not love it so much as to forgive sin until His justice and holiness had been satisfied to the uttermost. In all the aspects under which we can look at God's love, it bears one uniform appearance, the appearance of a love ready to manifest itself for the good of His creatures, but only when that love can be made compatible with His divine character.

It is very evident then, from all that we have said, that when the proposition of my text, "God is love," is used in any such manner as to place it about the sinner as a shield against the righteous anger of God, it is used without any foundation in the experience which we have of God's attributes or dealings. Never do we find that love exhibiting the weakness which is thus attempted to be attributed to it. Never do we find it conniving at sin, or passing it over as a matter which may be lightly treated. And this we see, not only in the Revelation of Christianity, but in the government of God as exhibited through society, considered merely as the moral Ruler of the Universe, putting revealed religion for the moment altogether aside. But nevertheless our text is true. "God is love:" only in a different sense from that in which you understand it.

"In this," says S. John, "was manifested the love of God toward us, because that God sent his only-begotten Son into the world, that we might live through him."[1] His love, then, is not to be found in any weakness of affection, nor in any connivance at sin: but in providing a Saviour from sin. In this sense our text is true: but not in the sense in which you desire it to be true. You desire God's love to be like human love, weak and passionate; blind to

[1] 1 S. John iv. 9.

all faults; overlooking all immoralities; partial to all indulgences; forgiving all sin unconditionally: but His thoughts are not as your thoughts. He knows your nature and its necessities; the terrible evil and bitterness of sin; the fearful punishment which awaits those who commit it; the certain condemnation of those for whom no Saviour is provided: and He manifests His love to you, by providing, at a cost past all price, a Ransom for you, and a Redemption in and through Christ Jesus. The contest which is always going on, is, that you require one kind of love, while He offers another. Which is the wiser? Who can look best into the past, and into the future? Who can judge what line of conduct is most necessary for the moral government of His universe? You think that you ought to be indulged in the propensities of your natures. He tells you that those propensities are all sinful, and must end in your eternal misery. You can see no love in a system which checks your desires, and interferes with your pleasures and interests. God, on the other hand, can place His love on nothing which shall not be remedial of your fallen condition, and conservative of your moral character. You pretend not to understand a love which administers punishment adequate to the sin. God cannot consider any thing as love, which is not consistent with the moral law of His creation and with the harmony of His character. And thus are you at antagonism with a God of love, because you will not consider that to be love which He considers as the highest manifestation of love, and will substitute for it a spurious counterfeit which He will disown at the last, and leave you without hope through a wretched eternity!

Look before you. What are those emblems? Emblems of the love of God in Christ. Why have they taken that tragic shape and form? Why do they represent the memorial of a Sacrifice? and that the sacrifice of an only and dearly beloved Son? and that the Son of the Most High God? What need of a sacrifice at all, if God be love in the sense in which you undertake to interpret the text? Why not a table covered with the flowers of the field, decked and adorned with the gems of earth and ocean? Why not priests, crowned with garlands, pouring out libations of perfumed wines before a God of simple indiscriminating benevolence? The very institutions of the religion in which you have been trained belie the idea of a God of love, who is so weak that He cannot punish, so unprincipled as that He will make no distinction between right and wrong. 'T is true, we do offer up at this Table, each time we meet here, a sacrifice of praise and thanksgiving; but for what? For a love which would satisfy an Universalist? — which would permit every man to expect salvation, no matter how opposite his life may have been to all virtue and to all truth? No! but for that manifestation of it which He gave us when He offered up His Only-begotten for our sins, that by such an offering He might make the forgiveness of sins consistent with His divine character. "Herein is love," said S. John, "not that we loved God, but that he loved us, and" — did what? Overlooked our sins? winked at our vices and immoralities? declined to notice or punish our wickedness? No, none of these, nothing like these; for the Scripture tells us that He cannot look upon iniquity: but He "sent his Son to be the propitiation for our sins."[1] What need for any propitiation for sin, if "God is love" in your conception of the expression? Propitiation is only necessary where there is an offended power, whose anger has been kindled, and whose wrath requires punishment and vengeance. No, my hearers; every thing contradicts your notion of God's love. The natural govern-

[1] 1 S. John iv. 10.

ment of the world as carried on by God through social and individual life contradicts it; for in them, love does not stay His hand from punishment, nor cut off the entail of sin from generation to generation. Your own feelings and judgments contradict it; for you establish and support governments, and laws, under which you do never permit love to turn aside the sword of an evenhanded justice. The Revelation of God contradicts it; for, in that, you find judgment laid to the line and righteousness to the plummet against His beloved Saints and His elect people. And the ordinances of the Church in which you are fostering this notion, contradict it; for they all point to the shedding of the most precious Blood of the Son of God as an atonement for sin which love could not pardon; and they keep it before you abidingly, that you may never be permitted to lose sight of the sublime truth, that God's holiness must be preserved inviolate. All these tell you that "God is love;" but that it is love as He has been pleased to manifest it, and not as you may be pleased to conceive it and insist upon it. Should you persevere in your idea, and rest upon it, meanwhile continuing in sin, you will find that "the bed is shorter than that a man can stretch himself on it: and the covering narrower than that he can wrap himself in it."[1]

SEPTEMBER, 1866.

[1] Isaiah xxviii. 20.

Forty-second Sermon.

See that thou make all things according to the pattern showed to thee in the mount. — HEBREWS viii. 5.

WE cannot examine the works of God as they exhibit themselves in Nature and in the constitution and course of the world, without perceiving very clearly that one or two main ideas pervade the whole structure, and give their hue and coloring to every thing which proceeds from the Divine Mind. From the minutest zoöphyte, whose very being has to be determined by the strongest glasses which the wit of man has contrived, up to the mightiest Angel who stands hard by the throne of God, we can trace one or two principles which are never deviated from, and which mark the presence of an eternal and unchangeable will. There is no anomaly anywhere, — no discord in the divine harmony. Every thing obeys laws which are uniform and persistent, indicating unity of conception and of purpose. All things seem to move around a divine Centre, which shoots its rays in every direction to the remotest circumference, diffusing light and life and order, and preserving the entire Universe in glorious unity and most necessary adjustment. Nothing too insignificant to have its own place in the series of things. Nothing too grand or sublime to be under the rule and direction of the Great First Cause. We can pierce no part of the chain which extends from earth to the throne of the Eternal without meeting these all-pervading principles; and we can find no point at which they begin, or in which they terminate.

We find them ruling in Heaven, and earth, and even in hell; and when we are lost, either in the infinite minuteness which baffles our powers or in the dazzling glories which shut in the presence of the Almighty, they have accompanied us to the confines which we could not pass, and have penetrated the recesses of light and of darkness which have shut out our senses and our conception. Types of the Divine Mind, they manifest themselves everywhere, because His presence and His will are without limit, and without change.

Among these all-pervading principles which indicate the presence of a single governing Mind, there are two which are especially distinct, and which can be traced without difficulty through every part of the Universe of God. These are *subordination* and *uniformity:* every thing in its due place, and operating in its own appointed sphere; and every thing, moreover, obeying the law of repetition, — that is, doing to-day what it did yesterday, doing this year what it did last year, doing this century what it did the last century, moving by a law which needs no change because it is the very best. Nowhere in all God's operations can we find any sphere of being which does not follow these invariable rules, which does not manifest and work upon these universal principles. The two evils which God seemed most to avoid in His arrangement of things, were insubordination and novelty. Without order there could be no peace; without uniformity there could be no security. The absence of these principles would at once unhinge all government and all domestic and social life.

If we begin at the very lowest point of creation, and examine inanimate nature as it is developed to us through the researches of science, we find a due subordination even among the masses of rock which form, as it were, the bones of the earth. These all have their due subordination following each other by such certain laws that science can always at once determine their place in the series, and can decide at a glance whether any thing useful to man or necessary to his wants is contained within their bowels, or underneath them, or above them. In this subordination those products which are most useful to man are always near the surface, within his reach, so adjusted as that he can procure them without insupportable toil. And when we study the extinct life, which is brought to light through the researches of geology, we discern the like subordination : animation exhibiting itself first in very inferior beings, such as fish and insects ; and extending upward in ever-ascending gradation of excellence, until man himself appears upon the stage. And when we consider the arrangement which Nature stamps upon man himself, we find the woman subordinate to the man, and the children subordinate to the parents, and the servants subordinate to the children, and the inferior animals subordinate to man in whatever state of social being he may chance to move. And if we follow this law of subordination out of the visible world, we find another series of being rising circle above circle, Angel and Archangel, Cherubim and Seraphim, Thrones, Dominions, Principalities, Powers, until we reach the Son of God Himself, who, although Lord of lords and King of kings, is yet, during the economy of grace, subordinate unto the Father, and acting according to His will. As the family cannot live in peace and harmony without due subordination of its parts, so cannot the State, so cannot even Heaven itself. It is the law impressed upon the Universe, manifest everywhere, operating everywhere, necessary everywhere.

The other law, of Uniformity, which I shall only touch in one of its most restricted senses, is quite as important as that of Subordination which I have just exhibited. I speak now of uniformity of action in natural and sensible things, in contradistinction to novelty and change. The sun, for illustration, has risen, to mortal eye, in the eastern heavens, ever since the creation, and has gone to its setting at the same spot, upon the same day, and at the same time of day, during every year from the moment when God set it in the firmament of Heaven to rule the day. The moon has, in her turn, exhibited the same phases to the eye of man, waxing and waning, waning and waxing, ever since her appointed place was given her among the heavenly hosts. The stars, which make their stately march around our little world, presenting to us, in turn, all their forms of beauty and of glory, have made no change in their celestial procession, since they sang together in the morning of Creation. Day and night are no different now from what they were when God saw that His works of creation were "very good," and when "the evening and the morning were the sixth day." Winter and Summer, Spring and Autumn, seed-time and harvest, have never changed; but they come and go with an unfailing certainty and an unerring uniformity. And as with Nature and her laws, so it is with all the laws which govern our natural and intellectual functions. We eat, we drink, we are born; we speak, we think, we communicate; we love, we hate, we sympathize; we are sick, and die: just as our kind has always done. Our very sins and punishments are uniform, and life itself is an unchanging cycle, in which all things come round to their place, forever changing yet forever the same, giving us experience and security. We ask not for novelty in these things: so far from it, any change in them produces alarm, shakes our nerves, disorders our calculations, and makes us feel insecure and uncertain. Uniformity is our delight, because upon it is founded all our experience: and the moment that is lost, we are upon an ocean without a compass and without a rudder; we know not what will come to us, or whither we shall go; we are adrift, having lost the guidance of God's law, and knowing not where the waves or the winds, or the poor pilot which man is, will carry us!

When this God of subordination and of uniformity was pleased to reveal Himself unto man, and to arrange a Church in the world, was it not likely, reasoning *a priori*, that in that Church there should be strikingly manifested these same principles, pervading it thoroughly, and showing very clearly that the God of Nature and of the Church was one and the same Being? Most likely: and accordingly we find that what a reasonable analogy would anticipate, did actually occur; and that the Church which He arranged in Israel and for Israel had, clearly stamped upon it, these indubitable marks of having come from Him. The law of subordination pervades every part of the Church government of the Mosaic dispensation, and the law of uniformity its whole ritual. In the one we find rank above rank of officers, from those who performed the lowest offices of the Church, up to the High-Priest who alone was qualified, or might dare, to enter into the Holy of Holies and meddle with the sacred mysteries of the Divine Presence. No one dared to interfere with the office which did not appertain to his rank; and the terrible punishments which destroyed Korah and his company, and which fell upon Uzzah, and which were threatened against any who presumed to intrude upon the sacred offices of the Church, plainly tell us how necessary did God deem order to be, in the arrangements of the Church. Every man had his appointed place. One tribe furnished the officers of the Temple. One family gave the priesthood to the Church. And thus it continued, until He came who fulfilled the law, and confirmed the promises, and made that ancient priesthood to pass away, having accomplished its work and foreshadowed Him who was the Temple, and the Priest, and the Altar, and the Sacrifice.

And as it was with the priestly arrangements of the Temple, so was it also with its ritual. That displayed the uniformity which is so marked in Nature, and which we should expect in a form of worship coming from God. Every part of that ritual was prescribed. Every sacrifice was arranged in its minutest details. Every formula was written down. For each occasion words were prepared, which were not deviated from. And all this continued, without variation, from the time of Moses until He, whose it all was, abolished it by His Almighty cry upon the Cross, "It is finished." Then passed away all that ritual, save as it might serve as furnishing a principle and a model for the Church of Christ, which was to spring out of its pregnant ashes.

In that Church of Christ we might naturally anticipate the same principles of subordination in the ministry and of uniformity in worship to manifest themselves. And so they do: and these principles lie at the basis of our order and of our worship. That arrangement which separates the Ministry into a threefold order, Deacons, Priests, and Bishops, was begun by Christ Himself, and was perfected by His Apostles, acting under the inspiration of the Holy Ghost. As there was no parity in earth or Heaven, so did Christ permit no parity in His Church. He appointed Apostles and Elders; and when He passed away, His Apostles added to these Orders of the Ministry that of Deacons, the office with which we are to-day concerned. Each of these had its respective functions, and each of them performed only those. When the deacon Philip had preached and done miracles and baptized at Samaria, he dared not proceed any further. He sent to Jerusalem, and laid his work before the Apostles, and they sent two of their number to Samaria *to lay hands upon them.* When S. Paul called the elders of Ephesus together, he bade them take heed to the flock over which the Holy Ghost had made them overseers, he exhorted them to every act of faithfulness as pastors and shepherds: but not a word did he say to them about ordination. But when that same Apostle directed his instructions to Timothy or to Titus, successors of the Apostles and Bishops of the Church, his main addresses to them were upon this very point of ordination. Each of these Orders in its place: Deacons for the lower offices of the Ministry; Presbyters for pastoral duties and the work of the flock upon earth; Bishops for ordination, and the laying on of hands, and the government of the Church.

And just as we should anticipate, in the Church, a subordination in the Ministry, because it was the type upon which every thing had been modelled, so might we look for liturgical uniformity as of a piece with all that had gone before. And while we do not consider liturgical worship as necessarily of divine institution, we do think that the analogy of God's works, and of God's Church under the old dispensation, would lead us to consider it as that mode of worship which should be most likely to meet and satisfy the wants of human nature. Why should our worship change, any more than the thousand other things in Nature and in society which go on perpetually in the same routine? Our wants are always the same: why not our prayers? Our relations to God and His Christ are unchangeable: why not our mode of expressing them? We come together to confess our sins: is not one comprehensive formula sufficient? We come together to offer up the sacrifice of praise and thanksgiving: are not a few psalms drawn from the treasures of inspiration, and associated with all the holiness of the past, and consecrated by the blood of confessors and martyrs, enough to embody those utterances of devotion? We come together to ask God for those blessings which are always the same, for that protection which is uniform and essential, for that guidance which needs no change in its power: why multiply words? why require novelty of expression? God certainly does not ask for them; does not show us, in His Revelation, that He requires them: nay, all the analogy of His Revelation and of His natural arrangement of things teaches us that He prefers uniformity. A well-ordered formula of prayer fulfills all its requisitions, and permits the introduction of nothing which may disturb the feelings or mar the solemnity of the occasion. A Liturgy is not absolutely called for by the Holy Scriptures: but the Church at a very early period is found universally using Liturgies, adducing as reasons for their adoption the fact that our Lord Himself had twice given His disciples the same form of prayer, and had guarded them against vain repetitions and much speaking in prayer. It is, to say the least, in unison with that order which we find stamped upon Nature, and the constitution and course of things.

The office of Deacon, to which we are about to introduce this young man, is the first step in that order which separates the Ministry from the laity. It was instituted by the Apostles, under the direction of the Holy Ghost, for the purpose of freeing themselves from certain matters of detail which interfered with the more important works of preaching the Gospel and of prayer. It seems, however, not to have been confined to those minor offices: for we soon find Stephen confessing, exhorting, and denouncing, for the sake of Christ, and giving himself up as the protomartyr of the Christian Church; and Philip baptizing, and performing miracles, and doing many things which stamped him as a Minister of Christ. The Scriptures, therefore, do not warrant us in considering it as an office of but little worth; for it has power to exercise many of the functions of the highest. He who is permitted to preach the Gospel, to baptize, to assist in the administration of the Lord's Supper, cannot be said to occupy a low place in the Church of Christ. He may have higher steps to take in the Church, but even this first step is full of dignity and honor. It brings him into contact with holy things; it admits him within the sacred precincts of the Altar; it connects him directly with Christ and His Church through the Sacraments; it invests him with the office of an ambassador from God to man. Surely these are functions which may satisfy any human being. Greater and more solemn other offices may be, but this is grave and solemn enough for one without experience and without practice. And the people should look upon it in this light: not as measured by its powers, but by its authority; not as determined by its functions, but by its origin and the commission which lies behind it. All the disabilities of the office are but temporary; its authority is eternal and enduring. All its inferiority and present lowliness will pass away with time; but its acts will endure, for good or for evil, throughout Eternity.

This office are you now about to take upon you, my young friend;—to take upon you at a time and under circumstances which will involve peculiar responsibilities, and require very earnest devotion. Those to whom you will be specially called upon to minister, will be men standing in constant jeopardy of life, to whom a day or an hour may be of the very utmost importance. You will have no time for trifling; no moment that you can waste in theory or speculation. With you, all must be work, earnest work; such work as men do when life rests upon it, and the danger is imminent. At any moment, those over whom you are placed by the Lord may be snatched away by the casualties of war; and you must therefore work "while it is called to-day." You will be where life is held very cheap, and where a brief cry of compassion is all that can be uttered over the fallen; but you must keep alive to the fact that the soul which wings its everlasting flight amid the storm of battle, goes to its account as surely, and upon the same principles, as that which is dismissed to its rest surrounded by weeping friends and encompassed by all the soothing processes of home and art. You, therefore, must speak and preach as if you were always speaking and preaching to dying men; as if the words you were uttering were the very last which you should utter to those who are listening to you that they may receive direction and advice. Your whole burden of work must turn upon a few brief sayings of the Bible, which must be pressed again and again with energy and with zeal; such as these: "Neither is there salvation in any other" than "Jesus Christ of Nazareth."[1] "Except a man be born again," "born of water and of the Spirit, he cannot enter into the Kingdom of God."[2] "Behold, now is the accepted time; behold, now is the day of salvation."[3] "Boast not thyself of to-morrow; for thou knowest not what a day may bring forth."[4]

With these themes you must mingle such instruction as can be given in the outskirts of a camp, and such a view of the economy of grace as one can mingle with exhortation and immediate turning to the Lord. Every Minister has his own work to do, and must do it according to the position in which he is placed, and the emergencies which encompass him. With you, as a Chaplain to the Army and ministering continually to the sick and the wounded, there must be great tenderness and a large-hearted charity; but

[1] Acts iv. 12, 10.
[2] S. John iii. 3, 5.
[3] 2 Cor. vi. 2.
[4] Proverbs xxvii. 1.

at the same time a stern adherence to truth and the requirements of God in Christ. Offer salvation; proclaim the tidings of great joy; press upon them the gracious invitation to come to Christ and be saved; preach grace, as you see it developed in the Scriptures: but at the same time do not forget to rebuke sin, to declare the necessity of the Spirit's work upon the heart, to announce fully that without holiness no man shall see the Lord. You will have no time to retrieve error. Once spoken, to those audiences, forever spoken. It is a seed sown for life and for death.

Your present position, and the work for which you are just now specially ordained, will carry you away for a time from the routine of the Church, and will introduce to occasions where you cannot fully carry out all her requirements. But, even there, you will find how beautifully her arrangements are suited to the necessities of man, and how rich is the Book of Common Prayer in furnishing prayers and supplications and givings of thanks. And then its objective worship is very attractive to those who are earnest and sincere; and its successive steps toward communion are great helps to those who are timid and distrustful. And in the hospitals, its rich prayers are most highly prized and its quiet earnestness goes to the heart and the soul. So far from the liturgical work of the Church being a hindrance to you, you will find it, if judiciously used, a great help, and a most potent auxiliary. But you must endeavor to adapt yourself to all occasions and all circumstances, and to act with the rites and ceremonies of the Church upon the same principle as that upon which our Saviour acted in regard to the Sabbath: that "the Sabbath was made for man, and not man for the Sabbath."[1] You must use them, but not abuse them. You must make them subservient to the salvation of the soul, and not permit them

[1] S. Mark ii. 27.

to clog that salvation. And thus, by the use of a sound judgment combined with an earnest devotion of purpose, you will gain a rich experience, that will be of immense service to you when the emergency which now presses upon you shall have passed away, and you be called once more to work in the ordinary channels of the Church. You are being ordained for a life's work; and that work will vary in kind, according to the path along which your Master shall lead you. What is required of you is, to be ready for to-day. Leave to-morrow to Him who has said: "As thy days so shall thy strength be."[1] Some positions require great and immediate activity, such as this which you are now to fill. Others call for careful culture: these may come, and with them God will give the time and the opportunity. What I wish to impress upon you is, to work in the present and for the present. Do not neglect the duty of the day, in preparing yourself for the possible duty of the hereafter. If you have leisure, use it well; if opportunity, grasp it and turn it to account: but do not neglect the salvation of the meanest creature upon earth, for any preparation that is to suit you for an imaginary future in the Church. "Work while it is called to-day."[2] "Gird up the loins of your mind, be sober,"[3] and "watch unto prayer."[4] God will guide you along the path which He has ordained for you to tread; will give you abundantly of the treasures of His grace; will strengthen and support you in times of weakness and infirmity; will make the light shine more and more distinctly upon your heart and life; and will finally give you the crown of everlasting glory. Cast all your care and weakness and infirmity upon Him, and He will carry it all for you.

JUNE, 1863.

[1] Deut. xxxiii. 25.
[2] Heb. ii. 13.
[3] 1 S. Peter i. 13.
[4] *Ibid.* iv. 7.

Forty-third Sermon.

Be still, and know that I am God. — PSALM xlvi. 10.

ONE of the hardest trials of our faith is that which is enjoined upon us by God in our text: to "be still," when He has laid the heavy hand of chastisement upon us, and "know that He is God." It is so much more natural, when our prosperity has been blighted, and days of darkness have blotted out the sunshine of our hearts and homes, to look at the secondary causes of our misfortunes and be angry with them, rather than see the rod in the hand of God, and then submit in quietness to the will of Him who has dispensed it: that it is justly reckoned one of the sublimest trials of faith to be enabled to say, in sincerity of heart, "Not my will, but thine, be done."[1] It is a marked indication that things unseen are getting the mastery over sense; and that God is becoming to us a reality, a present Deity, whose influence we joyfully recognize, and whose interest in our concerns we humbly and thankfully acknowledge.

This trial of our faith is brought home to us, my beloved people, at this moment of our reunion, in a most striking manner; and my earnest prayer both for you and for myself is, that it may end in a triumph of that faith, and that we may have grace given us to "be still," and to know that it is God who has overruled every thing to the purposes of His will, and that without His permission nothing could have happened which has happened.

[1] S. Luke xxii. 42.

To find any comfort in the consideration of human affairs, we must ever acknowledge a present Deity. Without Him, all is chaos, and all would be despair. Things would seem to go on without any rule, and folly and vice and wickedness to ride triumphant over the efforts of man. But when we soar above the sensible and the visible, and see Him seated upon His throne of righteousness and of mercy, holding in His hands the complicated threads of human action, and guiding and governing all wills and powers, as He thinks best for His creatures, we bow in humility and with thanksgiving: in humility, that we should presume to murmur when He is ruling over us; with thanksgiving, that the world has not been left to itself, but that He who has foreordained all things, is driving them on to their rightful consummation. So long as we fasten our thoughts upon secondary causes, upon human agents, upon earthly instruments, our most dangerous passions are kept alive: our anger, our wrath, our bitterness, our hatred, our uncharitableness; — the very feelings which inspired men have commanded us, as Christians, to put aside. It is not until God is permitted to fill our hearts, and to become — what He is — the Ruling Spirit of all worldly movements, and to shut out by His glorious Presence the human instruments through whom He works and punishes, that these unchristian passions can be soothed and quelled: soothed and quelled by the magical words, "Be still, and know that I am God." Just as Christ's words calmed the angry waves of the sea, when He arose and rebuked the winds: so when, in our peril and distress, we call upon Him, and He enters upon the scene, saying with the irresistible voice of Divinity, "Peace, be still," our passions sink before Him, and we are quiet, because we know that "He is God."

What, my beloved people, is our belief? What is it that we call our Christian faith? Is it not belief in a scheme, which, beginning in the cradle of the world, is to go on, until the kingdoms of this world shall become the kingdoms of Christ? Every link in the history of nations is a link likewise in the chain of events, which is to bring about that result. We know not how; we know not when: all we can do is, to act our part as seems to us right; to follow that path of duty, which opens itself before us. When we have done that, we have fulfilled our allotted task. The results and the consequences are with God. Should they be widely different from what we expected; should things take an altogether contrary course from what we thought they would do, or ought to do: we may be lost in amazement, but nevertheless the direction comes to us, "Be still, and know that I am God." We are not placed here upon earth to direct the purposes of God. We are the mere instruments created to carry them out; and while carrying them out, to save our own souls. We have only to look back, to trace the history of the Church through all its struggles with the world, to perceive how continually its instruments must have been lost in consternation at the dealings of God with them, and how their faith must have been tried as event after event developed itself in such seeming contradiction to their expectations and hopes. Noah must have been amazed when, as the fulfillment of the promises made to Adam and Eve at the expulsion from Eden, a flood covered the earth, and swept from it all living things save his chosen family. God's satisfaction of his amazement was no more than this, "Be still, and know that I am God." Abraham must have been amazed, when, as the fulfillment of the promise that in him should "all the nations of the earth be blessed," he was commanded to offer up his only son, the child of promise, as a sacrifice upon Mount Moriah. God's voice to him was no more than that which He still utters, "Be still, and know that I am God."

The children of the promise made to Abraham, Isaac, and Jacob, that the Messiah should come from them, and that "the sceptre should not depart from Judah, nor a lawgiver from between his feet, until Shiloh come,"[1] must have been amazed when both Israel and Judah were carried away into what seemed a hopeless captivity. The commandment still was, "Be still, and know that I am God." The followers of our blessed Saviour must have been in amazement, when He who proclaimed himself as the Son of God with power, and upon whose head were concentrated the promises and types and prophecies of all time as the Saviour of the world, was led away to be crucified between two thieves. "Be still, and know that I am God," was all the strength and consolation which they received. Why multiply instances? This has been the Church's and the Christian's experience, from the beginning. Man attempts to understand and interpret God's dealings: but it is not in his province "to know the times or the seasons which the Father hath put in his own power."[2] Man's duty is, when he has labored as God intended him to labor and has thus acquitted his soul, to acquiesce in the results; to have faith that God is wiser and holier than himself; and to be still, in contemplation of His dealings and in waiting upon His will.

We must not expect nor wish to be exempted from this condition of the Christian life. We must encounter many things, both in our national and personal experience, in which God's dealings will be very different from our expectations. His ways are not as our ways, nor His thoughts as our thoughts. We shall be called upon very often to look on in amazement at a course of proceeding on His part very contrary to what we supposed would be or ought to be; and under those circumstances, the attitude which Christianity calls upon us to take, is that indicated in our

[1] Gen. xlix. 10.

[2] Acts i. 7.

text. "Be still, and know that I am God," occurs just when He calls upon His Church to look upon the works of the Lord:—"Come, behold the works of the LORD, what desolations he hath made in the earth:"[1] so that it is no violent wrenching of the words from their context, but an application of them most suitable and appropriate.

And yet how hard it is to be still, in the full meaning of the expression as used by God in this glorious Scripture! For stillness is more than a mere submission because we cannot help ourselves; is more than acquiescence in His dealings, because He is the Author of them. To be still, in the full meaning of our text, is to believe that our affairs are in wiser and better hands than our own: and, while we look on in wonder and amazement, not to doubt but that we shall see and understand that He maketh all things to work together for good to them that love him,—to them that are called according to His purpose. We may be very still under calamity and humiliation, and yet very rebellious in our hearts against God; may utter no complaints in the hearing of man, while our hearts are swelling—and God searcheth the hearts—with irrepressible indignation. This is being still before man: but not still before God. The whisperings of the heart, of which man knows and hears nothing, are as loud before God as the surges of the ocean when they lash the rocks in their fury; and if those whisperings are rebellious, it is a conflict with God, which is incompatible with Christian peace. The stillness of the heart comes when passion has passed away, whether of grief or of suffering; when the spirit, quieted and soothed by the presence of the Holy Dove, sees God's love in all that has disturbed it; and mingles with its submission, a patient waiting upon the Lord for the manifestation of His goodness and wisdom.

[1] Psalm xlvi. 8.

It is that patient waiting upon the Lord which is now our duty, and at the same time our temptation. God says, "Be still:" but our throbbing hearts beat high with impatience. God says, "Your present condition is but a link in a chain of events which extends from eternity to eternity, and which is as necessary to My purposes as your personal faith is to your salvation; be still, and see the end:" but we are not in a temper for waiting; we are for judging and condemning God's dealings at once, — for it really amounts to that, — and for finding fault with all around us. This, my beloved fellow-Christians, is all very natural, very much in keeping with the feelings of the world: but is it very Christian? Is it in harmony with the teachings of Christ and His Apostles? Those teachings are the standard of the Church, the rule of its life and conduct. Often did they look in wonder at God's dealings with them, but their spirits yielded at once before the presence of God. Our Saviour Himself was "sore amazed"[1] at His Father's permission of the sufferings which He went through at the hands of men; but He never lost the divine charity which He came to teach and illustrate. "Father, forgive them; for they know not what they do,"[2] was His prayer in that moment of His agony. Our being still, involves all this, — patience, charity, forgiveness of injuries, the feeling that it is God and not man with whom we are concerned. And how much more noble and dignified it is — for true Christianity is the highest and sublimest dignity — to believe and feel that we are contending with God and not with man; to carry our cause from the battle-fields and courts of earth, and lay it down at the foot of the throne of God, and leave it quietly with Him. He knew our hearts; He saw our motives; to Him we committed ourselves; in His hands we placed every thing that was dear to us; we said in express words

[1] S. Mark xiv. 33. [2] S. Luke xxiii. 34.

that we were willing to abide by His decision and His judgment. Unless we are still under His decrees, we are taking all this back: we are appealing from Him — to I know not what, unless it be — to ourselves, as greater, wiser, and holier than He. We have done up to this time what we honestly and sincerely believed to be our bounden duty to God, and therefore to man. Let us not now swerve from what is the continuation of that duty. Quiet is to succeed activity; stillness to follow strife; patience to tread upon the heels of conflict. We were equal to the one: shall we not be equal to the other? We believed that we were Christians, while we labored for our cause: shall we not be Christians when called upon to acquiesce in God's decision upon that cause?

Nothing which occurs on earth is an end. It is only a means, leading on through antecedents and consequents, to the great and final purpose of human redemption. While that purpose is consummating, one thing follows another according to God's arrangement, and we become involved in them. Sometimes they are pleasing to flesh and blood; sometimes we suffer severely under them. But whether agreeable or disagreeable, they come alike from His hand, who has promised to make all things work together for good to them that love Him. While passing through them we have an end of our own, which is for us above all other ends; and that is, the salvation of our individual souls: and we must take care that we do not perish in the wilderness. Just as the preaching of the Word of God is the savor of life unto life to some, and the savor of death unto death to others, so are the events of God's providence — this sequence of which I am speaking — temptations involving our future condition far more than we are willing to acknowledge. We are now in a very trying position; one requiring great soberness and watchfulness; one in which we may be tempted with great ease to unbelief, to lukewarmness, to indifference, to coldness. Our besetting sins and temptations come to us, at this time, under such specious names and fair exteriors, that it requires a diviner touch, even that of Ithuriel — the touch of the Holy Spirit of God — to make them assume their real shapes. In the midst of it all, God calls upon us to "be still," and know that it is He who is dealing with us. Let us hear Him. Let us trust Him. Once when Christ was on earth, He sent His disciples away from Him into a ship, while He went up into a mountain apart to pray. But when the ship was now in the midst of the sea, tossed with waves, Jesus went unto them, walking on the sea. "And when the disciples saw Him walking on the sea, they were troubled, saying, It is a spirit; and they cried out for fear. But straightway Jesus spake unto them, saying, Be of good cheer; it is I; be not afraid."[1] Just so it is with us. We are in the midst of the sea, tossed with the waves, and the wind contrary. We see no horizon: all is dark and stormy. God in Christ, Our Father, appears before us, planting His footsteps in the sea, and riding on the storm. We are troubled at His presence. We do not recognize Him as God. We cry out for grief and fear. But His voice comes to us across the tempest, saying, "Be still, and know that I am God." Receive Me into your hearts, and you will find that the winds will cease, and the waves be calm. Let us welcome Him, my beloved people; and be not afraid, for He is our present help in every trouble.

But you may say, "It is easy to preach, but oh! how hard to practice!" But have I not, my people, to practice what I preach? am I not preaching to you that I may learn how to practice? Has any one found it harder to be still than I, and to admit that it is God? I find it just as hard

[1] S. Matthew xiv. 26, 27.

to practice as you: but I feel it to be my duty, and I shall always strive to do that. And I call upon you to do it, and will endeavor to lead you in the way. And if you ask, How is it to be done? my answer is: By not looking at the angry sea, or listening to the roaring winds; but by looking upon the God who is walking there, and listening to His tender voice when it says to you, "It is I; be not afraid." We shall never be at peace so long as we keep our eyes fixed upon the earth, and upon man. We must look up — up to God where He "sitteth upon the circle of the earth, and the inhabitants thereof are as grasshoppers,"[1] — ere we can attain that equanimity which becomes the child of God and the heir of heaven.

Our temptation is, my beloved fellow-Christians, that it is not our duty to "be still," and to recognize God as in the midst of our affairs. We rather think it our duty to be impatient and angry. Does man, then, rule in the affairs of nations? Are poor, weak, corrupt creatures like ourselves, the arbiters of the present and the future? God forbid! and every one of you would echo "God forbid!" For myself, if I were compelled to come to that conclusion, I should be in despair. I should have no hope for man, or for the world! And if man does not rule the world, who does? We have no answer left us, but God: for assuredly, while we acknowledge the power of the Devil and admit his influence in the affairs of men, we cannot believe him to be supreme over a world in which Christ's Church is enshrined. And if God rules over the affairs of men, and is overturning, overturning, overturning, "until He come whose right it is:"[2] why should we be angry because, in the onward movement of His chariot wheels, we may suffer, or even perish, in the flesh? Loss, suffering, chastisement, even death, are no tokens of God's displeasure. All

[1] Isaiah xl. 22.

[2] Ezekiel xxi. 27.

His chosen ones have suffered. All whom He ever loved, He chastised. Many of His most glorious saints perished by violence. Again and again were His chosen people subjected to direful captivity. We have no ground for despair. Things never stand still, either in the world, or in the Church. The scenes are perpetually shifting: and what to-day is encompassed with clouds and darkness, with mystery and amazement, is to-morrow rejoicing in light and sunshine, God having lifted up the light of His countenance upon it and made it clear! "Be still, and know that I am God," fills up the measure of our duty; and promises us the earliest relief, and the surest comfort.

> "Be still, my soul! Thy God doth undertake
> To guide the future, as He has the past.
> Thy hope, thy confidence, let nothing shake,
> All now mysterious shall be bright at last.
> Be still, my soul! The waves and winds still know
> His voice, who ruled them while He dwelt below."

October 15, 1865.

Forty-fourth Sermon.

In your patience possess ye your souls. — S. LUKE xxi. 19.

THERE are virtues which are suitable to all the circumstances of life by which we may be surrounded; duties, becoming every condition which God may place us under. There is a time, as the wise man tells us, for every thing: a time to weep and a time to laugh; a time to mourn and a time to dance: and our conduct is to be in harmony with our times. They are in God's hands; and as He appoints them, so must we adapt ourselves to them. What would be appropriate under one set of circumstances would be very inappropriate under another set. And this is very much dwelt upon in the sacred Scriptures. Both in the Old and the New Testament the people of God are commanded to watch carefully and thoughtfully the chain of events in which they are for the time involved; to examine their purpose and bearing, to study their meaning and coloring: and to adapt their behavior unto a suitable agreement with them. "In the day of prosperity," says the wise man, "be joyful," [1] give thanks and praise to God for His mercies and His blessings. Show forth gratitude by sacrifices of every kind. On the contrary, "in the day of adversity," when darkness lowers, and peril threatens, and the light of God's countenance seems hidden from us, "consider": [2] be sober and watchful, earnest and patient. When victory perched upon their banner and their enemies

[1] Eccles. vii. 14.

[2] *Ibid.*

fled before them, they were to sing the song of triumph with timbrels and dances. When days such as those which illustrated the reign of Solomon — halcyon days of peace and plenty — smiled upon the land, they were to manifest their sense of God's gracious mercy with festivity and a profuse return to Him of the gifts which He had poured into their bosoms. On the other hand, when dangers threatened their homes, when enemies thronged in rage upon their borders, they were to turn to God in humiliation and prayer, and to hide themselves under the shadow of His wings until their calamities were overpast. There was a proper and befitting carriage and conversation for every varying condition of events, and it was pressed upon them by God Himself, through the mouth of Prophets and Apostles and His own incarnate Son.

The verse from which I preach forms a part of the instruction which our Saviour was giving His disciples in connection with the days of fearful darkness which were approaching, — days which had been foretold ever since the time of Moses. Soon after His death the abomination of desolation was to stand in the holy place: the city and the Temple were to be razed to the ground. And these sad events were to be accompanied by unspeakable miseries and woeful trials: miseries and trials so great that He could find no fitter comparison for them than the horrors of the Judgment Day. While preparing them for the unheard-of calamities which should attend that catastrophe, He exhorts them to be firm and undismayed at their approach, and to meet them as reasonable creatures and children of the Most High. What were they to tremble at, seeing that the Lord God Omnipotent reigned, and that they were His chosen? After detailing the horrors of those days; the commotions and tumults and terrors which should herald them; the convulsions of Nature; the signs in heaven and on earth; the famine, the pestilence which should accompany them: He closes with the calm injunction of our text, "In your patience possess ye your souls."

What our Lord enjoined upon the disciples who walked with Him when upon earth, does He likewise enjoin upon all who, like them, may be passing through days of darkness and of affliction. Those are always times which require special watchfulness and consideration on our part,— special attention to our souls, and a cultivation of the grace of patience up to the very highest point to which it can be carried. "Affliction cometh not forth of the dust, neither doth trouble spring out of the ground."[1] They come from God, whether they be personal or national, and are meant to exercise our patience. At such times therefore, and under such circumstances,—especially if they be long continued, if they extend over weary years and we can see no prospect of their ending,—it becomes manifest that God intends patience to have her perfect work, and the exhortation becomes most important, "In your patience possess ye your souls."

In examining this text, you will perceive that its wording is peculiar. It is not a simple exhortation, "In patience possess ye your souls;" but it implies that, having already exhibited patience, you are, in the exercise of that patience, to perform a particular work,—you are to attain a point of great importance to yourselves and to the glory of Him who grants you the gift of patience. And that point is, to "possess your souls,"—to have them so in your own keeping, that you will not only save them at the last, but be masters of them while subjected to those evils which are brought upon you for your discipline and trial.

There have been given us two instruments by which we may be masters of ourselves,—reason and faith: the one

[1] Job v. 6.

distinguishing us from the brutes, the other lifting us above visible things. Either of these, when properly exercised, can place us above the frowns of fortune, and make us rise superior to those calamities which come upon us from the vicissitudes of temporal things. It shows but a very scant exercise of our rational powers, when we permit ourselves to lose the control of ourselves in the day of adversity. "If thou faint in the day of adversity," is the language of the Bible, "thy strength is small,"[1] — strength, not only of grace but of reason: for reason is given us, not merely to guide us in the path of life, but to sustain us when peril encompasses us, when troubles surround us, when fears harass us, when sorrow bows us to the ground. It is not as sufficient as grace; but among the Pagans it went far to make many of them worthy examples of fortitude and quiet possession of their souls in the hour of calamity. Fear, agitation, trembling, forfeiture of principle, inconsistency of conduct, loss of character in times of evil, are all unbecoming a being who has nothing more than reason to guide him: how much more unbecoming one who claims to have faith in addition to reason; who has not only the natural strength which comes with birth and culture, but the supernatural strength which comes from the Holy Spirit of God. Such persons fall short of the powers which God has given them, and fail in the very moment when they most need those powers.

The grace which we are to exercise in times like these upon which we have fallen, is patience. God is working out wonders of His own; wonders which we shall see and acknowledge in due time. We can show our faith in His wisdom and goodness by waiting upon His will, and, while waiting, by possessing our souls; keeping them calm and trustful through all the changes which may occur around

[1] Prov. xxiv. 10.

us; hopeful through the darkest hour; cheerful when all things seem against us. Our great advantages of civilization, of education, and of Christianity, are lost to us unless they give us these qualities when we need them. And when special grace has been vouchsafed us to wait upon God, we are recreant to our profession if we lose our Christian equanimity and fortitude because He delays the manifestation of His love and mercy. What is our discipline, if every thing is to happen just as we think it should; if no crosses are to meet us by the way; if no troubles are to harass our path; if no afflictions are to cast their dark shadows upon our households; if no desolation is to sweep athwart the track of our country's prosperity? What call is there for the exercise of our patience, if that patience is never to be tried either by man or God? How can we estimate its value, unless it be weighed in the balances with adversity and temptation? We may have the grace, but we shall not know it; we may be blessed with the elements of a high Christian character, but it will never be manifested to the world for the glory of God. Calamity, trouble, affliction, perplexity, are all necessary to bring out the beauties of grace, just as a dark background throws into prominent relief the beauties of nature and of art.

Patience has, like all other Christian graces, its gradations. Its perfectness is not reached at once. Its first step is in silent submission to God's will. We are quiet under His dispensations; we say nothing in contradiction to them; we do not murmur in words or in acts; we are dumb and open not our mouths: but still are there heights of patience above this, which we must reach ere we can be said in our patience to possess our souls, to be masters of them, to have them under our control. The second step is when we accept with thankfulness the strokes of God's fatherly rod; when we can see His loving hand in every blow He gives us; when we can say, out of grateful hearts, "It is good for me that I have been afflicted."[1] This is patience refined, purified, rising to a clearer perception of God's character as a God of love; of God's dealings as a Father, tender, pitiful, compassionate. This prepares us for the highest attainment, when we may be said, in the language of our Saviour, in our patience to "possess" our souls. We have climbed to this height when we have reached a serious cheerfulness under trials of whatever kind, rejoicing in tribulation, and counting it all joy when we fall into divers temptations. As faith gives us the possession of Christ, so does this patience give us possession of ourselves. An unbelieving man has no hold upon Christ: so an impatient man has no hold upon himself; "for what title soever we have to our own souls, we have no possession of them without patience." Then only are we masters of ourselves (and our souls are ourselves), when nothing can disturb us which is connected with the earth: our treasures, our hearts, our hopes, being all in heaven, whither our souls will follow them, and find them in the day of the consummation of all things.

This is our work, my beloved people, in the days which are continuing to darken over us. The Lord has promised us that "it shall come to pass, that at evening time it shall be light:"[2] but evening time may be yet distant; and meanwhile we must cultivate patience and possess our souls, even though all our other possessions be taken from us. Our souls are our own, out of the reach of any man, and cannot be lost, unless we lose them ourselves. And what is more encouraging to us than all, is the mysterious fact, that days of sadness and of adversity are just those which are most propitious to the saving of our souls. Man seems to be so constituted that days of prosperity and of

[1] Psalm cxix. 71. [2] Zechariah xiv. 7.

ease draw him away from any thoughts of his soul; fix his affections upon things of this world; employ him in matters which are sensual and earthly; turn his mind from his most solemn relations, — those to God and eternity. But when the world is tumultuous and agitated; when sorrow and distress are all around us; when the dark clouds which cover the heavens seem thick as night and give no signs of breaking; when Death is frequent and always threatening; when there is little joy to be found in home or society, and no rest for the tired spirit: then is it that the soul looms into importance both for this world and for the world to come. It is felt to contain the elements of true greatness; to be the sustaining power of the whole man; to rise superior to outward things and create a world of its own within the bosom; to be capable of serenity in the midst of tumult; of calmness in the fury of the storm; of courage when all hearts are failing; of self-control when things are combining to shake its constancy; of firmness when all is tottering around it. Above all, it is found to have a renewed existence beyond the grave, where every thing which made this life agreeable and desirable is offered to it as an eternal inheritance, enhanced by charms which this earth could not bestow, and stripped of those qualities which made them perishable and corruptible. These powers of the soul manifest themselves to us in our days of darkness, just as the stars shine brightest when night descends upon the earth and blots out the garish brightness of the day. They constitute the whole glory of the time of sorrow and affliction, and our eyes are riveted upon them as our only light and joy. We find within ourselves the source of our comfort and our hope; and learn, perhaps for the first time, that our real treasure of joy, both present and future, is locked up within ourselves, and has but little permanent connection with things outward and visible.

During the continuance of the circumstances under which we are living, patience is the grace which most becomes us. We can do no more than we are doing to change our condition, except wait upon God in cheerful submission. If He designs patience to have her perfect work, so be it. It is best for us, for He makes all things work together for good to those who love and fear Him. His purposes cannot be worked out in such brief time as our impatience desires. Even though all His will be to bless us and prosper us,—which I most firmly believe it is,—He may not be able, consistently with His mode of action, to bring His purposes to pass at once. We must be patient; and in our patience we must possess our souls. We must possess them in the sight of all men, for the uses of society. We must keep up the superiority of reason; must be sober, calm, earnest, resolute; must not permit passion to overcome us, nor fear to unnerve us, nor grief to overwhelm us, nor the loss of worldly things to cast us down. We are contending for great things; and we must be great ourselves, great especially in the possession of our souls. The greatest men of the earth have been distinguished for this self-possession in the midst of trial and adversity. It constituted the greatness of the ancient Cato, and was the controlling power of our peerless Washington. In such a conflict as this, passion is of no moment. It only disfigures the scene of action. Patience, endurance, self-control, self-possession, are our qualities for this world. But above all should every one of us, in our patience, see to the salvation of our souls,—to that higher possession which makes them ours forever: ours not only while we are struggling here, but ours while we are resting from all conflicts in the grave. God has made full provision for their salvation. He has given His most priceless possession, His only and well-beloved Son, for their redemption from sin and death and hell; and that Son has proclaimed to the world: "Him that cometh to me I will in no wise cast out."[1] "In your patience" in these days of trial and of adversity, employ yourselves in this great work. If every thing else should fail, and you should yet succeed in that, it will have been to you a work of greatness far exceeding any thing you could have achieved. Christ said, "What shall it profit a man, if he shall gain the whole world, and lose his own soul?"[2] and it is a question which you should weigh, and ponder upon, in these days when God is trying us in the furnace of affliction. Whatever else you lose, do not lose your own souls!

AUGUST 22, 1864.

[1] S. John vi. 37.

[2] S. Mark viii. 36.

Forty-fifth Sermon.

For this commandment which I command thee this day, it is not hidden from thee, neither is it far off. It is not in heaven, that thou shouldest say, Who shall go up for us to heaven, and bring it unto us, that we may hear it, and do it? Neither is it beyond the sea, that thou shouldest say, Who shall go over the sea for us, and bring it unto us, that we may hear it, and do it? But the word is very nigh unto thee, in thy mouth, and in thy heart, that thou mayest do it. — DEUTERONOMY xxx. 11–14.

SELDOM, my beloved hearers, have we been summoned to humiliation and prayer under more impressive auspices than those which have gathered us together this day in this sanctuary of God. The Representatives of a Sovereign State, newly come from their constituents, and carrying up to the Capital the detail of their sufferings and their trials, "Resolved," as their first complete act of legislation, that this day should be set apart as a day of fasting, humiliation, and prayer, upon which the people of the State should return thanks for God's mercies and blessings, should confess their sins, and should importune His favor. In addition to this "Resolution," the Legislature requested the Governor to issue his Proclamation calling upon the whole people to observe this day of solemn supplication, and with one heart and one voice to humble themselves at the Mercy-seat. And this Proclamation has been set forth in most eloquent and Christian language, giving us the key-note to the services of the day, and furnishing the materials out of which we are to weave our roll of lamentation and of woe. Our

State authorities have done their duty in most solemn fashion. God grant that the Churches and the congregations of this Christian country may not be one whit behind them in their appreciation of the necessity and value of this universal humiliation.

Such an authoritative and earnest appeal would not have been made, my hearers, to the people of our State, unless there had been ample ground for it in the condition of the country. Legislative bodies are not wont to occupy themselves with the arrangement of religious services, as their earliest act of importance. Their hearts, at their first meeting together after a long separation, are generally more full of friendly greeting and cheerful memories; and their minds, of the earthly topics of interest which concern themselves and their constituents. Each legislator brings with him some favorite measure which he deems most important for the welfare of the State; and he rushes at once to put in motion the machinery which is to give it success. The Message of the Executive, and the documents which accompany it, throw at once before them matters of new and deep importance, which usually absorb their attention, and give rise to immediate discussion. When therefore, as in this case, all these matters of private interest and of public concern are unanimously put aside for the sake of urging upon the people a solemn religious exercise, it is a striking proof that these legislators must have left their homes deeply impressed with the calamities which threatened their friends, and with the necessity of a public invocation of God's help in saving their desolated country from still further sufferings. Man had labored and struggled in vain: he must now turn to God; and, humbling himself to the dust, and confessing his guilt, must implore His Divine mercy.

And surely there is enough in our present condition to

humble us into the very dust: and in nothing more than in our own conduct. As the Governor tells us in his Proclamation, we are in the wilderness, suffering, and yet sinning; under the covenant mercy and guidance of a God of truth, and yet forever distrusting Him; receiving many tokens of His loving-kindness, and yet murmuring the moment any thing seems to be against us. For this unfaithfulness and impatience is He chastising us; and, until we are more submissive to Him and more resigned under His rod, He will continue to chasten us. We will not see that it is with God we have to deal, and not with man. We will not recognize, as fully as we should, that our controversy lies at the foot of His Throne, and has nothing to do with any earthly power. We will descend into the miserable arena of political strife, instead of looking up to Him who sitteth in the Heavens, and in whose eyes the nations of the earth are but as the dust in the balance. We will permit our hearts and our spirits to be agitated and irritated by matters with which we had better have no concern, instead of soaring quietly above them, and dwelling in the atmosphere of dignity and of peace which most becomes us. We should have no longer any thing to do with man, in the way of strife or contention. We should consider ourselves in the hands of God, our Father, and our providential Ruler; and should patiently await His dealings with us. A child might as wisely quarrel with the rod in a parent's hand, as we with the agents whom God is using to punish and to humble us. A man might as well endeavor to break in pieces the stone against which he has hurt his foot, as we to kick against the pricks which God has put in our way, to make us walk in the path He designs for us. When we act in this senseless manner, we are not only warring against our own prosperity, but against the preordinations of Him who ruleth every thing to the purposes of His own will. By such action we run against the thick bosses of God's buckler, and are destroyed.

For, if you will consider the words of the Proclamation under which we are here gathered together, you will perceive that the great causes which have led to this day of fasting and humiliation have come directly from His hand who rules the natural world, and at whose bidding the rain descends upon the evil and upon the good, and the sun shines upon the just and upon the unjust. "Our corn and our oil have failed of their abundance; our flocks and our herds are diminished. The cry of want is heard in our land: the manna and the quails come not yet." These are the motives which have induced our legislators to call us to humiliation; and these, surely, come from God. Man has no control over the Seasons: they are altogether beyond his influence. In our own beautiful prayers, we say: "O God, our Heavenly Father, who by thy gracious providence dost cause the former and the latter rain to descend upon the earth, that it may bring forth fruit for the use of man"; and again: "O Lord God, who hast justly humbled us by thy late visitation of us with immoderate rain and waters;" and again, in our service of Thanksgiving for the labors of the husbandman: "O most merciful Father, who hast blessed the labors of the husbandman in the returns of the fruits of the earth:" so that, in our Liturgical Services, we have beforehand ascribed plenty and want, scarcity and abundance, to God and not to man. And it is the same with sickness and with death, which have visited our State very severely during the past year. They come, most assuredly, from God; and are used by Him as instruments for the chastening of His children, — of those whom He loves, and cares for, and would keep near unto Himself. Man is far below any power of this sort. He may rule in the policies of earth. He may regulate such things as trade and commerce, as economy and wealth, as Law and Government: but thus far can he go, and no further. The heavens are out of his reach. The clouds which float in the heavens obey not his commands. Pestilence moves not at his decree; and Death submits not to his bidding. When Dearth, and Famine, and Poverty, and Disease are concerned, man has to contend with a higher Power than his fellow-man, — is being chastised by a rod which a fellow-mortal's hand is not permitted to wield. And when our fasting and our humiliation and our prayers are called for, to help us under calamities springing from these sources, we ought to know at once in Whose hand the rod is, and Who hath appointed it. In other respects, things have been better with us than they promised to be. Much of our landed property has been restored to its owners; our industry has been less interfered with than it was, and our trade and our commerce have resumed, in some measure, their ancient channels; our civil courts have been reopened and are administering a measure of justice. For these things we should be thankful; and if it be said, that a dark cloud seems to be gathering over us in the future, my answer would be: "Leave the future to take care of itself. We are concerned to-day with humiliation for the past, and with prayer under the sufferings of the present. Let us not look at the clouds, but at Him who rideth upon the clouds. Let us not fear the darkness, but enter into it, — if it be our duty, — knowing that God often dwelleth in the thick darkness.

Our controversy, therefore, my beloved people, is with God, and not with man: for it is He who has frowned upon our labor, and who has permitted our atmosphere to be laden with disease. And it is a great point to have satisfied you of this; for it removes from your hearts much of the pride and bitterness which might hinder you from humbling yourselves in the House of God this day. Man is much more unwilling to bow himself down before his fellow-man, than before God. With his fellow-man he enters into controversy about right and wrong, about justice and injustice, about merit and demerit: but with God, if he be at all right-minded, he raises no such questions. He bows his head and his heart at once before an all-wise and all-merciful God, who knoweth what is best for His creatures; and who has promised to make every thing work together for good to them that love Him. He quarrels with men: he dares not quarrel with God. Being satisfied then that it is God who has been inflicting upon you the successive blows under which you are suffering, you come to-day in a teachable temper, acknowledging that you have, in some way, offended God; and praying that He may send His Holy Spirit upon you, to search your hearts as with the candle of the Lord, and manifest to you your unfaithfulness.

Our being assembled together in this place this day, is an evidence to us that we ourselves acknowledge and feel the need of humiliation: and yet, each one may be a little doubtful what has been our offence as a people. As individuals, we are all conscious of our own particular sins; and of those we must repent: but it is not about those that we are to-day concerned. We are in the temples of God this day as a people, not as individuals. We have met to inquire of God wherein we have sinned against Him as a people, and to make our confessions and regain His favor. I will endeavor, so far as I have received light, to point out, with great diffidence and humility, some of the things in our conduct which may have offended God, and kept upon us His hand of chastisement.

Have we submitted to God's decision of the conflict in which we were, for so many years, engaged? This is the first question which comes up; and it has reference simply to God, and to the spirit of our minds towards Him. Without entering at all anew into the merits or demerits, the right or the wrong, the justice or the injustice, of that controversy, which have passed out of our hands into the hands of God, and have become a matter of eternal and immutable morality, we will all acknowledge that the conflict is ended, and ended by God, in a manner adverse to our wishes and to our interests. God has permitted it to end in one way, and not in another; and we must be convinced of that. The circumstances which accompanied its end were so plain and palpable, that God's hand could not be mistaken as being in it. Have we, my question is, acquiesced in our hearts in God's decision, or have we murmured and rebelled against His action, and counted it unjust and injurious? I do not ask whether it has changed your opinion of the justice or injustice of your action; — *that* has nothing to do with it: or, whether it has caused you to alter your views about the institution of slavery, which it overturned; — *that* likewise has nothing to do with it: but, whether you have submitted to God's will about the termination of the conflict. I know that, in many places and in many hearts, there has been an open quarrel with God upon this point; — that He has been charged with injustice, with a false view of right and wrong, with cruelty to the innocent and the godly. And while such feelings as these, and such language as this, have not been, to any common degree, openly indulged in, may there not have been enough of it seen by God, in the recesses of the heart, to arouse His indignation and excite His anger. For, to say the least of it, such murmuring and want of acquiescence in God's dealings argue faithlessness, and distrust in His love for His people. We have only to turn to the narrative of the exodus of the Children of Israel and their wanderings in the wilderness, to perceive how continually God's anger was aroused, and His indignation excited, because His people would not submit to His guidance, and acquiesce in His acts. God's people must be always tried; they will never be fit otherwise to be His people: and acquiescence in His dealings, — perfect trust and faith in His proceedings, — is the test of their faith. For God is working out larger ends than those which concern us as a people. His ends embrace the Universe: His purposes are co-extensive with Time. What may happen to us, is of great moment to us, because it is a trial of our faith: but is, at the same time, only a link in the chain of events which is working out a grander and sublimer purpose, in which we ourselves are at last to be most intimately concerned. The lesser end — our concerns — is absorbed in the greater: and if we have a sound and truly Christian trust in God, and in His purposes in Christ Jesus, we should feel that He is right in all He does, — gloriously right, divinely right; and that our duty is, however much His action may militate against our feelings or our hopes, to say: "It is well; for God has done it." It may be that we have not toned our hearts to this Christian submission; and that our heavenly Father may see in us an unbelief, and a mistrust, which have excited His anger and renewed His indignation. Let us this day examine our hearts upon this point; and if guilty, let us bow before His footstool, and say in sincerity of soul: "Not my will, but Thine, O God, be done."

Have we not cherished in our hearts a feeling of bitterness and uncharitableness against those who have been God's human instruments in bringing upon us humiliation, shame, poverty, exile, the various evils to which we, as a people, have been subjected? Have we not deemed it right to be unforgiving? Have we not cherished in our hearts a desire for their being punished in their turn, by God or by man? And if so, can you suppose that God will permit His children — those who are the professed followers and imitators of His Son — to indulge such feelings, without inflicting further chastisement upon them? How did our blessed Saviour act, when there was heaped upon Him every shame and every injury which man could inflict? "Father, forgive them: for they know not what they do."[1] What was His teaching, persistently, and the teaching of His Apostles? "But I say unto you, Love your enemies, bless them that curse you, do good to them that hate you, and pray for them which despitefully use you and persecute you."[2] "For this is thankworthy, if a man for conscience toward God endure grief, suffering wrongfully. For what glory is it, if, when ye be buffeted for your faults, ye shall take it patiently? but if, when ye do well, and suffer for it, ye take it patiently, this is acceptable with God."[3] This is the Christian's example; and this is what God expects from us; and if He find it not, and care for us, will produce it in us, through chastisements. The more right we may think we have been, the more incumbent upon us it is, if we desire to be acceptable with God, to imitate these feelings of the Master and His Disciples. It is hard, I know, upon flesh and blood: but grace is stronger than these; and neither flesh and blood, nor the feelings of flesh and blood, can ever inherit the Kingdom of Heaven. It is for yourselves, my people, that I am pleading, — for your own Christian characters; for your own earthly peace and welfare; for your deliverance from the rod; for your eternal salvation. Conquer these feelings! Look above the instruments; and see a loving Father's face, — loving while He strikes, pitying while He bruises. Hear the words of the Lesson which we have read to-day: "But if ye be without chastisement,

[1] S. Luke xxiii. 34. [2] S. Matt. v. 44.
[3] 1 S. Pet. ii. 19, 20.

whereof all are partakers, then are ye bastards, and not sons."[1] Let this day's humiliation place you right before God, with purified hearts, and spirits filled with charity for all men: — Charity, that divinest gift, which is above even Faith and Hope.

Have we not rushed back, as a people, to the worship of our old idols, — to an adoration of pride, of haughtiness, of position, of worldly-mindedness? Has not our deep adversity intensified these feelings? Has not our keen poverty made us still more sensitive than we ever were? There are no idols which God struck at, in his late humiliation of us, more openly than at the qualities of the carnal heart: have we learned the lesson? Have we endeavored to overcome these sins — for they *are* sins in the eye of God; or have we not rather thought it our duty to cherish and cultivate them more carefully than before? I am afraid that many of us have said: "Men may despoil us of our property, of our homes, of our rights, of our privileges; but they shall not deprive us of our pride, or our associations, or our memories. We will make these our idols, and will cherish and worship these in our inmost hearts!" Is not God visiting us for these things? Remember His language of old to Edom: "Whereas Edom saith, We are impoverished, but we will return and build the desolate places; thus saith the LORD of hosts, They shall build, but I will throw down. . . . . And your eyes shall see, and ye shall say, The LORD will be magnified from the border of Israel."[2]

These are the main points in our conduct, for which, perhaps, God is still laying His heavy hand upon us. There are others which time requires to pass over; such as the inordinate desire for wealth, which still clings to us as a people: the keeping back from the Lord of His offerings and His tithes; the permitting His houses to lie in ashes,

[1] Heb. xii. 8.

[2] Mal. i. 4, 5.

while all other things are being reconstructed; the seeming necessity for every thing save the sending forth of the Gospel of Jesus Christ. All these things are crying into the ears of the Lord God of Sabaoth, and will be heard: and what you will not give, shall be *taken*, — taken through rains, and drought, and caterpillar, and fire; and every purse shall have holes in it, through which ill-gotten or ill-hoarded gains shall leak out. God cannot be mocked, and will not be mocked! He will have what is His; and if not given for His sake, it will be taken for your own sake.

And He will not deal with a Christian State as with the heathen. "Like as I pleaded with your fathers in the wilderness of the land of Egypt, so will I plead with you, saith the Lord God. And I will cause you to pass under the rod, and I will bring you into the bond of the covenant."[1] For His will and His commandments are not hidden from you, my beloved people, neither are they far off. His "great commandment" is, "to love the Lord thy God, to walk in His ways, and to keep His commandments, and His statutes, and His judgments:"[2] and "it is not in heaven, that thou shouldest say, Who shall go up for us to heaven, and bring it unto us, that we may hear it, and do it? Neither is it beyond the sea, that thou shouldest say, Who shall go over the sea for us, and bring it unto us, that we may hear it, and do it? But the word is very nigh unto thee, in thy mouth, and in thy heart, that thou mayest do it." That is your privilege as a Christian people, — that God's commandments are in your keeping, familiar to you as household words; and that you have no excuse of ignorance, or of darkness. You sin in the broad light, when you do sin: you sin in the face of knowledge, of conscience, of the Church, of the Holy Spirit: and

[1] Ezek. xx. 36, 37.

[2] Deut. xxx. 16.

therefore is it that God thinks it worth while to chasten you. For chastisement, and humiliation, and adversity, and trouble, are often God's most faithful servants; — sent to you in love and mercy, to call you to the marriage supper of the Lamb. Continued prosperity is much more a token of God's displeasure than severe adversity: for prosperity, unbroken and unchecked, leads to the accumulation of wealth, to luxury, to immorality, to a carelessness of virtue and religion; and at last, passing from private to public life, to corruption and destruction. It is better to be chastened, than to be let alone. It is better that your land should be smitten with blasting and mildew; that the palmer worm should destroy your gardens, and your vineyards, and your fig-trees, and your olive-trees; better that the pestilence should come among you; better that your young men should be slain with the sword: than that you should hear the awful words, "Ephraim is joined to idols: let him alone."[1] May we never, my beloved people, hear that dread edict, either as a state, or as individuals. Rather let us pray, that we may be always kept in God's eye and under God's discipline, and that He may guide us as a people in the path He desires us to tread. Humiliation is good for us when it comes upon us from God's wisdom and God's rod. It is evil, only when we bring it upon ourselves through a fear of man, or through our own foolishness, or through looking at consequences when we should be looking at duty. Fear God, and keep His commandments, and your path will shine brighter and brighter unto the perfect day.

NOVEMBER 22, 1866.

[1] Hosea iv. 17.

Forty-sixth Sermon.

Although the fig-tree shall not blossom, neither shall fruit be in the vines; the labour of the olive shall fail, and the fields shall yield no meat; the flock shall be cut off from the fold, and there shall be no herd in the stalls: yet I will rejoice in the LORD, *I will joy in the God of my salvation.* — HABAKKUK iii. 17, 18.

A WEEK ago we assembled ourselves together in this place, under the solemn bidding of our State Authorities, to humble ourselves under the chastening hand of the Almighty, and with supplications to implore His forgiveness and mercy. To-day are we met again for prayer, but under very different auspices. Then we were urged to fasting and humiliation, because our fields had yielded no meat, and our flock had been cut off from the fold. Now we are called upon to keep a holy day of thanksgiving and of praise because, as a Nation, there has been a plentiful harvest and an almost universal prosperity. Then we were summoned to weep as a State with those who were weeping; now we are required to rejoice, as a Nation, with those who are rejoicing: and both upon the same principle, of obeying those who have the rule over us, and submitting ourselves "to every ordinance of man for the Lord's sake."[1] And these positions seem, at the first glance, very antagonistic to one another, and very difficult to be reconciled; but they may be harmonized, as I trust I shall be able to show you, upon the very highest Christian principles. For it is a law which pervades all the works of God, of whatever

[1] 1 S. Peter ii. 13.

kind, that things which, under a contracted view, appear at variance with each other; under a broader and more comprehensive one, are seen in beautiful harmony, the one being the natural complement of the other. No two things are seemingly more opposed to each other, when separately looked at, than the dark storm cloud and the brilliant rainbow, — the one the frowning type of wrath, the other the covenanted symbol of promise: and yet when the one lies upon the bosom of the other, bathing the last mutterings of the receding tempest in its hues of glory, they exhibit the perfection of heavenly beauty and the assurance of divine peace. The one was darkness, the other was light: together they figure righteousness and peace kissing each other.

Christ our blessed Saviour came into the world, not only to redeem us by His blood, but to introduce into it a principle at utter variance with the selfishness of human nature. This principle He was first to teach, as the true spiritual meaning of the commandments given by God to His chosen people; and then to exhibit in His own Person, by His humiliation, sufferings, and death for His brethren after the flesh. The world before His coming had heard enough of law and judgment, of sin and punishment: but nothing of love and sympathy; save as it came, in flashes through the clouds, light out of darkness: the Patriarchs and Prophets and Kings of the old dispensation giving the world faint glimmerings of what they knew themselves only through inspiration. "But grace and truth came by Jesus Christ;"[1] — the grace of divine mercy, the truth of God's immeasurable love! For "in this was manifested the love of God toward us, because that God sent his only begotten Son into the world, that we might live through him."[2] He gave His most precious and priceless possession, not

[1] S. John i. 17. [2] 1 S. John iv. 9.

only to rescue fallen man, but to teach him, as I said just now, that most divine of all lessons, the lesson of sympathy. Before Christ, man was an individual, or a part of a family, or perchance of a tribe, or even of a Nation: but since His coming, man has been taught that he is truly bound in bonds of love and sympathy with the whole world. As we say in our Creed that we believe in the Holy Catholic Church, meaning the Universal Church, so did Christ come to teach us that we must be catholic in our feelings towards all men; — must no longer measure our relationship by the old limits of blood, or interest, or earthly union, but by the limits of God's Love and Christ's Sacrifice. This is the broader and more comprehensive view, which corrects the narrowness of selfishness, and which makes us, while we weep for ourselves, still rejoice with the world where it rejoices, even though its joy may not extend to us in person or in interest. The same Heavenly Father who sends to us want and sorrow, sends to others plenty and joy: and shall we not sympathize with the dealings of God? The Prophet tells us, in my text, what his feelings were, and what his actions; and he comes to us as one of the accredited Messengers of the Most High, speaking as he was moved by the Holy Ghost: "Although the fig-tree shall not blossom, neither shall fruit be in the vines; the labour of the olive shall fail, and the fields shall yield no meat; the flock shall be cut off from the fold, and there shall be no herd in the stalls: yet I will rejoice in the LORD, I will joy in the God of my salvation." Here is, first, faith in God; trust in His wisdom and judgments; reliance upon His goodness and loving kindness: and then, satisfaction in what He was doing; no envy because He was giving to others and withholding from him; no jealousy because his neighbors were prospering and he was in adversity or suffering; no murmuring, because His hand lay heavy upon him, while others were eating and drinking and making merry: but an acquiescence in the love and mercy of the God of his salvation. His God had given him the assurance of that, at least. Whatever was in the present, the future was at least safe. However he might lack comforts or even necessaries in this world, he was assured that "the kingdom of God is not meat and drink; but righteousness, and peace, and joy in the Holy Ghost."[1] And this is the first lesson of the day,—to "rejoice in the Lord."[2] The powers that be have called us to thanksgiving. We think that we have but little to give thanks for (God knows how much mistaken we are in that, as I shall show you presently), and that there is no room for rejoicing in earthly matters. Be it so. Grant the position, for the present. Let us, then, "rejoice in the LORD," let us "joy in the God of our salvation." It is not much to give one day to spiritual joy—to thanksgiving for such a God as we have, the God of our salvation!

> Salvation! Oh, the joyful sound,
> Glad tidings to our ears;
> A sovereign balm for every wound,
> A cordial for our fears.

If we cannot rejoice in earthly things, let us rejoice in heavenly things. Let us leave Man, and his policies, and his devices, and let us climb up, on the wings of faith and love, and sing before the Throne and Him that sitteth on the Throne our song of thanksgiving and of praise. And our song might well take this shape: "We thank Thee, Father of Heaven and of earth, that Thou hast sent into the world Thine only begotten and well beloved Son, to die for us and our salvation; and that Thou hast, in His Person, spread over us the banner of love. We thank Thee that Thou hast separated the Nation to which we belong

[1] Rom. xiv. 17. [2] Phil. iii. 1.

from those nations which are lying in darkness and the shadow of Death; that Thou hast placed us where the Gospel is preached; and that, though Thou hast given us the bread of adversity and the water of affliction, Thou hast not removed our teachers into a corner; but that our ears still hear a word behind us, saying, "This is the way, walk ye in it, when ye turn to the right hand, and when ye turn to the left."[1] "We praise Thee, we bless Thee, we worship Thee, we glorify Thee, we give thanks to Thee for Thy great glory, O Lord God, Heavenly King, God the Father Almighty." And should we not rejoice — whether we think of the living or of the dead, of the past or of the future — that we can raise such a note of thanksgiving; and, leaving the world behind and all in it that is not agreeable to our views or harmonious with our desires, can revel in the great truth that "the Lord God omnipotent reigneth?" "Rejoice in the Lord alway,"[2] is the injunction of the Apostle, and comes to us as a voice from Heaven, when we think we see nothing to rejoice in on earth. Prophets like Habakkuk teach us the same glorious truth as Apostles like S. Paul; and the Church impresses it upon us when, every Lord's day, no matter what may be its livery, whether clothed in the garment of praise or the spirit of heaviness, she commands us to lift up our voice and unitedly to sing, "Praise the LORD, O my soul; and all that is within me, praise his holy Name."

This is one lesson of our text: but there is another and a harder lesson to learn, and that is, giving thanks for the prosperity of others, in the spirit of Christian sympathy. To rejoice in the Lord, to joy in the God of our salvation, comes easily to a spiritual mind; it is its daily food; it is the song which swells up from the heart while it draws water from the wells of salvation. But to overcome self-

[1] Isaiah xxx. 20, 21.

[2] Rev. xix. 6.

ishness so far as to rejoice with those who do rejoice, with people whom we have never known nor seen, who are united to us simply by a bond of governmental union, who have been lately in arms against us, who have inflicted upon us much suffering, who are still keeping us under the saw and the harrow: this requires not only the understanding, but the feeling of Christ's spirit; not only the perception of what He came to teach, but the assimilation to ourselves of the divine principle of sympathy which He illustrated in His Sacrifice and Death. And this is the mission of the Church: to produce, in those who name the Name of the Lord Jesus Christ and who call Him Lord and Master, this wide-spread charity; this love which suffereth long and is kind; which envieth not; which beareth all things, believeth all things, hopeth all things, endureth all things. The world utterly rejects it; but the Church cannot, so long as she breathes the Spirit of her Lord, and holds Him up for worship and imitation. He made no distinctions in His love; His sympathy was wide as the Universe. He died for all, and prayed, even when suffering cruel death at their hands, for their forgiveness, — the forgiveness of those very ones who were taunting and mocking and crucifying Him. And think ye that He did not mean the disciple to be as his Master? Surely He did: for, in that moment when He ceased giving His disciples His own form of prayer — our "Lord's prayer" — in which occurs the petition, "Forgive us our trespasses, As we forgive those who trespass against us," He returns to the subject, and selects that one alone of all the petitions to comment upon and enforce, saying, "For if ye forgive men their trespasses, your heavenly Father will also forgive you: but if ye forgive not men their trespasses, neither will your Father forgive your trespasses."[1] That certainly is plain

[1] S. Matt. vi. 14, 15.

enough; and I would ask you, Who has more trespasses to forgive than your Heavenly Father? Who has sins ascending to Him day and night more unceasingly from you, — from each one of you, from every one of you, — than your Lord and Master? While man sins against you once, you sin against God a hundred times. While man ruffles your temper or your peace of mind now and then, you are exciting His indignation, and arousing His wrath, unceasingly; and nothing but the Blood of Christ keeps that wrath from bursting forth against you. You must forgive, if you hope to be forgiven. There is no alternative: and if that true spirit of charity is in you, and with you, then can you keep your thanksgiving and your rejoicing, if not for yourselves, at least for your fellow-creatures. Christ said to His disciples: "Ye shall weep and lament, but the world shall rejoice;"[1] and therein was displayed the true genuine *status* of the Christian. He may be called upon to weep and lament; but he must so teach and so act as to make the world rejoice, and to rejoice with it himself, through his tears. "This is an hard saying; who can hear it?"[2] — but it is a true saying, and the only one which can ever leaven the world with love and peace.

It is only this sympathy, this Christian sympathy, of weeping with those who weep, and rejoicing with those who rejoice, which can meet the difficulties of our position. We are in a very painful position. Our hearts are sore with our troubles; our cheeks are yet wet with the tears of our mourning; our brows are wrinkled with care and anxiety; our feelings are daily harassed with the sufferings of those we love. Under these circumstances, we are called upon to give thanks and to rejoice, because, as a Nation, considering it as a whole, there is plenty and prosperity. What chord is there in the human heart that can vibrate

[1] S. John xvi. 20. [2] *Ibid.* vi. 60.

to such an appeal? The chord of Christian sympathy, and none other: that chord upon which the Spirit of Christ alone can play, and bring forth music. God has given us the principle, in His Divine love. Christ has commanded us to exercise it, and put it in practice. The Holy Spirit comes down upon the heart, and softens it, and bedews it with its own dove-like sweetness. And thus all the Persons of the adorable Trinity are combining to produce in us that state of feeling which belongs to the children of God. For "I say unto you," were the solemn words of Christ, "Love your enemies, bless them that curse you, do good to them that hate you, and pray for them which despitefully use you, and persecute you; that ye may be the children of your Father which is in heaven: for he maketh his sun to rise on the evil and on the good, and sendeth rain on the just and on the unjust. For if ye love them which love you, what reward have ye? do not even the publicans the same? And if ye salute your brethren only, what do ye more than others? do not even the publicans so? Be ye therefore perfect, even as your Father which is in heaven is perfect."[1] A lofty standard: a standard to which we may never attain, but nevertheless the standard to which we should be forever aspiring. It will not do to say: "It is unattainable; it is beyond flesh and blood; it was not meant for us; it is unnatural!" These propositions may all be true in themselves; and yet should have no weight in a Christian heart, or with a Christian spirit. We are making no appeal to flesh and blood, — no exhortation to the powers of nature. Our expectations of your improvement do not come from them. "I can do all things," said S. Paul, not through flesh and blood, not through the powers of nature, not through any strength of his own, but "through Christ which strengtheneth me."[2] That is his source of

[1] S. Matthew v. 44–48.

[2] Phil. iv. 13.

all Christian graces, and especially of this grace of love. He did not say, "I cannot be charitable; I cannot be forgiving; I cannot feel sympathy with so corrupt a mass of humanity as the world," and then rest upon his lees: but he turned to Christ, and strove in Him, faithfully, earnestly, prayerfully, to attain unto perfection,—the perfection of sympathy; for love is the fulfilling of the whole law.

But, my beloved people, you are mistaken when you say that you have nothing for which to be thankful in a national point of view. God is not to be looked at simply in the politics of a nation. He is to be considered as He rules Nature, as He restrains the actions of men, as He governs the Church, as He puts the bit in the mouth of the wicked and turns them about as it pleases Him. And surely we can be thankful that, while pestilence has touched us, it has not raged in its fury; that while want is felt, it has not reached the confines of famine; that while our industry has been, in a measure, blighted, there is still enough left to give us hope for the future. Turn to the records of pestilence and famine which are now coming to us from unhappy India,[1] and learn what we have escaped. We may again find cause of thanksgiving in that God's Spirit has soothed and calmed the spirits of many who were once bitter against us; and that friends have been raised up for us in high places, who have stood, and are still standing, as a tower of strength between us and those who would inflict upon us further evil. And then, surely, we who sit here should be unfeignedly thankful that the Spirit of God has been poured out upon His Church, and that we are seen to-day once more at unity over all this broad land, advancing with serried ranks against the enemies of Christ, "fair as the moon, clear as the sun, and terrible as an army with banners;"[2] putting the world under our feet,

[1] The Orissa famine of 1866.

[2] Solomon's Song vi. 10.

and loving the Kingdom of Christ more than the kingdoms of this world. And finally, we may rejoice that we are a part of a Christian Nation; and that prayer is forever ascending to God, from North and South and East and West, that He would guide us according to His wisdom, and as it seems best to Him; and that those prayers will be answered by Him in His all-wise Providence. There are good people everywhere, who are praying, "Thy will be done on earth, as it is in Heaven:" which is, at last, leaving things to His disposal, and placing them where they will most rightfully be ordered. All this is cause for thanks: and well may we unite therefore in giving thanks!

Let us never, my beloved people, turn away from giving thanks to God. His blessed Word says: "In every thing give thanks;"[1] in the darkness, as well as in the light; when the tear is trickling down the cheek, as well as when gladness rules the hour. We know very little, in this world, of the ways of God. He dwelleth often in the thick darkness. He plants His footsteps in the sea. We cannot follow Him: we must only trust in Him, and thank Him for such good as He clearly gives us. And that good is always more than we deserve; for it is visited upon us in a thousand ways that we do not notice. Every breath of air which fans our faces and brings health upon its wings; every movement of our bodies which is made without pain; every feeling and affection of the heart which gives us satisfaction and joy; every comfort of life which is permitted us: comes from His hand. "Do not err, my beloved brethren. Every good gift and every perfect gift is from above, and cometh down from the Father of lights, with whom is no variableness, neither shadow of turning."[2] We cannot pass God by, if we have true spiritual

[1] 1 Thess. v. 18.

[2] S. James i. 16, 17.

sensibility. He is with us, and around us, at every moment of our lives, blessing us in Nature, in Society, in our homes, and in our hearts. Therefore, in all things, let us give thanks!

NOVEMBER 29, 1866.

Forty-seventh Sermon.

And when these things begin to come to pass, then look up, and lift up your heads; for your redemption draweth nigh. — S. Luke xxi. 28.

THERE have been periods in the history of the Church of Christ upon earth which have well deserved the title of *Ages of Faith*, — periods in which the disciples of Christ have carried out in their daily practice the hardest sayings and the severest injunctions of their Master, — when they have verified the striking language of S. Paul, that "neither death, nor life, nor angels, nor principalities, nor powers, nor things present, nor things to come, nor height, nor depth, nor any other creature," were able to separate them from the love of God, which was in Christ Jesus their Lord. It has been with these giants in Faith as it has been with the giants of science and of literature. They have come in groups, come to meet great occasions or great opportunities, being raised up and filled with the Spirit of God to spread the Church through the blood of martyrdom, or to beat down heresy through valiant conflict and patient suffering for the Truth's sake, or to make utterance before the unbelieving nations of the deep things of God, — those things which the natural heart despises and rejects. These have been God's chosen witnesses, men who learned at the foot of the Cross to understand the value of the soul, and the sublime mystery of redemption, and the awfulness of Eternity; and to gauge all earthly things at their real price. The future was their point of observation, and not the present. The coming of Christ was their hope and consolation, not the coming of any thing worldly. Heaven and its promised glories filled up their hearts, and not man and his poor attempts at show and happiness. All the events of the world; all the circumstances which surrounded themselves; all the signs in nature, and all the confusion of the civil state: affected them only as so many portents which were to be interpreted in their relations to Christ's work upon earth. They looked above man, ever, to the Finger of God. They pierced through the darkness and the clouds which obscured this lower world, and saw the fire that was infolding itself, and the brightness that was round about it: and just when the hearts of the ungodly and the unfaithful were failing them for fear, they lifted up their heads and rejoiced in the tokens which announced the presence and the dealings of God. It was only when the world was left to itself, that they trembled. It was only when God seemed to be hiding Himself and giving up the nations to their own ways, that they were afraid.

These Ages of Faith, as I said just now, lie scattered all along the Church's path of life; and it was while creating the greatest of them that our Saviour uttered the words which I have selected for my text. His disciples were yet immature Christians; had most of them but lately entered the school of Faith; had none of them as yet received the power of the Holy Ghost; were more or less tinctured with the national error of supposing Him, their Messiah, to be coming soon to set up the reign of righteousness and of peace upon earth. They had no conception, in that early period of Christ's manifestation, of the long ages through which His Church was to be militant; of the many kingdoms which must rise and fall ere the Kingdom of Christ should come; of the strife and warfare and persecution and confusion which must reign over the world, ere their redemption should be accomplished. All this they had to learn: for if they knew it not, their faith might be shaken, and their love wax cold. And while schooling these early fruits of His divine Ministry, He has instructed us through them; and caused the lesson, which their necessities required, to reach even to us, and to comfort us in the midst of the changes and calamities which are forever disturbing the Church and the world.

It is the manner of the Scripture to convey its comfort or its warnings through words that have a double application, first to the times in which they were uttered, and then to any events in the future which might correspond with those in circumstance and import. And it is this method of teaching which makes the Bible a book for all times, an expanding voice, — if I may use the expression, — speaking to men of every age and suiting itself to the necessities of every period. What was comfort to the early Christians, becomes comfort for us. What was explanation to them, is explanation for us. And expressions which had reference in their delivery only to matters that were local or temporary, become, through this presence of an inspiring Spirit, applicable to events of a more general and exalted nature, reaching from earth to Heaven, and embracing within their grand development events as remote as the ending of the whole Christian economy.

Our text is a passage from one of these remarkable discourses, — partly a word of comfort, and partly a word of prophecy. It was spoken by our Lord when preparing His disciples for the wonders and tribulations which should accompany the destruction of Jerusalem: and it hurries on, in the fullness of its comprehensiveness (for with the Lord a thousand years are as one day) until it includes in its warnings and exhortations all Christians, even to the moment when He Himself shall come a second time in the clouds of Heaven to judge the world. And His lesson to both them and us is, that Christians have nothing to fear even in the worst times; nay, that their moment of exultation and of glory shall be when others are trembling with fear, — when there is "distress of nations with perplexity."

If we examine our text in connection with the whole discourse of our Saviour, it will sound strangely in the ears of unbelief, and even in the ears of many who profess to be the followers of our Lord. These last will find it almost as hard a saying as those who disbelieve the Gospel, and will confess that they have not reached up to that height of faith which will make them exult amid such scenes of awful terror. For Christ bids them, "when these things begin to come to pass, then look up and lift up your heads." What things? The world at peace around them, persecution having ceased, and humiliation and shame having taken their flight? What things? Christianity victorious, and seated in the pride of power? What things? Their Lord, the conquering hero they had expected, beginning to reign upon Earth? None of these: for looking up and lifting up their heads at such things would not have constituted them a peculiar people, nor made them giants in faith. But they were commanded to look up and lift up their heads, just when every one else was trembling with fear, and calling upon the rocks and the mountains to fall upon them and hide them from the wrath of the Lamb: "And there shall be signs in the sun, and in the moon, and in the stars; and upon the earth distress of nations, with perplexity; the sea and the waves roaring; men's hearts failing them for fear, and for looking after those things which are coming on the earth: for the powers of heaven shall be shaken. And then shall they see the Son of man coming in a cloud with power and great glory. And when these things begin to come to pass, then look up, and lift up your heads; for your redemption draweth nigh." What a religion, that can give comfort amid such convulsions of nature and such lamentations of man! What Faith, that can make a human creature face such omens of destruction, and exult amid the wreck of the heavens and the earth!

And yet if we really only were what we profess to be, believers in Christ and in His work, why should we be moved at any thing, save the victory of Satan? If he could once again turn back the tide of battle which Christ rolled upon him when He came from Bozrah in garments dyed with blood, travelling in the greatness of His strength, a Christian might be shaken to the depth of his soul: but nothing else can harm him! All things else are but links in that chain of events which stretches from the Cross of Christ to His second coming in glory; — are but onward movements in that redemption of our race which, beginning in the love of God, shall end in the exulting triumph of Christ, when death and hell shall be cast into the lake of fire. What are signs in the sun, and in the moon, and in the stars, to a Christian when his Lord has told him that they are hung out in the heavens as tokens of His love to him, of His divine work in his behalf? They are like the signal-fires which were flashed in ancient days from tower to tower, and from mountain to mountain, heralding on wings of light the advent of some mighty conqueror, carrying joy to the hearts of all his faithful followers, and striking terror only into those who had proved traitors to his cause. It is but right that the morning stars, which sang together when the Almighty laid the corner-stone of the Earth and planted its everlasting foundations, should once more signal forth their joy at its re-creation in righteousness. It is but fitting that the sun, which was shrouded in darkness when the Son of Man was crucified, should blaze with redoubled glory when He comes in the Majesty of His Godhead. And what, to the Christian, is "distress of nations with perplexity;" is "men's hearts failing them for fear:" when he remembers that those nations have been the stern opponents of Christ's Kingdom; those men, the scoffers who have said unto God in the pride of their hearts, "Depart from us; for we desire not the knowledge of thy ways?" Is not their humiliation his glory? Is not their terror — the only time, perchance, that they have truly feared God — his hope! What has he been struggling for, all his days? Upon what have his feeble yet earnest efforts been concentrated? The consummation of the work of the Lord, — the in-bringing of that glorious Conqueror, when every eye shall see Him, and every knee shall bow before Him, and the shout of glory shall ascend, of blessing, and honor, and glory, and power, unto Him who hath redeemed us out of every nation and kindred and people, and hath made us to be kings and priests unto God! And shall he be afraid of the accompaniments of this his crowning desire and prayer? Strangely inconsistent should he be, to tremble when he should look up with joy and hope, — to be of a fearful heart when his Lord has commanded him to lift up his eyes and see the glory of His Cross!

It may seem strange that the reason given in my text for the exultation of Christ's followers in that day should be "because their redemption draweth nigh." And those who have not well considered the economy of Grace may ask: "Was not our redemption procured when our Saviour died upon the Cross and rose again for our justification? Have not all those who have died in faith gone to the land of peace and of rest? Are not we, who still live, rejoicing in the hope of our deliverance from sin and death and hell?" I would not, my beloved hearers, mar a single joy, or blight a single hope, in your Christian life; but I must nevertheless tell you that your redemption, and the redemption of those who have gone before you, will not be consummate until the second coming of our Lord. "For we know," says the Apostle S. Paul to the Romans, "that the whole creation groaneth and travaileth in pain together until now. And not only they, but ourselves also, which have the first fruits of the Spirit, even we ourselves groan within ourselves, waiting for the adoption, to wit, the redemption of our body."[1] 'T is true that we can never again, save by our own consent, be made the servants of sin and the captives of Satan: for Christ has conquered through His blood. 'T is true that all who have died in faith are living in an assured hope of everlasting glory. 'T is true that we can raise the cry of victory even here upon earth, and ask, "Who is he that condemneth? It is Christ that died, yea rather, that is risen again, who is even at the right hand of God, who also maketh intercession for us." 'T is true that we can face our fiercest enemies, and triumphantly challenge death and the grave. But nevertheless, "the last enemy that shall be destroyed is death," and he holds and will hold all bodies in his grasp, until the trump of the archangel and the voice of God shall summon all the bodies of all the dead from earth and sea, and the faithful shall be caught up to meet their Lord in glory. This will be our redemption. This was the redemption which drew nigh, when these signs in sun and moon and stars, and this distress of nations, burst upon the watching eyes of Faith. We must not mingle confusedly the steps of our redemption. We must watch upon the Lord, and rejoice that He is bringing us nearer every

[1] Rom. viii. 22.

day to the period when He shall set His Son upon His holy hill of Zion.

And this is the comfort which is offered to us, my fellow-Christians, when we see signs in the heavens and signs in the earth, when distress of nations with perplexity is visible in the world, when men's hearts are failing them for fear. They are tokens that God's work is speeding to its consummation, that the curtain is rolling up which is to introduce another act in the drama of the world's spiritual history. Religion, Christianity, are too much wrapped up in all the questions now agitating the world, to be left out of our calculations in weighing events and anticipating consequences. And although I am not silly enough to suppose that such events are indicative of the immediate coming of our Lord to His final Judgment, still they are enough to render Christians thoughtful and watchful; and to comfort them, when trouble may come upon them in the future, with the belief that their redemption draweth nigh.

I trust, my beloved people, that there are many of you who are longing for that redemption, — who, weary of sin and sorrow, are looking, with anxious hearts, for their rest. How mournful it is to see immortal creatures weaving forever new webs of hope, and fastening them to objects which are actually crumbling while they rest upon them. What is this world, with all its noise and tumult, with all its seeming importance and majesty, but a stage upon which God is moving its actors to and fro according to the purpose of His will, and dismissing them at His pleasure when their parts have been played out? And yet most of them think only of themselves, and forget Him who is overruling every thing, and who has said: "I will overturn, overturn, overturn, until He cometh whose right it is." But there are some, I know, who see and acknowledge an overruling Providence; who can perceive an order in the midst of apparent confusion; who can trace a divine plan through all the complications of human affairs. To such there can be no fear. In the hearts of these children of God there can be no distress. They can see God in the whirlwind, and in the storm; and they can trust to Him who is forever working to bring in their redemption. Man is looking only at man. God is looking at sin, and death, and hell, and him who has the power of death. Man is contending for power, for territory, for rights, for liberty: God is overruling all that, to give His Son dominion over all, and to bring in that liberty wherewith Christ hath made us free. When the nations are distressed and perplexed, when men's hearts are failing them for fear, when the sea and the waves are roaring: then may God's children look up and lift up their heads, for they may rest assured that their redemption draweth nigh,— that their salvation is nearer than when they believed.

Forty-eighth Sermon.

In thy light shall we see light. — PSALM XXXVI. 9.

THE peculiar and unceasing boast of the present time is, that it is an age of light. All our public declaimers, whether they take for their platform the rostrum, the lecture-room, the legislative hall, or the pulpit, invariably strike the same key-note, and congratulate their audiences upon the wonderful advancement of the world in knowledge, in intelligence, and in right reason. It is a thing taken for granted; about which there can be no dispute; which needs only to be enunciated, to be assented to: and if any question should arise upon the subject, that question would have no reference to the matter of fact, but only to some special difference about the kind of light which has streamed in most plenteously, or has weighed most in the scale of interest or importance. In proof of its great improvement in knowledge, one is pointed to the modern discoveries in physical science; to the marvellous achievements wrought through the application of steam; to the yet more wonderful applications of electro-magnetism; to the labor-saving machines which are reducing man to a mere regulator; to the exquisite beauty and finish of the arts; but above all to the universal comfort which has spread itself through society. In order to demonstrate this advancement in intelligence, its school-systems, its lyceums, its lecture rooms, its teeming press, its ever increasing libraries, its general diffusion among the masses of truths and secrets and privileges which used to be confined exclusively and mysteriously to the favored few, are triumphantly advanced as incontrovertible evidence. The growth of right reason is marked, in the public estimation, by the superiority of its arrangements in Government; by its inventions in Religion; by its assertion of rights which have been long kept under the foot of political or ecclesiastical or domestic tyranny; by its universal outcry against every thing old and established. To controvert these pretensions, is to place yourself out of the pale of acknowledged truth, and to be assuming a position contrary to the conclusions of the advancing world and the glorious spirit of the age. To deny that all this stuff is light, seems, to the rushing world, like the denial of a first truth; like the contradiction of something obvious to the very senses of mankind. And so the world dashes on, flattering itself with its progression, exulting in the brightness which encircles its onward career, and promising itself an approaching perfectibility which is to fulfill the predictions of Poets, Philosophers, and Statesmen.

How startling, or else how ridiculous, it must sound to such a world, to be told that it is lying in darkness; that so far as all true light is concerned, these references and illustrations are of no account, because they do not touch the question which is of most interest to an immortal creature, the question of moral and religious advancement. That there is a vast and daily progression in physical knowledge; that there is an unceasing application of the principles of science to the comfort of life; that there is a vast multiplication of the apparatus of literature and of the means of intelligence; that the intellect is active and busy beyond all precedent; I will not deny: but no more can I admit that these things necessarily increase man's knowledge of God, and of that true Light of which He is the Fountain and eternal Parent. "That which hath been is now; and that which is to be hath already been,"[1] saith the wise man. And, while the investigations of modern travellers and antiquarians are satisfying us that we know very little of luxury which the ancients knew not, and possess very little of the security of life and property which they possessed not, and are very little advanced beyond them (if we be advanced at all) in literature and the arts, while yet they lay imbruted in foul idolatry and in the blackness of darkness upon religious topics: I cannot acknowledge that the improvement in our day, in these respects, necessarily involves a like improvement in matters relating to the heart and to the spirit. The Christian, and above all the Christian Minister, cannot be too cautious about confounding progress in physical science and in social life, with progress in morals and religion. They do not always go together; and illustrations innumerable, did time permit their introduction, might be furnished from the events of the current time, to satisfy any reasonable man of this truth. The statistics of crime have established the fact beyond all controversy, that a diffusion of education, as it is called,—where that education was merely intellectual, in which there was not a decided admixture of religious instruction,—had invariably produced an increase of villainy and corruption. And with reason; for man's nature being strongly inclined to evil, mere intellectual culture only sharpens corrupt faculties, and furnishes them with means and appliances of wickedness. And these statistical results, brought out by individuals having no alliance with religion, coincide strictly with the *a priori* reasonings of true philosophy; and are just such as a Christian would have anticipated, with no other basis for his foresight than the simple truth of man's fall and consequent corruption, as revealed by the Holy Scriptures. No, my hearers, the world may reach, and

[1] Ecclesiastes iii. 15.

probably will reach, a yet higher position in physical power and physical comfort; will attain still loftier flights in intellectual eminence; will improve still more in social organization: while yet it shall fulfill what S. Paul said of the Romans in their Augustan age of luxury and literature: "Because that when they knew God, they glorified him not as God, neither were thankful; but became vain in their imaginations, and their foolish heart was darkened. Professing themselves to be wise, they became fools, and changed the glory of the uncorruptible God into an image made like to corruptible man, and to birds, and four-footed beasts, and creeping things;"[1] or what the same Apostle said, with equal truth, of the refined Ephesians: "having no hope, and without God in the world."[2] All these manifestations of physical and intellectual progression do not in the least degree forbid my saying that the world, even in its active and progressive advancement physically and intellectually, is lying in darkness.

But you may ask: "How can such a position be reconciled with the fact of a Christian Revelation, with the apparatus of Religion staring us in the face at every turn? How can the world be lying in darkness, when the Sun of Righteousness has arisen upon it with healing in His wings; — when He who called Himself 'The Light of the world,' has scattered the beams of truth over the groaning and travailing creation?" Ah! my hearers, as well might you ask how the inmates of an asylum for the blind can be said to be lying in darkness, when the sun of Nature has arisen with brightness in his train, and has diffused the glory of his effulgence over earth and air and ocean. What is all the radiance of the heavens, — what the rainbow hues which are painted with the pencil of the Almighty in rich luxuriance upon the outspread creation, — to beings defec-

[1] Rom. i. 21–23. [2] Eph. ii. 12.

tive and deprived of the organ of perception? Light is all around them, and beings like themselves are rejoicing in that light: but to them, it is as though it were not. They hear of it with the hearing of the ear, and perchance give it the credence of the understanding: but they can form no conception of it. And as it is with them, so is it, I grieve to say, with by far the larger proportion of those who are living in the Light of the Gospel, and under the very shadow of Christian institutions. The glorious Light of the Gospel of Jesus Christ is irradiating the world; is blessing with its preciousness the children of God; is clothing with the anticipated robes of heavenly glory those who have been washed in the Blood of the Lamb: while, to these blinded multitudes, — blinded by the God of this world, — there is neither Light, nor preciousness, nor beauty in the revelation of the Almighty. "Eyes have they, but they see not."[1]

It is in this sense, my beloved hearers, that I am bound to preach the broad distinction which there is between that wisdom which is earthly and sensual, and that wisdom which cometh from above; between a world pressing forward in the race of physical advancement, and that same world lying in religious darkness: and to labor to impress upon you the truth of our text, addressed by the Psalmist to the Lord God of Israel: "In thy light shall we see light." This distinction is beautifully drawn in the twenty-eighth chapter of Job, where this very train of thought seems to have been passing nearly four thousand years ago through the mind of the man of Uz: "Surely," writes he, "there is a vein for the silver, and a place for gold where they fine it. Iron is taken out of the earth, and brass is molten out of the stone. . . . As for the earth, out of it cometh bread: and under it is turned up as it were fire.

[1] Psalm cxxxv. 16.

The stones of it are the place of sapphires, and it hath dust of gold."[1] This, you perceive, is a knowledge of natural things; is the development of physical science as known in his time: but the inspiration which lighted upon him would not permit him to stop there, — to confound this with true wisdom and religious light. "But where," goes he on to ask, "shall wisdom be found? and where is the place of understanding? Man knoweth not the price thereof; neither is it found in the land of the living. The depth saith, It is not in me: and the sea saith, It is not with me. It cannot be gotten for gold, neither shall silver be weighed for the price thereof. . . . Whence then cometh wisdom? and where is the place of understanding? Seeing it is hid from the eyes of all living, and kept close from the fowls of the air. Destruction and death say, We have heard the fame thereof with our ears. God understandeth the way thereof, and he knoweth the place thereof. . . . And unto man he said, Behold, the fear of the Lord, that is wisdom; and to depart from evil is understanding."[2] He knew well that natural knowledge was one thing, and that religious knowledge was quite another thing; and his rich and magnificent summary concluded at the same point with that of David in our text: "The fear of the Lord, that is wisdom." "In thy light shall we see light."

Supposing now, for a moment, that I have persuaded you to receive this distinction, and to acknowledge that there is a wide difference between the onward march of the world in intelligence and knowledge, and the progress of that same world in religious light: it will still seem incredible to you, that you can be living in the midst of such a system as Christianity, supporting its institutions, partaking of its blessings, and yet not be a recipient in any

[1] Verses 1, 2, 5, 6. [2] Job xxviii. 12–15, 20–23, 28.

degree of the Light which is its distinctive glory. "I believe," you may say, "upon evidence, the truth of the Christian religion, and its divinity; I have been instructed in its truths from childhood; I read my Bible, and admire its moral teachings and its profound wisdom; I practise, as fairly as I can, the duties which it inculcates: and am I to be told that I am lying in darkness, and have no religious light?" You may have more my hearer, than I am aware of. I stand not here to judge you: I rather desire that you should judge yourself. In answer to your indignant question I have only to say, as one who desires you to be a partaker of that Divine Light, that you may have proceeded quite as far as you represent yourself to have done, and yet be in darkness about all that relates to spiritual things. For, as to your believing in the Revelation of God as a matter of fact, S. James tells us that "the devils also believe, and tremble."[1] And as to the reading of your Bible, there were those in the Apostles' days who read them, and yet wrested them to their own destruction.[2] And as to your performance of the moral duties of the Bible, you can read there of a young man who was so good that when our Saviour saw him He loved him; who could answer to a very strict catechism upon these points: and yet to whom He was compelled to say, "One thing thou lackest."[3] And as to your baptism and youthful instruction in these things, we have S. Peter saying to Simon Magus, whom Philip had baptized upon a profession of faith, and who had seen the wonderful works of the Lord: "Thy heart is not right in the sight of God. . . . For I perceive that thou art in the gall of bitterness, and in the bond of iniquity."[4] A remembrance of these Scriptural examples forces me to say, that you may have proceeded

[1] S. James ii. 19.
[2] 2 S. Pet. iii. 16.
[3] S. Mark x. 21.
[4] Acts viii. 21, 23.

all this length, and yet may not be in the Light. But mark! I say "may not be;" — I say that it does not follow as a matter of course, that such religious exercises as you plead must necessarily determine that you are in the Light. That must depend upon other tests drawn from the Bible itself, which must at last settle all the questions relating to our spiritual life.

The Bible proceeds throughout upon the position that the Godhead has been revealed to man only in and through Jesus Christ. "No man hath seen God at any time," saith S. John; "the only-begotten Son, which is in the bosom of the Father, he hath declared him."[1] And S. Paul speaks of Him as "dwelling in the light which no man can approach unto; whom no man hath seen, nor can see."[2] So that when the Lord Jesus Christ proclaimed Himself as the "Light of the world," He developed the true meaning of the Psalmist: "In thy Light shall we see light." Just as in Nature, we see not light by looking into the dazzling brightness of the orb of day, but rather gather darkness: so is it ordered that we shall not drink in religious light directly from the glorious Fountain of Light before whom Cherubim and Seraphim veil their faces, lest we be overpowered by its effulgence and perish: "for there shall no man," saith Jehovah, "see me, and live."[3] But when that light of Nature is reflected from the myriad points on which its rays impinge, and comes to us a liquid molten flood of glory, mellowed and softened to our senses, how perfectly in that light do we see light! What, in itself, when we dared to raise to it our presumptuous eye, was too dazzling for our weakness, is now, in its diffusion, mild, beneficent, beautiful, precious above all price. What, in itself, destroyed our vision, now fills it with perfect satisfaction and unalloyed delight. And just so is it, when we turn

[1] S. John i. 18. [2] 1 Tim. vi. 16. [3] Exodus xxxiii. 20.

from the ineffable, invisible and unapproachable Godhead, to "God manifest in the flesh,"[1] — to Him who took upon Him our weaknesses and carried our sorrows, who calls Himself our Brother, and gathers about Him all the tenderest affections of our nature. O how mild, how beneficent, how precious does the Divinity shine forth in Him! How quickly do we learn from Him, and in Him, and through Him, the character and the attributes and the purposes of that Godhead which we cannot otherwise approach! What words of wisdom flow from His lips! He speaks as never man spake. What floods of light are cast upon life and immortality! How all the mysteries of our being open under His Divine teachings, leaving nothing mysterious, save the great mystery of godliness itself! How all the wants of our nature are satisfied: wants manifested by man in the thousand devices he has adopted to bring the Godhead down to earth, and put into words by Job when he said: "O that I knew where I might find him! that I might come even to his seat! O that one might plead for a man with God, as a man pleadeth for his neighbor!"[2] Truly can we say that the Psalmist uttered the truth of prophecy when he said: "In thy light shall we see light;" and that the Nicene Fathers expressed most happily the idea of Scripture, when, in the Creed which is called after their Council, they designated our blessed Lord as "Light of Light."

My answer, then, to your question of mingled wonder and indignation, will depend, as I said just now, upon your capability of meeting the tests of Scripture which are placed by inspiration right across your pathway. In that sublime introduction to his Gospel, in which S. John opens so magnificently the essential Divinity of our Lord, "In the beginning was the Word, and the Word was with God,

[1] 1 Tim. iii. 16. [2] Job xxiii. 3, and xvi. 21.

and the Word was God:"[1] he says, "In him was life; and the life was the light of men. And the light shineth in darkness; and the darkness comprehended it not."[2] Here is your first test. Do you comprehend the light which has been brought in through Jesus Christ, to wit, His wisdom, His righteousness, His sanctification, His redemption? Do you perceive and confess the Cross of Christ to be the power of God, and the wisdom of God, unto salvation? All light short of this is no Light at all. Salvation is what Christ came to procure. Whatever may be the collateral blessings of Christianity — and they are many — this is its absorbing purpose. And though you understand all mysteries, and all knowledge, if you understand not this, you are yet in darkness. The promise was: "Howbeit, when he, the Spirit of truth, is come, he will guide you into all truth. . . . He shall glorify me: for he shall receive of mine, and shall show it unto you."[3] Hath this Spirit of Truth dealt with you, my hearer? Hath this perception of Light been given you, so that you can say, "One thing I know, that, whereas I was blind, now I see"?[4] If it has not, then are you still in darkness, although encompassed with light; and you have yet to beseech God to enable you to say: "In thy Light do I see Light."

Let me apply another test. S. John tells us very plainly concerning the Son of God: "He that believeth on him is not condemned: but he that believeth not is condemned already, because he hath not believed in the name of the only-begotten Son of God. And this is the condemnation, that light is come into the world, and men loved darkness rather than light, because their deeds were evil."[5] Here, again, belief in Jesus Christ is made salvation, and unbelief condemnation. Now apply this test to yourself, my

[1] S. John i. 1, 2.
[2] *Ibid.* 4, 5.
[3] *Ibid.* xvi. 13, 14.
[4] *Ibid.* ix. 25.
[5] *Ibid.* iii. 18, 19.

hearer, and do it honestly: apply it in no superficial way, in no such way as shall permit you to deceive yourself. Frame not out of your imagination a system which you may choose to call Christianity, and then, comparing that with your feelings, tell me that you have no unbelief in Christianity, no dislike of the Light of Truth, no love for darkness! That will not do. David did not say, "In *our* Light shall we see light." He appealed to a Holy God, who searcheth the heart, and said: "In *thy* Light shall we see light;" and therefore, when you would understand your spiritual condition, you must place your feelings under the blaze of that Revelation, which our Lord, Light of Light, has given us for our instruction. A man cannot serve two masters, for he will certainly love the one and hate the other: and no more can you dwell in two such states, at once, as Light and Darkness. The one will extinguish the other. And you will find, when you are forced to make the choice between Light and Darkness, that, unless enlightened by the Spirit of God, you will confess that, if this be Light, you prefer darkness, and embrace condemnation.

Taking these two tests as our rule of judgment, let me ask you, of what avail will progression in physical science, will improvements in the comforts of social life, will advancements in the arts and refinements of civilization be to you, in removing your darkness, and giving you Light? What perception can they give you of spiritual life? "For what man," says the Apostle, "knoweth the things of a man, save the spirit of man which is in him? even so the things of God knoweth no man, but the Spirit of God."[1] The more you strive to find out God through intellectual processes, the more will you have to acknowledge, if you are really in earnest in your search: "Such knowl-

[1] 1 Cor. ii. 11.

edge is too wonderful for me; it is high, I cannot attain unto it."[1] Your progress will be like that of a child, who thinks that he could touch the heavens by climbing to the summit of some lofty mountain. He would find to his dismay, could he compass his desire, that the higher he climbed the further would the skies seem to withdraw themselves from him, and leave him in a cold, thin atmosphere, where there would be no comfort, no ease, no peace, and where he might find destruction. You, my hearer, may pile reason upon reason, and argument upon argument, but you will not be able to compass your vain desire. God will be as far away from you when you shall have done all this, as He was when you began your toilsome search; and your intellectual efforts will place you every moment in a more comfortless and hopeless position. Think you that you are the first who has tried this experiment? We have the experience of one who tried it near four thousand years ago, and his record is: "Canst thou by searching find out God? . . . . It is as high as heaven; what canst thou do? deeper than hell; what canst thou know?"[2] Light, as the Psalmist tells us, is sown for the righteous: but nowhere are we told that it is sown for the intellectual, or the refined, or the civilized, merely as such.

And now, in conclusion, let me point you to Him, who proclaimed from that central spot of earth which God had chosen for His Temple and His Altar: "I am the light of the world: he that followeth me shall not walk in darkness, but shall have the light of life."[3] Let me beseech you to lay aside this useless struggle after Light through natural processes; and at once, while you have the light, pray to God to give you His Holy Spirit, that He may manifest Christ unto you. Out of Christ there is no Light for man. "The LORD said that He would dwell in the thick dark-

[1] Psalm cxxxix. 6. [2] Job. xi. 7, 8. [3] S. John viii. 12.

ness;"[1] and what He said, He will perform in any case where His Light is attempted to be put aside. In Christ is Light: out of Christ is darkness, gross darkness. God has no light for the proud: He "resisteth the proud,"[2] says S. James. "Behold, all ye that kindle a fire," are the words of Isaiah, "that compass yourselves about with sparks: walk in the light of your fire, and in the sparks that ye have kindled. This shall ye have of mine hand; ye shall lie down in sorrow."[3] But, on the other hand, he says: "For thus saith the high and lofty One that inhabiteth eternity, whose name is Holy; I dwell in the high and holy place, with him also that is of a contrite and humble spirit, to revive the spirit of the humble, and to revive the heart of the contrite ones."[4]

And let us not forget, my fellow-Christians, who profess that we are in the Light, that we ourselves were "some time in darkness," and that by the grace of God we are what we are. Let us not be high-minded, but fear. Remove that grace, and our candle would go out. Depend for a single day upon ourselves, and darkness will begin to gather around us. Let us keep abidingly with us the glorious truth of our text, "In thy light shall we see light," and strive to walk unceasingly in the stream that radiates from the Cross of our Saviour. "The path of the just, " says Solomon, "is as the shining light, that shineth more and more unto the perfect day:"[5] and that was before the Sun of Righteousness arose upon the earth. How much more now, when that Sun is casting its full sunshine upon the world! While we have the Light, let us walk in the Light: lest darkness come upon us, and our "feet stumble upon the dark mountains."[6]

AUGUST 12, 1866.

[1] 1 Kings viii. 12.
[2] S. James iv. 6.
[3] Isaiah l. 11.
[4] *Ibid.* lvii. 15.
[5] Proverbs iv. 18.
[6] Jer. xiii 16.

Forty-ninth Sermon.

Wherefore seeing we also are compassed about with so great a cloud of witnesses, let us lay aside every weight, and the sin which doth so easily beset us, and let us run with patience the race that is set before us, looking unto Jesus the author and finisher of our faith. — HEBREWS xii. 1, 2.

IT is exceedingly difficult for us as Christians, struggling after victory, to conceive how it is possible for us to finish our course with joy. We read of such conquerors in the Bible; we see their names embalmed in the pages of Inspiration; we hear their songs of triumph as they enter into rest: but we separate them from ourselves by a distance as great as that which separates the heavens from the earth. Abraham, and Isaac, and Moses, and David, and Paul, it is true, have fought the good fight, have kept the faith, and deserve the crown of righteousness which is laid up for them. But while we admit this, we do not, in reality, consider these Saints of the Bible as flesh and blood. We elevate them, as ideal beings, into some imaginary condition; and take neither example nor comfort from their struggles, and their success. We consider them as a part not of the history but the machinery of our religion; — not as men born in sin, heirs of corruption, and redeemed by the Blood of Christ: but as superior beings, occupying a higher sphere, breathing a more spiritual atmosphere, and holding a closer and more intimate communion with God. As the books of the Bible were instrumentally composed by them, we invest them with the awe and the veneration which properly surrounds the inspiration of God; and, in spite of our own understanding, give them a place in the scale of being something akin to that which intermediate deities hold in the systems of paganism. It is only after a great struggle that we can be brought to admit any likeness in nature or situation between them and ourselves, and to look upon them as witnesses of the promises and hopes of the Gospel.

This is unfortunate; for, in running the race which is set before us, we do need all the encouragement which we can receive from man as well as from God. The Bible will not permit us to consider the acquisition of the crown of righteousness as an easy victory. It places it within our reach; it surrounds it with all the glory which language or conception can give it; it invites, it encourages, it entreats us with all the eloquence of tongues touched with a live coal from off the altar, to strive after it: but tells us at the same time, in language which cannot be misunderstood, that it is no easy conquest. All the words which express a great struggle are used to convey to the mind of the Christian the understanding and the experience of the sacred writers in regard to it. It is a fight, in which Christians are urged to put on the whole armor of God; it is a race, in which they are warned to cast aside every weight and the sin which doth most easily beset them; it is an agony, in which we wrestle not against flesh and blood, but against principalities, against powers, against the rulers of the darkness of this world, against spiritual wickedness in high places. Descriptions like these do not look as if the authors of them considered victory as a very certain or a very light thing; and therefore is it that they surround the arena with all the light, and hope, and promise, that they are permitted to heap together for the encouragement of the combatants. For this purpose S. Paul, in writing to the Hebrews, summons up from the past all the heroic men who had fought the good fight of faith, and passes them before his readers as witnesses to the great truths of the Gospel, — as palpable evidence of the power of grace in sustaining men like ourselves in the unequal strife which they were called to wage. "Seeing then," says he, "that we are compassed about with so great a cloud of witnesses, ... let us run with patience the race that is set before us." Now it would be no encouragement at all, if these witnesses were not men of like infirmities and like condition with ourselves. The success of an angel would give no warrant of success to us. The triumph of an imaginary being would ensure no triumph to a being of flesh and blood. The whole force of the illustration rests upon the truth of the position that these Scriptural witnesses were as sinful, as frail, as weak as ourselves, and have conquered through like means with those which are placed within our grasp. They stand as a connecting link between us and our Saviour, breaking the awful distance, and bidding us hope, that as they have conquered in His strength, so may we, if we are patient and watchful, one day carry the palm branches of victory in our hands.

The truth is, that so far from these witnesses not being real and proper examples to us, we really enjoy higher privileges of a religious kind than they did. "These all," says the Apostle, after enumerating by name some of this cloud of witnesses, and grouping a multitude of others under various titles of suffering, "having obtained a good report through faith, received not the promise: God having provided some better thing for us, that they without us should not be made perfect."[1] They lived under the Law; we live under the Gospel: "for the Law," says S. John, "was given by Moses, but grace and truth came by Jesus Christ."[2] They were partakers of the Old Covenant: we

[1] Heb. xii. 39, 40.

[2] S. John i. 17.

are the partakers of the New, according to that rich promise of God in Jeremiah: "Behold, the days come, saith the Lord, when I will make a new covenant with the house of Israel, and with the house of Judah. . . . I will put my laws into their mind, and write them in their hearts."[1] They had earthly priests and an earthly tabernacle: priests who needed daily to offer up sacrifices first for their own sins and then for the people; — a tabernacle which, though made according to the pattern showed to Moses in the mount, was yet made with hands. We have an High Priest with an unchangeable Priesthood, consecrated for evermore, and ever living to make intercession for us; — and a Tabernacle which the Lord pitched, and not man. Surely, therefore, if these conquered under all these disadvantages, much more may we hope to conquer, if we follow them as they followed Christ. If they, resting merely upon promises, had grace and strength sufficient to overcome the world: we, who have the fulfillment of that promise in the outpouring of the Spirit of God, may ask with confidence, "Who is he that condemneth? It is Christ that died, yea rather, that is risen again, who is even at the right hand of God, who also maketh intercession for us. Who shall separate us from the love of Christ? Shall tribulation, or distress, or persecution, or famine, or nakedness, or peril, or sword? . . . . Nay, in all these things we are more than conquerors through him that loved us."[2]

This cloud of Saints surrounds us, then, as a cloud of witnesses, testifying to us for example, for encouragement, for comfort; testifying as men testify when they sympathize in each other's troubles and struggles, and cheer each other up against adverse fortune. They are represented by the Apostle as a cloud compassing the living, struggling Church of God, animating their weary and desponding

[1] Heb. viii. 8, 10. [2] Rom. viii. 34, 35, 37.

spirits not merely by words, not merely by promises, but by their presence, — a presence seen by the eye of Faith, even as the servant of the Prophet saw, when his eyes were opened, horses and chariots of fire innumerable round his master: and when the Christian asks, —

> Who are these in bright array?
> This innumerable throng,
> Round the Altar, night and day
> Tuning their triumphant song?

the answer comes, — "Sir, thou knowest:"[1] this is that great cloud of witnesses mentioned by S. Paul as compassing the struggling Church. These are they which came out of great tribulation, and have washed their robes, and made them white in the blood of the Lamb."[2] It is as when a poor shipwrecked creature, who is buffeting with the waves and is almost ready to perish, sees those who were in like condition with himself standing in safety upon the shore, and hears their cheers of animating hope ringing above the blasts of the tempest, —"Fear not! When thou passest through the waters, they shall not overflow thee: for His everlasting arms are underneath thee."

And what do they bear witness to? What says this cloud of witnesses to the struggling soul? "As thou art," Owen has beautifully worded it, "so were we; so guilty, so perplexed, so obnoxious to wrath, so fearing destruction from God. And what way did you steer, what course did you take, to obtain the blessed condition wherein now you are? Say they, we went all to God through Christ for forgiveness, and found plenty of peace, mercy, and pardon in Him for us all. The rich man in the parable thought it would be a great means of conversion if one should rise from the dead and preach. But here we see that all the Saints departed and now in glory do jointly preach this fundamental truth, that there is forgiveness with God."

[1] Rev. vii. 14. [2] *Ibid.*

And have you, my hearer, no personal interest in that cloud of witnesses? Are there no sacred forms there that have once upon earth guided you in the ways of virtue and religion? Are there no familiar voices coming to you from that land of spirits, and cheering you onward to Heaven? Are there none there who have walked side by side with you in this vale of tears, and talked with you of the land of rest and peace? See you no mother there? Recognize you no tone that carries you back to the freshness of childhood, when in innocence and in faith you looked up into that beloved face, and drank in the teachings of Truth? See you no wife there? Hear you no gentle voice, sweet as the memory of love can make it, whispering to you words of urgency and of hope? Are there no cherubs amid that group beckoning to the smitten hearts from which they have been torn, calling, in those accents of tenderness which can never be forgotten, upon father and mother to look to Jesus and be saved? They are all there: although unseen, — unheard perhaps for lack of faith, — still there, a portion of that cloud, witnessing to you through memories dearer than any present joys, speaking to heart and to conscience of the love of God in Christ. If the Patriarchs are there; if the sweet Psalmist is there; if the great Apostle to the Gentiles is there: then are all of ours who have died in faith there, and we may realize in their spiritual presence the encouragement, the hope, the joy, which their triumphant victory can give us!

"Poor souls," says the author from whom I quoted a little while ago, "are apt to think that all those whom they read or hear of to be gone to Heaven, went thither because they were so good and holy." Are not these your present thoughts, my hearer? Does not this rise up in your mind whenever this cloud of witnesses is mentioned? "And yet," continues Owen, "not one of them, not any one that is now in heaven, Jesus Christ alone excepted, did ever come thither any other way but by forgiveness of sin; and that will also bring us thither, though we come short of many of them in holiness and grace." Those witnesses are not sent, my hearers, to discourage us by their imaginary holiness. They are sent as illustrations of the great truths of the Gospel; as bearing testimony that mercy and grace have come by Jesus Christ; as examples of the patience, of the long suffering of God. They encompass us, so that which ever way we look we may see the image of the glory of God in the face of Christ Jesus reflected from the beaming, triumphant looks of those we have loved, and taken sweet counsel with, upon earth.

How little do we realize this privilege! How the earth and things earthly shut out these divine visions! We need every help and every encouragement which the Bible can give us, and we permit sense to obscure the most cheering prospects which it opens before us. Alas for our weakness! Let us no longer use this cloud of witnesses to dishearten us, but to animate us. Let us henceforward be taught by it the practical lesson of our text, — "to run with patience the race that is set before us."

When we take up this cloud of witnesses individually, and separate one of them from the group with which he stands connected, we perceive that he has reached his present position of triumph by having passed, in faith and with patience, through the course along which God has led him. A being of like infirmities and passions with ourselves, born in sin, clothed with flesh and blood, a citizen of the same world we contend against, hunted by the same adversary who goeth about like a roaring lion seeking whom he may devour: he has so lived, and so acted, as to have been made meet for the inheritance of the Saints in light. He had a life to live upon earth, having the like temptations, the like duties, the like trials with those which beset us: and his position among the cloud of witnesses teaches us that he has been enabled to say, "I have kept the faith." As with them, so with us. A race is set before us. A course is marked out for us. Not a temptation there, from which He has not made a way of escape. Not a trial, in which His grace is not sufficient for us. Not a burden, which He has not promised to carry for us. Our part is, not to quarrel with our lot, not to murmur against the arrangements and dispensations of Providence, not to imagine concerning the fiery trial which is to try us as though some strange thing happened unto us: but to run with patience whatever race may be set before us. It may prove a severe struggle. We may have to win the crown through much suffering. Tears and groans and agony may mark much of the way. But this should not move the Christian from his integrity, — should not shake the faith of the combatant in his final victory. His Saints have all suffered. It has been their universal lot; nay, it is made the very condition of reigning. "It is a faithful saying: For if we be dead with him, we shall also live with him: if we suffer, we shall also reign with him."[1] "The Spirit itself beareth witness with our spirit, that we are the children of God: and if children, then heirs; heirs of God, and joint heirs with Christ; if so be that we suffer with him, that we may be also glorified together."[2] "Take, my brethren," says S. James, "the prophets, who have spoken in the name of the Lord, for an example of suffering affliction, and of patience. Behold we count them happy which endure."[3] Job knew this well when he said, "Though he slay me, yet will I trust in him."[4] Our

[1] 2 Tim. ii. 11, 12.
[2] Rom. viii. 16, 17.
[3] S. James v. 10, 11.
[4] Job xiii. 15.

work is to press forward in the race: not halting to weep over the ruggedness of the way; not fainting because difficulties beset the path, not turning back because there is a lion in the track: but if we must needs weep and groan and tremble, let us do it while we yet run, if so be it end in patience. God knows better than we do what is our necessary share of chastisement, and what form it shall put on; and He sees likewise, what we find it very hard to see, how much of it is brought upon us by ourselves. If any thing should teach us patience, it is this consideration, — that while there is much of affliction and of suffering which is trial, there is also a very large share which our Heavenly Father puts upon us as chastisement for our sins. Let us not faint nor grow weary, therefore, when we are rebuked of Him; for afterward it yieldeth the peaceable fruit of righteousness to them who are exercised thereby.

This patience in running the race that is set before us is not attained, however, unless we observe the injunctions of the Apostle in our text. This cloud of witnesses inspires us with hope, renews the ardor of our first love, kindles afresh the zeal which urged us to enter upon the Christian race. Let us therefore cast aside every weight, and the sin which doth so easily beset us! The candidate for the olive crown at Olympia stripped himself of every incumbrance that might for an instant clog his movements. He cast every thing away that might hinder, in the least, his chance for triumph in the contest he was waging. Earnest in his purpose, single-minded in his object, heart and soul absorbed in the hope of victory, he counted every thing as a weight which impeded his onward movements. In like manner does the Apostle enjoin upon us who desire to finish our course with joy, to cast aside every thing which may hinder our heavenly race, and especially that besetting sin of unbelief. But alas! how different is our practice!

Instead of stripping off and casting aside feelings, tempers, habits, desires, imaginations, which are adverse to the life of God in the soul, we are perpetually renewing them, even when God has again and again smitten and crushed them. He says to us, as plainly as he said of Edom of old, — "They shall build, but I will throw down:" and we weave afresh, in the very face of the tempests which are beating upon us, the webs of fancy and of hope which keep us on enchanted ground! How sad it is to see the children of God taking up burdens instead of laying them down, — twining their affections around objects which hinder them in their race, and from which they must be violently torn, with suffering and anguish, ere they can run with patience their allotted race! And yet nothing is more common than this struggle against God; — this putting on as fast as He strips off; — this adding weight to weight, while He bids us cast every weight away. There can be no patience while this contest is going on. It is our will against God's will. It is a strife in which there will be murmuring, and perchance rebellion, against the arrangements of God. Patience comes when this strife is ended; when the will of man is merged into the will of God; when, humble as a little child, the Christian yields implicitly to the guidance of his Heavenly Father, sees all his idols broken without a single murmur, and through tears of thankfulness acknowledges with David, — "It is good for me that I have been afflicted."

The hardest of all hindrances to our patience is the sin which doth most easily beset us! It is not, as it is often carelessly understood, some particular besetting sin of the individual: but it is the sin that doth so easily beset every one of us, the sin of unbelief! Men often flippantly say when the Gospel is preached, when grace is magnified, when Faith is held up and pressed as the sole instrument of justification with God, that it is making religion too easy,

Heaven too attainable, — encouraging sin, that grace may abound! Alas! my hearers, there is a dead faith that it is easy enough to lay claim to, and to boast of: but the faith which worketh by love is the hardest thing in heaven or earth to procure or maintain. Unbelief is natural to us. It besets us, as the Apostle intimates, on every hand; and at all times, it is forever assailing us, from the cradle to the grave. No matter how graciously God may have dealt with us, in how many ways we have experienced His loving-kindness: we are perpetually doubting His love and mercy! We cannot believe that He has sent His only Son to die upon the Cross, that we, through faith and the sprinkling of Blood, may find forgiveness and acceptance! When that is forced upon us by irresistible evidence, why, *then* we cannot believe that forgiveness will be given of grace, without money and without price! When, through a grateful experience, we become convinced of this, we cannot believe that we shall be guided along our path to Heaven by the same love which hath placed us in it! Every dark hour that lowers upon us, — every fiery trial through which God passes us, — all the deep waters through which He makes us wade, — are so many evidences of His having forsaken us! The richest processes of His love are converted, through this alchemy of the natural heart, into causes of distrust; and we go, halting, through our whole pilgrimage, because we cannot rise up to the height of that love of Christ which passeth knowledge. Although He tells us: "My thoughts are not your thoughts, neither are your ways My ways:"[1] we will clothe Him with the attributes of our own wretched natures, forgetting that He is God and not man, and that He has proclaimed His Name as "The Lord, The Lord God, merciful and gracious, long-suffering, and abundant in goodness

[1] Isaiah lv. 8.

and truth, keeping mercy for thousands, forgiving iniquity and transgression and sin."[1] This sin, the Apostle especially declares, must be cast away ere we can run with patience the race that is set before us; for the heart of unbelief transforms the Gospel into a yoke of bondage, — our Father into a consuming Fire, — the very throne of Grace itself into a throne of Judgment!

But you will say, How is all this to be done? — Whence is to come the power that will enable me to cast aside every weight, and especially the sin of unbelief? The Apostle answers: "Through Jesus:" — "Looking unto Jesus as the Finisher, no less than the Author, of our Faith." It was He, by His Spirit, who awoke within us the first glimmerings of belief. It was He, who roused us from the death of trespasses and sins, saying, "Awake thou that sleepest, and arise from the dead, and Christ shall give thee light."[2] It was He, who changed the heart of stone into a heart of flesh, and wrote upon it the supernatural words of faith and of love. It was He, who by that same Spirit has been working persistently with that same heart, sanctifying and purifying it, and changing it into His own image, from glory to glory. And having begun in the Spirit, shall we end in the flesh? Having received the Lord Jesus as our Wisdom, our Righteousness, our Sanctification, our Redemption, shall we turn again to the beggarly elements, and desire again to be in bondage? God forbid! Jesus Christ must be the Finisher as well as the Author of our Faith; must perfect that in glory which He has begun in grace! If you need faith, look unto Jesus. In Him is the fullness of that grace which freely giveth Faith! If you need spiritual strength, look unto Jesus. You can do all things through Christ strengthening you! If you need mercy, look unto Jesus. Mercy and Truth

[1] Exod. xxxiv. 6, 7.

[2] Eph. v. 14.

came by Him. Keep your eye fixed upon Him, and all else will prove easy! Weights will fall off, and not tarry to be cast away. Unbelief will wither under the brightness of His light, and shrink away abashed before His glory! Keep your eye fixed steadily upon Him: for He is the brightness of His Father's glory, and the express image of His Person; and "we all, with open face beholding as in a glass the glory of the Lord," shall be "changed into the same image from glory to glory, even as by the Spirit of the Lord."[1]

[1] 2 Cor. iii. 18.

Fiftieth Sermon.

For the Son of Man is as a man taking a far journey, who left his house, and gave authority to his servants, and to every man his work, and commanded the porter to watch. Watch ye therefore: for ye know not when the master of the house cometh, at even, or at midnight, or at the cock-crowing, or in the morning: lest coming suddenly he find you sleeping. And what I say unto you I say unto all, Watch. — S. MARK xiii. 34–37.

OUR Saviour had taken occasion from an observation of one of His Disciples as He went out of the Temple, — "Master, see what manner of stones and what buildings are here," — to foretell the destruction of Jerusalem; and to mingle with the sufferings of that time, and the need of watchfulness against them, the still more awful terrors of the Judgment day, and the still more urgent necessity of a constant preparedness for it. It was one of the secret things of the Almighty, — the coming of that day, — known to no man; but for that very reason made more terrible, for it might burst at any moment with its accompanying doom upon their heads. "Take ye heed," therefore, "for ye know not when the time is."

But our Lord never taught only for one time or for one occasion; and in this case, so soon as He had pressed upon His Disciples the instruction He would give them, He transforms the topic into the parable which forms my text, and addresses it to all future generations, closing with a solemn admonition: — "And what I say unto you I say unto all, Watch."

How little the world looks as if it was watching for any such event as the coming of Christ! To look at it as it sweeps along in its fullness of life, it appears as if its inhabitants expected it, with themselves, to endure forever. How many ties of affection are daily forming! How many plans, extending far into the future, are arranging and executing! How many hopes, cherished in the sanctuary of the heart, are looking for their fulfilment to long years ahead! The world is eating and drinking, marrying and giving in marriage, buying and selling, as if nothing was ever to change it from its usual routine. Ask its people what they dread, why their hearts are fainting within them: and they will answer you: — "We tremble at the loss of property; at the loss of office; at the loss of position; at the loss of reputation:" but seldom "Because we remember the coming of the Lord." That has but little influence over their minds. Whenever it crosses their thoughts, it is like a far-off thing, floating in dim uncertainty. Although it is quite as much in the ordinary and probable routine of things as any event before which they tremble, they cannot see it, and will not dwell upon it. They are borne along by the swelling, rushing tide of life, and fear nothing so much as being separated from its roar and tumult. But few seem to be considering whence they came, or whither they are going, — who placed them here, or for what purpose. They act for the most part as if they were mere bubbles, rising by chance out of the bosom of Life's Ocean, to float for a time upon its surface, and then to burst and vanish forever! No thought of the past; no thought of the future; but little thought of God: the world and the present make up every thing.

From this unsound and untrue condition of things Christ would arouse those for whom He died, and would press upon them consideration and watchfulness. He would disabuse *you* among the rest, my hearers, of the idea that you are without responsibility to God; that you have merely to pass through life as it pleases you; and at the end lie down in peace without any accountability. He would awake you to a higher, nobler view of things, point out to you your true work on earth, and impress you with a full sense of your glorious destiny. He cannot consent that those for whom He shed His precious blood, for whom He opened an access to the throne of God, for whom He prepared a future of unspeakable glory, should pass through life without a single spiritual aspiration, and then die without a well-grounded hope of everlasting life. He speaks to you, therefore, this parable, and tells you that you all have a work to do, and an account to give: a work not simply for yourselves, but for God; an account to be rendered not when you may please to be ready, but at any moment He may choose to call for it, whether in youth, or in life's prime, or in the ripeness of old age.

The great mistake we all make is in confounding the work we do for the world and for ourselves, with that which we are required to do for God. Work for ourselves and for the world is as much our duty as any other moral or social obligation which God may have laid upon us: but it is not all of our duty. We hold two relations in life, one to this present world, the other to the world which is to come; and we perform our duty aright when we harmonize the two, and while, living for our families and for society, live also for God. If we err on either side, we are wrong. If we permit the one rod, even though it be the rod of God, to swallow up the rest, we run into error. When our Saviour was asked, "Which is the greatest commandment of the Law?" His answer was: "Thou shalt love the Lord thy God with all thy heart, and with all thy soul, and with all thy mind: this is the first and great commandment. And the second is like unto it; Thou shalt love thy neighbor as thyself. On these two commandments hang all the law and the prophets." Mark! on these two commandments: not on one, but on both. And the error man is constantly committing is to seize on one of them, and make that every thing. The work which God gives us to do is a happy conjunction of these; — is to love Him so that a devout character shall be carried into all the relations of life; and then to do our duty in that station to which He has called us, so as to glorify His name upon earth. When we achieve this harmony, then are we indeed the true children of Him, the combination of whose attributes is holiness.

The difficulty which we encounter in directing the minds of men aright in religion, is in persuading them that they have an especial work to do for God, — a work in which He is to be glorified for Himself. The work which is laid upon you by your earthly relations is so forced upon your notice by the conditions of life, treads so pressingly upon your heels, that you cannot overlook it. If you do, the world clamors at you so loudly that you are fain, for very comfort's sake, to take up your burden and travel under it. But not so with the work which you have to do for God. That stands upon a different footing. It is a work, at least in its springs, very much of feeling. It is occupied with prayer, with supplications, with thanksgiving, with praise, with ascriptions of glory. If not performed, you do not hunger, nor thirst, nor lack raiment, as a necessary consequence. The world does not reprove you, nor cry out upon you. You appear to go along as usual, without suffering any of those immediate ill effects which flow from the neglect of your worldly work. And therefore it is that you forget it, and overlook it, and imagine that it will never be required of you. But Christ explains the law of God's government by the parable which we are considering. He tells you that the Son of Man is as a man taking a far journey, who left His house, and gave authority to His servants, and to every man his work. "Watch ye therefore: for ye know not when the Master of the house cometh, at even, or at midnight, or at the cock-crowing, or in the morning." The work is left you to do: but it is a work of the will. God obliges you to work for yourselves, that you may keep famine from your doors, vice from your households, evil from yourselves: but He does not force you to work for Him. His service, to be of any value, must be a willing one, a service of the heart; and so no temporal punishment of an immediate kind is laid upon your neglect of it. David frequently in the Psalms complains of the prosperity of the ungodly. This work therefore has to be perpetually enforced upon your remembrance. You have to be reminded that you have duties distinct from the duties of life, not having their beginning nor their end with man, but with God. God is a Father, and He will not have all the love and service of His children given to the world. He forces them to go abroad and fulfil their work of social duty; but they must return home and cheer Him with their love, their gratitude and their devotion, in return for all that He has done for them. He wants you, when you have finished your lawful and necessary work, to turn your thoughts to Him, and praise Him for all His benefits.

Much of our work is common to us all. The curse of labor is upon us, and labor we must, in some way or other. But each individual and each position in life has something peculiar to itself, and our duty is to understand what that work is. And whatever it is, it stands connected with that which is the paramount work of man, — the salvation of his soul, and the glorifying of God upon earth. It can never be fully performed unless that element is developed in harmony with it. For however pressing the necessity of daily and worldly work, Christ has Himself told us that there is but one thing absolutely needful, — but one thing which, if neglected, has no remedy!

Our Lord has given every man his work, — every man his own peculiar work. Sometimes it is a work of active service; sometimes of patient endurance. Now it is a work to be done in some very obscure position; and then again are we called to fill and illustrate some lofty station. In one instance, that work is confined to the quiet monotonous routine of domestic life; and in another, it is performed in the public eye, with all men gazing upon us. In all, God may be glorified, and the name of Christ honored; and in all God must be glorified, if we would perform our work as He intends that it should be fulfilled. Our primary task, therefore, is to ascertain what our peculiar work is, and how we may perform it so as to carry out the purposes of God, and secure the benefits and blessings of its faithful performance to ourselves. For who gains by the salvation of the soul, my hearer? "Look unto the heavens, and see; and behold the clouds which are higher than thou. If thou sinnest, what doest thou against Him? or if thy transgressions be multiplied, what doest thou unto Him? . . . Thy wickedness may hurt a man as thou art; and thy righteousness may profit the son of man."[1] Is not all the benefit to inure to yourself? Are you not to be the recipient of that life and immortality which your Saviour has brought to light? Are you not to escape that fearful doom which is denounced against those who lose their souls? How many days and nights you spend for the attainment of objects which are insignificant when compared with those which are to be attained through salvation! How much ease do you sacrifice! How much danger do you risk!

[1] Job xxxv. 5, 6, 8.

How much hardship do you encounter! And all willingly and cheerfully. If you would only give half the pains to the soul which you give to the body, you would find that your work of life would be far easier, while your soul would be rejoicing in its redemption from the bondage of sin and the fear of death.

My hearer, have you ever asked yourself what is your especial work? What is that which the Lord has given you to do, while He has gone upon that far journey from which, at any unexpected moment, He may return? Some work you have to do for the Lord. What is it? If you do not know; if you have never yet paused in the advance of life to find out; if you are plunging forward in darkness and in ignorance: woe unto you! — for your Lord will surely come back and search into your life and actions. For we are only servants, and must give the account which masters require of their servants. He will come upon us unexpectedly; and then shall we be questioned of the past. Oh, that terrible past! It has been told us by those who have been recovered from the unconscious state of drowning, that in the few moments when they were passing from life into that condition, every event of the past came over them in distinct succession. They saw vividly, as in a moving panorama, every act of the life which they deemed long buried in oblivion. They had themselves forgotten them; yet there they were, evoked from the mysterious chambers of the mind by the agony of that moment. And so shall it be when our account is called for. "God requireth that which is past." And His power will be greater than even the power of Death. Not only shall events come before us then, but every thing which can in any measure stand connected with sin; — words, thoughts, imaginations, desires, motives, all shall be summoned to testify of your life and your work: — "What have you done in fulfillment of the work which I committed to you? What return is there for the trust which I reposed in you? How have you acted in the station of life in which I placed you?" It will not do to say, "Lord, I was not idle; I busied myself day and night at my counting-house, or in my shop, or with my worldly work of whatever kind, and I made my family comfortable, and I left my children well to do in the world." The answer will be:—"That is all very proper to a certain extent; but that was not all the work which I appointed you to do. I commanded you to love Me, and you have entirely forgotten Me; to believe in My Son Jesus Christ, and you have neglected or despised His claims to save your soul; and you have never thought of it, but have left it to decay, perhaps to destruction." There will be no discharge in that war. We shall all have to come up to that bar, and be judged according to the works done in the flesh. No plea shall be of any avail then, except that we have done our work,—the work appointed us,—in great weakness perhaps, and with much infirmity, but trusting in the love, mercy and grace of Jesus Christ our Saviour.

And is it not well that our Saviour bids us watch? Who can foresee when the Master will come? His messenger Death is busy all around us, summoning our fellow-creatures to His presence. His darts are ever falling in the homes which stand so thick around us; why not in yours, my hearer? No week passes but some familiar name comes wafted to us in connection with that terrible Destroyer. When each week begins, who can tell whose name will follow next? It is the darkest of all lotteries. We know only this, that his harvest is forever going on; that his sickle is never idle; and that he is gathering in the fields of the world for judgment. Shall we, for this, live always in the fear of Death? No! but for this reason we should live in preparedness for it. We should measure life; number our days; examine our work; see that all is ready for the Master. Life is too solemn a thing to be trifled with. Death is too terrible an enemy to be met unexpectedly. Both demand watchfulness: life, that we may spend it aright, and do our allotted task; Death, that we may meet it calmly, feeling that it has no sting.

Are there any of you, my fellow-Christians, who have permitted the circumstances of the times to tempt you into carelessness, — to cause you to cease your watchfulness and your expectation of the sudden coming of your Lord? Let the solemn warnings which you have received, from time to time, arouse you from your lethargy and bring you back to watchfulness! These are no times for sleeping! Death seems unsatisfied with the carnage of the past, and is gathering himself for fresh slaughter among the children of men. Pestilence often follows war, and already it is hovering upon our coast. Winter may check it for a time, but if it has its work to do, the breath of spring will come laden with its poison. The sorrows of the time, which have overwhelmed and made torpid so many hearts, are sent by God to prepare you for coming evil. Of all times, the present calls for watchfulness and not for apathy! Arouse yourselves, children of God; and while you humble yourselves under the mighty hand of God, forget not that you are Christ's servants, bound to do His work in the Church militant upon earth, and to advance His kingdom wherever He may spread the banner of the Cross. Instead of permitting suffering to overcome your faith, let it rather lead you on to perfection. Instead of fainting in the day of adversity, gird up your loins, and be sober, and strong in the Lord. Instead of sleeping because the world is troubled and agitated, rather stand upon your watch-tower, and await in faith and patience the Coming of your Master.

The Apostolic Succession.

An Extract from a Sermon preached at the Consecration of S. John's Church, Savannah, on Saturday, the 7th of May, 1853, *on the words: "And lo, I am with you alway, even unto the end of the world, Amen."* — S. MATTHEW, xxviii. 20. *After matters of local interest, and enlarging on "soundness in the faith" and the "due administration of the Sacraments" as two "Notes" of the Church, the Preacher thus continued:* —

THE third note which we offer as evidence that we are of that Church with which Christ has promised alway to be, unto the end of the world, is the *Ministerial Succession.* Nor is this an idle matter, for it involves no less than the whole question, whether there be any Ministry at all. If the authority which Christ left with His Apostles has been suffered to expire, whence hath it been renewed? And if it hath not been renewed, where is the Ministry? What right hath one man more than another to baptize, to preach, to administer the sacraments, to absolve from sin? Why may not each say to his neighbor, "Come and baptize me" — "come and consecrate the elements, and give me to eat and drink of the Body and Blood of my Saviour"? This seems preposterous; nay, blasphemous: and yet, if there has not been a Succession in the Ministry from the time of the Apostles, — if the golden chain has ever been broken at any point, at any time, — this very thing must have occurred; and having occurred, all ministerial authority has ceased: for an assumed authority can never have become rightful, through how many soever links it may have been transmitted. Unless each Minister can trace up to the Apostles, he must reach a point at which the authority he exercises was usurped; and that usurpation must vitiate all that has succeeded. But there *is* unbroken ministerial Succession. There is a chain that can be followed, link by link, up to the Apostles, along which hath descended the authority which Christ intended should be vested, for the ordinary purposes of His Church, in the sacred Ministry. We can give you name by name, Bishop after Bishop, until we touch S. John at Ephesus, and S. James at Jerusalem, and S. Mark at Alexandria; — until we join on to the very men on whose heads Christ laid His hands, when He sent them out and commanded them "to preach, to heal the sick, to cleanse the lepers, to raise the dead, to cast out devils." The arrangement of the three Orders is broken nowhere. It commences with the first establishment of the Jewish Church, when the High Priest, the Priests and the Levites made up the ministry of the Temple. It continues when Christ with His Twelve and the Seventy made up the Orders of the nascent Christian Church. The gap is instantly filled, when Christ, having ascended to the right hand of the Father, left the Twelve and the Seventy on earth, by the appointment of Deacons. And as the Apostles died away, we find holy men selected to fill their places, and Timothy and Titus performing those offices which Paul and Peter and James had performed, and bidden to transmit them to others who should stand in their room: so that the Fathers of the third and fourth centuries could boldly affirm that there was not a See of any magnitude that could not trace its Bishops up to the Apostles themselves. And what they said then, we can affirm now. And however the Succession may have run at times through unworthy channels, that no more proves that it came not from the Apostles, than the muddiness or even filthiness of a stream in some particular part of its course would satisfy us that the pure water which we are drinking cannot be traced, through that very polluted spot, up to its crystal fountain in the mountain top. How vain is such argumentation against the truth! Was Jesus Christ not the Messiah because He came through Tamar and the wife of Uriah? Did these unworthy wombs pollute the Promise so that the Seed of the Woman did not bruise the serpent's head? Why, the first principle of Protestantism is, that it is the office and not the man which has authority; and that, so there be faith in the breast of the recipient, the unworthiness of the Priest can effect no more than his own condemnation!

These are the tokens and signs of such a Church as our Saviour has promised to be with alway, to the end of the world. But this promise is not unconditional. In the Epistle to the Romans, the Apostle, in writing to them, says:—"And if some of the branches be broken off, and thou, being a wild olive tree, wert graffed in among them, and with them partakest of the root and fatness of the olive tree; boast not against the branches. But if thou boast, thou bearest not the root, but the root thee. Thou wilt say then, The branches were broken off, that I might be graffed in. Well; because of unbelief they were broken off, and thou standest by faith. Be not highminded, but fear: for if God spared not the natural branches, take heed lest he also spare not thee."[1] The only Church which shall stand forever is that which is called in these verses of S. Paul, the ROOT of the Olive Tree. Particular Churches, such as the Jewish Church, or the Roman Church, or the Anglican Church, are only branches from that ROOT: the first, the natural branch; the latter, the branches graffed in when the other was broken off and cast away. When

[1] Rom. xi. 17–21.

Christ therefore promised that He would be with His Church alway, to the end of the world, it was to no particular Church that He made this promise: it was to any and every branch of the Root, which He might please to graff in. It gives warrant to no particular branch of this Church of God to say that Christ will be with it alway, to the end of the world, unless it preserve within itself the faith of Abraham, — the righteousness of faith, as it is called in the Scriptures. Take, for example, the very Church to which this Epistle was written, the Church of Rome, the very Church to which the Apostle wrote the words: "Be not highminded, but fear. For if God spared not the natural branches, take heed lest he also spare not thee," and see why it is that God's people were obliged to come out of her. It was not because she had not the Ministry, for that she certainly has in all its Orders. It was not because she had not the Sacraments, for she has preserved both those which Christ ordained. It was not because she did not hold the great doctrines of the Trinity and the Atonement, for nowhere are they more decidedly taught than within her bosom. It was not that she did not possess and retain the Scriptures as the Word and Truth of God, for she has faithfully kept them for the Churches which have purged themselves of her abominations. It was because she had overlaid the righteousness of faith, and had thus become a corrupt branch, although God has not yet broken her off from the root of the Olive Tree. It was upon this ground the Reformation planted itself, that Rome had abandoned the righteousness of faith; and to sustain that abandonment, had added to all these characteristics of a true Church — the Ministry, the Sacraments, the Scriptures — novelties not authorized by the Word of God or the customs of the Churches which had been planted by the Apostles and their immediate successors.

Pastoral Letter

From the Bishops of the Protestant Episcopal Church to the Clergy and Laity of the Church in the Confederate States of America; delivered before the General Council, in S. Paul's Church, Augusta, Saturday, November 22d, 1862.

AT your request, brethren of the Clergy and Laity, we conclude the session of our First General Council by presenting to you and reading in your presence a Pastoral Letter, addressed to the members of the Protestant Episcopal Church scattered throughout the Confederate States. By the mighty power of the Holy Ghost we have been permitted to bring our deliberations to a close in a spirit of harmony and peace which augurs well for the future welfare of our branch of the Church Catholic; and our first duty is to thank Him who has promised to be with His Church to the end of the world, for His presence with us during our consultations, and for the happy conclusion to which He has brought our sacred labors.

Seldom has any Council assembled in the Church of Christ under circumstances needing His presence more urgently than this which is now about to submit its conclusions to the judgment of the Universal Church. Forced by the Providence of God to separate ourselves from the Protestant Episcopal Church in the United States, — a Church with whose doctrine, discipline and worship we are in entire harmony, and with whose action, up to the time of that separation, we were abundantly satisfied — at a moment when civil strife had dipped its foot in blood, and cruel war was desolating our homes and firesides: we required a double measure of grace to preserve the accustomed moderation of the Church in the arrangement of our organic law, in the adjustment of our code of Canons, but above all, in the preservation, without change, of those rich treasures of doctrine and worship which have come to us enshrined in our Book of Common Prayer. Cut off likewise from all communication with our sister Churches of the world, we have been compelled to act without any interchange of opinion even with our Mother Church, and alone and unaided to arrange for ourselves the organization under which we should do our part in carrying on to their consummation the purposes of God in Christ Jesus. We trust that the Spirit of Christ has indeed so directed, sanctified and governed us in our work, that we shall be approved by all those who love our Lord Jesus Christ in sincerity and in truth, and who are earnest in preparing the world for His coming in glorious majesty to judge both the quick and the dead.

The Constitution of the Protestant Episcopal Church in the Confederate States, under which we have been exercising our legislative functions, is the same as that of the Church from which we have been providentially separated, save that we have introduced into it a germ of expansion which was wanting in the old Constitution. This is found in the permission which is granted to existing Dioceses to form themselves, by subdivision, into Provinces; and by this process gradually to reduce our immense Dioceses into Episcopal Sees, more like those which, in primitive times, covered the territories of the Roman Empire. It is at present but a germ, and may lie, for many years, without expansion; but being there, it gives promise, in the future, of a more close and constant Episcopal supervision than is possible under our present arrangement.

The Canon Law, which has been adopted during our present session, is altogether in its spirit, and almost in its letter, identical with that under which we have hitherto prospered. We have simplified it in some respects, and have made it more clear and plain in many of its requirements; but no changes have been introduced which have altered either its tone or character. It is the same moderate, just, and equal body of Ecclesiastical Law by which the Church has been governed on this continent since her reception from the Church of England of the treasures of an Apostolic Ministry and a liturgical form of worship.

The Prayer Book we have left untouched in every particular, save where a change of our civil government and the formation of a new nation have made alteration essentially requisite. Three words comprise all the amendment which has been deemed necessary in the present emergency, for we have felt unwilling, in the existing confusion of affairs, to lay rash hands upon a Book consecrated by the use of ages, and hallowed by associations the most sacred and precious. We give you back your Book of Common Prayer the same as you have entrusted it to us, believing that if it has slight defects, their removal had better be the gradual work of experience than the hasty action of a body convened almost upon the outskirts of a camp.

Besides this actual legislation which we now submit to you, our assembling together has given us a view of the condition of the Church throughout the Confederate States which renders it our duty to speak to you as Chief Pastors over the flock of Christ: reminding you of the peculiar encouragements which surround us; specifying the points towards which our efforts, as a Christian Church, should be directed; and pointing out the deficiencies which require instant correction and amendment. No moment seems so propitious for the performance of this duty, as that in which we are beginning a new life in the Church, and are preparing to stamp ourselves upon the world for good or for evil.

Our highest encouragement is derived from the fact that we hold the sacred trust of the Faith once delivered to the Saints, and that we hold it in connection with a Ministry whose succession from Christ and His Apostles is undoubted, and with a form of worship simple and pure yet sublime and Scriptural. These are not gifts to make a boast of, but to use for the glory of God and the advancement of Christ's kingdom. Far from filling us with vain glory, their possession should humble us to the dust, unless we approve ourselves faithful stewards of such inestimable treasures. To whom much has been committed, from him will much be required; and it remains for us to prove whether we have deserved so spiritual an inheritance. But possessing them, we may rightfully feel that we enter upon our warfare with the world, the flesh, and the devil, having all the strength that Divine Truth and a Divine Commission can give us. We can press on, without any doubts resting upon our hearts as to the Truth which we are teaching, as to the validity of the Sacraments which we are administering, or as to the authority of the Orders which we are transmitting. Upon all these points we are secure; and we can go forward offering to all men, with boldness and confidence, the Gospel of our Lord Jesus Christ and the fellowship of the Saints. Whatever hindrances we may meet, or whatever contradiction of men we may encounter, we can rest assured that truth will finally prevail, and that God will set His Son upon His holy hill of Zion.

Our next source of encouragement is that we enter upon our work with our Dioceses fully organized, and with the means which Christ has instituted in His Church well distributed throughout the Confederate States. When we remember the very different auspices under which the venerated Fathers of the American Church began their work, and mark how it has grown and prospered, we should indeed take courage and feel no fear for the future. In their case all their ecclesiastical arrangements had to be organized: in our case we find these arrangements all ready to our hand, and with the seal of a happy experience stamped upon them. In their case every prejudice of the land was strong against them: in our case we go forward with the leading minds of our new Republic cheering us on by their communion with us, and with no prejudications to overcome, save those which arise from a lack of acquaintance with our doctrine and worship. In their case they were indeed few and separated far from one another in their work upon the walls of Zion: in our case we are comparatively well compacted, extending in an unbroken chain of Dioceses from the Potomac to the confines of the Republic. Despite all those disadvantages, "the little one became a thousand and the small one a strong nation," and shall we despond? If we be watchful, and strengthen the things that remain, our God will not forsake us, but will "lengthen our cords and stretch forth the curtains of our habitations." In visible token of this fact, we have already, since our organization, added to the House of Bishops the Rt. Rev. Dr. Wilmer as Bishop of Alabama, and received into communion with the Church the Diocese of Arkansas.

Another source of encouragement is that there has been no division in the Church in the Confederate States. Believing, with a wonderful unanimity, that the Providence of God had guided our footsteps, and for His own inscrutable purposes had forced us into a separate organization, there has been nothing to embarrass us in the preliminary movements which have conducted us to our present position. With one mind and with one heart we have entered upon this blessed work; and we stand together this day a band of brothers, one in faith, one in hope, one in charity. There may be among us, as there always must be, minute differences of opinion and feeling, but there is nothing to hinder our keeping the unity of the Spirit in the bond of peace. We are all satisfied that we are walking in the path of duty, and that the light of God's countenance has been wonderfully lifted up upon us. He has comforted us in our darkest hours, and has not permitted our hearts to faint in the day of adversity.

These striking encouragements, vouchsafed to us from the Father of our Lord Jesus Christ, should fill our hearts with earnest devotedness, and should make us even now to inquire, "Lord, what wilt thou have us to do?" And the answer to this question will lead us, your Chief Pastors, to specify the points towards which our efforts, as a Christian Church, should be especially directed.

Christ has founded His Church upon love: for God is Love. It is the highest of all Christian graces. "And now abideth Faith, Hope, Charity, these three, but the greatest of these is Charity." Charity! not mere alms-giving, which is only one of its manifestations: but love, Christian Love! As Christ our Lord loved the world so divinely that He was satisfied to suffer all things for its redemption: so does He command us to love one another, and to be ready to do all things for each other's salvation. This was His especial commandment: "A new commandment give I unto you, that ye love one another." And this is truly not only the new commandment, but the summary of all the commandments. The whole Gospel is redolent with it, with a broad, comprehensive, all-embracing love, appointed, like Aaron's rod, to swallow up all the other Christian graces, and to manifest the spiritual glory of God in Christ.

A Church without love! What could you augur of a Church of God without Faith, or a Church of Christ without Hope? But Love is a higher grace than either Faith or Hope, and its absence from a Church is just the absence of the very life-blood from the body.

Our first duty, therefore, as the children of God, is to send forth from this Council our greetings of love to the Churches of God all the world over. We greet them in Christ, and rejoice that they are partakers with us of all the grace which is treasured up in Him. We lay down to-day before the Altar of the Crucified all our burdens of sin, and offer our prayers for the Church militant upon earth. Whatever may be their aspect towards us politically, we cannot forget that they rejoice with us in the "one Lord," the "one Faith, the "one Baptism," the "one God and Father of all," and we wish them God-speed in all the sacred ministries of the Church. Nothing but love is consonant with the exhibition of Christ's love which is manifested in His Church; and any note of man's bitterness, except against sin, would be a sound of discord mingling with the sweet harmonies of earth and heaven. We rejoice in this golden cord which binds us together in Christ our Redeemer; and, like the ladder which Jacob saw in vision, with the angels of God ascending and descending upon it, may it ever be the channel along which shall flash the Christian greetings of the children of God.

But while we send forth this love to the whole Church militant upon earth, let us not forget that special love is due by us towards those of our own household. To us have been committed the treasures of the Church; and those of our own kindred and lineage, who have sprung from our loins both naturally and spiritually, who are now united with us in a sacred conflict for the dearest rights of man, ask us for the bread of life. They pray us for that which we are commanded to give, — the Gospel of the grace of God. They put in no claim for any thing worldly — for any thing alien from the mission of the Church. Their petition is that we will fulfill the very purpose of our institution, and give them the means of grace. Every claim which man can have upon his fellow-man, they have upon us; and having these claims, they ask only for the Church. They pray us not to let them perish in the wilderness; not to permit them to be cut off from the sweet communion of the Church. "If," says the Apostle, speaking of Christian professors, and alluding to mere earthly things, "any provide not for his own, and especially for them of his own house, he hath denied the faith, and is worse than an infidel." What, then, shall we say of that Church which shall not provide for its own children? How can it hope to be watered itself with gracious rain from Heaven, when it hoards up for itself the river of life, which is ordained to flow through its channels of grace?

Many of the States of this Confederacy are Missionary ground. The population is sparse and scattered; the children of the Church are few and far between; the Priests of the Lord can reach them only after great labor and privation. Hitherto has their scanty subsistence been eked out from the common treasury of our united Church. Cut off from that recourse by our political action, in which they have heartily acquiesced, they turn to us and pray us to do at least as much for them as we have been accustomed to do for the Church from which they have been separated by a civil necessity. We can do what they ask, and we ought cheerfully to do it. Unless we take care that the Gospel is sent to these isolated children of the Church, who will heed their cry? They have no Church to cry to, but the Church which we now represent; and they cast themselves upon us in full faith that we will do our whole duty towards them. They are one with us in faith, in care, in suffering; they are bearing like evils with those which disturb us; and they have no worship to cheer and support them, no Gospel to preach to them patience and long-suffering. For Christ's sake they pray that they may be given at least a Mother's bosom to die upon.

Voices of supplication come to us also from the distant shores of Africa and the East: but only their echo reaches us from the Throne of Grace. The policy of man has shut out those utterances from us. How it can help their cause to separate the children of God from one another, He only knows: but we can hear them when we kneel in prayer, and commune with their spirits through the Spirit of Christ. But God is perchance intending, through these inscrutable measures, to shut us up to that great work which He has placed at our very doors, and which is, next to her own expansion, the Church's greatest work in these Confederate States. The religious instruction of the negroes has been thrust upon us in such a wonderful manner, that we must be blind not to perceive that not only our spiritual but our national life is wrapped up in their welfare. With them we stand or fall; and God will not permit us to be separated in interest or in fortune.

The time has come when the Church should press more urgently than she has hitherto done upon her laity, the solemn fact, that the slaves of the South are not merely so much property: but are a sacred trust committed to us, as a people, to be prepared for the work which God may have for them to do in the future. While under this tutelage He freely gives to us their labor, but expects us to give back to them that religious and moral instruction which is to elevate them in the scale of being. And while inculcating this truth, the Church must offer more freely her ministrations for their benefit and improvement. Her laity must set the example of readiness to fulfill their duty towards these people; and her clergy must strip themselves of pride and fastidiousness and indolence, and rush, with the zeal of martyrs, to this labor of love. The teachings of the Church are those which best suit a people passing from ignorance to civilization; because, while it represses all fanaticism, it fastens upon the memory the great facts of our religion, and through its objective worship attracts and enchains them. So far from relaxing, in their case, the forms of the Church, good will be permanently done to them just in proportion as we teach them through their senses and their affections. If subjected to the teachings of a bald spiritualism, they will find food for their senses and their child-like fancies in superstitious observances of their own, leading too often to crime and licentiousness.

It is likewise the duty of the Church to press upon the masters of the country their obligation, as Christian men, so to arrange this institution as not to necessitate the violation of those sacred relations which God has created, and which man cannot, consistently with Christian duty, annul. The systems of labor which prevail in Europe, and which are, in many respects, more severe than ours, are so arranged as to prevent all necessity for the separation of parents and children and of husbands and wives: and a very little care upon our part would rid the system, upon which we are about to plant our national life, of these un-Christian features. It belongs, especially, to the Episcopal Church to urge a proper teaching upon this subject, for in her fold and in her congregations are found a very large proportion of the great slaveholders of the country. We rejoice to be enabled to say that the public sentiment is rapidly becoming sound upon this subject, and that the legislatures of several of the Confederate States have already taken steps towards this consummation. Hitherto have we been hindered by the pressure of abolitionism. Now that we have thrown off from us that hateful and infidel pestilence, we should prove to the world that we are faithful to our trust; and the Church should lead the hosts of the Lord in this work of justice and of mercy.

Another duty, which, for the present, devolves upon the Church, is an oversight of the children of God, as they lie without religion and without Christian care in the camps and hospitals of our Government. Far be it from us to say that there has been no Christian supervision of our soldiers; and we cheerfully concede all praise and thanks to those who have done their duty through danger and privation: but we must affirm that there is still a great lack of service on the Church's part in this connection. From whatever cause it has arisen, whether from the scarcity of clergymen, or from unwillingness to bear the hardships of the soldiers' life, we are obliged to acknowledge that we have been unable to find men who were willing to answer this call, and to take their places, not as soldiers fighting for their country, but as soldiers fighting for the victory of Christ over sin and death. In the opinion of the House of Bishops, no position is more suited, at this moment, to the true spirit of Christ and His Church, than that of a faithful minister of the grace of God and of the Sacraments of the Church to the soldiers in the field, or in the hospital: and we would urge it upon those ministers who have been exiled from their parishes, to enter upon this work as their present duty, trusting for support to Him who has said, "I will never leave thee nor forsake thee."

The most striking deficiency in the Church's work which

we perceive in looking at the Church's life, is a lack of zeal in spreading the influences of the Church through her Services and Sacraments. Our ministry has become too local and sedentary, too well satisfied to sit down and do the work which it has undertaken to do, overlooking the fields white for the harvest which are spread out all around them, and which cannot be cultivated save through their agency. Every well-established congregation should consider itself as a centre of Missionary work, and should encourage its pastor to extend his usefulness beyond its own limits, and while he is a Priest to them, to be, in some measure, a Missionary to all about him. As long as the selfish idea is indulged, that a minister is tied down to a local congregation, and has no business to work around him, the Church must languish, or increase but slowly. Missionaries cannot be furnished for every village and neighborhood; and these must remain uncared for by the Church, unless the settled clergy will make up their minds to extend the sphere of their operations beyond the narrow limits of their own immediate cures.

Another deficiency which requires amendment, is the little spiritual intercourse which takes place among the Clergy in their work for the Church. Each man works in his sphere: but for the most part he gives nothing to his brother clergyman, and receives nothing from him in return. When our Lord sent forth His Apostles, He sent them two by two, for the evident purpose that they should support, strengthen, and comfort each other. The spirit of this action is very much overlooked in the Church, and the Clergy are weakened by it. While the House of Bishops would not specify any mode by which this defect should be remedied, it would recommend to the Clergy a more free, spiritual intercourse, a more frequent interchange of clerical services, greater communion in prayer and in counsel.

Many a despondent heart would thus be cheered, and many a weak brother would be comforted and strengthened.

Another deficiency which requires amendment, is the little spiritual help which is given to the Clergy by the Laity. We have no reference now to the temporal support of the Clergy, although we might well dwell upon that: but to the spiritual help which a Christian Laity might give to the Clergy. In reading the Acts of the Apostles, we find many illustrations of this truth; and we perceive how the greatest of the Apostles was not above the help of his yoke-fellows in the Gospel. There are many ways in which spiritual and earnest Laymen can help their Clergy in the work of the Church, and under their guidance and direction, can become valuable Missionaries of Christ, even while unordained. It requires sacrifice and self-denial; but we must all remember that we are not our own, but are bought with a price, and belong to Christ, body, soul and spirit.

But over and above all these special deficiencies, looms up that greatest of all deficiencies, the lack of the Holy Spirit in and with our Churches. Because of the degree to which spiritual influences have been abused in our land, we have been tempted to run into the other extreme, and to forget that we are living under what the Apostle calls the dispensation of the Spirit, and that the Church's work must derive all its power from His presence. Our danger is, to merge the Holy Ghost into the means of grace, and overlook the important fact that He is a personal agent, acting indeed through those means, but not necessarily tied to them. Our Saviour said: "The wind bloweth where it listeth, and thou hearest the sound thereof, but canst not tell whence it cometh, and whither it goeth: so is every one that is born of the Spirit." And as with the individual, so with the Church. The Holy Spirit will be in the

Church, if His presence is kept there by an acknowledgment of His power, by a sense of His necessity, by a constant prayer for His presence; but the addresses to the Churches in Asia Minor instruct us to be watchful over ourselves, and to hold fast by Him, who is the representative of Christ upon earth, while Christ is interceding and advocating for us in Heaven. Let the Church and her Ministers always bear in mind, that the growth of the Church and the vitality of the Church are "not by might, nor by power, but by my Spirit," saith the Lord.

And now it only remains for us to bid you, one and all, an affectionate farewell. We cannot but remember that when we last separated from you, there stood among us two venerated brethren, dearly beloved in the Lord, who have since entered into their rest. When we parted we knew it must be so, but we could not foresee where the hand of Death would fall. And now again we know, that separating once more for the like space of time, we shall not all meet again. Whose shall be the summons? Well for us that the curtain of God's providence hides this knowledge from us, teaching us the lesson of Christian truth, that we must all watch and be sober, because we know neither the day nor the hour when the Son of Man cometh. May God's gracious Providence guide you in safety to your homes, and preserve them from the desolations of war. And should we not be permitted to battle together any more for Christ in the Church militant, may we be deemed worthy to be members of the Church triumphant, where with Prophets, Apostles, Martyrs, Saints and Angels, we may ascribe honor and glory, dominion and praise to Him that sitteth upon the Throne, and to the Lamb, forever!

An Address

At the Funeral of the Rt. Rev. Nicholas Hamner Cobbs, *D. D., late Bishop of Alabama, delivered in S. John's Church, Montgomery, Alabama, on Sunday, January 13th,* 1861.

THE year has opened upon us, Fellow-Churchmen and Fellow-Christians, with a great public sorrow. This smitten congregation, this vast assemblage of sympathizing friends, this crowd of bereaved Clergymen, this Church clad in the deep habiliments of mourning, all attest that the grief which lies heavy upon us is of no private character. It is not a single family, or a single circle, which mourns to-day; but it is every family, and every circle, of a large and wide-spread communion. It is not one congregation only, that bows its head in the dust, and sits silent under the chastening hand of God; but it is every congregation of this extended Diocese. And beyond its limits are thousands of the good and the devout, who share with us our grief for the death of this holy servant of God, and whose prayers are this day ascending to Heaven on the wings of the Holy Dove in behalf of his widow, of his children, of his people, of his Clergy, of the Church of the Living God. And through this wide land are hearts weeping for him to-day, as for a Father; are voices uttering blessings upon his name for all the good he has done to them. And many, who never looked upon his face, are placing upon his grave the tribute of love, for the gentle goodness whose fragrance reaches even unto them; of reverence, for the holiness which made him precious among the saints of God. We, who stand here weeping over his dead body, are but the representatives of multitudes, who are shedding their tears in the privacy of their own households. We, who utter in this place our broken words of love and sorrow, are only the leaders of hosts, who are lifting up to God the voice of supplication for strength and comfort under this sore affliction. For there is yet, thanks be to God! virtue enough left among men to enable them to recognize the embodiment of goodness, and grace enough to lead them to pay homage to the reflection of their Saviour's image.

And well does his memory deserve all this love, and all this gushing tribute of affection. From his youth, up to the moment when the silver cord was loosed, was he himself a creature of unselfishness, lavishing upon all around him the bounties of his goodness and the warmth of his affection. Never has he sought his own things, but always the things of others. Wherever in his ministry the Spirit of God has called him, that sphere has been warmed by the kindliness of his nature, and the earnestness of his piety. Whether toiling as a Missionary among the valleys of his own beloved Virginia, or laboring as a Pastor in the exacting congregations of towns and cities, or standing beside the fountains of Science and sweetening their waters with the truths of Christianity, or building up the Church in this almost virgin Diocese: he has left everywhere the like impress of himself. He has ever walked in an atmosphere of love; and those among whom he has wandered rise up, even to this day, and call him blessed. Heartfelt gratitude has followed him all his days. Affection has sweetened his whole pathway of life. Devotion has filled Heaven with prayers in his behalf; and now that he has sunk to his rest, there is showered upon his grave all this pent-up tribute of sincere devotion. He verified in his life, and in his death, that striking beatitude: "Blessed are the meek: for they shall inherit the earth."

How comforting it is to stand beside the dead, and see that Christ's promises have been fulfilled in life and in death! And in no one has this been more strikingly exhibited, than in our beloved brother. He was enabled by faith, first to overcome the world; and then, by a like faith to overcome Death and the Grave. Few men have been more in the world than the holy Bishop whose life we are illustrating, while few men have been less of the world. A soldier of the Cross from early manhood, a warrior for Christ all his life through, — a warrior, too, who never shrank from any post, or any duty, a Missionary, a Priest, a Chaplain, a Bishop, — he yet was kept unspotted from the world. It had no charms for him; or, if it had, he trampled them under foot with an unsparing severity. He moved among men always as the Minister of God, as the Ambassador for Christ. No one could ever mistake his character, or his purpose. While he was gentle unto all men, he was never pliant; while he was wary in the pursuit of the great purposes of Christ's Kingdom upon the earth, nothing turned him aside from their consummation. Baffled to-day, he resumed his efforts to-morrow. Disappointed in his spiritual aims, he renewed his heart through prayer, and worked afresh. His whole soul was thrown into the advancement of Christ's Church, because he believed that Church to be the pillar and ground of the Truth. He was never ashamed of the Gospel of Jesus Christ, but preached it ever as the Wisdom of God, and the Power of God unto Salvation. Worldliness he rebuked; ungodliness he denounced; and maintained a strict discipline over the Church of Christ. And God rewarded his faithfulness in life by His Presence in death, and bore him in peace through the valley of the shadow of death to that "rest which remaineth to the people of God."

Bishop Cobbs was remarkable in every feature of his ministerial life: remarkable, because peculiar. As a Pastor, he was unrivalled. Carrying into every house the gentle, loving spirit of which we have spoken, he wound himself about the hearts of young and old, so that their affection for him became an indissoluble tie. It was not in his case, as too often it is, a mere transient admiration of a Clergyman's powers, or a Clergyman's manners, but it assumed the unchangeable form of a relationship. It continued through life. It died not out with his removal to another sphere, but he remained the beloved Pastor until death destroyed the bond. No subsequent tie could ever obliterate that first spiritual love. Wherever he went, or whatever he became, his children in the Lord followed his wanderings with the eye of unchanging affection, and never swerved from their allegiance. And this was the result of his earnest self-devotedness to the interests of his people, combined with that indescribable power of insinuating himself into their deepest affections. It is useless to attempt to analyze it, because, even if analyzed, it could not be imitated, for it belonged to the man. It was that which constituted, as a Pastor, his peculiar power. And this rich, unceasing fountain of sympathy made him a true comforter in affliction or disease; a welcome visitor in every abode of poverty or sorrow. It was a living manifestation of the power of Christian love. He carried with him none of the artificial manners of the world; he took no pains to be a courtier, or a truckler; he spoke with honest fearlessness, yet with discretion, the words of truth: yet everybody loved him, and no one was ashamed to be governed by his counsel. He moved in and out among his people, the servant of all, and yet the head of all; the humble man of God, and yet the unopposed Ambassador for Christ and His Church.

Bishop Cobbs was remarkable as a Preacher: remarkable again, because peculiar. And that peculiarity consisted in two things, one of which came to him by nature, and the other by grace. He possessed, naturally, a clear insight into character; and this, combined with a daily examination of his own heart, made him one of the clearest and most searching pulpit orators of the Church. He tracked sin through all its hiding-places with an unerring sagacity, and laid bare the defects of the life of God in the soul with the skill of a spiritual anatomist. It required a very spiritual state of mind to follow him; and sometimes the hearer was lost, because the speaker was passed beyond his depth. To the growing Christian his pulpit instructions were surpassingly useful; and many, whom in his earlier days he led into the way of life, would never consent to compare anybody's teaching with his. This was one peculiarity; the other, I grieve to say, is still more uncommon: the presence, in his preaching, of the unction of the Holy Spirit. Alas! how few attain that mighty power! How seldom are the words of the preacher steeped in the oil of the Sanctuary, so that they glide into the hearts of the hearers, and become as nails driven into a sure place! He possessed it in an eminent degree, and his sermons upon ordinary occasions always impressed the hearer with the feeling that the preacher had woven them, not out of his mind, but out of his spirit in communion with the Spirit of God. And these peculiarities constitute the elements of pulpit excellence. With these, many defects of manner and style can be forgiven: without these, our words, however harmonious and rhetorical, are but as sounding brass, or a tinkling cymbal.

Our beloved Bishop was remarkable, likewise, in his Episcopal character: remarkable again, because peculiar. And that peculiarity consisted in his ruling everybody through the power of gentleness. No Bishop of our Church has ever had around him a more devoted Clergy, or a more united Laity; and yet no Bishop has ever assumed as little authority over either Clergy or Laity. Their devotion to him was the spontaneous tribute of affection, to one whom they perceived to be spending himself in their service, and who had no aims save those which he believed to be the aims of Christ and His Church. His prudence and his wisdom were manifest to all; and when these are combined with a sincere and unselfish piety, they are irresistible. No points ever arose between him and his Convention; and when he was drawn, against his will and against his nature, into the controversies of others, his wise conclusions were always sustained. And this is the true influence of a Bishop, when he wields authority, not because the Law gives it to him, but because his people are assured that he will assume none which is not clearly his; and will exercise even that, wisely and discreetly. This entire confidence in their Bishop was manifested only a year or two since by the Convention of this Diocese, when it placed, unhesitatingly, its whole Missionary operations in his hands, trusting implicitly to his better knowledge of the wants and necessities of his Diocese. And well might they have reposed this perfect trust in him, for he spared no pains in the oversight of his Episcopate. He was ever on the wing, travelling through heat and cold, through storm and sunshine, in the highways and byways, exposed to every inconvenience to which one may be subjected in these days of improvement; seeking out the children of the Church wherever they might be found scattered in the waste places of the land. His journeys were unceasing, his labors enormous, and no fear of personal discomfort ever kept him from his duties. And when he indulged himself with a little rest in the home of his affections, his active mind was busy in the device of glorious things for the Church of God. He worked out, in these moments of repose, an ideal for the future, which was to concentrate around the Bishop, in the heart of this Metropolis, all the efficient agencies of Church work: schools for the lambs of the flock; seminaries for students of every kind; nurseries for instruction in all the routine of benevolence; and, rising from their midst, a Cathedral Church, from which should daily ascend the prayers and praises of God's people, and from which should radiate to the extremities of the Diocese the holy influences of Christianity. This ideal has Death scattered, for the present, as it does so many other ideals; but seed sown by the righteous, and watered by their prayers, never perishes. The time will come, when he will be remembered as the wise and holy man of God, who looked far into the future, and saw in vision the glorious things of the Church of his Redeemer.

And God has richly blessed the work and labor of his hands. Receiving this Diocese from the hands of its energetic Missionary Bishop some sixteen years ago, he has moulded it into its present strength and compactness. It has increased more than five fold under his untiring labors, carried on through numberless disadvantages. In the early part of his Episcopate he was subjected to great toil in reaching his places of appointment, for, even to-day, it is a most laborious Diocese to traverse. But through it all he persevered, establishing this point, confirming that; planting new Churches in the wilderness, and reconstructing the old; upholding the weak; comforting the perplexed; cheering the despondent: a true leader of the hosts of God, whose trumpet never gave an uncertain sound. No one, who has not passed through the experience of a Missionary Bishop, can understand or appreciate the severity and variety of his labors. Set apart to build up the Church of Christ in an unkindly soil, it would be an arduous task, even though he were helped with all the appliances of human agency. But when he is sent alone, without the aid of proper assistants, without money at his command, to assist the feeble parishes and animate the strong; encountering here lukewarmness, and there indifference, and everywhere ungodliness: it demands a heart of steel, and a spirit warmed by the perpetual sunshine of God's countenance, to accomplish the work of the Lord. That our beloved brother was enabled so gloriously to fulfill his mission, he owed to the grace of God, working in and through his rare personal qualities. These he laid, in all humility, at the foot of the Cross, and received in return the strength which cometh from Jesus Christ, the Crucified Saviour, the Risen Advocate and Intercessor.

In the higher Councils of the Church, our brother held an enviable position. His character gave him great power among his brethren of the Episcopate, and in the House of Bishops his opinion always carried great weight. He did not mingle much in its debates; but when he chose to speak, no man was more attentively listened to, or more generally approved. It was a matter of regret that he did not express his views more freely; but his great humility displayed itself in this, that he esteemed others better than himself. "He was willing," he said, "to be instructed by those who were older in the Episcopate," and thus held his tongue, even from good words. But when he would permit himself to give utterance to his opinions, he was sure to make his mark; for wisdom sat upon his lips, and integrity swayed every movement of his heart. Good sense, deep wisdom, and unchanging kindness of utterance, were the characteristics of his speeches: and never did he rise without casting light upon the subject which he treated; and — what was better — never did he close, without casting over the assembly the spell of his loving heart. We shall mourn the absence of his spirit from our Councils, for, we shall never see again precisely his counterpart.

And, if missed from the General Council of the Church, how much more deeply shall we feel his absence in that narrower, but more intimate Council, in which he has communed with his brethren in behalf of the interests of Literature and Science in our Southern Dioceses! It was there we felt his value, for he cast his whole heart and soul into the elevation of the standard of learning in the Church and in the Country. He was totally dissatisfied with the superficial education of the United States; and his earnest wish was, to bring back the olden times of English learning, when scholarship and piety were indissoluble companions. Often have we talked over this hope, in intercourse which I can never forget; and how his eye would kindle, and his form dilate, as he opened his views for the future of our University, and lifted up a standard of scholarship such as few men even conceive of in this present day! It was upon occasions like these that I first discovered the latent enthusiasm of his character; — how he kept down, under the restraints of duty and of grace, a spirit which could flame forth, when time and opportunity permitted, into an ardor that was electric, and that filled his hearers with amazement and admiration. And this enthusiasm he was prepared to cast into the work of the University, and promote, with his wise counsels, its early establishment. It was getting very near his heart: but now, all that is left us is the memory of his sagacity, and the duty of enshrining him as one of its earliest friends and wisest architects.

Such a heart, and such a soul, so gentle, so loving, so full of goodness, could only arise out of a Religion that was deeply personal.

His theology was fixed and definite; but it was his personal piety which distinguished the man. He was one of the holiest men I have ever met, and the very radiance of his face told the passer-by that he lived with Jesus. In the last communication which he made to his Clergy, he says: "As to my hope of justification with God, tell them that 'This is a faithful saying, and worthy of all acceptation, that Christ Jesus came into the world *to save sinners.*' I have been called a good man, a kind man, from my youth up. I do not say whether justly, or otherwise. I have *tried* to show kindness and sympathy to all, especially to the poor, to the afflicted, and to the bereaved; and I am certain that I do not now bear malice, or cherish unkind feelings, towards anybody on the face of the earth. But, if I have done any kind deeds, or any good works, I am sure I make no merit of them, but cast them all behind my back, and nauseate them, and spit upon them as 'filthy rags;' and counting myself an 'unprofitable servant,' I look only unto Jesus, the Author and Finisher of our Faith, and say:

'In my hand no price I bring,
Simply to Thy Cross I cling.' "

And this was a fitting close to a life of entire devotion to the cause of Christ. He knew no other master than Jesus Christ, and Him crucified: and "next to Christ who is the Head, he loved the Church," to use his own language, "which is His Body, with his whole heart." Trusting thus in the Blood of the Atonement; rejoicing that Christ had died for his sins, and risen for his justification, he submitted himself to the Sovereign Will of God. "I know not yet, with certainty, what is to be the issue of this sickness. I have no will nor wish in the matter. 'Nor life nor death I crave'; but simply to do, to bear, to suffer, and to glorify the will of God." And with this humble, submissive spirit, he went his way to his Father's home.

And well may you, my hearers, and all the Church over which he had the oversight, lament to-day, in dust and ashes; for you have lost, at this most critical period of your civil and ecclesiastical affairs,* one whose prayers were mighty before God, and whose counsels were prevalent among men. Most grievous is the affliction, when, at any time, and under any circumstances, a faithful Bishop is taken from his flock; but it is overwhelming, when his light is put out just as that flock is entering into the dark cloud of trouble and of perplexity. Yet such is your condition to-day. Just when his people most need consolation; just when his Clergy most require the counsels of a wise experience; just when the Church is to be guided through a period of change, and therefore of peril: your earthly guide and counsellor is taken to his rest. And such a guide! so gentle, yet so wise; so loving, yet so firm; so modest, yet so influential; so full of the Spirit of God, yet knowing how to move warily among the children of men.

It is indeed — for I end as I began — "a great public sorrow;" and well may the State, equally with the Church, lament that so holy a man has been taken away in this her hour of trial, perchance of peril. For such men as he — men of prayer, and men of truth — constitute the strength and power of a State. They are "the horses and the chariots of Israel." Well, therefore, may the tears of Statesmen mingle with the tears of women, and the grief of age be uttered side by side with the grief of childhood. It is a conjunction worthy of him, who came so near to his Saviour's ideal of conduct, that he should be "wise as a serpent, and harmless as a dove."

But he has not left you without counsel in this emergency. He has counselled you, year after year, from this

* Bishop Cobbs departed in peace about fifteen minutes before the cannon announced that the "Ordinance of Secession" had passed.

pulpit, telling you where to look for wisdom and for strength, in every hour of your necessity. His finger has pointed you unswervingly to the Throne of Grace; and all his lessons have taught you, that the Lord God Omnipotent reigneth, and that He holdeth in His keeping the hearts of all men. He has counselled you in his daily intercourse with you, teaching in season and out of season, that God is Love, and that He watches over His children, with a tenderness surpassing the love of woman, keeping them as the apple of an eye. He has counselled you by his daily walk and conversation, showing you, in his own life, what it is to move daily and hourly in the faith of God, and in the righteousness of Christ. And now has he counselled you by his death, showing you how one, born weak and sinful and corrupt, can glorify God, even in his infirmities; can triumph over sickness, and pain, and death; can lie down in peace, assured that "them also which sleep in Jesus, will God bring with Him."

For you, brethren of the Clergy, has he left a more particular and special blessing. He had you in his heart, all through his weeks of suffering: for he knew your sorrow, and he could sympathize with it. "Give to each and every one of them," are his own touching words, "individually, my love and my blessing; and tell them, that as, during my whole Episcopate, it has been my earnest purpose and constant endeavor to be, and to show myself to be, the personal friend and helper of every Clergyman in my Diocese: so now, I have them still in my heart. And, with my farewell blessing upon them, upon their families, upon their parishes, and upon my whole Diocese, tell them, that their dying Bishop exhorts them, in Christ's name, to study to be men of God: men of peace, men of brotherly kindness, men of charity; self-denying men, men of purity of character, men of prayer; men striving to perfect holiness in the fear of God, and laboring and preaching with an eye single to His Glory, and the salvation of souls."

I dare not intrude myself into the sacred sanctuary of his home. Private loves and private griefs belong not to the public eye. They are for the heart, and for God. But I may be permitted to say to you, out of the fullness of a loving heart, that his widow and his children have the sincerest sympathy of the Church of Christ, and that their names will be carried upon the wings of prayer to that Comforter, who alone knoweth how to comfort all them that are afflicted. Your richest legacy is his character: your surest trust, the promises of God, made to the seed of the righteous. May His peace, that peace which passeth all understanding, abide with you, now and forever!

And now, let us take the aged warrior to his rest. His time of work is over. The sun has set upon his day of labor. The hour of rest has come: and he is given that blessedness, which none but a Christian warrior can know, —the blessedness of the transition state from the work of earth to the work of Heaven. Oh the sweetness of that word *rest!* To cease from all the weariness of life; to be done with its cares, its perplexities, its sorrows, its miseries; to have fought the good fight of faith, and ended the struggle; to have finished the work which God has given us to do: and now to lie down, and be at peace. The Psalmist expressed it, when, in the weariness of his struggles, he cried, "Oh that I had wings like a dove, for then would I flee away and be at rest." S. Paul expressed it, when, aged and worn, he exulted in his approaching end: "For I am now ready to be offered, and the time of my departure is at hand. I have fought a good fight, I have finished my course, I have kept the faith: henceforth there is laid up for me a crown of righteousness."[1] S. John

[1] 2 Tim. iv. 6–8.

proclaimed it, as an utterance from Heaven, when he said: "I heard a voice from heaven, saying unto me, Write, Blessed are the dead, which die in the Lord from henceforth: Yea, saith the Spirit, that they may rest from their labors; and their works do follow them."[1] It was rest that our beloved warrior craved; — rest from sin, rest from warfare, rest from responsibility, rest from temptation, rest from the solemn work of life: and God gave him the boon when He dismissed him from his post: "Go thou thy way, till the Great Day: faithfully hast thou done thy work. Now shalt thou rest, and stand in thy lot at the end of the days."[2]

[1] Rev. xiv. 13.

[2] Daniel xii. 13.

www.ingramcontent.com/pod-product-compliance
Lightning Source LLC
LaVergne TN
LVHW021059110826
845150LV00001B/124

* 9 7 8 1 4 2 5 5 6 6 3 2 6 *